The *Arthaśāstra* in a Transcultural Perspective

Comparing Kauṭilya with Sun-Zi, Nizam al-Mulk, Barani and Machiavelli

The *Arthaśāstra* in a Transcultural Perspective

Comparing Kauṭilya with Sun-Zi, Niẓam al-Mulk, Barani and Machiavelli

Editors

Michael Liebig

Saurabh Mishra

INSTITUTE FOR DEFENCE STUDIES & ANALYSES
NEW DELHI

PENTAGON PRESS

The *Arthaśāstra* in a Transcultural Perspective
Comparing Kauṭilya with Sun-Zi, Nizam al-Mulk, Barani and Machiavelli

Editors: Michael Liebig and Saurabh Mishra

First Published in 2017

ISBN 978-81-8274-938-2

Published by

PENTAGON PRESS
206, Peacock Lane, Shahpur Jat,
New Delhi-110049
Phones: 011-64706243, 26491568
Telefax: 011-26490600
email: rajan@pentagonpress.in
website: www.pentagonpress.in

In association with
Institute for Defence Studies and Analyses
No. 1, Development Enclave,
New Delhi-110010
Phone: +91-11-26717983
Website: www.idsa.in

Printed at Aegean Offset Printers, Greater Noida, U.P.

Contents

Preface

This edited volume continues the series of publications of the Institute for Defence Studies and Analyses (IDSA) that address the pre-modern Indian political theorist Kauṭilya and the relevance of his thought for contemporary strategic thinking and practice. The three conferences on Kauṭilya's *Arthaśāstra* organised by IDSA since 2012 are documented in three edited volumes.* These contain analyses of the core ideas and concepts of Kauṭilya's *Arthaśāstra* and investigate their relevance for India's strategic culture.

This particular volume takes us a step further by situating Kauṭilyan thought in a comparative perspective. That means, first, taking a trans-temporal, mainly intra-cultural perspective on the significance of Kauṭilyan thought for the evolution of India's political institutions and practices. Here, the concepts of intra and trans-cultural hybridity, and the 're-use of the past' are key. In addition, a comparative perspective involves correlating Kauṭilya to pre-modern political thinkers of other civilisational spaces and historical contexts, such as Sun Tzu, Ziauddin Barani, Niccolo Machiavelli, and Nizam-ul-Mulk.

The impulse for these publications came from a brainstorming in spring 2014, when a group of researchers from IDSA and the South Asia Institute (SAI), University of Heidelberg, met in New Delhi. They shared the view that the academic evaluation of the core concepts of Kauṭilya's *Arthaśāstra* – and their contemporary relevance – remain inadequate, and devoid of a comparative dimension. As a result, two trilateral workshops were held: one in May 2015 at IDSA in New Delhi, and another in February 2016 at ISAS in Singapore – the latter titled 'Evolution of the Modern State in India: Comparing Kauṭilya, Machiavelli, Nizam-ul-Mulk, Barani and Sun-Tzu.' Meanwhile, Prof. Subrata

*Gautam, P.K. / Mishra, S. / Gupta, A. (Eds.) (2015, 2016a/b): *Indigenous Historical Knowledge – Kautilya and his Vocabulary*, vols. I, II, III. New Delhi: Institute for Defence Studies and Analyses/Pentagon Press.

Mitra moved from Heidelberg to the Institute of South Asia Studies (ISAS), National University of Singapore.

The project has been enriched by the researchers and their research subjects drawn from different cultural and national traditions. The research results presented at the workshops are both interesting and novel – offering fresh insights into the evolution of the science of politics, statecraft, and inter-state relations. We are delighted that these research findings are being shared with a wider audience.

Jayant Prasad
Director General, IDSA

Subrata Mitra
Director ISAS, NUS

Contributors

Col. Pradeep Kumar Gautam (Retd.) is currently a Research Fellow in the Military Affairs Centre at the Institute for Defence Studies and Analyses (IDSA), New Delhi, India.

Dr. M. S. Prathibha is currently an Associate Fellow in the East Asia Centre at the Institute for Defence Studies and Analyses (IDSA), New Delhi, India.

Dr. Medha Bisht is an Assistant Professor in the Department of International Relations at the South Asian University, New Delhi, India.

Dr. Michael Liebig is a Fellow and Lecturer at the South Asia Institute, Heidelberg University, Germany.

Dr. Saurabh Mishra is a Research Assistant at the Institute for Defence Studies and Analyses (IDSA), New Delhi, India.

Dr. Seyed Hossein Zarhani is a Fellow and Lecturer at the South Asia Institute, Heidelberg University, Germany.

Prof. Subrata K. Mitra is the Director of Institute of South Asian Studies, National University of Singapore, Singapore.

1

Introduction

Michael Liebig and Saurabh Mishra

In writing this introduction, we have to take a somewhat bigger sweep. This edited volume is already the fifth in a series of books published by the Institute for Defence Studies and Analyses (IDSA) that are addressing Kauṭilyan thought and its contemporary relevance.[1] This volume, however, is the first in the series that has an international character right from the beginning – both with respect to the researchers involved and its subject area – looking at Kauṭilya's *Arthaśāstra* in a comparative, transcultural perspective. Yet, it needs to be emphasised that it was a long way until the 'comparative moment' was reached.

The contents of this edited volume are derived from two workshops on Kauṭilyan thought – one in May 2015 at the IDSA in New Delhi and the other one in February 2016 at the Institute of South Asian Studies (ISAS), National University of Singapore. However, the genesis of this book goes back to 2012, when a group of Political Science researchers from India and Germany[2] came to the conclusion that the idea-contents of Kauṭilya's *Arthaśāstra* are far too important for Political Science – political theory, International Relations (IR) theory, Security Studies and Intelligence Studies – as to be solely left to Sanskrit philologists. Unquestionably, Indology has done most valuable scholarly work on the *Arthaśāstra* – including making it accessible to the social sciences. But we thought that a fresh approach was overdue that situated Kauṭilyan thought firmly in a Political Science frame. After all, the *Arthaśāstra* deals with political theory and theorised statecraft and Kauṭilya himself calls it a work of 'Political Science'. We felt that we should work with respect to Kauṭilya's *Arthaśāstra* in a directionality that somewhat paralleled that of Amrita and Aruna Narlikar with respect to the *Mahābhārata*.[3] We had, still somewhat vaguely, three research areas in mind:

(a) Exploring the relevance of Kauṭilyan ideas and concepts for the present – that is, the foreign and domestic policies of post-independence India.
(b) The interpretive explication of the central ideas and concepts of Kauṭilya's *Arthaśāstra* with respect to its domestic and foreign policy dimension.
(c) Exploring the significance of Kauṭilya for the genealogy of political thought and the evolution of Political Science and IR theory.

Back in 2012/13, the focus of our research had been the relevance of Kauṭilyan thought for present-day India.[4] What influence, if any, does Kauṭilyan thought have on post-independence India's institutional evolution and political culture as well as on Indian strategic culture? Through expert interviews and the (content) analysis of contemporary political and strategic texts, our research finding was rather clear-cut: Yes, Kauṭilyan thought-figures are a significant ideational ingredient of modern India's politico-strategic culture. This applies to the manifest influence of Kauṭilyan thought via the conscious and deliberate 're-use of the past' (Mitra) in addressing contemporary challenges by politico-strategic actors – embedded in India's paradigm of the 'modernity of tradition'.[5] Equally significant is the latent influence of Kauṭilyan thought within the 'habitus' (Bourdieu) of political and strategic actors as well as within 'popular politicising'.[6] Subrata K. Mitra's article in this volume provides the theoretical entrée to the question of the relevance of Kauṭilyan thought for modern India's political institutions and behaviour.

However, we quickly came to a second and quite sobering finding – the consequence of which is this volume: In order to explore the contemporary relevance of Kauṭilya, it is indispensable to thoroughly study the *Arthaśāstra* – which means analysing and explicating its central ideas and concepts. That is actually a simple and logical correlation: Without an in-depth understanding of the *Arthaśāstra's* idea-contents, there can be no adequate understanding of its (continual) efficacy in present-day political and strategic contexts. Yet, we realised that, to the extent Political Science has addressed the contemporary relevance of Kauṭilyan thought at all, this simple and seemingly self-evident fact has been mostly disregarded.

In a philological framing, Indologists have debated endlessly about the authorship and dating of the *Arthaśāstra*, while, not surprisingly, showing only sparse interest in its idea-contents in terms of Political Science and IR theory. Yet, Kauṭilya does state consistently that his *Arthaśāstra* is a work of 'Political

Science' and, indeed, with respect to its subject areas, its explicitly stated methodology and its philosophical underpinnings, the *Arthaśāstra* has to be characterised as a (pre-modern) work of Political Science and IR theory. But most political scientists and IR theorists, including in India, have either ignored the *Arthaśāstra* altogether or have been content with merely superficial knowledge of the work via secondary literature. Such ignorance and sciolism in the Political Science milieu has embarrassing consequences: crude misrepresentations of the idea-contents of the *Arthaśāstra* and unsubstantiated ideological attributions to Kauṭilya like expounding anti-secular 'brahmanical political theology', panegyrising the caste system[7] or pushing cynical power politics devoid of any ethical constraint.[8] Kauṭilya is being paraded as the golden boy of those pushing for 'indigenism' and 'nativism' in Indian Political Science and thus, albeit indirectly, reactionary Hindutva ideology.[9] We come back to such misrepresentations and ideological projections in some more detail below.

While we keep the question of Kauṭilya's relevance for both contemporary India's politico-strategic behaviour and for the evolution of Political Science firmly in the back of our minds, we first concentrate on the *Arthaśāstra's* idea-contents. In this introduction, we first sketch the conceptual gestalt of the *Arthaśāstra* as a whole. Then, we analyse and explicate, in a concise fashion, its central thought-figures. The enterprise of analysis and explication of the core ideas and concepts of Kauṭilya's *Arthaśāstra* leads inevitably to the necessity to introduce a comparative dimension. Without the inclusion of a comparative approach, the analysis and explication of Kauṭilya's core ideas and concepts would remain one-dimensional and miss out on their actual intellectual substance and value. But that is not really an issue for this introduction, but the subject of the essays in this volume.

In a Political Science perspective, the main characteristics of Kauṭilya's *Arthaśāstra* in its entirety can be listed as following:

(a) Foundational text of (pre-modern) political theory and theorised statecraft (Political Realism).

(b) Scholarly exposition of its contents (Book XV deals exclusively with methodology).

(c) Basic assumption: autonomy, normative eigenvalue and inherent logic of the political sphere and statecraft.

(d) No 'ideological' presuppositions in religious, metaphysical, moralistic or eschatological terms.

(e) Experience-saturated (Kauṭilya's own participant observation in state affairs).

(f) Theoretical text featuring an ideal-type polity (ideal-type in Max Weber's sense).
(g) No historiographic account of the politics and institutions of the Maurya Empire.
(h) Instructional, but no utopian construction.
(i) Holistic understanding of the state and statecraft (Grand Strategy): governance, administration, economy, legal system, foreign affairs, intelligence and military strategy.
(j) Ideal-type polity based on the patrimonial state (monarchy).
(k) Agency perspective in foreign affairs: The Kauṭilyan 'revisionist' ruler (*vijigīṣu)* pursues the unification of the politically fragmented Indian subcontinent.

Next, we need to sketch our interpretive explication – in the framing of Political Science and IR theory – of the central ideas and concepts of Kauṭilya's *Arthaśāstra*. While, within our group, Saurabh Mishra possesses basic knowledge of Sanskrit, we had to rely on translations of the *Arthaśāstra* from the Sanskrit. We could draw not only on English translations, our clear choice being R.P. Kangle's 1972 translation, but also on Johann Jakob Meyer's 1926 German translation from the Sanskrit original.[10] Beyond the problem that both (excellent) translators are unfamiliar with Political Science/IR terminology, we were faced with the problem of explicating latent meanings of some Kauṭilyan narratives and his sometimes rather metaphorical vocabulary.

For example, the 'idea' or conceptual meaning (*sinngehalt*, as Max Weber would put it) of raison d'état is ever present in the *Arthaśāstra*. Yet, the category of raison d'état is still absent – both in the Sanskrit original and the English and German translations. Thus, the explication of latent idea-contents in this pre-modern text of political theory is not simply a matter of 'correct' translation, but necessitates the interpretive utilisation of categories and concepts of modern Political Science. Such interpretive approach is no anachronism since the (political) subject matter addressed by both the pre-modern idea and the modern category is ontologically self-similar and time-transcending. And, equally important, the modern category is genetically rooted in the pre-modern idea. One might say, the 'idea' is the category 'in its youth' – both share the same basic meaning, but the category has a more complex semantic morphology in terms of dimensions of meaning and their delineations.

The validity of our approach – 'Political Science Hermeneutics', as one might say – for interpreting a pre-modern text of political theory is supported by the puzzling fact that in Machiavelli's political writings too the category of raison d'état is missing. However, as in the case of Kauṭilya some 18 centuries earlier, the idea of raison d'état permeates *The Prince* and the *Discorsi*. No cognoscenti of Machiavelli's writings would dispute that, and many people, even political scientists, assume that the term raison d'état was coined by Machiavelli. In fact, the category raison d'état [*ragion di stato*] was first developed by Giovanni Botero some six decades after Machiavelli's death. Botero defined raison d'état as "the knowledge of the means and measures that are necessary to establish, preserve and enlarge a state." We may add: Botero's definition of raison d'état is fully homologue with both Kauṭilya's and Machiavelli's idea of it.[11]

The Core Concepts of Kauṭilya's *Arthaśāstra*

The Political Science-vectored analysis and interpretation of Kauṭilya's *Arthaśāstra* yields a core set of ideas, concepts and concept clusters. These central concepts do not map the actual comprehensiveness and richness of valuable and time-transcending thought-figures in the *Arthaśāstra*, but understanding them is the necessary precondition for any meaningful engagement with the text itself as well as the exploration of the relevance of Kauṭilyan thought in historical and contemporary contexts. Therefore, we provide in the following a brief sketch of these concepts and concept clusters:

(a) Political anthropology: the basic disposition for material gain and power – and consequent conflicts of interest and anarchy (*mātsya-nyāya*).

(b) The *saptānga* theory: the 'seven state factors' (*prakṛti*) constituting the power of the state

(c) The *ṣāḍguṇya* theory: the 'six methods of conducting foreign policy'.

(d) The *upāyas* cluster: 'the four basic means of politics'.

(e) The *maṇḍala* scheme: the ideal-type constellation of friendly, adversary and neutral states.

(f) The Kauṭilyan idea of raison d'état based on the *saptānga* and *ṣāḍguṇya* theories.

(g) Kauṭilya's political realism.

(h) The normative foundations of Kauṭilyan thought.

(a) Political Anthropology

Kauṭilya accepts the pursuit of lust, material gain and power ('the six enemies') as 'facts of life'. These basic anthropological dispositions must be hedged, argues Kauṭilya, but cannot be denied nor durably eradicated. Thus, politics must soberly take the anthropological realities of seeking wealth and power into account. Kauṭilya writes: "Material gain, spiritual good and pleasure: this is the triad of gain. Of that, it is better to attain each earlier one in preference to each later one." And: "Since material wealth is the root of spiritual good and has pleasure for its fruit, the attainment of that utility means attainment of all gains."[12]

Kauṭilya's political anthropology has a second basic feature: Human beings, individually as well as in social groups, pursue 'selfish' interests because of their basic dispositions of greed and striving for dominance. Therefore, conflicts of interest are inevitable and they often lead to (violent) conflicts. For Kauṭilya, conflicts of interest and subsequent non-violent and violent struggles between individuals and social groups (family, clan, tribe or state) are an anthropological constant in human existence.[13] Usually, the resolution of conflicts of interest and struggles derived thereof means that the stronger party enforces its will upon the weaker party. This basic anthropological situation – *mātsya-nyāya* or anarchy – is expounded by Kauṭilya already at the beginning of Book I of the *Arthaśāstra*: *[T]he law of fishes (mātsya-nyāya). For, the stronger swallows the weak in the absence of the wielder of the rod.*[14]

To summarise: Kauṭilya's political anthropology rests on two basic theorems: the preponderance of the pursuit of material gain and power and the conflictual nature of social and inter-state relations. These anthropological constants are neither philosophically elevated nor ethically abominated. As basic 'facts of life', these anthropological dispositions must be carefully considered in political theory as well as in practical statecraft.

(b) Saptānga Theory

In Books VI and VIII of the *Arthaśāstra*, Kauṭilya expounds the *saptānga* theory which refers to the seven 'constituents' (Kangle) or 'state factors' (Meyer). The seven *prakṛtis* are:

1. *swāmī*: the ruler
2. *amātya*: the Minister [government and administration]
3. *janapada*: territory & the people [in the countryside]
4. *durga*: the fortress [capital city]
5. *kośa*: the treasury [economy]
6. *daṇḍa*: armed might
7. *mitra*: the ally [in foreign policy]

The *saptānga* theory is the conceptual foundation of Kauṭilya's theory of the state as well as statecraft (with respect to domestic as well as foreign policy): *The king and his rule [state], this is the sum-total of the seven constituents of the state.*[15] For Kauṭilya, all seven *prakṛtis* constitute (state) power, not just armed might. The *saptānga* theory means that state power is an aggregate of material and immaterial variables. Thus, state power can, if not precisely measured, at least be adequately evaluated and estimated. Kauṭilya provides a substantive concept of state power, which is comprehensive as well as differentiated in itself. Kauṭilya's holistic and substantive concept of state power is a truly outstanding theoretical achievement.

The singular significance of the *saptānga* theory for the evolution of Political Science becomes evident when we compare Kauṭilya's *Arthaśāstra* with the political writings of Niccolo Machiavelli. In *The Prince,* the 10th chapter is titled: 'How the strength of all states should be measured,' but what Machiavelli writes there does not even approximate the theoretical quality of Kauṭilya's *saptānga* theory. Kauṭilya's *saptānga* theory becomes even more impressive when we relate it to Hans J. Morgenthau's theory of Political Realism in the mid-20th century. In his most famous book, *Politics Among Nations*, Morgenthau develops the concept of 'national power' which shows remarkable homologies with Kauṭilya's concept of state power. Morgenthau's concept of 'national power' includes the following components which are partly material and quantitatively measurable variables, partly immaterial, intellectual-mental factors: 1) the geographical setting of a state (while sharply rejecting the theory of geopolitics); 2) the availability of raw materials and agricultural products; 3) the industrial potential; 4) the population size; 5) the military potential of a state; 6) 'national character'; 7) 'national morality' and 8) the 'quality' of government and diplomacy.[16]

(c) Ṣāḍguṇya Theory

In Book VII of the *Arthaśāstra*, Kauṭilya sets forth the *ṣāḍguṇya* theory: a state has six policy options for the conduct of its foreign policy – nor more, no less: "These are really six measures, because of differences in the situations", says Kauṭilya.[17] The 'six methods of foreign policy' are:

1. peace (*saṃdhi*)
2. war (*vigraha*)
3. 'staying quiet', 'wait and see', neutrality (*āsana*)
4. 'marching', coercive diplomacy, mobilisation for war (*yāna*)
5. 'seeking shelter', alliance building (*saṃśraya*)
6. 'dual policy', diplomatic duplicity (*dvaidhībhāva*)

The *ṣāḍguṇya* cluster can be understood as a continuum of which peace and war are the poles. However, neither peace nor war is normatively charged up by Kauṭilya. Yet, for reasons of purposive political rationality, a policy of achieving policy aims without going to war, is preferred by Kauṭilya, because war inevitably means the destruction of personal and material resources: one's own and the enemy's.

The selection of one of the six methods of foreign policy is wholly dependent on situational factors, yet it follows an inherent logic. The guiding principle, in determining which of the six foreign policy options is to be adopted, derives from the intrinsic connectivity between the *sāḍguṇya* and *saptānga* theories: *The circle of constituent elements [the seven prakṛtis] is the basis of the six measures of foreign policy [ṣāḍguṇya].*[18]

Kauṭilya wants an objective assessment of the situation in policy planning. In inter-state relations, there are necessarily at least two independent actors involved. Therefore, it is not one's own state's power potential (*prakṛti* aggregate) that is decisive, but the ratio of the *prakṛti* aggregates of two (or more) states. Before making decisions in foreign policy, the task of the ruler and his advisers is *ascertaining the relative strength or weakness of powers.*[19] The ratio of *prakṛti* aggregates or the correlation of forces is the key concept of the Kauṭilyan theory of inter-state relations. The seven parameters of the *saptānga* theory provide objective and substantive criteria for making a sound assessment of the correlation of forces between competing or adversary states and deciding on the course of action in foreign policy. The correlation of forces (in terms of *prakṛti* aggregates) determines which of the six foreign policy methods has to be chosen:

1. peace > the rival state is stronger and will remain so in the foreseeable future.
2. war > the rival is vastly inferior in power.
3. neutrality > the correlation of forces is balanced.
4. coercive diplomacy > one's own power is rising vis-a-vis the rival state.
5. alliance building > the rival state's power is rising faster than one's own.
6. diplomatic double game > the constellation among rivals and allies is highly fluid.

Kauṭilya's insistence that the conduct of foreign policy is restricted to a fixed array of policy options, is shared by Hans J. Morgenthau: "Governments might have been wise or unwise in their choice of policies, successful or unsuccessful in their execution; they could not have escaped the rational necessity of selecting one of a limited number of avenues through which to bring the power of their nation to bear upon the power of other nations on behalf of the national interest."[20]

(d) The Upāya Cluster

The *upāyas* are not an original Kauṭilyan concept, but go back to the oldest sources of ancient Indian political literature.[21] In the *Arthaśāstra*, the *upāyas* are explicitly introduced in the 10th chapter of Book II, but Kauṭilya refers to them many times in course of the text. *The means [of politics] are conciliation (sāma), gifts (dāna), dissension (bheda) and use of force (daṇḍa).*[22]

Following Max Weber, one may say that the *upāyas* state how a political actor can enforce his will against the resistance of another actor(s). While the *upāyas* – the four basic principles of political action – apply to all fields of politics, the *ṣāḍguṇya* cluster can be seen as a derivative of the *upāyas* in the field of foreign policy. For Kauṭilya, there is a ranking among the *upāyas*; its criterion being the amount of effort necessary to enforce one's will upon the other party.

This is the group of four means. Each preceding one in the enumeration is the easier and lighter one. Conciliation is simple. Gifts are twofold being preceded by conciliation. Dissension is three-fold, being preceded by conciliation and gifts. Use of force is four-fold, being preceded by conciliation, gifts and dissension.[23]

(e) The Maṇḍala Scheme

The Kauṭilyan *maṇḍala* conception is based on an ideal-type constellation of states: In the centre of concentric circles of states, the 'activist' or 'revisionist' state of the *vijigīṣu* is located – like the hub of a wheel. Grouped around it, are the immediate neighbour states, which are regarded as enemy states (*ari*). In the rear of the first circle of (enemy) states, there is a second circle of states. These indirect neighbours are friends (*mitra*) or potential allies, because their relation to the first circle states – their direct neighbours – is hostile. Beyond these two circles of states, come two more. The ordering principle of the *maṇḍala* scheme is: direct neighbour equals to enemy, and indirect neighbour equals to friend.[24] For the 'activist' state, the first and third circle tends to be hostile, while the second and the fourth circle is friendly. However, beyond friends and enemies, there are middle states (*madhyama*), bordering the 'activist' state and its allies as well as its enemies. And, there are distant powerful or neutral states (*udāsīna*), which (at least temporarily) stay out of the conflicts in which the 'activist' state is involved.

The *maṇḍala* conception is often described as the 'essence' of the Kauṭilyan theory of foreign policy. However, we do not think that the *maṇḍala* scheme defines a rigid friend-foe relation in the sense of a quasi-geometric and/or 'geopolitical' determination. The *maṇḍala* scheme is designed to provide a dynamic foreign policy orientation for the *vijigīṣu* – the ruler who is trying to form one dominant state out of a multitude of smaller states. After all, once the direct neighbour has been conquered or made a vassal, the erstwhile (second-circle) friend becomes an enemy. Kauṭilya's foreign policy theory is 'revisionist', because it aims at the elimination of political fragmentation on the Indian subcontinent – and the *maṇḍala* scheme provides a conceptual framework for the strategy of forming a pan-Indian state structure. Once the *vijigīṣu* has completed the unification of the subcontinent, he becomes the *cakravartī* – the 'ruler of the earth'. But for Kauṭilya, the 'earth' is the Indian subcontinent *between the Himalaya and the sea.*[25] Beyond India's geo-cultural boundaries, with respect to Tibet, China, Iran, Central Asia or the Indian Ocean rim states, the political status quo is not called into question by Kauṭilya.

In Kauṭilya's strategic agenda of politically uniting the Indian subcontinent, we find a striking parallel with Machiavelli, whose political writings must be seen in the light of the strategic goal of Italy's political unification and liberation from foreign domination.[26] In Machiavelli's time, at the turn of the 15th to the 16th century, Italy was not only politically fragmented, but suffered from serial foreign interferences and outright military invasions. Drekmeier rightly notes: "Kauṭilya was faced with the same need for political union in the face of disorder and external threat that confronted Machiavelli in northern Italy...Northern India was comparable in this respect to the Italy of Machiavelli's time."[27] And Adam Watson writes:

> Just as Machiavelli wrote a treatise called *The Prince* as a guide to a man who might be able to conquer and unite Italy, so Kauṭilya wrote a manual called *Arthaśāstra* or Book of the State. In this, he described in detail the nature of the Indian states system and the relations between one ruler and another, and explained how a prince, whom he called the conqueror [*vijigīṣu*], might exploit the pattern in order to bring all India into a Persian-type of Empire. Kauṭilya also found a man capable of doing this [Chandragupta Maurya], which Machiavelli did not.[28]

(f) The Kauṭilyan Idea of Raison d'État

We noted above that the category raison d'état is absent in the *Arthaśāstra*, while the idea of raison d'état permeates the work. The Kauṭilyan idea of raison d'état is inextricably linked to the *saptānga* theory. The directionality of change that Kauṭilya demands for the state factors (*prakṛti*) is unambiguous as he wants the optimisation of the seven state factors. The fundamental benchmark for the conduct of policy – in domestic as well as foreign politics – is the optimisation of the state factors. Preserving and expanding the power of the state, is the basic understanding of raison d'état shared by Kauṭilya, Machiavelli and Botero as well as most modern IR theoreticians. For Kauṭilya, the aggregate of the seven state factors constitute state power and the first imperative of statecraft is the optimisation of the seven *prakṛtis* – in quantitative and qualitative terms. *And when the king is possessed of excellences, he makes the state factors perfect with their respective excellences.*[29] This optimisation imperative means that the Kauṭilyan idea of raison d'état entails a substantive definition of the maintenance and expansion of the state's power. Thus, the Kauṭilyan idea of raison d'état loses the character of an abstract proposition and indeterminate maxim. Instead, Kauṭilyan raison d'état acquires substantiality and can be operationalised.

However, there is also a normative dimension of the Kauṭilyan idea of raison d'état. Kauṭilyan raison d'état not only means maintaining and expanding the power of the state via the optimisation of the seven state factors, but also ensuring the welfare and security of the people. This normative pillar of Kauṭilyan idea of raison d'état is not declaratory. In Book I of the *Arthaśāstra,* Kauṭilya states unambiguously: "In the happiness of the subjects lies the happiness of the king and in what is beneficial to the subjects is his own benefit."[30] Thus, the ruler is both the 'first servant of the people' and the 'first servant of state'. In the sphere of statecraft, Kauṭilya denies a fundamental contradiction between purposive political rationality – the inherent logic of the state, i.e. raison d'état – and normativity, i.e. assuring the welfare of the people. Moreover, in Kauṭilya's view, each of the two value ideas underpinning raison d'état has a dimension of purposive political rationality and a dimension of political normativity.

The Kauṭilyan idea of raison d'état is rooted in the *saptānga* theory. And, equally so, the *ṣāḍguṇya* concept cluster is based on the *saptānga* theory because the choice of one of the six policy options depends on correlation of forces in terms of the state factors. Thus, we see a logical and substantive connectivity between the *saptānga* theory, the *ṣāḍguṇya* concept cluster and the Kauṭilyan idea of raison d'état.

Kauṭilya's idea of raison d'état represents a ground-breaking intellectual achievement in the history of political thought. Referring to ancient Indian political thought and particularly to Kauṭilya, Charles Drekmeier rightly notes: "Thus does the problem of raison d'état develop [in ancient India]– before its appearance in the West."[31] While the category of raison d'état is an intellectual child of early European modernity, the idea of raison d'état was developed in pre-modern India and Kauṭilya was the first to substantially theorise it.

(g) Kauṭilya's Political Realism

Kauṭilya's realist attitude in analysing political phenomena, is homologue with what Machiavelli writes in his *The Prince*:

> But my intention being to write something of use to those who understand, it appears to me more proper to go to the real truth of the matter than to its imagination; and many have imagined republics and principalities, which have never been seen or known to exist in reality; for how we live is so far removed from how we ought to live, that he who abandons what is done for what ought to be done, will rather learn to bring about his own ruin than his preservation.[32]

Kauṭilya submits that his political theory is grounded in empirical analysis of political reality and scientific in that his theory-building proceeds methodologically and according to the principles of causality and logical consistency. Consequently, his theorems are not derived from any 'ideological' presuppositions. Kauṭilya sees politics as an autonomous sphere with an inherent rationality in terms of theory and practice. Thus, we can recognise the contours of the Kauṭilyan idea of political realism, even though the category of 'political realism' is absent in the *Arthaśāstra*.

From the above explication of Kauṭilya's political anthropology and his central thought-figures, we can identify the following ideas and concepts as constituting Kauṭilya's idea of political realism that encompasses the whole sphere of politics, not only the field on inter-state relations:

- The preponderance of the pursuit of material gain and power as anthropological constant.
- (Self)interest and consequent conflicts of interests as anthropological constant.
- Understanding of politics as struggle and the anarchic nature of inter-state relations (*mātsya-nyāya*).
- The centrality of power in politics expressed through the *saptānga* theory as well as the *upāyas* and *ṣāḍguṇya* concept-clusters.
- Politics as an autonomous sphere with inherent logic and normative eigenvalue.

Based upon this set of Kauṭilyan idea-clusters, we argue that the *Arthaśāstra* is the foundational text of the theory of Political Realism, even though the antecedent *The Art of War* of Sun-Zi and Thucydides' *The Peloponnesian War* do already contain important realist thought-figures.

If structural homologies between central ideas and concepts of the *Arthaśāstra* and key concepts of early modern and modern political realism, as represented by Machiavelli and Hans J. Morgenthau, can be verified, the logical conclusion would be that modern theory of Political Realism is (also, and maybe significantly so) built upon the pre-modern political realism of Kauṭilya.

Morgenthau locates the conceptual starting point of his theory of Political Realism in ancient political philosophy – not only of Greece, as one would expect, but also of China and India: "Human nature, in which the laws of politics have their roots, has not changed since the classical philosophies of China, India, and Greece endeavoured to discover them. Hence, novelty is not necessarily a virtue in political theory, nor is old age a defect."[33] Morgenthau does not name any authors or works of classical Chinese and Indian philosophy, but we know of his intellectual familiarity with Kauṭilya from his book *Dilemmas of Politics,* which contains five explicit references to Kauṭilya.[34]

Is it not really puzzling that, for the past sixty years, no political scientist or IR theorist – in India or elsewhere – has followed up on Morgenthau's own statements about the intellectual roots of his theory of Political Realism in ancient India or his direct references to Kauṭilya?[35] Less surprising is the fact that the 'established' genealogy of political thought in general and the intellectual history of political realism in particular are flawed and Eurocentric.[36]

(h) The Normative Foundations of Kauṭilyan Thought

A wide-spread perception about Kauṭilya's *Arthaśāstra* is its supposed amorality and some scholars go as far as judging the text as immoral. But, even a cursory reading of the text would reveal strands of morality and ethical considerations throughout the *Arthaśāstra*. And, its in-depth reading and analysis would reveal the ethical logic underpinning the text. The *Arthaśāstra's* ethical logic can be derived from key elements constituting the intellectual and philosophical context of the *Arthaśāstra* since Kauṭilya elucidates, elaborately, these elements in the text. He unambiguously declares his text as standing in the line of the great *Arthaśāstra* tradition that can be traced to the *Vedas*, *Rāmāyaṇa* and *Mahābhārata*. These works are considered to be the repositories of philosophical and mundane reflections from the most ancient political tradition on the Indian subcontinent. Howsoever historical or mythical these texts are, they are situated within the whole of the Indian philosophical traditions addressing the fundamental questions of existence and human behaviour – notably including those of the social and political spheres.

The notion of *rājadharma* in the ancient Indian political traditions, especially in the *Mahābhārata*, as a normative yardstick to evaluate governance, compels us to search for the ethical structure in the *Arthaśāstra*. Right at the beginning of Book I of the *Arthaśāstra,* we find references to texts and traditions as well as behavioural prescriptions for the ruler, which are loaded with ethical deliberations. Next, we find the ancient Indian notion of *puruṣārthacatuṣṭya* – the balance of *dharma, artha, kāma, mokṣa* – which considers ethics (*dharma*) as one of the essential elements of a life to be complete and fulfilled. Therefore, the claim that the *Arthaśāstra* would outrageously flout ethical principles is simply unsustainable. How can an author, who, at very outset of his book, respectfully acknowledges the importance of antecedent texts on ethics and political morality, be a propagator of immorality! However, the ethical logic of the *Arthaśāstra* is different from the logic of the various 'idealist' schools of ancient as well as contemporary philosophies, yet that ethical logic is clearly identifiable – and Kauṭilya offers us intellectual tools to that end.

In Book I, Chapter 2, of the *Arthaśāstra* Kauṭilya talks of "*establishing (the necessity of) philosophy*", and continues, "*Sāṃkhya, Yoga and Lokāyata– these constitute philosophy (ānvīkṣikī).*" Here we find the conceptual key that gives us access to the ethical logic of the *Arthaśāstra.* Kauṭilya further says that "*philosophy is ever thought of as the lamp of all sciences, as the means of all actions (and) as the support of all laws (and duties).*"[37] Philosophy, here, is the "*science of enquiry*" and laws and duties mean *dharma*. The *dharma*, in context of the political sphere, becomes *rājadharma* in the Indian tradition. Thus, Kauṭilya considers the *ānvīkṣikī* as the central tool ('lamp') for generating valid knowledge and judging ethical behaviour. For Kauṭilya, the 'science of enquiry' or *ānvīkṣikī* is the benchmark for ethical behaviour and thus leads to *dharma*, including *rājadharma*. The chapter titled "*Rājadharma*, Legitimacy and Sovereignty in the *Arthaśāstra*" discusses the normative and ethical logic of the text in detail.

Kauṭilya and the *Arthaśāstra* as a Foil for Ideological Projections

The *Arthaśāstra* is not an easy text to study (we too went through that experience). At the first onset, the novice is unlikely to get a conceptual grasp of the text. However, patience and self-discipline (not settling for *Cāṇakyanīti* or commentary books) pays off; and soon the *Arthaśāstra's* logical and substantive structure reveals itself to the reader. The *Arthaśāstra* is a book that seems designed for multiple reading: time and again, when paging through it, one runs into fresh ideas, aspects and puzzles, and gains new insights. One may agree or disagree with some (or many) ideas or concepts contained in the *Arthaśāstra*, but one can be rather sure that they won't be shallow and banal.

Unfortunately, many political scientists (and social scientists more generally), who have expressed at times, firm views on the *Arthaśāstra* and its author, are suspected of having never studied the work. Similarly, the rich and complex intellectual gestalt of Kauṭilya gets reduced to the 'Chanakya metaphor': 'the cunning statesman who gets things done whatever it takes' –

and without any ethical considerations. When surveying articles on Kauṭilya and the *Arthaśāstra* – both journalistic and academic – we have often rubbed our eyes in disbelief: Is it possible that apparently smart authors are actually innocent of any deeper knowledge of the *Arthaśāstra's* idea-contents?

Closely connected with the superficiality syndrome with respect to Kauṭilya's *Arthaśāstra*, is another virulent phenomenon among political and social scientists: projections and attributions upon the *Arthaśāstra* which are evidently neither derived from the text's content nor its structure. The usual modus operandi for such projections and attributions consists in first constructing some ideological bugaboo – 'indigenism', 'brahmanical political theology', 'adulation of caste system' or 'cynical, amoral power politics'. Once the ideological bugaboo has been erected, Kauṭilya as an intellectual gestalt and/or the *Arthaśāstra* (in toto or selected thought-figures thereof) are swiftly subsumed under the bogeyman label.

We analyse here two academic articles to demonstrate how the bugaboo method is operating. The first article that we analyse attributes to Kauṭilya 'brahmanical political theology'.[38] We also examine Atul Mishra's article *Indigenism in Contemporary IR Discourses in India: A Critique*, in which Kauṭilya's *Arthaśāstra* is presented as a key asset of 'indigenism' in Indian Political Science and IR theorising.[39]

... Kauṭilyan Secular Politics Twisted into 'Political Theology'

A key problem regarding Kauṭilya's perception is the controversial issue whether Kauṭilya is a 'Hindu' or a 'political' thinker. An article by Stuart Gray has drawn our attention because he makes great (rhetorical) efforts to reinforce the perception that Kauṭilya is first and foremost a 'Hindu' thinker. He ascribes to Kauṭilya a 'political-theological' ethic, which, in his view, is identical with the 'brahmanical' settings of rigid *varṇāśrama-dharma* – stratification of the society in the hierarchy of four castes (*brāhmaṇa, kṣatriya, vaiśya* and *śūdra*) and four stages of life (*brahmacarya, gṛhastha, vānaprastha* and *sanyāsa*). Gray sees the brahmanical caste cum *dharma* system as the determining frame of the *Arthaśāstra* within which the king has to perform all his political functions and tasks. Supposedly based on this interpretation, Gray introduces the term 'political theology' that was coined in the early 1920s by Carl Schmitt in Weimar Germany. It seems unlikely that Gray was not aware of the negative (proto-fascist) connotation of the term 'political theology' that he tries to superimpose upon Kauṭilya and the *Arthaśāstra*.

Gray's understanding of philosophical foundations of the *Arthaśāstra* and his imposition of the label 'political theology' on Kauṭilya are profoundly flawed. It is quite true that the caste system is based on mythology constructed through the *puruṣasūkta* of the *ṛgveda* and that it was the hegemonic social order in Kauṭilya's times. But, to say that the caste and caste *dharma* system had a deterministic value and leverage for all decisions and actions of the Kauṭilyan king, is not only an exaggeration, but a misplaced idea. Right at the beginning of the *Arthaśāstra*, Kauṭilya explicitly states that *ānvīkṣikī* is the indispensable tool [*"lamp of all sciences, as the means of all actions (and) as the support of all laws (and duties)"*] for the ruler's prudent decision-making and action. Gray completely misses *ānvīkṣikī* (the 'science of enquiry') which is explicitly presented and explained in the *Arthaśāstra*. Although *ānvīkṣikī* is the source of the text's inner logic, and none of its analyses or recommendations makes sense without it, Gray ignores it. He seems to be driven by the idée fixe that texts written by *brāhmaṇas* or 'Hindus' are primarily, if not exclusively, based on theological axioms and considerations.

The *Arthaśāstra* predominantly features the *Lokāyata* current of Indian philosophy. Kauṭilya accurately acknowledges the stalwarts of the *Lokāyata* school at the very outset of his book by stating: "*Salutation to Śukra and Bṛhaspati*". Both Śukra and Bṛhaspati have the status of political gurus of the *dānavas* and *devas* respectively. While both have been considered *brāhmaṇas*, quite ironically, *Lokāyata* is probably the most anti-*brāhmaṇ* philosophy among the Indian traditions of thought. The *Lokāyatas* (or *Cārvakas)* openly and explicitly label the *brāhmaṇas* as 'scoundrels', 'knaves' and the like. Thus, it is illogical to assume that a text which explicitly praises the *Lokāyatas* should be a pure manifestation of brahmanical ideology aiming solely at the continuation of the *varṇa* order. For any unbiased reader of the *Arthaśāstra*, it is evident that other state goals are the primary focus of the text and Kauṭilya names them precisely as *yogakṣema* – acquisition and protection – of wealth. Even though the spiritual well-being of the people is also a state goal in the *Arthaśāstra, yogakṣema* has primacy. However, Kauṭilya never forgets the fundamental philosophical frames of *ānvīkṣikī* that are needed for the rational selection of the objectives and endeavours of statecraft.

Gray tries hard to demolish the image of Kauṭilya as a secular thinker who attributes to the king's edicts the authority to transgress, if necessary, established religious law and custom. Gray cites the *Arthaśāstra* stating: "*A matter of dispute has four feet – law, transaction, custom, and royal edict; (among them) the later one supersedes the earlier one*."[40] Gray disputes this statement of Kauṭilya by contrasting it with another quote from the *Arthaśāstra*: "(Carrying out) his own duty by the king, who protects the subjects according to law, leads to heaven; of one who does not protect or who inflicts an unjust punishment, (the condition) is the reverse of this."[41] Gray interprets this citation as revealing Kauṭilya's overwhelmingly strong brahmanical impulse, who thus supposedly states what any *brāhmaṇ* advisor would offer as advice to the ruler. Moreover, the king is to follow his *svadharma* or 'his own duty'; that means his caste (*kṣatriya*) duty and not his obligations to the state and the people in terms of statecraft guided by *ānvīkṣikī*.

According to Gray, Kauṭilya is a full-fledged advocate of 'political theology' and a conservative who is focused on the preservation of the caste system and the caste duties as the means to achieve the ultimate soteriological goal – 'heaven' (*swarga*). However, the ultimate goal of 'Hindu' life is *mokṣa*, not *swarga*. Heaven plays an important role as a spiritual tool for guiding and moulding the minds of 'ignorant people' towards an (established) order. But the (Kauṭilyan) king is certainly not expected to be suffering from such ignorance (*avidyā*). In Book I of the *Arthaśāstra*, Kauṭilya submits the elaborate provisions for the training of the king in different sciences, especially the 'science of enquiry' (philosophy). The king is expected to be a *rājarṣi* who knows the depths of *ānvīkṣikī* (*Sāṃkhya, Yoga* and *Lokāyata*) – which surely does not prioritise heaven (*swarga*). For the first two of the three philosophical schools, heaven is the realm of 'unrealised/ignorant people who need further attitudinal evolution to attain *mokṣa,* while *Lokāyata* does not recognise either a real or a conceptual existence of anything like heaven. Thus, Gray's prioritising the second cited statement by Kauṭilya mentioning heaven over the first that mentions the supremacy of the king's edict over other legal or customary matters seems to be based on a profound misconception since *ānvīkṣikī*, not the brahmanical construction of something like heaven, is supposed to lead towards the attainment of the *mokṣa*. Kauṭilya has clearly identified *ānvīkṣikī* as the science of truth-seeking that is providing the rationalising tool for the conduct of human life in general as well as for the king's 'royal edicts' and thus his legitimacy. Since *ānvīkṣikī* is a complete non-issue for Gray, he won't notice its priority over any mythological and customary issues in the *Arthaśāstra.* And, by blanking out *ānvīkṣikī*, Gray can claim that Kauṭilya was devoutly brahmanical – and little else.

Adequately defining the term 'Hindu' requires a significant intellectual effort, but in his article, Gray does not offer any definition of the term. The reader is left with his own imaginations of the term without any criteria of their adequacy. The definition of a 'Hindu' or 'Hinduism' is a much-debated and controversial issue. Gray's article gives an impression that he associates the 'Hindu' religion with theist brahminical Aryan order vectored on the *varṇāśrama-dharma.* He effectively equates *varṇāśrama-dharma* with 'Hindu'. Such understanding of the term 'Hindu' is bound to lead any analysis of the *Arthaśāstra* astray because the text contains strong atheist strands throughout. Among the three composites of *ānvīkṣikī, Sāṃkhya* and *Lokāyata* are recognised as atheist philosophical systems, while the third (*Yoga*) is an adaptation of the *Sāṃkhya* by the theists.[42] Thus, any idea of declaring the spirit of the *Arthaśāstra* as 'theological' or labeling the text as 'political-theology' is utterly misplaced.

Analysis shows that the spirit of the *Arthaśāstra* is unquestionably secular, i.e. discussing ways and means of acquisition and protection of wealth that do not derive their validity from religious or theist texts, but from refined systems of (atheist) philosophy – *ānvīkṣikī*. Moreover, Hinduism is no equivalent to the 'religions of books' because it includes theist and atheist (yet orthodox) schools of philosophy. Hinduism also deeply interacts with the non-orthodox systems that are at loggerheads with the orthodox systems in many aspects. Hinduism is a conglomeration of different schools of philosophies co-existing together, not just the 'brahmanical' Aryan order based on mythology and sustained by a socially and politically dominating section of *brāhmaṇs* in the Indian society. Kauṭilya mentions the Aryan order as both the ideal-type and the self-evident social order of his times that needed no further explanation or justification. But even in his times, India had not a homogenous social structure. One important thing to remember here is that if Kauṭilya was a conservative due to pragmatic necessities with respect to the social order of his time, so were Plato, Aristotle and Machiavelli. They did not challenge the social order and stratification of their times, sometimes even legitimising abominable institutions like slavery.

Gray's allegations that Kauṭilya does not separate politics from religion and does not prioritise politics over religion, necessitate the clarification what religion is. In our understanding, religion is a set of ideas for conducting personal life and organising the social order that is based on some mythological constructions or some miraculous revelations by some almighty supreme being that is infallible and ought not be questioned and disobeyed. If we accept these basic characteristics of religion, then the *Arthaśāstra* is far from anything religious or theological since it is based on empirical experience and analytical thinking. The text is completely free of the assumption of or the guidance by an almighty supreme being, even though Kauṭilya favours *brāhmaṇas* and mentions the preservation of *varṇāśrama-dharma* as one of the king's duties.

We always need to keep in mind that Kauṭilya is simultaneously a grand political analyst, rigorous scholar, and an experienced political practitioner. He can be called a political theorist since he has analysed and theorised – i.e. transformed into coherent conceptual configurations – antecedent political traditions of which we have only selective and thus incomplete knowledge. Kauṭilya, as a political practitioner and actor of statecraft in the context of the existing social and ideological realities had to take into account the dominant social and ideological order backed by the political elite. Hence, the *varṇāśrama-dharma* is preserved as one of the king's duties in the *Arthaśāstra*. His stance seems to be due to practical constraints rather than philosophical considerations – and certainly not any so called 'theological' commitment. Caste and religion are subjects only treated en passant in the *Arthaśāstra* and discriminatory caste-connected provisions are marginal compared to the idea-contents of the *Arthaśāstra* as a whole.

The disputed lineage of Chandragupta Maurya, who founded the Maurya Empire with Kauṭilya's help, and is still widely celebrated as a 'non-*kṣatriya*' king, only adds up to support the proposition of Kauṭilya's secularism and relativisation of caste status. What is remarkable in the *Arthaśāstra* are the many references to 'lower' castes emphasising the meritocratic perspective versus some 'inherent value' of caste status. Gray, while discussing the sources of political legitimacy in Kauṭilya's and Machiavelli's writings, states: "While Kauṭilya appeals to a particular theology and aims to preserve traditional brahmanical socio-political order, Machiavelli appeals to secular aims (glory, liberty) and seeks to acquire and maintain a new state in a delegitimised world without the help of Christianity or any other religious tradition."[43] This statement reveals Gray's misunderstanding of the *Arthaśāstra,* in which the ultimate goal is political – the preservation and expansion of the power of the state and the welfare of the people – and not the adulation of 'a particular theology' and the 'brahmanical social order'. Kauṭilya was not intent to challenge the social order or the social stratification of the day, but to theorise polity and governance on the basis of secular philosophical tools – *ānvīkṣikī*. The secular political goals driving Machiavelli – surely not just 'liberty' and 'glory' – were quite similar to those of Kauṭilya's eighteen centuries earlier: preservation and expansion of the power of the state and the welfare of the people.

Verse 2.1.11. of the *Arthaśāstra* further proves Kauṭilya's rational stance by demanding the use of reasoning in determining what is good and bad even in the 'Vedic lore'. This idea of reasoning and questioning even the *Vedas*, which Gray proclaims to be the foundation for Kauṭilya's alleged brahmanical "political theology",[44] shows his profound misunderstanding not only about the nature of the *Arthaśāstra*, but of the *Vedas* as well. He seems to project the nature and status of the 'books of revelation' of the great 'religions of books' onto the *Vedas* that have a very different character altogether. *Vedas* are, in general, revered for being repositories of the whole spectrum of knowledge – mundane, philosophical as well as mythical – but not as any infallible and thus dogmatic religious texts. The mythologies associated with the *Vedas'* origins are evidently later creations by certain brahmanical groups which are disputed in texts like the *Arthaśāstra* by subjecting them to rational enquiries. So, Kauṭilya's acknowledgment of the value of *Vedas* does not mean that he views them as infallible religious texts. Instead, Kauṭilya suggest that the whole gamut of traditional knowledge should not only be learned, but interrogated by the king using the tools of reason as to strengthen his insights in the theoretical and practical realms of politics. Thus, theology has no place in fundamental theoretical understanding of polity. Rather, it has an instrumental role in the pragmatics of social and political affairs. The issue of legitimacy as a secular value in the political ethics of the *Arthaśāstra* is elaborately dealt within the chapter "*Rājadharma*, Legitimacy and Sovereignty in the *Arthaśāstra*".

To sum up, obviously, Kauṭilya is a 'political thinker' not a 'Hindu thinker' as such. Kauṭilya is 'Hindu' or 'brahmanical' just to the extent that he gives religion and the *dharmaśāstras* a certain space as customary law in the political realm. But the freedom of practicing any religion is the secular principle that in Kauṭilya's view belongs to the people. However, in case of political necessity, all matters of religion can be overruled by royal edicts. But decisive is that such edict, just like all other political decisions of the ruler, must be based on philosophical truth-seeking that is inherently secular. In all that, Kauṭilya stands en par with Plato, Aristotle or Machiavelli.

... The Smokescreen of 'Indigenism' in Political Science and IR Theory

The intellectual bogeyman called 'indigenism' seems to have its exclusive habitat in the academic milieus of contemporary India. Imagine you read in a refereed journal the following statement:

> Indigenism involves the claim that a select corpus of ancient European resources – the heritage of classical European political thought ranging from Thucydides to Aristotle, Cicero and to Saint Augustin – are relevant for understanding contemporary politics in Europe and international relations.

Most likely, you would think that both the author and his referees have a serious intellectual problem with touting the term 'indigenism' for Europe's classical legacy. Yet, if you are in India and proclaim the same sentence, except for substituting the words 'European' and 'Europe' with 'Indian' and 'India' and naming Kauṭilya, the *Mahābhārata*, Manu and Kamandaka instead of the Greek and Roman thinkers, you apparently stand on respected academic ground when extolling the term 'indigenism'.

Within present-day Indian social sciences, there seems to exist some eerie disposition to put up with the term 'indigenism' or to be more precise, the alleged need to combat 'indigenism' in Indian Political Science and IR theory. One reason might be the term's nebulosity, so people can have the most diverse associations with 'indigenism'. Still, the Indian 'indigenism' discourse remains a kind of mystery. Think of the Italian Niccolo Machiavelli, who at the dawning of modernity was convinced that only by engaging with the classics of Roman antiquity would Political Science be able to advance. How right he was!

Those who uphold the academic combat term 'indigenism' pretend to oppose the 'indigenist' claim of superiority of endogenous political-cultural sources over 'Western' resources.[45] Thus, the impression is created as if Western political thought would be negatively privileged in Indian academia. In reality, the exact opposite is the case. Atul Mishra finds the 'indigenist' assertion outrageous that Kauṭilya's much older *Arthaśāstra* would be more comprehensive and conceptually dense than Machiavelli's much later political writings. He even polemicises against Max Weber for holding such view.[46] He also expounds the need to protect endogenous 'sub-altern' and post-modernist resources against an alleged onrush of 'indigenism' – listing Christian, Muslim, low-caste, tribal, female and 'alternative modernity' sources as endangered species. Behind these smokescreens, something quite different is lurking: 'indigenism' is used as a deliberately vague, but clearly pejorative umbrella term under which India's pre-modern politico-cultural resources are to be subsumed. The purpose of such classification seems to be the academic marginalisation of these pre-modern resources. The actual message carried by the academic combat term 'indigenism' is: stay away from whatever or whoever has been labelled as 'indigenist'.

In his article, right from the beginning, Mishra leaves no doubt about the prime target of his campaign against 'indigenism': the intellectual engagement of Indian social scientists with Kauṭilya's *Arthaśāstra*. He is indignant that Raja Mohan would call Kauṭilya "a true founder of what we now call Political Science", that other (unnamed) Indian political scientists would present the *Arthaśāstra* "as the definitive classical text in Indian political thought". He also rejects the proposition that the *Arthaśāstra* is "the earliest treatise on Political Science, statecraft and 'realism' in the world."[47] However, these three statements on Kauṭilya by putative Indian 'indigenists' are perfectly valid and can be corroborated by anyone who has actually studied the *Arthaśāstra* and analysed it in comparative perspective. In his article, Mishra mentions Kauṭilya and/or the *Arthaśāstra* 24 times, yet in the references, the *Arthaśāstra* is not listed.

Mishra seems to hold the view that the intellectual engagement with classical, pre-modern Indian texts in a Political Science context, is eo ipso an 'ahistorical', if not anachronistic, enterprise. Or, in simpler words: India's ancient political classics are utterly irrelevant for analysing or designing policies and strategies in the 21st century. His polemics against the 'ahistoricity' of 'indigenism', however, misses the basic character of all classical authors – Indian or not – relating to the political theory and statecraft. Their works have originated in specific historical and cultural contexts, yet they have remained thought-provoking classics across time and up to the present, precisely because their idea-contents transcend the historical and cultural contexts of their origination. It is doubtful that Mishra would risk interrogating the contemporary theoretical and political relevance of Thucydides, Plato, Aristotle, Cicero, Dante, Machiavelli or Shakespeare in the same dismissive manner he addresses the relevance of the *Mahābhārata*, *Rāmāyaṇa*, *Pancatantra* or *Arthaśāstra* for political theory and practice in modern India.

Mishra flatly denies that Political Science and, in particular, IR theory have pre-modern origins and evolved over more than two millennia. For him, Political Science and IR theory are a pure offspring of Western, notably Anglo-American modernity. Once again, adopting such a position is only possible if there is solid cluelessness with respect to classical pre-modern politico-strategic texts beginning with Sun-Zi, Thucydides and Kauṭilya. Against Political Science and IR theory, firmly embedded in Anglo-American modernity, Mishra claims, Indian 'indigenism' is seeking the establishment of an ('indigenist') 'Indian school of IR theory'.[48] This assertion is simply untenable. Quite a few Indian political scientists and IR theorists have deplored their discipline's passive and sterile dependency on Anglo-American theories, but an exhortation to bring about an 'Indian school' – separated from and opposed to the global IR mainstream – is nowhere to be seen in Indian academia.[49] Atul Mishra's actual worry is not a fictional 'Indian school of IR', but the potential of classical Indian political theory like Kauṭilya's *Arthaśāstra* to "become the basis for reimagining IR in India".[50]

The real issue is intellectual engagement with India's pre-modern resources of political thought in order to critically draw from them and/or conceptually catalyse through them vocabulary, thought-figures, ideas and nuances that widen the Western-dominated canon of Political Science and IR theory (and not substitute it).

Atul Mishra not only denounces the alleged 'indigenist' adulation of classical Indian texts of political thought as such, but equally so the 'indigenist' proposition that "a corpus of brahmanical texts and traditions from early India can…inform India's domestic politics and foreign policy."[51] The idea that India's classical political thought should be relevant for contemporary politics and strategic analysis is anathema to Mishra. For him, doing that comes down to "mechanistically apply a Kauṭilya to contemporary affairs".[52] Here, he targets, in particular, IDSA's project 'Indigenous Historical Knowledge', because it has been "engaging the text [Kauṭilya's *Arthaśāstra*] for directions on policy studies, and argu[ing] that it is relevant to strategic and academic international studies too."[53] Since Mishra categorically denies the theoretical and practical relevance of classical Indian political thought for the present, he equally refutes the "claim that a text like the *Mahābhārata*, that represents India's national culture, sheds light on the [present-day Indian] state's bargaining positions and negotiating strategies in international affairs."[54]

Atul Mishra disputes, with respect to India's pre-modern political-cultural resources, their "translatability to our modern times".[55] Instead, he advocates an approach which "is distinctive for its privileging of the modern" and thus rejects "ideas and practices from the past that may create (often debilitating) disadvantages for contemporary India's constituent populations such as Dalits, religious minorities, women and tribal people."[56] Pre-modern Indian political classics must be negatively privileged – i.e. marginalised – since they advocate "brahmanical excesses on subaltern populations", including torture, judicial inequality, caste system and gender discrimination.[57] A careful study of Kauṭilya's *Arthaśāstra* would have revealed quite a few more prescriptions which do not fit the political and ethical standards of the 21st century. In Political Science, critical analysis knows how to distinguish what is time-bound and obsolete from what has enduring conceptual value. But Mishra seems intent to confuse critically drawing on India's politico-cultural classics for innovative conceptualisations in Political Science and IR with devout endorsement of each and every aspect contained in these pre-modern political texts.

Once again, we may ask if the intellectual engagement with Plato or Aristotle is reactionary 'indigenist' undertaking because the two ancient Greek political thinkers refrained from any critique of slavery which they viewed as the 'natural condition' for the majority of human beings. Yes, the caste system is still a serious problem in today's India, but it is rather absurd to blame a classical political thinker for not having rejected the *varṇa* system about 2300 years ago.

To sum up, the term 'indigenism' does not represent a substantive and sustainable concept. Instead, it is an ideological and pejorative term designed to taint India's pre-modern politico-strategic resources and to compromise the intellectual engagement with them. As an ideological smokescreen, 'indigenism' is meant to obstruct Political Science and IR theory critically drawing on India's pre-modern resources for innovative conceptualisations. And we should note, the bogeyman 'indigenism' is upheld at the very moment when political scientists and IR theorist actually do begin to study Kauṭilya's *Arthaśāstra*, the *Mahābhārata* and other endogenous pre-modern writings for addressing contemporary political issues in South Asia and beyond.

Kauṭilya's *Arthaśāstra* in a Comparative Perspective

We now leave behind the ideological bugaboos designed to marginalise India's pre-modern politico-strategic resources and turn back to actual *Arthaśāstra* and its author. In the course of the analysis and explication of the *Arthaśāstra's* core ideas and concepts, we noted already, albeit en passant, that there evidently exist some homologies between Kauṭilyan thought-figures and those of much later political theorists like Niccolo Machiavelli and Hans J. Morgenthau. Almost a century ago, Max Weber[58] had already pointed to structural homologies between Kauṭilya and Machiavelli and so did Jawaharlal Nehru in his 1944 *The Discovery of India*.[59] Since, a growing number of Indologists and political scientists have compared Kauṭilya and Machiavelli and found similar thought-figures between them.[60]

Machiavelli is a political theorist of early modernity in Renaissance Europe, while Morgenthau is a representative of political thought of 'mature' modernity in 20th century Euro-Atlantic space. If homologies between the pre-modern Kauṭilya and political thinkers of modernity can be observed, it seems reasonable to do two things:

1. A thorough and more systematic comparison of Kauṭilya's *Arthaśāstra* and Machiavelli's *The Prince* and the *Discourses.*
2. Compare Kauṭilya with other pre-modern political thinkers.

We chose the three politico-strategic theorists/practitioners, listed below, because they come from Asia and seem to share a disposition of political realism with Kauṭilya. It is only for constraints in time and logistics that we did not include a political thinker from pre-modern Europe; otherwise, our choice would have been Thucydides and his *The Peloponnesian War*. But as things were, we settled for:

a) The ancient Chinese military strategist Sun-Zi and his *The Art of War* [*Sunzi Bingfa*].[61]

b) The medieval Persian-Islamic political theorist Nizam al-Mulk, author of the *Siyāsatnāmā* [The Book of Government].[62]

c) The medieval Muslim-Indian political philosopher Ziya Barani and his work *Fatāwā-ye jahāndāri* [Rulings on Temporal Government].[63]

If there are structural homologies between key ideas and concepts of Kauṭilya and Machiavelli, Nizam al-Mulk, Barani and Sun-Zi, two basic explanations seem plausible:

(a) An independent, 'parallel' generation of thought-figures in different cultural and historical contexts. For this explanation, Helmuth Plessner's 'covariance' approach[64] and Eric Voegelin's 'equivalences' approach would be relevant.[65] Both authors think that ideas and concepts which have been independently generated in historically and culturally distant contexts, can be structurally homologous. As Adda Bozeman notes: "However, certain other non-Western modes of comprehending the incidents of government seem, on examination, to refer to precisely, or nearly, the same values that Western nations are now trying to convey."[66]

(b) The second explanation would be a trans-temporal and transcultural 'flow' or 'migration' of Kauṭilyan thought-figures – albeit in hybrid recast. Trans-temporal and even more so transcultural idea-migration inevitably involves hybridisation – modifications and adaptations of the original concepts to changing historical and cultural contexts, which, however, do not alter (and compromise) their essential idea-contents.[67]

We feel no need of making conclusive determinations whether homologies between Kauṭilyan thought and ideas and concepts of Sun-Zi, Nizam al-Mulk, Barani and Machiavelli indicate either a case of 'covariance' or of 'idea-migration'. Ultimately, as we have suspected all along, with respect to homologies among the five political thinkers, we will find indications for both covariance – independent and original idea generation – and transcultural as well as intracultural idea-flow along with hybridisation. However, the relative weight of covariance and idea-migration underpinning homologies may differ sharply. Homologies in the writings of Sun-Zi and the later Kauṭilya may indicate a case of predominant covariance rather than transcultural idea-flow. Conversely, in the cases of Nizam al-Mulk, Barani and Machiavelli the indications for a westwards migration of Kauṭilyan thought are rather strong and outweigh those for covariance. If a trans-temporal and transcultural 'migration' of Kauṭilyan thought from South Asia to Europe has occurred, Persian and Arab cultural spaces would be key 'transit points' in terms of both the migratory route and hybridisation.

However, trans-temporal idea-migration must not necessarily be transcultural, but can equally so occur within a cultural space. In our context, it is to be noted that Kauṭilya himself states explicitly that his *Arthaśāstra* is based on antecedent *Arthaśāstras*, which have unfortunately been lost, as well as other antecedant *dharmaśāstras* and philosophical texts. In his essay to this volume, Saurabh Mishra examines the influence of these sources upon Kauṭilya's *Arthaśāstra* – thus, we can assume a case of intracultural migration of key ideas of political philosophy. Another, rather obvious case of intracultural idea-flow would be the staying-power of the idea-contents of Kauṭilya's *Arthaśāstra* in South Asia over roughly eight centuries, after which they decisively influenced, if not shaped Kāmandaka's *Nītisāra* [The Elements of Polity] – pre-modern India's second most important text on political theory and guidance in statecraft.

In his essay to this volume, Pradeep Kumar Gautam reconstructs the flow of Kauṭilyan thought through India's history of political thought and its political history – during the ancient, medieval, colonial and post-independence period. His text is a convincing argument against claim that Kauṭilya's *Arthaśāstra* had been 'lost' for over two millennia till it was 'rediscovered' in 1904 by R. Shamashastry. The *Arthaśāstra* was transmitted mainly orally, but also as written text during the whole period beginning at the end of the 4th century BCE up to the beginning of the 20th century CE. Gautam's essay also covers the migration of Kauṭilyan thought to geo-cultural spaces that are close to the Indian subcontinent and have a close affinity to the Indian culture.

Subrata K. Mitra, in his essay, shows how the Kauṭilyan state conception has impacted the institutional design of post-1947 India. A case both of intracultural idea flow from the pre-modern era into the present and hybridisation – the fusing pre-modern Kauṭilyan political concepts with 'imported' British institutions and political practices. Trans-temporal and intracultural idea-migration is theoretically captured by Mitra's concept of 're-use of the past' and Bourdieu's 'habitus' conception. The first refers to the deliberate 're-use' of pre-modern thoughts and practices to meet contemporary political challenges, while the second refers to the subconscious diffusion of pre-modern political ideas, values and behaviour in the present.[68]

Often, intracultural and transcultural idea-migration go hand in hand. Not only is Kauṭilya's *Arthaśāstra* based on antecedent Indian *Arthaśāstras* and other endogenous texts of political philosophy (a case of intracultural migration), but there are substantive indications that the *Arthaśāstra* has also been influenced by antecedent Persian-Achaemenid statecraft.[69] While there are no extant theoretical texts on statecraft from Achaemenid Persia, the Achaemenid Empire controlled large parts of the today's Pakistan from ca. 500-326 BCE and such geographical vicinity implies cultural exchanges with the northern Indian states of that period, which would encompass the transcultural migration of political concepts as well.

As Hossein Zarhani shows in his essay in this volume, the case of Barani's *Fatāwā-ye jahāndāri* too would indicate a combination of transcultural and intracultural idea-flow. Zarhani's hypothesis is that Kauṭilyan thought-figures migrated to pre-Islamic Persia during the Sassanid era and got hybridised there into the pre-Islamic Persian Mirror for Princes political literature. In spite of the collapse of the Sassanid Empire and the country's Islamisation, the Kauṭilyan idea corpus 'survived' and got further hybridised into the Islamic-Persian Mirror for Princes genre. Barani's *Fatāwā-ye jahāndāri* – written in the era of the Delhi Sultanate – would indicate a re-migration of hybridised Kauṭilyan thought-figures from Persian and Arab cultural spaces, to which it had diffused earlier on. Thus, we have a case of multi-directional transcultural idea-flows. Yet, there are also indications that Barani was 'directly' influenced by the lively tradition of Kauṭilyan thought within the Indian cultural context – thus intracultural idea-migration.

Both cases of idea-migration – intracultural and transcultural – necessarily involve the hybridisation of idea-contents. However, the essays of this volume seem to indicate, not surprisingly, that hybridisation is far more accentuated in transcultural idea-migration than in intracultural idea diffusion.

The above sketch of the concept of transcultural idea-migration and intracultural idea-diffusion and its illustrations drawing on the essays of the volume, are not meant as conclusive evidence. Instead, we think that we can demonstrate: With respect to evident homologies between Kauṭilya and Nizam al-Mulk, Barani and Machiavelli, during the pre-modern and early modern era, the conditions of the possibility did exist that Kauṭilyan thought migrated westward and exerted tangible influence on these three political theorists.

Stating this, is also the appropriate moment to express our profound appreciation for the political scientist/historian Adda Bozeman (1909-1994) and her seminal study *Politics and Culture in International History* (1960).[70] In this work, Bozeman put together a comprehensive genealogy of political thought and statecraft in Eurasia – from early antiquity to early modernity. She covers culture, state structure and political thought of the ancient Middle East, Achaemenid Persia, Greece and the Hellenistic empires, China, India, the Roman Empire, Byzantium, the Southern Italian state of Frederick II Hohenstaufen (that wasn't medieval any longer) and the Westphalian state system of early modernity. Bozeman's admirable achievement lies not in the historic accounts as such, but her penetrating sense for transcultural interfaces in political theory and practice. Firmly rooted in the European intellectual tradition, she left Eurocentrism behind (without making a fuss about it) and engaged in comparative politics and comparative political theory long before these approaches became fashionable in Political Science. Indicative for her sense of the essential amidst incidental occurrences, is her recognition of the continuing significance of the political legacies of Chinese Legalists, Kauṭilya, Achaemenid-Persian statecraft or Nizam al-Mulk. The academic specialists in each of the research areas covered by Bozeman will surely find faults with her, yet she had courage to pinpoint the great lines of development – all having a transcultural character. While her academic colleagues remained content with the myopic view on their respective areas of expertise, Bozeman had the intellectual courage to draw a grand picture of the pre-modern Eurasian transcultural "communications networks".[71]

Yet, Adda Bozeman has also a sobering effect in that she reminds us of the relative incompleteness of our research. Even if we know that the established genealogy of global political thought is Eurocentric and deeply flawed; and even if we know that Kauṭilya's *Arthaśāstra* is a key 'synapse' in the pre-modern communication network with respect to political thought in Eurasia; the still 'missing links' are many and so are the research lacunae.

END NOTES

1. Gautam (2013), Gautam P.K. / Mishra, S. / Gupta, A. (Eds.) (2015, 2016a/b).
2. The group includes Col. P.K. Gautam (Retd.), Dr. Saurabh Mishra, Dr. M.S. Prathibha from the Institute for Defence Studies and Analyses (IDSA), New Delhi; Dr. Medha Bisht from South Asian University, New Delhi; Prof. Dr. Subrata K. Mitra, Dr. Michael Liebig and Dr. Hossein Zarhani of the South Asia Institute (SAI), Heidelberg University. In 2015, Prof. Mitra became the Director of the Institute of South Asian Studies (ISAS), Singapore National University (NUS).
3. cf. Narlikar and Narlikar (2014).
4. cf. Gautam, P.K. (2013a), Liebig (2013).
5. Rudolph and Rudolph (1967).
6. Mitra and Liebig (2016).
7. cf. Gray (2014).
8. cf. Boesche (2002a).
9. cf. Mishra (2014).
10. cf. Kangle (2010b/1972), Meyer (1977/1926).
11. Botero (1589: 169).
12. Kangle (2010b: 431-432), [9.7.60-61, 9.7.81]. Citations from the *Arthaśāstra* are in italics.
13. Without reference to Kauṭilya, E.H. Carr, the 20th century British political realist, echoes the Kauṭilyan standpoint: "The clash of interests is real and inevitable; and the whole nature of the problem is distorted by an attempt to disguise it" [Carr (1981: 60)].
14. Kangle (2010b: 10), [1.4.13-14].
15. *Ibid.*
16. cf. Morgenthau (1951/1978: 105-170).
17. Kangle (2010b: 321), [7.1.5].
18. *Ibid.*: 321, [7.1.1].
19. *Ibid.*: 406, [9.1.1].
20. Morgenthau (1958: 66f).
21. Hillebrandt (1923: 150).
22. Kangle (2010b: 95), [2.10.47].
23. *Ibid.*: 425, [9.6.56-61].
24. The friend/foe taxonomy in Kauṭilya's *maṇḍala* scheme reflects the evident fact that conflicts of interests (and violent conflicts) are more likely between immediate neighbour states sharing a common border than geographically distant states.

25. Kangle (2010b: 407), [9.1.18].
26. The final chapter of Machiavelli's Prince is an 'exhortation' to end Italy's political fragmentation and domination by foreign powers.
27. Drekmeier (1962: 206, 208).
28. Watson (2009: 78).
29. Kangle (2010b: 386), [8.1.16].
30. *Ibid.*: 47, [1.19.34].
31. Drekmeier (1962: 203).
32. Lerner (1950).
33. Morgenthau (1978).
34. Morgenthau (1958).
35. E.H. Carr – with his *The Twenty-Years Crisis* – is the other central figure of 20th century political realism. Carr roots his theory in the political writings of Machiavelli, but there are also conceptual homologies among key concepts in the *Arthaśāstra* and Carr's *The Twenty-Years Crisis*. In contrast to Morgenthau, there is no indication that Carr knew of Kauṭilya's *Arthaśāstra* (or Sun-Zi's *The Art of War*) Yet, both Carr and Morgenthau are standing on the intellectual shoulders of Kauṭilya and the *Arthaśāstra*.
36. Kauṭilya and his *Arthaśāstra* and Sun-Zi and his *The Art of War* are not even mentioned in the edited volume *Roots of Realism.* cf. Frankel (1997).
37. Kangle (2010b: 5-7).
38. cf. Gray (2014).
39. cf. Mishra (2014).
40. Gray (2014: 640).
41. *Ibid.*
42. The whole philosophy in *Yoga* remains the same as that of the *Sāṃkhya* except an assumption of the almighty consciousness. But, technically and functionally, everything else remains the same.
43. Gray (2014: 642).
44. *Ibid.*: 638.
45. "Efforts to establish the superiority of these select resources from India's remote past over Western and Chinese traditions of reflections on politics are hard to miss" [Mishra (2014: 122)].
46. Mishra (2014: 122, 125, 133). Mishra's view that Kauṭilya is no match for Machiavelli is also expounded by Kanti Bajpai. cf. Bajpai, Kanti/Basit, Saira/Krishnappa, V. (2014: 10).
47. Mishra (2014: 120, 121, 122).
48. According to A. Mishra, Indian 'indigenists' are imitating Chinese 'indigenism' in IR theory which aims at establishing a 'Chinese school of IR theory' against the Anglo-American dominated IR mainstream.

50. Navnita Behera's seminar 2007 article, cf. Behera (2007).

50. Mishra (2014: 119).
51. *Ibid.*
52. *Ibid.*: 124.
53. *Ibid.*:120. Mishra refers repeatedly to IDSA's Indigenous Historical Knowledge project and Col. P.K. Gautam's 2013 book *One Hundred Years of Kauṭilya's Arthaśāstra*.
54. Mishra (2014: 121). Here, Dr. Atul Mishra targets Narlikar and Narlikar (2014).
55. *Ibid.*: 125.

56. *Ibid.*:126.
57. *Ibid.*
58. cf. Weber (1994), Weber (2000).
59. Nehru (1981: 123).
60. cf. inter alia: Sarkar (1919), Drekmeier (1962), Sil (1989), Boesche (2002b).
61. Sun Tzu in *The Art of War*, cf. Giles (1910).
62. cf. Nizām al-Mulk (2002).
63. cf. Barani (1972).
64. cf. Plessner (2003).
65. cf. Voegelin (1990/1971).
66. cf. Bozeman (1960: 7).
67. cf. Mitra (2012).
68. cf. Mitra (2011), Bourdieu (1990).
69. cf. Zimmer (2011).
70. cf. Bozeman (1960). Born in Latvia, as the daughter of a German-Baltic general serving in the Czarist army, Bozeman studied in Heidelberg, Paris and London, before she moved to the United States in the late 1930s. From 1947 to 1977, she taught at Sarah Lawrence College, New York.
71. McNeill (1993: xi).

2

Kauṭilya *Redux*? Re-use, Hybridity, Trans-cultural Flow and Resilience of the State in India*

Subrata K. Mitra

Introduction

Does Kauṭilya's *Arthaśāstra* – a treatise on state theory and statecraft, written over two millennia ago – have any significance in contemporary India? What heuristic role do the lessons of this classical text play in understanding the 'modern' state, and the contentious politics of contemporary India?[1] Those unfamiliar with India's classical heritage might see this question as so much romantic nostalgia for a Hindu 'golden age'[2], or even worse, as a patriotic urge to revive a past that has no resonance with the present.[3] This paper engages with this contested field. We argue here that the post-independence state of India and the strategic thinking of India's political leaders draw on the intellectual bequest of the *Arthaśāstra*, and the political culture of ancient India of which this text is an integral part. We argue, further, that the resilience of the Indian state – whose durability is an exception in the ephemeral world of post-colonial states – arises from the ability of the designers of modern Indian institutions to tap into the endogenous reservoir of stateness.

The main argument of this chapter is that the state and politics in India today are the results of seamless evolution[4] from the pre-modern past. Modern

---

* Prepared presentation at the joint ISAS-IDSA Workshop on "Evolution of the Modern State in India: Comparing Kauṭilya, Machiavelli, Nizam al-Mulk, Barani and Sun-Tzu" (ISAS), Singapore, February 25-26, 2016.

India's institutions are the result of a strategic adaption of some imported institutions in order to make them compatible with the Indian political 'habitus',[5] and the hybridisation of some exogenous institutions and practices with their endogenous homologues. The exegesis of the re-use of the Kauṭilyan state conception in the institutions of modern India is the main goal of the chapter. Its second goal goes beyond the specific case of India and aims at a generalisation of state-formation in transitional societies. We argue that the designing of the modern state in India through strategic re-use, hybridity, trans-cultural flow and the innovative politics of Gandhi, Patel, Nehru and their lesser known acolytes is not an idiosyncratic feature of Indian history and culture. Instead, we assert that this narrative is a variation on the general theme of state-formation in transitional societies. This, the chapter develops in terms of a brief introduction into the key concepts of hybridity, habitus, re-use and resilience, and a brief perusal of institutional arrangements of the state in India in terms of these categories.

Form and Content: Hybridity and Resilience of Post-Colonial States

The state in India has a tendency to bounce back. Wars, secessionist movements, breakdown of orderly rule in violent inter-community riots or constitutional coups like in the Emergency imposed by Indira Gandhi (1975-77) might give it a momentary jolt but the basic structure remains stable, albeit with suitable strategic changes that eventually contribute to its resilience. This is explained by the functional symbiosis that the modern state and traditional society have developed through their co-evolution.

India, though in most senses a modern state with an emerging market, still retains some features of a 'third world' country. Modern politicians in ethnic garb, mass poverty, urban squalor, traditional rituals in the public sphere and subsistence agriculture co-existing next to state-of-the-art technology mark the landscape of the vast country. With her continental dimensions, ancient traditions, living religions, huge ethnic and linguistic diversity, expanding market, steady economic growth and an effective but noisy democracy, modern India is a bundle of contradictions. Even for visitors who come equipped with prior knowledge of the country, surprises abound. The whole idea of the 'modernity' of India's politics can therefore raise critical eyebrows among western students of Indian politics for whom politics is exotic and confusing.

Contradictions abound, the country that still cherishes the non-violent legacies of Gautama Buddha and Mahatma Gandhi, India is nonetheless a proud possessor of the atom bomb. The bickering within India's political establishment over nuclear policy and ambiguity of the nuclear doctrine leads to confusion about the real objectives of India's nuclear policy. India's general elections, the largest in the world in scale, are mostly free and fair but armed troops are needed to be deployed for safe conduct of the polls. Power changes hands peacefully through democratic elections, but an alarming number of legislators at local and regional levels carry criminal records. Beyond politics, one comes across the same welter of images that are at once baffling and contradictory. Internet cafes, slums and beggars jostle for space in crowded cities; vicious inter-community riots and terrorist attacks come and go, and yet life continues at an even pace, apparently undisturbed. The modern state, secular by law and in spirit, still appears to equivocate about the role of religion in politics.

India, the 'bomb and Bangalore' notwithstanding is a transitional society and an emerging economy where the symbols of radical change in the short span of one generation are clearly visible. The significant point here is the deeper cultural unity and political consensus that underpin the strife at the surface of the political landscape. The combination of diversity and inequality, the bane of many developing societies, does not appear to disturb the stability of India's political system. The distinctive style of Indian politics is the result of hybridisation of the pre-colonial past and the modern European politics that colonial rule introduced into the vast Indian Empire. The rulers of post-independence India to whom the British transferred power, have chosen to re-use this legacy in their design of the modern institutions of India. India, we learn from Rudolph and Rudolph, Nandy, Ron Inden and Bozeman[6] is not alone in the strategic incorporation of the past into the present in order to generate a modernity that is both legitimate and appropriate for the context.

To explain the hybrid Indian system as coherent to skeptical western students of Indian politics is a challenging task for which the contribution of Bozeman is a significant landmark. To quote:

> Most of the indigenous patterns of life and thought became *blurred* during the centuries of European supremacy, when they were being *integrated* to Occidental scheme of things. Many were officially discarded because they seemed to impede the attainment of the political and social goals associated with the cause of progress, as suggested by voluntary or involuntary contacts with the West. Others simply withered away with the social structures to which they had given support. However, when the non-Western peoples began to assume their places as modern political communities in the world so largely shaped by Western thought, it became increasingly apparent that the *Western ideas were not the exclusive mainsprings of their political attitudes and actions*. Whether in India, Egypt, or Nigeria, men have been generally stimulated by the spread of literacy and the growth of nationalism to probe their own pasts and to *resurrect the realities and myths that antedated their knowledge and acceptance of Western ways.*[7] (Emphasis added)

Why have Bozeman's prescient comments on the nature and course of political change in ancient civilisations facing the challenge of modernisation, voiced five decades back, not been taken up more widely? This general incomprehension of 'the modernity of tradition', or more particularly in the case of India, the democratic achievements of the country based on a political system that some specialists of democratic theory dismiss as 'merely hybrid' (e.g. Wolfgang Merkel) results from a deeply held belief in the superiority of the 'pure' as against the 'impure'. Hybrid species – cross-breeds, half-castes, amalgams, and bastards – do not have an easy time in most societies. High cultures, high society, high art and the high church dictate purity as the norm. Hybridity – a generic expression for its opposite – is seen as the aberration that one has to put up with for practical and pragmatic considerations.[8] Beyond the pale of everyday life, purity is also the norm of modern science. Clear concepts, precise measurements, and causal models constitute the essential tool kit of the modern scientist. Purity is essential to order; and the modern state is the ultimate upholder of purity and order. In the iconography of ideological purity, Danton, Robespierre and the unfailing guillotine, meting out revolutionary terror to the 'un-citizen' and the impure, remain the quintessential symbols of the Jacobin state, and defenders of its single minded quest for virtue and perfect citizenship.[9]

The normative asymmetry of the pure and the hybrid where the former is automatically endowed with superiority has marked the comparative of politics of transitional societies. Just as apprentice physicists must learn to define and measure atoms and even smaller particles, chemists, the periodic table, biologists – genes and chromosomes – so must the beginners in comparative politics learn to distinguish between democracy and dictatorship, the modern and the traditional, the developed and the developing as 'pure' categories, and to measure the hiatus between the ideal and the actual with quantitative, qualitative or discursive tools.[10] However, the world seen through the lens of comparative politics based on 'pure categories' can produce unsatisfactory results. The catch – landed by the net of comparative analysis – is often difficult to classify, while some big fish escape the net of measurement altogether.[11] The interstices of 'pure' categories like democracy and dictatorship are full of substances that are real but not measurable in terms of the pure categories that define the polar opposites of the scale, that too, only in terms of the ideal types that define them normatively.

In the era of globalisation and trans-cultural, border-crossing citizenship, the political landscape of post-colonial societies, and vast pockets of the western world bear witness to the existence of hybrid structures – of institutions, practices and artistic design – that are fence-sitters, straddling different worlds, and difficult to classify in terms of the canon of comparative politics. 'Caste associations', 'fixers (culture brokers)', 'mixed economies', '*satyāgraha*' (the concept of mass civil disobedience coined by Gandhi in South Africa, and subsequently introduced to India) and '*grām pancāyats*'[12] (modern, elected village councils that are based on a classical concept of village self-governance) – each carrying a tenuous link to their original (root) concepts to which new impulses and experiences have been strategically added – are part and parcel of the vigorous political life in these countries.

The chapter questions the normative asymmetry of purity and hybridity in the light of Indian experience. It is organised around three questions whose empirical domain extends beyond the case of India. What are the salient hybrid features of the state in India, what led to their incorporation into the modern state that the constitution aimed at, and how do they connect to the core concepts of Kauṭilya? Is hybridisation of the state – resulting from the strategy and vision of modern political actors in re-using the past – the essential factor behind the resilience of the Indian political system? Finally, in everyday life, is hybridity the essential reality behind the chimera of a universal modernity, not bound by time and space? Since the article applies these questions to the core concepts of the Kauṭilyan state, we briefly describe some of them in the next section.

Classical Meets the Contemporary: Kauṭilya and the Modern State in India

(a) Eigenvalue of the state and raison d'état

The state, as expounded in Kauṭilya's *Arthaśāstra*, is an ideal-type. As such, it is no description or 'imagination' of the historical state structure of the Maurya Empire or any other polity in ancient India. However, that does not mean that Kauṭilya's ideal-type conception of the state is a 'utopian' construct. The polities of ancient India do provide the foil for constructing the ideal-type Kauṭilyan state. And in that, Kauṭilya draws on state conceptions of earlier political theory in ancient India, most of which got lost.[13]

To be precise, the Kauṭilyan state is a 'patrimonial state', in Max Weber's terminology. That means that the ruler and the state are conflated, however one that is drifting apart. The ruler still 'embodies' the state, but the state has already gained significant eigenvalue which manifests in an institutionalised 'state bureaucracy' that performs 'objective' functions dictated by the inherent logic of the state. Moreover, the eigenvalue of the Kauṭilyan state transforms the nominally absolutist ruler into the 'supreme functionary' or 'first servant' of the state – the very opposite of 'Asiatic despotism'.[14]

If the state bureaucracy is the institutional expression of the state's eigenvalue, the inherent logic of the state is expressed in raison d'etat: preserving and expanding the power of the state. The 'power' of the state is neither limited to its ability to use force (*daṇḍa*) nor is it an abstract, relational magnitude. Instead, Kauṭilya puts forth a substantive definition of the state's power via the seven 'state factors' (*prakṛti*): *swāmī*, the ruler; *amātya*, the minister or the government; *janapada*, the people (in the countryside); *durga*, the fortress or capital city; *kośa*, the state treasury; *daṇḍa*, the armed forces (plus police and the secret service) and *mitra*, the ally or foreign policy. The aggregate of the seven *prakṛtis* constitutes the power of the state. If Kauṭilyan raison d'état is preserving and expanding the power of the state, the 'operationalisation' of raison d'état means preserving and expanding each of seven *prakṛtis* and thus their aggregation. The optimisation of the seven *prakṛtis* – and thus the qualitative and quantitative expansion of state power – is Kauṭilyan raison d'état.

However, Kauṭilyan raison d'état is not only the expression of the intrinsic logic of the state's existence, but the 'basic norm' guiding the state's actions. Raison d'état is the ruler's *dharma*. The foreign policy of the Kauṭilyan state appears to be 'pure' power politics. However, it has a directionality which is both 'strategic' and normative: the political unification of the Indian subcontinent. Kauṭilyan foreign policy aims at altering the status quo in inter-state relations: neighbouring states are to be 'conquered' – i.e. to be annexed or to be turned into vassals. In such foreign policy expansionism, however, military conquest is not the prime option. Instead, Kauṭilya favours diplomacy and 'covert operations' via the intelligence service. Of Kauṭilya's 'six methods of foreign policy' (*ṣāḍguṇya*), war is only one – and definitely ultima ratio.

Kauṭilya's apparent expansionism and revisionism does not see the territorial 'aggrandisement' of the state as end in-itself. For him, overcoming the political fragmentation of the subcontinent can only be realised, if there is one state with the will and power to 'incorporate' the anarchic multitude of states into one pan-Indian state. In ancient India, that state was Magadha which was transformed into the Maurya Empire by Kauṭilya and Chandragupta.

Beyond the geo-cultural space of the Indian subcontinent, Kauṭilyan foreign policy knows neither revisionism nor imperial expansionism. With respect to China or the Graeco-Persian states, Kauṭilyan foreign policy is vectored on non-revisionist 'balance of power' realpolitik.

(b) The Kauṭilyan state and the people: The King-Divine Agent, trustee or product of a social contract?

As indicated above, Kauṭilyan raison d'etat is not reducible to 'pure' power politics, but has a normative dimension as well. The ruler's *dharma* is not only to strengthen state power, but to assure the security and the material well-being of his subjects:

> In the happiness of the subjects lies the happiness of the king and in what is beneficial to the subjects is his own benefit...Therefore, being ever active, the king should carry out the management of material well-being.[15]

The state's obligation of improving the welfare of the people, constitutes a normative eigenvalue, but one that Kauṭilya sees inextricably linked to the basic norm of raison d'état: only the optimisation of the seven *prakṛtis* will secure the welfare of the people and only under conditions where the people's lives are secure and prosperous, can the state build up its power in terms of the seven *prakṛtis*. The strong state will provide internal security and the rule of law as well as external security against foreign aggression. If the people feel secure and are prosperous, they will be politically content and the state remains stable.

Kauṭilya sees the relationship between the ruler – the patrimonial state – and the people in almost contractual terms: the ruler delivers vital services – security and a political framework conducive to economic prosperity – and, in return, he can demand the payment of (non-excessive) taxes and duties.

(c) Kauṭilya's political economy

For Kauṭilya, the economy is the material foundation of state capacity – a truly extraordinary theorisation at the time. The state has the obligation to promote economic development and growth, because increased economic output translates into increased tax revenue (without unduly burdening the people). Tax revenue fuels state capacity: government and administration, the armed forces, the legal system and infrastructure. In accordance with Kauṭilyan raison d'état, the state promotes economic development, notably through the expansion of arable land and infrastructure building.

The Kauṭilyan political economy is a 'mixed economy'. Most of agriculture, crafts and trade are private, but the state is an economic actor in its own right that controls and runs the 'strategic sectors' of the economy: mining and metallurgy, manufactures for military goods, precious metals and infrastructure. Notably, the state also runs the 'entertainment industry' – taverns, brothels and gambling. Kauṭilya demands that all state enterprises must be profitable and thus provide a second source of state income on top of taxes and duties.

To a large degree, the Kauṭilyan economy is a money economy with a state monopoly of coinage. The Kauṭilyan state is conducting comprehensive supervision and regulation of the private sector, including consumer protection, trade control, labour inspection, weights and measures, animal protection and nature conservation.

The economic policy of the Kauṭilyan state is etatist and dirigiste and exhibits remarkable similarities with mercantilism in Europe between the 16th and 18th century.[16]

(d) The Kauṭilyan state: Centralisation and autonomous spaces

The Kauṭilyan state aims at centralisation, but not maximum centralisation. The state accepts diversity and plurality in terms of ethnicity, language and religion – the central characteristics of Indian cultural space. The state pursues no homogenisation drive: no 'state language' is enforced, nor is there a 'state religion'. In short, the Kauṭilyan state is a secular state. As Max Weber rightly observed, Kauṭilya exhibits an extraordinary degree of indifference towards religions and 'ideologies' of any kind.[17]

The Kauṭilyan state respects a certain degree of autonomy of village communities in the rural areas and professional 'guilds' in urban contexts. Kauṭilya strongly advocates a policy of respecting local customs and habits in areas that have been conquered and annexed. This applies even more so for states that have been made vassals by diplomatic or other means.

However, on a deeper level, the Kauṭilyan state in-and-for-itself has 'de-centralised' structure. First, the state's foundation is the caste system (*varṇa*) and its preservation is explicitly proclaimed a state goal by Kauṭilya. The senior positions in government and administration are reserved for the *kṣatriya* and *brāhmaṇa* castes, but between the two castes there is a barrier which prevents that political and religious-cultural power conflates into one 'ruling class'. Moreover, economic and financial power lies mainly with the *vaiśya* caste which in turn is separated from the *kṣatriya* and *brāhmaṇa* castes. Thus, there is a singular distribution of power and corresponding 'checks and balances' within the state structure. Consequently, the ruler of the Kauṭilyan state is neither an 'Asiatic despot' nor a Roman empire-style 'pontifex maximus' who unites worldly and religious-ritual power.

While strongly affirming the *varṇa* order as the social foundation of the state, Kauṭilya expounds some pragmatic relativisation with respect to an a-priori valuation of caste status. For him, caste status has to be earned. In the balance of meritocratic and caste considerations, Kauṭilya tends to favour professional competence. His merit-based attitude to caste, is visible with respect to the *śūdras* whom he sees as the actual producers of national wealth and the bravest of soldiers in combat.

(e) The Kauṭilyan state and its legal system

The Kauṭilyan state has an expansive and elaborated legal system. Three chapters ('Books') of the *Arthaśāstra* are devoted to legal matters: one for civil law, one for criminal law and one for extra-judical prosecution of 'enemies of the state'.

The justice system is a core task of Kauṭilyan state and jurisdiction is the occupation of state-salaried judges. Kauṭilya specifies the requirements for fair trial and the prevention of perversion of justice. Sentencing follows the principle of retribution (talion), but, except high crime, corporal punishment – mostly mutilations – can be converted into money fines which are cashed in by the state.

State crimes, such as treason, counterfeiting, corruption or embezzlement of state property, are punished extra-judicially by decision of the ruler and his closest advisers. 'Enemies of the state' are killed by special operatives of the secret service and their death is made appear as natural death or accident.

In summary, it can be stated that the Kauṭilyan legal system, as part of the state apparatus, provides certainty of the law, but no equality before the law. For the same offences, different penalties are imposed, depending on the caste status. However, the punishment of 'state crimes' lies outside the regular legal system.

(f) Social hierarchy and rational bureaucracy

As mentioned above, the society on which the Kauṭilyan state rests, is de-aggregated via the caste order. While the upper hierarchy of governance and administration is the prerogative of the *kṣatriya* and *brāhmaṇa* castes, 'the people' is segregated into *vaiśyas*, *śūdras*, *dalits* and *ādivāsis* in social, economic, legal and ritual terms – each having its own, specific *dharma*.

The de-aggregated society is framed through the multi-layered state bureaucracy whose functions include inter alia: tax collection, law enforcement and supervision and regulation of economic activities. The Kauṭilyan state bureaucracy is subject to the principles of rationality and efficiency. Its members need to have professional expertise in their area of functional responsibility which means that most of them have to be literate.

The state bureaucracy is often organised in 'competing units'. For example, the finance administration is divided in a department for tax collection, a department of the treasury and an audit department that controls the two other departments. That is to increase efficiency and combat corruption and embezzlement – two paramount concerns of Kauṭilya. Moreover, all elements of governance and administration, irrespective of their hierarchical status, are monitored by the secret service. Interestingly enough, the secret service itself is compartmentalised in two units – one attached to the ruler, the other to the 'chancellor' (*mantrī*).[18]

Science, philosophy and other 'higher knowledge' is reserved for the *brāhmaṇas*, but literacy is not the privilege of the upper castes. Practical knowledge is deemed necessary for all people.

(g) *The Kauṭilyan capital city*

The *Arthaśāstra* contains a rather detailed description of the Kauṭilyan state's ideal-type capital city (*durga*). Remarkable in this city design, is Kauṭilya's exclusive focus on considerations of security and functionality. The fortification of the city is described at length and in detail. And, equally so, the design of the royal palace is primarily following security concerns, i.e. concentric security zones, secret escape routes, etc. Otherwise, the ideal-type design of the capital is guided by strictly functional considerations: fresh water supply, waste management, hygiene, fire protection, rectangular streets and housing blocs, etc. The one 'ideological' factor in Kauṭilya's city design, is its division into four districts, one for each of the castes. Aesthetic considerations are completely missing in Kauṭilya's design: both with respect to the royal palace and with other public or sacred buildings.

Kauṭilya exhibits a keen interest in science and to a somewhat lesser extent technology, but the arts are a non-issue in the *Arthaśāstra*. Political authority and legitimacy derives from the austere leader's competence in statecraft backed by a well-functioning state bureaucracy. Political aesthetics like monumental architecture and other forms of politically charged symbolism, seem irrelevant for Kauṭilya. Is that so because Kauṭilya is genuinely disinterested in (political) aesthetics or is it something so obvious for him that it is not worth writing about?

Trans-cultural Flow of Kauṭilyan Thought, 'Political Habitus', and Strategic 'Re-use'

The Kauṭilyan state as presented in the *Arthaśāstra* provides a vast reservoir of ideas and concepts with respect to state theory and theorised statecraft. Even a cursory review of the political patterns of thinking and behaviour as well as the institutional make-up of contemporary India reveals manifold 'traces' and 'echoes' of the Kauṭilyan state and its modes of behaviour. What is the 'connection' between such an ancient text and political reality in contemporary India? How does hybridity of pre-modern political thought and modern political practice come about?

Bozeman uses the concept of syncretism in order to express the result of a dialectical interaction of the traditional and the modern in order to generate an authentic, context-relevant 'modernity'. To quote:

> Each nation, each culture, each region is...today a separate stage upon which local, communist, and Western European systems of reference and belief interact;

and, barring the contingency of an ultimate obliteration of one or the other by conquest, each is likely to evolve its own syncretic system for the ordering of life within its contours and the projection of its interests abroad. In other words, the realities of world affairs today are not adequately rendered when conveyed in the simple myth of a bipolar world; for between the poles of the contemporary cultural and political map of the world there are numerous well-defined civilisations as well as many others that are just beginning to define themselves.[19]

Conventional theoretical approaches of political science tend to offer sceptical silence on that question. We adopt here an 'unconventional' theoretical approach by turning to Pierre Bourdieu's concept of 'habitus': the efficacious presence of ideas, patterns of thought and behavioural attitudes that formed in the past in the present. That includes the 'active presence' of past ideas and concepts which as such have been 'forgotten' because they have become 'natural' or 'common sense'. The habitus is the repository in which past ideas are 'aufgehoben' – silent and forgotten as such – yet being preserved and efficacious.[20]

Our assumption is that Kauṭilyan thought has 'lived on', albeit mostly latently, in the 'collective memory' of not only Indian elites, but also of the population-at-large.[21] As Maurice Halbwachs, who developed the concept, stresses collective memory involves a 'conscious' as well as a 'subconscious' or 'semiconscious' dimension.[22] Nehru cogently described India's collective memory as a "mixture of popular philosophy, tradition, history, myth, and legend" and with respect to the active presence of the past ideas in the present, he uses the term "palimpsest".[23]

We argue that Kauṭilyan ideas are indeed influencing the basic patterns of thought, dispositions and preferences in the field of Indian politics and strategic affairs. Kauṭilyan thought figures are integral part of the habitus of those involved in Indian politics and strategic affairs. In other words, Kauṭilyan thought is a key component of India's politico-strategic culture.[24]

However, besides or 'on top of' the latent presence of Kauṭilyan thought, there has been its manifest presence – phenomenologically and discursively. The text of the *Arthaśāstra* has been continuously transmitted over the past 2300 years – orally and in writing. Throughout this timespan, there have been Indian cognoscenti who studied, learned by heart or copied the *Arthaśāstra*, albeit to varying degrees at various times. Moreover, Kauṭilyan thought has been addressed and absorbed in a multitude of scholarly writings, literary works, playwrights and popular narratives across the centuries. In 1904, the *Arthaśāstra* was 're-discovered' for Indological science and for political actors of the Indian independence movement, but it had never been 'lost' in the preceding centuries.

As the Kauṭilyan thought has 'nested' in India's collective memory – both its unconscious and conscious sphere – it can be efficiently 're-used' in addressing the political challenges of the time. Thus, our proposition is that Kauṭilyan thought has been re-used throughout India's political history – in the Maurya Empire, the Gupta Empire, the Mughal Empire and in post-1947 India. In other words, re-using (politico-strategic) traditions is a deep-rooted Indian tradition.

The relevance and efficacy of the Kauṭilyan thought for contemporary Indian politics derives from a singular constellation: Those political actors who have consciously and intentionally taken recourse to Kauṭilyan ideas and concepts in order to use them for resolving current problems, can build upon their latent presence in the 'political habitus' among the elites as well as the people of India. The case in point is Jawaharlal Nehru who thoroughly studied the *Arthaśāstra* and presented his findings in *The Discovery of India*. In whatever Nehru learned from studying the *Arthaśāstra* and then applied to building the modern Indian state, he could count on a ready receptivity towards Kauṭilyan thought. Due to the dialectical entanglement between 'political habitus' and 'political re-use' in India, the practical political outcomes of the re-use show such high degree of viability and resilience – in terms of hybrid institutions and institutional practices, notably the strategic directionality of foreign and security policy.

The Post-colonial Condition and Hybridity of the 'Modern' State in Transitional Societies

There are four parameters that underpin the state and modern politics in India, each with a bearing on the Kauṭilyan heritage: a bureaucratic state machinery that combines policy responsiveness and law and order management; contribution to agenda setting by local protest movements; political elites using two-track strategies that combine both institutional and non-institutional modes of action; and, constitutional change as a political resource.[25] The most important aspect of the modern state in India is that it draws on the Kauṭilyan heritage of the King as a provider of order, a party to an implicit social contract, and a guarantor that disorder and civil war – *mātsyanyāya*, a condition of incessant conflict where big fish eat small fish – does not break out. This is the legacy on which Indian democracy and the political culture of election draw on – which makes it possible for India to develop an endogenous democratic culture. The important contribution of Bozeman (1960) helps appreciate the links between India's pre-modern political culture and context and their re-use in the modern Indian state.

The state in pre-modern India made a distinction between righteousness (*dharma*) and material power (*artha*). The priestly group (*brāhmaṇas*) and rulers (*rāja*) were responsible, respectively, to strike the balance between the two.[26]

Royal power, thus, rather than being identified with the divine mandate of the King – like the Pharaoh of Egypt or Chinese son of Heaven – was the outcome of a social contract. "Anointed by the Brāhmaṇa high priest, the king was an executive, but in himself, he was nothing."[27] Kings who exceeded their authority were subject to multiple censures. This pre-modern idea of countervailing forces has been re-used in the modern constitution where the Supreme Court of India has emerged as the ultimate arbiter of right and wrong, and the referee in the incessant competition for power between individuals, groups, regions as well as the whole process of representation and election.

The application of these core ideas has led to a hybrid political system that is both modern and deeply traditional. The norms generated through this strategic and critical re-use of India's cultural heritage has created a modern Indian nation that can aspire to membership of the global society and yet remain ensconced in its own tradition. These norms which are constantly evolving have helped the Indian state and society to 'lock-in'[28] and generate democratic governance.

This Indian state model, which approaches the problem of challenges to political stability distinguishes itself from the structural-functional approaches because of its methodological individualism, the incorporation of rules as an endogenous variable and the specification of cultural and historical contexts as exogenous constraints that account for the bounded rationality of the actors. In this model, the new social elites, themselves the outcome of a process of fair and efficient political recruitment through democratic elections, play a two-track strategy and institute processes of law and order management, social and economic reform and accommodation of identity as an operationally testable model. The key function of this model is to help establish an agenda for empirical research into the policy process by focusing on the key decision-making elite (See Figure 1).

Figure 1: A Dynamic Neo-institutional Model of State Formation and Innovative Governance

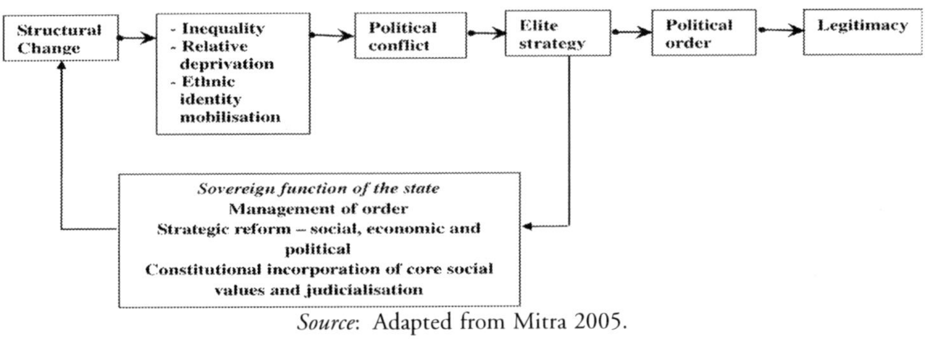

Source: Adapted from Mitra 2005.

The Indian achievement of democratic governance is by no means trivial, and deserves a brief explanation as to how the conditions that led to them were institutionalised. Much further research is necessary to understand how and for which strategic reason the founding fathers of modern Indian politics such as Gandhi, Nehru and Patel adapted the pre-modern past to the challenges thrown up by colonial rule and Indian resistance to it and how the resultant institutional insights found their way to the Indian constitution. While the three leaders often diverged in their responses to specific issues, what held them together was their understanding of the need to re-use the past to produce an authentic Indian modernity. That made them more receptive to the whole notion of hybridity – an idea that was not so popular either for the leaders of revolutionary anti-colonial movements or for those whose sole objective was to gain power through the mechanical imitation of the norms and institutions of colonial rulers. Since the notion of hybridity is relatively unknown in comparative politics, we make a brief mention of this concept in other disciplines.

In terms of its origin in biological sciences, hybridity is an attempt to overcome binary opposites through the creation of a third species that combines some characteristics of the two. Critical theorists find a positive appreciation of syncretism in this phenomenon.[29] Hybridisation is a motivating factor – an attempt to devise a 'third space' (e.g., between coloniser and the colonised or dominance of race and nationalism) which combines elements of the original duality, but folds them together in a functional, coherent way. Bhabha, to whom we own this seminal concept, transforms hybridity by adding the concept of the imaginary from Fanon, Lacan and Bakhtin.[30] Fludernik comments, "The term hybridity, from its moorings in sexual cross-fertilisation, racial intermixture and intermarriage, has now drifted free to connote (rather than denote) a variety of interstitial and antagonistic set-ups which are clearly linked to a 'subaltern'[31] perspective and a positive re-evaluation of hybridity."[32]

The research on hybridity runs parallel to the concept of re-use, emanating from art history, which has gradually found its way into the larger field of social and political investigation.[33] Referring to the presence of the past in the interstices of the present, Morris-Jones, a leading early chronicler of politics in India says, "The political systems of modern states are usually developments from earlier, sometimes much earlier, times. The systems undergo change in response to changes in other aspects of human behaviour and thought; they also have the capacity to exert independent influence on these other aspects. If, in haste, we speak of a political system 'reflecting' social conditions, we would recognise that the process of reflection is one which changes both the instrument and the subject."[34] Further, "India's political leaders inherited under this heading of government still more than the accumulated sum of psychological capital; they received the more tangible equipment and machinery of government. These may be considered first as organisation, structure and procedures, and, secondly, as personnel."[35]

The availability of some new concepts has considerably enriched the tool-kit of comparative politics in its attempt to bring post-colonial regimes under the domain of political analysis. The first of these concepts, trans-cultural, asserts that even the seemingly most local phenomena are part of trans-cultural flows of concepts and things. Cultures are not merely social groups or geographies, but they are constantly constructed and reconstructed 'social imaginaries' that express the fluctuation of political forces. However, even assuming that cultures and cultural spaces are not autarchic, they do exist as distinct empirical phenomena based upon diverse histories, collective memories, traditions and habits. Among cultures, we can distinguish two basic types: cultures that are vectored on 'ethnic', lingual, religious and 'ideological' homogenisation (Europe, USA, Japan or China), and those characterised by inclusive plurality in terms of ethnicity, language, religion and ideology – Indian culture being the case in point of inclusive plurality.

The hybrid institutions and practices are empirical evidence of what Bhabha calls the 'third space'. Hybrid institutions are necessarily a part of a larger political project, one where elites and counter-elites seek to amend the rules to produce new designs and imbue them with a new spirit, geared to a political goal. The flow diagram in Figure 1 depicts how elites might seek to do this in the context of a changing or challenged society through the combination of three tactics, namely, the political management of identity, strategic reform of laws and the constitutional incorporation of core social values.

In their solicitude to gain legitimacy and enhance governance, elites look broadly across the social spectrum, and deeply into local, regional and national history, to identify useful resources for governance and legitimacy, and bring them into the mainstream. Not bound by doctrine or ideology, India's colonial rulers, the nationalist leaders and subsequently, the leaders of the post-colonial state could afford to be 'trans-lingual, trans-cultural and trans-disciplinary' in the sense that there was no political or scientific taboo against the search for things that would work.[36] These huge experiments in colonial dominance, anti-colonial resistance, nation-building, democratic transition, economic growth and justice, governance and legitimacy produced a whole new range of hybrid political institutions and practices. The empirical analysis below will focus on colonial hybridisation as an act of imperial domination of the Indian population; Gandhian counter-hybridisation as an act of resistance; and post-colonial hybridisation as a project of nation-building and legitimacy in the context of a deeply divided and diverse society that takes democracy seriously.

Hybridisation as a Political Strategy of Dominance, Co-optation and Resistance

The British, masters at indirect rule, innovated a number of hybrid institutions to rule India in an orderly manner. While this sustained the raj over two centuries – never in history have so few ruled so many with such little use of overt force – this came at the cost of arrested growth, and the severing of India's colonial present from the pre-modern past. We learn from scholarly accounts of everyday life in classical India that the society, polity and the economy evolved in continuous symbiosis in course of the millennia of its early, settled existence.[37] While self-contained, India was not insulated from external inspiration because there were various forms of conceptual flow that continuously enriched Indian life. There were pilgrims and visitors from abroad, some international trade and military invasions. However, society had mastered the art of accommodation of difference, and re-use of the past to construct new, hybrid structures that could cope with changing times.[38] With the loss of political autonomy and destruction of the knowledge-generating universities, and scholarly communities around temples through Islamic invasions that began in the 8th century CE, India started losing this capacity for endogenous self-renewal. There were local instances of fusion and innovation in art and architecture between Islam and Hinduism, Jainism and Buddhism, a process which reached a national scale under the rule of the Great Mughals.[39] But society as a whole had lost the vibrant capacity for efficient, endogenous evolution. The coup de grâce to this moribund structure was dealt by the colonial intrusion from Europe, starting in the eighteenth century. By 1858, with the defeat of the Sepoy Mutiny, the victorious British proclaimed the ultimate intellectual, moral and political subjugation of the Indians at the Delhi Durbar.

While India has been no stranger to invasions through the Northwest passes in the high Himalayas, British rule was special in terms of its representation of the Indian past. Up to the arrival of the British, in India, the past and the present had lived in a complex and dynamic symbiosis. But, under the British, the past really became the past.[40] The point is made by Metcalf (1998) in a seminal article on aesthetics and power under colonial rule.

While the British continued the tradition of "appropriating the politically charged forms of their predecessors as a way of legitimising their own regime",[41] their method of depicting the past differed radically from their predecessors. Previous rulers of India had added their visions and symbols to existing designs so that the past and present could appear as part of a continuous flow. However, in British public buildings and political institutions, the past was depicted definitely as the 'past' whose only function was to serve as a foil, on which the British present could shine brighter, while staying aloof and distant. In a memorable passage Metcalf recounts how the British durbar was traditional in form but thoroughly modern in content:

> In his 1903 durbar, Curzon sought to utilise the 'familiar' and even sacred form of 'the East'. As he proudly proclaimed, the entire arena was 'built and decorated exclusively in the Mogul, or Indo-Saracenic style'. Yet Curzon refused to sanction an exchange of presents, or nazrs which had formed the central binding element of pre-colonial durbars. Instead, he had each prince in their turn mount the dais and offer a message of congratulation to the King-Emperor. Curzon then simply shook hands with the chief as he passed by. Incorporation and inclusion, so powerfully symbolised by khillat and nazr, had given way, despite the Mughal scenery and pretence, to a wholly colonial ritual.[42]

In aesthetics, as in politics, the colonial strategy consisted in the incorporation of the past – Indian tradition in this case – within the present in a subsidiary capacity. Nandy adds in the same vein "Modern colonialism won its great victories not so much through its military and technological prowess as through its ability to create secular hierarchies incompatible with the traditional order."[43] The British told Indians that their past was truly a past: the way forward consisted in learning new, modern ways from European science, technology, institutions and morals. The hybridisation of the Mughal Durbar in this case was part of the colonial strategy to seal off the vital links of the colonial present with the pre-colonial past. A cluster of European publicists combined forces to teach the 'childlike' Indians new, better, modern ways, and to punish them when they were 'childish', refusing to learn.

The hybridisation of the Mughal Durbar was part of the successful strategy of ruling the Empire through native intermediaries with very little use of overt force. The successful experiment spawned its variations in many other areas of administration, architectural design and city planning, and in public life. The examples of re-use of colonial institutions in post-independence politics are plentiful. Though not always so clearly visible to those who are unfamiliar with India's colonial interlude, specialists recognise the British derivation of the rules, procedures and rituals of the Indian Parliament.[44] The Devaswom Boards in South India and their equivalents in other parts of the vast country – departments of religious property, also set up during the British rule – are in charge of administration of old temples as of the new. Government ministers of democratic India hold court – much like their colonial and pre-colonial predecessors held durbar – and transact state business with a motley crowd of visitors, with the same display of power, privilege and pomp. Independent India has clearly moved on, and shown, once again, the country's capacity to achieve change without revolution.

Prelude to the Contemporary State: *Satyāgraha* and the Conflation of Modernity and Tradition

This trend of uninterrupted and unhindered conceptual flow from Europe to India was challenged once Gandhi got to the centre stage of India's politics, fresh from the successful application of *satyāgraha* as a novel, hybrid form of peaceful political resistance. Under his moral and political leadership, Indian freedom fighters learned to gain new insights on their home ground, which found singular expression in Nehru's *The Discovery of India*, including his treatment of Kauṭilya therein. The process of introspection and selective re-use intervened during the process of the writing of the Indian constitution. The defining moment came with the celebrated Nehru speech 'Freedom at Midnight' in which he announced to a sceptical world the birth of the Indian nation state when he said, "when the soul of a nation, long suppressed, finds utterance". Today, the Indian state – cutting edge of the process of self-assertion of Indian society – is both structure and agency of the indigenous evolution and resilience of the political and social systems.

The Congress party, at the height of colonial rule, had become the vehicle of the synthesis of the two main strands of Indian nationalism – the liberal constitutionalists like the 'moderate' Gopal Krishna Gokhale – and the radical 'extremists' led by Bal Gangadhar Tilak. Following its foundation in 1885 by a retired British civil servant – Sir Alan Octavian Hume – the Indian National Congress gradually acquired a complex, hybrid character – of collaborator and competitor, movement and party, purveyor of modern rules, committee meetings, minute taking and sporting the khadi, charkha and *satyāgraha* as its main political instruments – combining participation and protest action as a two-track strategy of power.[45] After Independence, when its rival Muslim League left India for Pakistan, the Congress, complete with its party organisation, Nehru as Prime Minister-in-waiting, its core ideas about planning, foreign policy and state-building already shaped, was more than ready for succession to power.

Mahatma Gandhi, the most outstanding leader of India's struggle for independence and a continued source of moral inspiration, was trained as a barrister in England. He developed the method of *satyāgraha* – a quintessentially hybrid concept that re-used a Jaina ritual, turning it into a tool of nonviolent resistance – while he was in South Africa working for an Indian law firm. The South African experience also taught Gandhi the importance of cross-community coalitions, a theme that he subsequently transformed into 'Hindu-Muslim unity'. This became a salient feature of Gandhi's politics upon his return to India in 1915, and a hallmark of the politics of the Congress party which found it useful as a political instrument to fend off its challengers – the

Hindu Right, the Muslim League and their British patrons. Under his leadership, the Indian National Congress became increasingly sensitive to the gap between the predominantly urban middle-class Congress-party and the Indian masses, and shifted its attention to the Indian peasantry. Under Gandhi's leadership, the Indian National Congress steadily broadened its reach both in terms of social class and geography. To mobilise mass support, Gandhi introduced a number of indigenous political practices like fasting and general strikes or hartal (a form of boycott accompanied by a work stoppage). He combined the techniques of political negotiation with more coercive direct action (such as hartal, *satyāgraha*, etc.) – one wonders whether his staging of mass civil disobedience is not a variation of 'power politics'. Gandhi derived both the political resources and the methods from within Indian culture and history and he knew the potency and stamina that these endogenous resources had among the Indian masses.

The distinct character of Indian politics derives in no small measure from the trickling down of the norms of British constitutionalism and hybrid colonial institutions, and the 'trickling up' of Indian tradition and custom, and hybrid forms of cooperation and contest. The most important of the legacies consists of the modern political institutions and the process of parties, interest groups as well as the quintessential Indian political strategy that combines institutional participation and political protest. The main legacy of pre-independence politics to post-independence practice is the effort on all sides to bring political competition into the ambit of the rule of law, moderate politics and political institutions. When rules appear too restrictive or not sufficiently legitimate and the game threatens to get out of hand the state intervenes with its own mixed strategy of suppression and accommodation, in a manner that is both akin to that of its British predecessor and Kauṭilyan statecraft. With some exceptions such as the continuing conflict in Kashmir, and the Northeast, this strategy has worked out successfully, adding layers of new elites and political arenas into the political system. The modest origin of decentralisation has matured into a full- fledged federal system, comparable to the now defunct Soviet federal system in its institutional complexity but endowed with far more vitality, as one can see from its resilience.

The Hybrid Post-colonial State as Both Structure and Agency

With the coming of independence, the state emerged both as the structure within which nation-building and development were to take place, and the main agency for these projects. Just like their British predecessors, the leaders of independent India put the institutions of the state to task to achieve these political objectives.

But democracy made the difference; the national agenda got taken over by the subaltern social groups who increasingly moved on to the offices of power and prestige. However, the game continued to be played on the rules laid down by the independence generation. These new elites – people with ambition and skills, emerging from lower social orders – became the vital link between the modern and the traditional India, and, as a hinge group in Indian society, charged with the task of acting as culture-brokers, innovated new political practices, implemented through hybrid institutions. This section illustrates the core argument by drawing some examples from the structure of the modern state in India and the process of its interaction with traditional society and traditions of political thought and practice going back to Indian antiquity. The section below discusses why and how the post-colonial state has come to play a catalytic role in reviving the interrupted links of the present to the past, and through it, to restore the vital process of self-reflexive and authentic evolution through its hybridisation.

(a) Ontology of the state: Individualist and communitarian

Though the Constitution of India was greatly influenced by its British origin (two-thirds of the written constitution came from the Government of India Act, 1935, passed by the British Parliament), it nevertheless established its departure from colonial practice by conflating the individual and the community, modernity and tradition, the exogenous cultural flow and the indigenous tradition in a novel manner. Article 1 of the Constitution announced: India, that is Bharat, shall be a Union of States, thus affirming the dual origin of the Indian political system from the cultural flow from Europe through the conduit of colonial rule, and the resurrection of the ruptured links with Bharat – the mythical kingdom of pre-modern India. Similarly, the choice of the Aśokan 'Lion Capital' and the 'Aśoka Cakra' (wheel with 24 spokes) as the state emblems of independent India is an example of hybridisation. The hybrid constitution, part liberal, part communitarian, provides a third space between the rational, utility maximising individual and the collectivity, keen on solidarity and policing the common bonds.

The Indian state moved beyond the canon of its liberal name-sake and ascribed to itself a variable space between the ideals of the neutral enforcer of norms – the essential feature of Weberian, bureaucratic modernity – and the partisan defender of the traditional, marginal and the patrimonial:

> Like Hindu conceptions of the divine, the state in India is polymorphous, a creature of manifold forms and orientations. One is the third actor whose scale and power contribute to the marginality of class politics. Another is a liberal or citizens' state, a juridical body whose legislative reach is limited by a written constitution, judicial

> review, and fundamental rights. Still another is a capitalist state that guards the boundaries of the mixed economy by protecting the rights and promoting the interests of property in agriculture, commerce, and industry. Finally, a socialist state is concerned to use public power to eradicate poverty and privilege and tame private power. Which combination prevails in a particular historical setting is a matter of inquiry.[46]

The two authors also note that "state in India was not a European import", but the "historical legacies of imperial states on the Indian subcontinent in the pre-Christian era established state conceptions and institutions that provided models for the subcontinental multinational state of modern India."[47] Needless to say, the Kauṭilyan conception of the state, is an important factor of influence on the design of modern Indian state – not only in terms of 'state philosophy', but basic institutional structures and procedures as well.

(b) The Congress 'System': Bridging colonial rule and competitive politics

The transition from colonial rule to competitive party politics within a democratic framework was facilitated by a conglomerate of interests, personalities and beliefs that drew as much on the indigenous idiom as on liberal democratic politics. With Jawaharlal Nehru at the helm of affairs, the Indian National Congress (INC), located at the fulcrum of national politics, constituted the core of a one-dominant-party system. For about two decades, the INC ruled from Delhi and practically in all the Indian federal States. Elections were free and held regularly but the Congress which never won a majority of votes, thanks to the first past the post voting system, regularly won a majority of seats, and came to be known as the party of governance. The opposition parties, scattered around it, practically never held office but exercised power and influence in implicit coalition with factions within the Congress party. This made it possible for India to reinforce a political culture of bargaining, reform and orderly social change without party alternation. This unique constellation of forces came to be known as the Congress System, which, in retrospect, was the vital link between despotic and democratic rule.

In the diagrammatic representation of the Congress System (Figure 2), the axes represent major issues facing the country, at the centre of which stood the Congress Party. On each issue, left and right wing opinions were arrayed on either side of the Congress represented by the dark inner circle. The next circle stands for the opposition parties. The Congress System held the Indian National Congress in legislative power but a power which could not swing the country in a clear political direction.

Figure 2: The Congress System of India

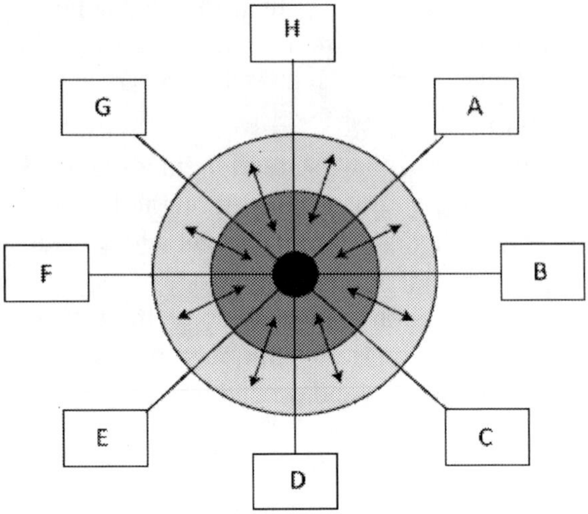

Source: Adapted from Morris-Jones (1966) 'Dominance and Dissent' in *Government and Opposition,* p. 219.

(c) The economy: Modern, traditional, liberal and Gandhian, all at the same time

The 'Mixed' economy, combining features of Soviet style planning and the free market with rather articulate echoes of Kauṭilyan economics became the main frame of India's economic life. The 'Indian' model of democratic development emerged from a series of strategic choices made during the early years after independence. These choices, in turn, were based on a set of compromises that attempted to blend the experience of wartime planning and controls, domestic pressures for a policy of economic nationalism, and the liberal, Gandhian and socialist ideological crosscurrents that existed within the nationalist movement. The model that grew out of these strategic choices evolved incrementally into a set of policies that became the basis of India's development consensus. It called for a system of centralised planning and a mixed economy in which a government owned public sector would dominate basic industry and the state would control, regulate, and protect the private sector from foreign competition. Foreign capital would be permitted, but only under highly controlled and restricted circumstances. The objectives of India's development were to achieve rapid economic growth, self-reliance, full employment and social justice. Irrespective of the actors' pragmatic considerations, the choice of the mixed economy and economic development model, clearly indicates 'Kauṭiylan echoes' in defining the strategic directionality of economic policy: qualitative and quantitative economic growth must serve building 'national power'.

These key concepts were understood in the same sense much as the European social history during the period of rapid change which witnessed the rapid transformation of traditional agricultural society into the modern industrial society. The former was characterised by the predominance of ascription, multiplex social relations where one individual would play a variety of roles, a deferential stratification system, ensconced within primordial kin networks. A modern society, on the other hand, was seen as one based on the predominance of universalistic, specific and achievement norms, high degree of social mobility, specialisation and occupational differentiation, an egalitarian class system based on generalised patterns of occupational achievement and the prevalence of association of specific groups not based on ascription.

The mixed economy gave an institutional shape to the liberal, socialist and communitarian values that constituted the three main strands of the Freedom Movement and dominated the proceedings of the Constituent Assembly. The liberal values were given a clear and incontrovertible shape in the Fundamental Right to the freedom of trade, occupation and ownership, Article 19 of the Constitution. The socialist values were less explicit, but nevertheless, clearly discernible. Instead of the concept of due process – open to judicial interpretation – the Constitution settled for the concept of 'procedure established by law' which made 'national' interest more compelling than the interest of the individual, a doctrine that paved the way for land reforms, and laws aimed at curbing the full play of capitalist enterprise. Articles 39, 41, 43, 46 of the Directive Principles of State Policy recommended that the state pursue policies aimed at bringing about right to an adequate means of livelihood, the distribution of the ownership and control of material resources of the community in a manner that best serves the common good, and to avoid the concentration of wealth, a living wage, decent standards of living and full enjoyment of leisure and social and cultural opportunities for the entire population. Finally, even though there was no staunch 'Gandhian lobby' in the Constituent Assembly, communitarian values such as welfare of Harijans, backward classes, women and children, village and cottage industries, educational and economic interests of weaker sections, cattle welfare, banning slaughter of milch cattle found their way into the body of this elaborate text.

(d) Self-rule and shared rule: Combining cultural diversity and the federal structure

Apart from academic disputation about the nature and even the 'authenticity' of India's federal system as defined in the constitution[48] lies the reality of an enormous country whose cultural heterogeneity is expressed in the federal organisation of power. Since state reorganisation in 1953 and 1956, state boundaries have roughly coincided with historically rooted linguistic and cultural regions. The differences reinforce the effects of size and continue in the federal system the tensions between regional kingdoms and subcontinental empire that have characterised the history of the state in India. Federalisation – the subject of numerous studies, conferences, and commissions – beginning in the early seventies with the Rajamannar Committee (1971) in Tamil Nadu[49] and continuing till today – reflects the crucial role it plays in national politics. The fact of the matter is that Indian federalism is very much a hybrid Indian creation, combining imported concepts of power-sharing with indigenous methods of consensus and accommodation. During the dominance of the Congress party, the 'Union' government (a sign of hybridity – for the constitution recognised the federal government simply as the Union) and most State governments were ruled by the same party and conflict resolution could take place informally within party channels, causing some specialists to question the purity of the Indian brand as authentically federal. However, federalism Indian style has gained endurance and legitimacy; found a new lease of life by developing an intricate set of informal channels and formal mechanisms to continue effective conflict resolution. The territorial state has seen many changes, particularly at the level of the regions. New regions have been created to give more salience to regional identity, language and economic needs. But, unlike in neighbouring Pakistan, which mainly as a result of regional imbalance, split into two in 1971, the territorial integrity of India continues to be stable.

(e) Indian Personal Law: Conflating the secular state and sacred beliefs

India's Personal Law, governing family, marriage, divorce, adoption and succession is a unique blend of the double commitment of the state to the rights of the individual and commitment to group identities.[50] Ironically, the collective rights and group identities were rooted in the history of representation under British rule. The British, who at home conceived of the political community in terms of equal citizens, in India saw it in terms of distinctive groups, which was taken to be a unique feature of Indian society. The same held also for the leaders of India's freedom movement who sought to realise a political community composed of equal citizens but early on realised that they could not build a nationalist movement without recognising cultural and territorial communities. Political safeguards to minorities were a key element of British efforts to represent groups in Indian society. They were first elaborated in the Morley-Minto constitutional reforms of 1906, then in the Montagu-Chelmsford scheme of 1919, and finally in the constitutional framework that received the royal assent in 1935.[51]

The constitutional design and the structure of institutions that were intended to give concrete shape to the idealistic goals of the Republic, enshrined in the preamble, adopted methodological individualism as the cutting edge of social change. However, such principles as individual rights, representation based not on group identities but individual interests and structured along the lines of political majorities, seen in the context of a society based on hierarchy and tightly-knit social groups, could only lead to conflicts based on values and interests of everyday politics. Free and fair elections, universal adult franchise and extension of the electoral principle into all realms of social power were intended to articulate, aggregate and eventually incorporate endogenous political norms and alien political institutions within the structure of the political system of the post-colonial state.

The fuzzy, hybrid practice of combining individual rights and group identity came to a sore test in the Shah Bano case where the Supreme Court upheld the appeal of a divorced Muslim woman for her individual right to alimony against the practice prevailing in the Muslim community of India of leaving such matters to the community. However, in the face of strong opposition to the extension of a 'pure' construction of individual rights to the Muslim community, Prime Minister Rajiv Gandhi introduced the [Muslim women] Protection of Rights on Divorce Bill in 1986, and restored the hybrid solution to the complicated relationship of Islam and the secular state.

(f) The modern state and cultural diversity: Three language formula

Many post-colonial states, following independence, set up a single national identity – one state, one legal system, one national language and one state religion – as the basis of their statehood. Pakistan – the land of the pure – became an advocate of this form of purity whereas India stood for a more inclusive identity. In its solicitude to distinguish itself from secular and diverse India, Pakistan opted for Urdu as the national language, refusing to dilute this unity through official recognition to other major languages like Bengali. India, on the other hand, after a brief spell of disorder on the issue of national language, devised a formula in course of the States' Reorganisation Commission to encourage large sections of the people to learn a language other than one's mother tongue. The idea of hybridity has found a hospitable corner.

(g) Social hierarchy and rational bureaucracy

The modern men and women to whom the British transferred power in 1947 had their task cut out for them. Echoing the spirit of the times, India's first Prime Minister Jawaharlal Nehru, outlined his vision of the future of Indian state, society and the economy, in a famous oration that has since become a landmark on modern India. Nehru, a quintessential renaissance man, had presented this modernist agenda on the background of the carnage that followed the Partition of British India into Pakistan, carved out as a homeland for India's Muslims, and the Indian republic that chose to remain a secular state. As India's first Prime Minister, Nehru, a social democrat by temperament, intensely aware of the urgency of a concerted effort to remove mass poverty and ignorance, sought legitimacy through the promotion of general welfare. Democracy, a sense of community and modernisation were values that were to lead the way into the promised future. The fact that these principles were of alien provenance did not matter at that moment of euphoria.

The modern message of Nehru and his generation of leaders was carefully wrapped in traditional, Indian symbols, and conveyed through the hybrid institutions that formed part and parcel of the Indian political system. Nehru's generation of leaders who took over the mantle of hybrid modernity from their predecessors has been able to institutionalise the genre of the *neta* – typically Indian leaders. At the crucial nodes of this complex system, one increasingly found the quintessential Indian *neta* – Hindi for leader – who became a two-way culture broker, constantly conflating the modern and traditional idioms of Indian politics. As much in their rhetoric, as in their person, these *netas* represented a quintessential Indian genre. The hybrid *neta*, much like Mahatma Gandhi before Independence – a picture of charismatic Laloo Prasad Yadav shows how these political entrepreneurs combined traditional symbols and modern institutions and technology to produce a superb conduit for the flow of power, communication and legitimacy.

A key feature of the modern Indian state is its centralised bureaucracy. Both Nehru and Patel recognised the indispensability of a centralised state bureaucracy. They made sure that the Indian Civil Service of colonial times was wholesale taken over by the new state – just like the armed forces, police and the intelligence service. However, centralised state bureaucracy in India was not invented by the British. India has an endogenous tradition of state bureaucracy that goes back to the Maurya Empire – and its conceptual design is laid down in the *Kauṭilīya-Arthaśāstra*. As Panikkar notes:

> The age-old political tradition in India before Independence was that of an administrating state. At all times, from the time of the Nandas in the 4th century BCE, it was a vast bureaucracy that governed the country, collected its revenue, looked after the irrigation system and maintained law and order. Basically the British system was not different from that of Mauryas or the Moghuls.[52]

(h) Public buildings and images of the hybrid state

The architecture of public buildings of India, and city planning provide the final evidence of hybrid modernity. The British colonial rulers laid down the plans of capital buildings with broad avenues (optimal for military marches as much as for showcasing the street plans of modernity) but nevertheless, adorned with symbols of traditional India (in this case, the Mughal water garden, the Buddhist *stūpa*, the Islamic minarets and the Hindu *chatrīs*) that would make the native feel comfortable in the modern set up. The 'traditional' designs and architectural forms that the British drew on were themselves hybrid in nature, based on a re-use of local and regional forms as well as conceptual and cultural flow from outside the country.[53]

The British strategy of domination which took into account the enormous gain in legitimacy through the re-use of the institutions and sacred symbols of those defeated by it, consisted of selected incorporation of some elements of the Indian past and conspicuous rejection of the rest. Imperial design and utilitarian ideology converged in the Anglo-Indian style – in architectural as much as institutional – design. The sole opportunity for colonised Indians to advance, as they saw it, consisted in the acceptance of modern (i.e. European) science, technology and values. The coming of Gandhi, and subsequently, India's independence, challenged it, opening up, in the process, the flood-gates into India's pre-modern past for those fighting for freedom from colonial rule.

Colonial aesthetics and colonial politics were of one piece. The architecture of colonial rule worked to one common purpose – of selective incorporation, de-linking traditional elites from their ancestral moorings, and justifying their power in terms of the common purpose of Progress, of which colonial rule was but an instrument. The Archaeological Survey of India preserved India's monuments – both sacred and administrative – in a state of "arrested decay"[54] isolated and distanced from the community of which they used to be an integral part. So did the new British established political and administrative institutions which presented the Indian past as inferior to the British present, and by the same analogy, the modernity symbolised by colonial rule as the superior future.

The British designers of India's capital and the public buildings drew on the designs and symbols of modernity, as well as traditional symbols of India – the Hindu *chatrī*, the Islamic *mīnārs*, Buddhist *stūpas* and the Islamic water garden.[55] The intention here was to make the subject feel comfortable in his new abode, and generate legitimacy for British rule in the process. The 'Transfer of Power' to the successor regime of Nehru passed on this hybrid structure. The new stakeholders – many from lower social orders who quickly adapted themselves to their new social and political circumstances – found a useful tool of order and legitimacy in these new, modern institutions, and re-used them by incorporating minimal but necessary changes in the inner architecture of space.

The Pure and the Hybrid: Significance of Kauṭilya for State Resilience in the Age of Global Terror

In its search for pure categories in terms of which to compare the diversity of states, comparative politics has left behind the pragmatic empiricism of Aristotle which saw experience (and as such, actors' preferences) rather than superior knowledge as the basis of legitimacy.[56] Instead, the inspiration of Plato's 'ideal' state construction has dominated the field. Examples of the ever present search for pure categories, and the failure to fit the world into them, are plentiful. A seminal attempt to classify contemporary political regimes (192 of them, to be precise) into democracy and authoritarian categories found 38 per cent belonging to the pure class of liberal democracy. The rest were distributed over 'electoral democracy' (16%), ambiguous regimes (8.9%), competitive authoritarian (10.9%), hegemonic electoral authoritarian (13%), politically closed authoritarian (13%).[57] A subsequent attempt at a similar classification came up with a deeply pessimistic conclusion with regard to the tendency of transitional regimes to move firmly away from the lure of authoritarianism, smuggled into the structure of pure democratic institutions by the way of hybridisation.[58] These unfruitful attempts to bring errant hybrid regimes into the net of neat classification hold out the portents of hope for trans-disciplinary analysis and a wider model encompassing insights gained from the new research on cultural flow[59] that can take in 'pure' as well as hybrid cases.

The status of the state in India as a modern, consolidated, electoral democracy is well established.[60] But, while the country responds positively to most items on formal check lists of stateness and democracy, doubts persist about its authenticity as a democracy because of its anomalous character. The authoritarian 'emergency' provisions built into India's constitution, the practice of relinquishing state power to the military under the Armed Forces Act, hybrid legislation that combine features of modern and religious laws, capitulation to social actors and ethnic groups in communal riots and most importantly, glaring failures to protect secularism and individual rights – the ultimate symbols of high modernity – are pilloried as 'functional' lapses by the defenders of modernity. India's political system, which combines liberal democratic institutions and elements of her pre-modern past – notably Kauṭilya's theory of the state – continues to puzzle.[61]

In their prescient essay on the 'modernity of tradition' which analysed some ambivalent aspects of modern Indian institutions[62] Lloyd and Susanne Rudolph had laid down the ground work for issues raised in this article. India, thanks to the mismatch between pre-conceived categories and her empirical complexity,[63] occupies an ambiguous position in global ranking of democracies. The empirical analysis of the features of the Indian state shows, however, that rather than being merely a diminished sub-type of liberal democracy, the state in India is a modern state in its own right, but one which diverges from the western state "in the importance it accords to 'pre-modern' political forms...because they express different cultural values and traditions that form part of the cultural heritage."[64] It is the quintessential unity in diversity, for the state is the fulcrum around with diverse ideologies, cultures, beliefs and economic regimes revolve. In the words of Lloyd and Susanne Rudolph (1987), the state in India is a manifold – an embodiment of the "avatars [incarnations] of Vishnu".

The hybrid elements in the modern state of India are the outcome of the historical genealogy of the state tradition and its discontinuities, cultural and geographic diversity, and the deep class conflict that underpins Indian society. Before we analyse these conditions that have affected the emergence of the state, we need to consider the theoretical bridge that connects the process of state formation to its ultimate product, namely the institutional structure of the state.

Conclusion: Implications of the Indian Case for a General Theory of State Formation in Transitional Societies

The anomalous character of India in terms of the comparative politics of democracy helps link a debate specific to comparative politics with the larger issue of hybridity that has dominated critical theory and post-colonial literature. A brief foray into the larger theoretical landscape can help to establish a course for empirical analysis of the Indian case and provide the basis of an analytical tool-box that extends the conventional rational choice neo-institutional model of the state by drawing on trans-lingual, trans-cultural and trans-disciplinary aspects of state formation. On the basis of this heuristic model, we can analyse the underlying process that has made the state in India what it is, and explain why the state has become a key element in the resilience of India's political system.

The states of contemporary South Asia emerged from the area that corresponds to the spatial domain of Kauṭilya's *Arthaśāstra*. Why did the Indian state follow a different course of evolution than that of the other South Asian states? Deeper exploration of the issue is beyond the remit of this paper. However, in view of the comparative significance of the issue it is important to indicate that at critical junctures of state formation and evolution, the leadership in question made choices that led to state consolidation as in India, and state fragmentation like in Pakistan 1969-70 and state paralysis in Sri Lanka whose seeds can be seen in the choices made by the policy of 'Sinhala only'. The conclusion returns to the issue of the relationship of the pure and the hybrid in Political Science, and opens it up for a general, cross-disciplinary debate.

The focus on hybrid structures generates the space for the understanding of phenomenon of cultural and conceptual flow, and the emergence of hybrid institutions as a consequence of the conflation of the endogenous and the alien categories and institutions. In this article, we have outlined the theoretical puzzles associated with the 'modernity of tradition' of the post-1947 state in India. And we have specifically sketched the contours of the intellectual influence and tangible impact of the Kauṭilyan theory of the state and statecraft upon the modern Indian state. The elaboration of the latent impact of Kauṭilyan thought via the habitus of modern political actors as well as the active re-use of Kauṭilyan thought by modern political actors and the institutional consequences thereof will follow further on in the text.

With the state and the political system of India as the main focus, we have explored the components of India's hybrid state, and attempted to account for them in terms of the strategies followed by the main political actors of India. We have argued that hybridisation is part and parcel of politics as actors, in their search for autonomy, coherence, resilience and development, transform rules and designs as they see fit. A solution where the bulk of stake-holders simultaneously reach or expect to reach their best outcomes, once achieved, yields a 'lock-in' from which they would find it difficult to exit. Each hybrid institution carries a 'lock-in' at its core.[65] Not all innovations or amendments work, of course, but when they do, or as North puts it, when a cluster of actors 'lock-in' around a particular design or set of rules, the result – a new hybrid institution – can become enduring.

Left to their own devices, people connected to these hybrid institutions do not necessarily see them as aberrations, or diminished forms of the real thing. Despite their stretched, mixed or altered forms, or precisely because of them, hybrid political structures have a real life, full of vitality, social significance and the capacity for self-regeneration. Rather than being merely transient, many flourish over long stretches of time and space.

Not all hybrid structures are treated kindly by different scientific disciplines; their academic standing varies from one discipline to another. The intellectual indulgence that critical theory, post-colonial literature, cultural anthropology and social history have shown to hybrid structures, concepts and institutions is missing in comparative politics. In its Jacobin mode, comparative politics usually approaches the political process of post-colonial states with 'pure' categories of European provenance, thus running the risk of parts of the empirical world escaping the classificatory project altogether, or worse, the analyst, having failed to classify or explain, out of sheer desperation, turning into a moralist![66] Little does one realise, however, that concepts – when they travel beyond their place of origin – still carry their birth marks of cultural and contextual assumptions built into them. The mechanical application of 'pure' concepts of European origin to alien soil can lead to 'conceptual stretching'[67] or violent retribution by the way of radical rejection of all that go under the banner of such concepts, leading to violent post-revolutionary frenzy.[68] Inducting hybridity and cultural flow in to the pure categories of comparative politics might contribute to firmer measurements, and a more benign world.

Looking back at the Indian past through hybrid eyes yields surprises. One comes to realise that modern institutions of India, nationalist sentiments notwithstanding, are a true British legacy. In the second place, a critical analysis of British rule and Indian resistance to it helps explain why democratic institutions have worked more effectively in India as compared to her neighbours.[69] That the synthesis of British constitutional norms and political forms with India's indigenous political tradition led to a different outcome than the other successor states ensues from India's tradition of re-use, where the past continues within the present as a fundamental politico-cultural reality that is being drawn upon by deliberate political design. The British pursued their own colonialist variation of re-use with respect to Indian tradition, but that eventually collided with the Indian nationalists' strategy of re-use. Avid re-users, post-independent India's leaders have not only re-used their endogenous politico-cultural resources, but also appropriated many of the symbols and institutions of their colonial predecessors, and cloaked them in Indian garb. This blending of indigenous tradition and imported institutions explains both, the ability of the British to rule for so long with little recourse to overt force, as well as the smooth transition from colonial rule to multi-party democracy.

Effective accommodation of the past within the structure of the present is not necessarily a problem of mechanical accumulation. It also entails the need for leaders to strategically pick and choose; the process is marked by violence and leaves behind a trail of bitterness and anxiety. This helps explain the juxtaposition of successful state formation and persistence of inter-community conflict and regional secession movements in India.[70]

Seen in this light, the claim of high modernity in its Orientalist avatar to the 'pure' and use of the resultant power to authenticate its claim to the high moral ground, and fending off any claims to familiarity by the subaltern (in the sense of the hybridity, pollution *métissage*, solecism, mimicry...), comes across as theory playing the hand maiden to politics.[71] The research on hybridity questions the dominance of one society over another in the name of modernity and "Whereas for Hegel, Marx and Weber there appeared to be but one race and the West had strung the tape at the finish line for others to break, for us it has become apparent that there are multiple races and many finish lines, and the tapes are manufactured also in Tokyo and Beijing".[72] The symbolic presence of the past constitutes a link of modernity with collective memory. Susanne Rudolph generalises from these observations to the need to look at the universal claims of a particular variant of modernity afresh.[73]

Where, then, does comparative politics go from here? A number of theoretical developments in the social sciences and humanities since the halcyon days of structural functionalism – conceptual stretching, bounded rationality, two level games, entangled history, habitus, re-use, and the flow of culture – point in the direction of new pastures that one can visit in order to enrich the basis of comparison that is relevant to our times.[74] The biggest challenge is to bring the two worlds – of comparative politics and conceptual flow – together and make it methodologically possible for them to draw strength from one another. Even as we celebrate the value added character of hybridity for conventional research on the state and modernity, one should, nevertheless be weary of too hasty a rejection of the rigour of logical positivism at the core of comparative politics. Hybridity research stands to gain enormously from retaining the epistemological links with historical development of comparative politics as a distinctive field. Re-use rather than replacement is the best scientific way forward, because, important as the heuristic value of hybridity is, progress in the field of research on modernity and the state is contingent on rigorous fieldwork that is the most valuable legacy of structural-functionalism. To measure the length, breadth, depth and stability of hybrid substances, we still need categories and tools that are themselves not hybrid. The alternative is to bring in a form of radical relativism that denies any possibility of inter-personal communication or replication.

The crucial issue is not to lose sight of the fact that political concepts and institutions – pure as well as hybrid – are political constructions – and as such, contingent on a cluster of interests, stakeholders, and their contextual setting. As long as the values, beliefs, interests of the stakeholders are served well, and the world at large leaves it alone, an institution and its underlying concept can remain stable over long periods of time. However, today, in the age of trans-national citizenship and global communication, they are as much subject to the inward flow of concepts as to the outward. Most of all, thanks to the new research on hybridity, the ontological status of the 'pure' has become contested. Hybrids do not necessarily think of themselves as impure, and, it is quite conceivable that the 'pure', so-called, is actually a special case of the hybrid. As one notices the helpless search for a way to accommodate Islam on European soil, with the Jacobin state and global Islam locked into a stalemated conflict, one looks wistfully at the success of the hybrid Indian Personal Law and the hybrid modern state with a Kauṭliyan core that has kept the divisive issues of the sacred and the secular within the bounds of the rule of law.

END NOTES

1. For a critical analysis of modernity in the Indian context, cf. Rudolph and Rudolph (1967) and Mitra (Ed.) (2009), five vols.
2. K. M. Munshi founded Bharatiya Vidya Bhavan in 1938 with the blessings of Mahatma Gandhi with the intention of reviving interest in India's past as part of the larger goals of India's freedom movement.
3. "The past has to be seen to be dead; or the past will kill". See Naipaul (1979: 174).
4. Evolution is a concept used in biology to describe long term developments that are undirected and have a common point of origin in the past. An approach to apply this concept to political science is Evolutionary Institutionalism (EI). In this application institutions are analysed analogous to organs from an evolutionary perspective. Institutions evolve, according to EI, influenced by ecological factors (exogenous change) or through re-interpretation and re-implementation in the course of daily routines (endogenous change); cf. Gould (2002), Lewis and Steinmo (2012).
5. Following Pierre Bourdieu's concept, 'habitus' is understood here as the repository of past ideas and patterns of thought and behaviour that sub- or semi-consciously influence, if not steer present thinking and acting in the politico-strategic field. The habitus enables the 'flow' of ideas and attitudes across time – independent of their transmission in discursive contexts. cf. Bourdieu (1990: 52-97), Michael Liebig (2014a: 90-96, 276-312).
6. The reference here is to Rudolph and Rudolph, *The Modernity of Tradition*, Ashis Nandy, *The Intimate Enemy* and Adda Bozeman, *Politics and Culture in International History*. Each of these three texts presents the pre-modern past as a vital reservoir of knowledge that the designers of modern India have re-used in order to create the institutional arrangement that has shown its resilience over the past six decades.
7. Bozeman (1960: 5).
8. cf. Douglas, Mary (1966/1996 reprint: I), for a lucid and "universal analysis of the rules of purity which applies equally to secular and religious life as to primitive and modern societies."
9. [On the wake of the Revolution] "Suddenly, subjects were told they had become Citizens; an aggregate of subjects held in place by injustice and intimidation had become a Nation. From this new thing, this Nation of Citizens, justice, freedom and plenty could be not only expected but required. By the same token, should it not materialise, only those who had spurned their citizenship, or who were by their birth or unrepentant beliefs incapable of exercising it, could be held responsible. Before the promise of 1789 could be realised, it was necessary to root out Un-citizens" [Schama (1989: 859)]. The search for purity functions as the essence of legitimacy for totalitarian rulers, from Stalin to the Taliban.
10. The political development literature of the 1960s is replete with such developmental schemata which in turn draw on older categories such as *Gemeinschaft* and *Gesellschaft* (Toennies) that cast developing and developed societies in a model of developmental nexus. The responsibility to provide guidance to the developing societies was taken up by the institutions in charge of policing purity – experts, colonial masters or their post-colonial pupils to whom power was transferred at Independence – who were expected to detect, punish and eliminate impurity.
11. cf. Diamond (2002a).
12. Fürstenberg (2015).
13. cf. Kangle (2010c), Liebig (2014a), Zimmer (1969), Hillebrandt (1923), Sil (1989).

14. Max Weber was the first western social scientist to recognise Kauṭilya's significance. See Weber's '*Politics As A Vocation*' and his sociology of religion studies on Hinduism and Buddhism. cf. Weber (2000); Weber (1988).
15. Kangle (2010b: 47), [1.19.34-35].
16. cf. Weber (2000: 161).
17. *Ibid.*: 146.
18. cf. Scharfe (1968: 233-276).
19. Bozeman (1960: 5-6).
20. cf. Bourdieu (1990: 52-97).
21. cf. Dixit (2004); Menon (2013).
22. cf. Halbwachs (1991).
23. Nehru (1981: 59, 67).
24. cf. Zaman (2006).
25. Mitra (1999b); Mitra and Singh (2009b).
26. Politics in classical India "distinguished between dharma, a concept carrying the broad general meaning of righteousness and best rendered in legal literature as the divinely ordained norm of good conduct, and artha, which signifies utility and property. The sources of Indian political thought are thus essentially two-fold: the dharmashastras, or treatises on law and political theory, among which the *Code of Manu* is the most renowned, and the Arthaśāstra which deal with practical politics on the national and international level." Bozeman (1960: 120).
27. Bozeman (1960, 121).
28. North identifies two major factors that are responsible for incremental institutional change, namely, "the lock-in that come from the symbiotic relationship between institutions and the organisations that have evolved as a consequence of the incentive structure provided by those institutions, and the feedback process by which human beings perceive and react to changes in the opportunity set." North (1990: 7).
29. Fludernik (1998: 10).
30. "Bhabha himself has complicated the notion of hybridity even further by resorting to the Lacanian category of the imaginary, a move which hearkens back to Franz Fanon's work. For Bhabha the coloniser and the colonial subject both undergo a splitting of their identity positions, a splitting that occurs through their mutual imaginary identification (pictured in terms of mimicry). Bhabha's model also relies on Derrida and Bakhtin, bringing together a variety of poststructuralist concepts which are then catachrestically applied and juxtaposed in a variety of contexts and settings. I refrain at this point from a more detailed explication of Bhabha's *The Location of Culture* since his model is discussed in great detail in the essays of Fludernik and Ray" [Fludernik (1998: 14)]. cf. Bhabha (1994).
31. A Gramscian term, adopted by Gayatri Spivak and the Subaltern Studies School.
32. Fludernik (1998: 21-22).
33. Hegewald and Mitra (2008).
34. Morris-Jones (1964: 13).
35. *Ibid.*: 17.
36. The Chinese came to the same conclusion – "It does not matter what colour the cat is, as long as it catches mice!" - three decades after the Great Proletarian Revolution.
37. cf. Auboyer (1965); Edwardes (1965).
38. This spirit of renewal, essential to the conservative dynamism of pre-modern India, is

summed up in an often-repeated *śloka* from the Gīta: *Whenever, scion of Bharatas! Righteousness declines and unrighteousness prevails, I manifest Myself.* (Bhagavadgītā 4.7).

39. For examples of re-use during the period of the decline of India's political autonomy, cf. Hegewald (2006: 517-523); Hegewald (2005: 179-190).
40. Metcalf makes this point in his interpretation of the decorative role of past artefacts in the modern architecture of Lutyens [Metcalf (1998)].
41. Metcalf (1998: 14).
42. Metcalf (1998: 24) sums up the reciprocal relation of Orientalism and Empire in the following passage: "Perhaps Curzon's lamp [which he got designed in Egypt and arranged to be placed on the grave of Mumtaz in the Taj Mahal] might be taken to represent the colonial aesthetic. It is an aesthetic of difference, of distance, of substantiation, of control – an aesthetic in which the Taj Mahal, the mosque of Cairo, even the *Arabian Nights*, all merge and become indistinguishable, and hence are available for use however the colonial ruler chooses. It is an aesthetic in which the past, though ordered with scrupulous attention to detail, stays firmly in the past. It is an aesthetic Shah Jahan [the Mughal emperor who built the Taj Mahal as a memoriam to Mumtaz Mahal, his deceased Queen] could never have comprehended".
43. Nandy (1983: IX).
44. The signs of the lingering British presence – Sunday as the official holiday of the week, left-hand-drive of the Indian traffic, and the ubiquitous Ambassador car, a hybrid British Austin Rover adapted to Indian roads which had become the sturdy emblem of Indian officialdom, are everywhere. The Dak Bungalows, outposts of the British Raj out in the country, temporary homes for the British civilian officers on tour, are tended with the same attention to details by the PWD – the Public Works Department, also of British vintage – just as are the post-independence guest houses of the national and state governments.
45. Rudolph and Rudolph (1987), Parekh (1999).
46. Rudolph and Rudolph (1987: 400f).
47. *Ibid.*: 63f.
48. cf. Mitra (2000).
49. Government of Tamil Nadu: *Report of the Centre-State Relations Inquiry Committee, 1971*.
50. cf. Mitra (2002), Ghosh (2007).
51. cf. Coupland (1944:128, 134, 151), for the evolution of statutory communalism.
52. Panikkar (1963: 228).
53. Tillotson comments: "The visual culture of the Mughals, so distinctive and instantly recognizable, was not conjured out of nothing. Its success was the product of the skillful blending together of the many different traditions that were available to the artists to draw on, including the Mughal's own central Asian heritage and the expertise and many long-established styles of India itself. The empire's greatest legacy is perhaps this composite culture; and that culture's most outstanding masterpiece is the building [Taj Mahal]" [Tillotson (2008: 44)]. The architectural designs "drew inspiration from three related traditions: the architecture of the Mughals' central Asian homeland; the buildings erected by earlier Muslim rulers of India, especially in the Delhi region; and the much older architectural expertise of India itself." (*Ibid.*: 46)
54. Metcalf (1998: 18).
55. Hegewald (2012).

56. Aristotle felt that "too great a departure from common experience probably has a fallacy in it somewhere, even though it appears to be irreproachably logical" [Sabine (1973: 99)].
57. cf. Diamond (2002a: 26).
58. "[However] empirical evidence increasingly suggests that to a significant extent the third wave of democratisation could become less of a triumph of political liberalism and liberal democracy than a success story for 'hybrid' or 'ambiguous' regimes, 'delegative', 'defective', 'semi-' or 'illiberal' democracies, 'competitive authoritarianism.' These political systems include the 'Potemkin democracies' where a democratic façade conceals an authoritarian leadership and those that are 'ethnocratic', 'plebiscite-populist, often even with sultanistic components, and which therefore may be identified as 'false democracies'" [Croissant and Merkel (2004: 2)].
59. See below for the concepts of trans-lingual and trans-cultural research. Students of comparative politics engaged in the classificatory analysis have much to learn from similar attempts in history, particularly the research on 'histoire croisée'. cf. Werner and Zimmermann (2006).
60. cf. Mitra and Singh (2009) for diachronic data on legitimacy and efficacy in India which shows a steady rise from 1971 to 2004 for which we have evidence from survey data. Participation in free and fair elections has gone up steadily from 1951 when the first general election with universal adult franchise was held, and has reached levels that are respectable by the standards of liberal democracies.
61. cf., for example, Lijphart (2009).
62. For a succinct analysis of how 'modernity and tradition' do 'infiltrate and transform each other', cf. Rudolph and Rudolph (1967: 3).
63. cf. Mitra (1999b).
64. Mitra (1990b: 6).
65. North (1990: 94). I have drawn on North to ask, "why do institutions work in South Asia, sometimes?" [cf. Mitra (1999a): 422)].
66. cf. Mitra (1988: 318-337) and its companion piece Mitra (1994). Both essays have been reprinted in Mitra (1999).
67. Conceptual stretching takes the shape of hybrid categories such as 'people's democracy', 'guided democracy', 'Islamic democracy', etc. "When scholars extend their models and hypotheses to encompass additional cases, they commonly need to adapt their analytic categories to fit the next contexts...[However] the overly strict application of a classical framework can lead to abandoning to category prematurely or to modifying it inappropriately" [Collier and Mahon (1993: 845)].
68. The motley crowd of resisters, united to fight the 'intrusive other', come together under hybrid categories such as 'the Church' (see Charles Tilly's analysis of the counter-revolution in the Vendee) or Islam, in contemporary Afghanistan.
69. Purists like Jinnah and Bandaranaike, following their pure visions of Islam and Buddhism respectively, have run their states – Pakistan, the land of the pure, and Sri Lanka, the sacred land of Sirindip – to political dead-ends.
70. "Two salient areas of Indian politics that call for critical attention and possible re-evaluation are the relations of the state and the market, and the attitudes of the state towards religion. The former has attracted some attention already. The Indian economy has belatedly come to terms with the necessity of taking painful decisions about restructuring and accepted the need for internal and international competition. But considerable confusion and outmoded assumptions still dominate the attitudes of the

state towards religion" [Mitra (1990a: 92)]. "For its survival and growth, the state in India will need to go beyond simple accommodation and to transcend some contentious interests – religious, social, economic and political – when the occasion so demands" [Mitra (1990a: 93)].

71. It is about time that the students of the modern state re-read Elias, Foucault, Nandy and Metcalf to decide for themselves how much there is to un-learn so that they might learn properly how the modern state in India has acquired its 'European' resilience without the benefit of European history.

72. Rudolph (1987: 732).

73. "When empiricists, structuralists or political economists look at what they consider the mere flimflam of the symbolic realm, they want to know where the real stuff is: the village, the irrigation network, the coalition between king and noble, the extractive mechanism. They ask, how many divisions does the pope have? I also want to answer to choose questions. But as we address the state in Asia, we must treat the symbolic as a phenomenon. We must try to create theoretical frameworks that combine a demystified, rationalist worldview with an understanding of the phenomenology of the symbolic in societies where the gods have not yet died. And we must combine it with the understanding that we too construct and act within cosmologies and that we only deny the myths we live by because we cannot see or articulate them" [Rudolph (1987: 742)].

74. Several articles points in the direction of the wider dimensions of this project. These include: Gallie (1955/56), Sartori (1970), Collier Mahon (1993), Collier and Levitsky (1997), Diamond (2002b), Lindberg (2007), Stepan (2008).

3

Understanding Kauṭilya's *Arthaśāstra*: Origination, Migration and Diffusion

Pradeep Kumar Gautam

Introduction

This chapter is about understanding an ancient Indian text on statecraft called Kauṭilya's *Arthaśāstra*.[1] Its relevance today makes it a significant text to pursue. According to Johann Jakob Meyer, the German Indologist and translator of Kauṭilya's *Arthaśāstra* from Sanskrit to German, in 1927,[2] "the *Arthaśāstra* was not a book but a library of ancient India."[3] I think this assessment was very correct. Each time you pick up the text something new and novel emerges in the understanding – like browsing through a good well stocked library. Benoy Kumar Sarkar, one of India's leading scholars in early 20th century had deeply engaged with Indian political traditions and had compared them to the Western ones. As an ice breaking work, on Kauṭilya's *Arthaśāstra*, he had aptly said that the work spans across "principles and methods", and is also "theoretical and philosophical".[4] For translation from Sanskrit into English, the best source is that of R.P. Kangle, who had undertaken its translation comprehensively which also includes a study on the subjects covered in the text.[5] He probably devoted his whole life to this endeavour. It is to his credit that although he was a scholar of Sanskrit, he could relate the text to matters of Political Science, statecraft, security, philosophy and comparative world politics in great detail. He categorised the nature of the text to argue that the text:

> is not a theoretical treatise on Political Science. It does not cover the origins of

> the state, its nature and functions. It does not inquire how some men come to rule over others and how a majority of men are content to be governed by a few.[6]

So, a question comes to mind, what is the scope of Kauṭilya's *Arthaśāstra*? Kangle addressed this to mention that:

> *Arthaśāstra* is understood as the science of dealing with state affairs in the internal as well as external sphere; or in other words, it is the science of statecraft or of politics and administration.[7]

In his conclusion to the study, Kangle sums up to say:

> It is essentially a treatise on the art of government. It assumes monarchy to be the form of government; hence it is primarily addressed to the king, advising him on how the administration of his kingdom should be carried on and how he should adjust his foreign policy to the best advantage of his state.[8]

Kauṭilya's *Arthaśāstra* survived in oral traditions and fragmentary commentaries till its discovery in 1904 and its publication in 1915 into English, and later into other languages as well. The international community of scholars was considerably stimulated by this development.[9] However, one great hurdle was an answer to the question as to how come such a manual found its way in Indian traditions which appeared to be 'other-worldly'? Let us examine this.

In the past, it had often been incorrectly assumed by some Indologists that Indians are a nation of just philosophers. Dr. D.R. Bhandarkar in his analysis of the work of two such Indologists – Max Muller and Bloomfield (who felt that there was a total absence of statecraft) – gives Kauṭilya's *Arthaśāstra* as an evidence to negate the myth that "India made no contribution to the science of politics and has therefore no place in the political history of the world." Bhandarkar challenges this to say:

> For we learn from Kautilya that up till his time no less than four schools of the science of polity were known, and no less than seven individual authors of great eminence flourished, who were in no way connected with any school...Again, what were the *vidyas* or sciences prevalent in his time? They were *anvikshaki*, Philosophy, *trayi*, Theology, *varta*, Economics, and *danda-niti*, Polity....Does this not clearly show that before the advent of the Mauryan power the Indians cultivated the science of politics with as much boldness and alacrity as they did theology and philosophy...[10]

In the context of Indian civilisation enriching the knowledge of the world, Max Weber was one of the first German scholars to have noticed in 1917 that India "has come to have something of the significance that ancient Greece has had in the West".[11] Although Max Weber had sensed the unique role of the text early in 20th century, the initial debates and interest over its rediscovery in early 20th century got addressed mostly amongst only linguists, Sanskritists and ancient historians. This may not be enough to make the text relevant as concepts still remain understudied. Myron Weiner in 1984 had noted that absence of contemporary relevance in scholarship. The argument was:

> Commentators on the contemporary Indian political, social and economic scene almost never draw their analytical concepts explicitly from the literature of classical Indian political thought. Although Indians who have analysed this literature – K.P. Jayaswal, U.N. Ghosal, B. Prasad, D.R. Bhandarkar, R.S. Sharma, A.S. Altekar, K.M. Panikkar, B.K. Sarkar, T.N. Ramaswamy and B.A. Saletore – may have been eager to show that the literature had contemporary relevance, they were not primarily concerned with the study of contemporary politics and society.[12]

Surely the near absence of relating the text and its wisdom to contemporary politics, statecraft and diplomacy few decades ago was a fact. But why was this not done in the past? One reason is that the initial debates and interest over its rediscovery in early 20th century got addressed amongst only linguists, Sanskritists and ancient historians. Probably this unfortunate practice continues even today due to rigid departmental habits. To relate this text now to Political Science has been a task not fully done and the chapters in this book attempt to just do that. It is because anything 'classical' cannot vanish or disappear. Therefore, this knowledge needs to be systematically transferred to the realm of Political Science. Colin S. Gray reminds us that the "classical texts of political realism provide sound education. Of course, every text bears the stamp of its place, time and particular culture – for example, Thucydides, Sun Tzu, Kauṭilya, Machiavelli, Morgenthau and Aron all offer timeless wisdom because they all shared an accurate enough vision of enduring reality."[13]

It seems that Kangle did not engage in depth and detail with 'theories' which lie buried in the text. But after half a century of research that followed Kangle's study in the text, theories of economics are being discovered and together with the "superstars of eighteen century" such as David Hume, Adam Smith, James Stuart, and John Stuart Mill: Kauṭilya's contribution has been acknowledged through history of non-Western sources.[14] Sihag demonstrates that Kauṭilya is the founder of a number of economic theories and concepts.[15]

The mention of the text to be the source material of many other disciplines like diplomacy and military science has also been alluded to in the seminal and multivolume *History of Science, Philosophy and Culture in Indian Civilization.*[16] Today, this rich ancient text does not fail to excite and interest readers, especially as it still requires significant study and interpretation by political scientists– a challenging task. In recent times, political scientists and pundits from India well-versed in both International Relations (IR) and Kauṭilya's *Arthaśāstra* have taken very important steps to figure out which theory of IR best fits the text, beyond just classical realism. Akhilesh Pillalamarri[17] equates it with offensive realism without mentioning but implicitly having in mind its proponent like the theorist John J. Mearsheimer's *The Tragedy of Great Power Politics* (2001). Mahendra Prasad Singh, a former Professor and Head of Department of Political Science of Delhi University, is more direct. He compares it with Kenneth N. Waltz's *Man, the State, and War* (1959) to argue:

> There is a parallel between the theories of *saptanga* state and *rajmandala* of Kautilya in the modern neo-realist or structural-realist theory of international relations formulated by Kenneth N. Waltz.[18]

Further, to release the text from the stranglehold or paradigm of only political realism (and thus freeing him of being used only as an adjective a la Machiavelli),[19] Deepshikha Shahi argues that *Arthaśāstra* is essentially a work of "eclecticism" as it does not exclusively endorse a realist worldview; it rather also incorporates the theoretical propositions of Social Constructivism in comprehending and practising international relations.[20] Likewise, Medha Bisht argues to illuminate the idea of power, order, political virtue and state in IR and political theory;[21] and in this volume, shows the concept of "world system theory". Like art appreciation, finding similarities with many important strands of IR shows that the text or the 'masterpiece' is not only a gold mine but has other rare materials for which special intellectual tools are required. Thus, Michael Liebig shows the rich implicit concepts of the discipline of Intelligence Studies such as analyses, assessments and estimates in the text.[22] And later, with Dany Shoham, another scholar of contemporary Intelligence Studies, conclusively proves it again.[23]

Thus, Kauṭilya's *Arthaśāstra* as a normative text of instructions with various principles and ideas that are still relevant today, is being introduced in this study. The manual offers a vast range of topics and disciplines, of which defence, security, statecraft, international relations, and foreign policy and diplomacy stand out. The *Arthaśāstra* consists of 15 books called *adhikaraṇas*. Each book has chapters, which have sections comprising of prose called *sūtra(s)*.[24] The first five books known as the *tantras* deal with internal administration of the state, the next eight deal with *āvāpa* or its relations with neighbouring states and the last two are miscellaneous in character.[25] A breakdown of Kauṭilya's *Arthaśāstra* is given in the Appendix.

This study attempts to provide an understanding on the enduring and rich nature of the text, and accordingly its relevance. Besides foreign policy, issues on war and peace in the text can supplement and reinforce international laws of war. The first part covers, what is Kauṭilya's *Arthaśāstra*; and who is Kauṭilya? The second part explains key concepts of foreign policy and statecraft. The third part includes the continuation and migration of tradition in different forms within and outside India. The fourth part provides a case study on Kauṭilya and war.

Part I: What is Kauṭilya's *Arthaśāstra*; and Who is Kauṭilya?

The Key Role of Artha

"Since very early times *artha* has been regarded as one of the *trivarga* or three goals of human existence, the other two being *dharma* (ethical and moral) and *kāma* (worldly desires and expectations)."[26] *Arthaśāstra* is regarded as a *śāstra* concerned with general well-being on earth. "And since state activity alone can make such general well-being possible, the protection of earth and its acquisition, which are essential parts of state activity, are declared the province of this *śāstra*. It is thus defined as the *śāstra* which shows how this activity of the acquisition and protection of the earth should be carried out."[27] *Arthaśāstra* is a political manual. It is the science which is the means of the acquisition and protection of earth. The rulership of the 'earth' contemplated in the text does not however necessarily imply the conquest of the whole world. The field open for the operations of the would-be conqueror (*vijigīṣu*) appears restricted to the region lying between the Himalayas and the sea. Territories beyond the borders of India are not included in the 'territory of the Sovereign Ruler'.[28] In this setting of political unification of common cultural Indian subcontinent, the *Arthaśāstra* has a twofold aim. "First, it seeks to show how the ruler should protect his territory. This protection (*pālana*) refers principally to the administration of the state. Second, it shows how territory should be acquired. This acquisition (*lābha*) refers principally to the conquest of territory from others".[29] "The ends which the *Arthaśāstra* has in view are the *yogakṣema* (protection of what is acquired) and *rakṣaṇa* (protection) of subjects."[30] *Yogakṣema* is the purpose and the responsibility of the state by avoiding *mātsyanyāya* (big fish swallowing the smaller fish). Kauṭilya enjoins the king to adopt policies that would lead the state to *vṛddhi* (prosperity) and avoid those that result in *kṣaya* (decline).[31] The normative dimension is the political unification of the Indian subcontinent with no imperialist expansion beyond the subcontinent. In the text, there are two dominions (*viṣayas*): the *sva-viṣaya* (the dominion of the conqueror-to-be) and the *para-viṣaya* (dominion of the enemy). It is possible that city dwellers had a clear understanding of citizenship while those in the countryside (*janapada*) had overlapping jurisdiction as *sūtra* 8.1.26-27 indicate:

> And city-dwellers are stronger than the country people and being steadfast (in loyalty) are helpful to the king in times of trouble (8.1.26). Country people, on the other hand, are common to the enemy (8.1.27).[32]

Text on Artha, Date and Author

Romila Thapar who considers the text to be a Mauryan document wonders: "It has long been a puzzle as to why, if Kauṭilya had known a large imperial state, his work should be concerned with smaller states".[33] On the other hand Mark McClish argues that it is not a Mauryan document.[34] Hermann Kulke and Dietmar Rothermund in their *A History of India* provide a workable political system of the *Arthaśāstra*. They argue:

> Kautalya depicts a situation in which several small rival kingdoms each have a chance of gaining supremacy over the other if the respective ruler follows the instruction given by Kautalya. In ancient Indian history the period which corresponds most closely to Kautalya's description is that of the mahajanapadas before Magadha attained supremacy. Thus it seems more likely that Kautalya related in normative terms what he had come to know about this earlier period than his account actually reflected the Mauryan empire during Chandragupta's reign. Thus the *Arthasastra* should not be regarded as a source for the study of the history of the empire only but also for the history of state formation in the immediately preceding period.[35]

The History and Culture of Indian People: The Age of Imperial Unity highlights that between the small states in the ancient period there was an interplay of centripetal and centrifugal forces. Every state tended to encroach upon its neighbours. A big empire could not last long. Outlying regions were tempted to drift away to start an independent career and make a bid for supremacy. There were compromises and a fusion of federalism and feudalism.[36] It is in this approximate context that the famous circle of kings was constructed in Kauṭilya's *Arthaśāstra*. I argue that it is a good and unique scenario planning tool when used with other concepts such as *ṣāḍguṇya* and *upāyas*, and the seven pillars of *prakṛtis* and their state of health or ill health (*vyasanas* or calamity or disasters) of one's own, friends and foes.

For *artha* the one and only text is *Arthaśāstra,* attributed to a number of authors among whom Kauṭilya's is the final and supreme version.[37] Professor Upinder Singh of Delhi University in summation, basing it on all evidence including that of Thomas R. Tarutmann, *Kauṭilya and the Arthaśāstra* (1971), [who conducted a computer-aided statistical analysis of the *Arthaśāstra,* focusing on the differences in the frequencies of ordinary, frequently occurring word such as *ca* (and) and *va* (or) in different books of the work assume that different word frequencies point to different authors], takes a middle path. She concludes:

> Although the *Arthaśāstra* does have a certain element of unity, it is very likely that there were later interpolations and remouldings. The crux of the problem is: In view of debate over its age and authorship and its normative nature, how is this text to be used as a source of history? There do not yet seem to be sufficient grounds to abandon the idea that *some part* of the text was composed in the Mauryan period by a person named Kauṭilya, allowing for later interpolations stretching into the early centuries CE. Since it has some moorings in the Mauryan

period, the *Arthaśāstra* can be used as a source for certain aspects of the period. At the same, we have to be careful not to read the book as a description of Mauryan state or society.[38]

Chandragupta, the founder of the Maurya dynasty, succeeded to the Nanda throne in about 321 BCE at the age of 25. Indian traditions have it that the Kauṭilya, also known as Chanakya or Vishnugupta, was his mentor and guide. The origin and early life of Chandragupta remains obscure, though according to the prevalent view he belonged to the Moriya tribe and his caste was low. Both Indian and classical Greek sources state that he overthrew the last Nanda ruler and occupied his capital Pataliputra (modern day Patna). The Greek accounts add that he moved to north-west India and subdued the Greek garrison left behind by Alexander.[39] Narayan Chandra Bandyopadhyaya has given a comprehensive account of the stories related to Kauṭilya from *puraṇas,* Jain and Buddhist traditions, mention of his name and work by Daṇḍī the poet of sixth century CE, by Baṇa – the biographer of king Harṣa in 7th century CE (though not in praise but "a violent denunciation"), use of language bearing close resemblance to Kauṭilya by Kalidas, Kamandaka, Somadeva-Suri the Jain, parallelism with his work by later *smṛti* writers such as Yājñavalkya Smṛti, Kātyāyana Smṛti, Mallinātha, Kulluka Bhaṭṭa the commentator of the Manusaṃhita, Kathā-sarit-sāgara, and the drama Mudrārākṣasa.[40]

As is well known, Viṣṇugupta[41] or Kauṭilya, otherwise known as Cāṇakya,[42] was not only celebrated as a king-maker but is now regarded as the greatest exponent of realistic policies of governance and of methods of diplomacy as applicable to the period of foreign impact and internal dis-unity.[43]

Kauṭilya's *Arthaśāstra* survived in oral traditions and in fragmentary commentaries till its discovery in 1904 and its publication in 1915 in English and other languages later. Traditionally, Kauṭilya is considered the author of the *Arthaśāstra.* He is also known as the one who destroyed the power of the Nandas and placed Chandragupta Maurya on the throne of Magadha.[44] According to ancient Indian history, in 320 BCE, Chandragupta Maurya was the first Indian king who consolidated the Indian subcontinent into a cohesive country with the foundation of the Mauryan Empire.[45] Prior to him, Alexander had reached the fringes, and after defeating the rulers of the Indian borderland at Punjab, had left Greek governors to administer the area. During this time, the rest of India to the east was ruled by the Nanda kings who were unpopular and despised; nevertheless, their military strength was formidable and probably deterred further advance by Alexander's overstretched troops. The legend goes that the Nanda king, the then ruler of Pataliputra (modern Patna), had insulted Kauṭilya who fuelled by this insult later succeeded in uprooting the Nanda Dynasty and establishing the Mauryan one in its place.

The date of the opus is not known precisely.[46] But the tradition that Kauṭilya was the author of *Arthaśāstra* seems to have been generally accepted since fairly ancient times. Kamandaka's *Nītisāra* (*The Essence of Politics*), for example, asserts that the wise Viṣṇugupta, who had destroyed the Nandas by his magic lore and given the earth to Chandragupta, extracted the nectar of *Nītisāra* from the ocean of *Arthaśāstra*.[47] This consolidated and updated Kauṭilya's *Arthaśāstra* in the form of *Nītisāra* can be situated at the threshold or advent of the early medieval period (c.500-700 CE).[48] Sources of the Gupta period, such as the famous Sanskrit play *Mudrārākṣasa* (*Minister's Signet Ring*) by Viśākhadatta, give credit for Chandragupta's rise to his political advisor Kauṭilya, the author of the *Arthaśāstra*.[49]

We do not engage in this debate here as the Sanskritists and ancient historians are divided over it. And a resolution seems unlikely. For our purpose, we may assume a broad bracket as the year of its compilation varies amongst authors from the 4th century BCE to the 3rd century CE. We focus and see for ourselves what the concepts in the text tell us today or in other words as also argued by Michael Liebig – "engage substantially with the *idea contents* of the *Arthaśastra*."

The Characteristic of Indian Historiography

Of the four source materials of Indian History (archaeology, epigraphy, numismatics and literary sources), literary sources are the most abundant. This chapter, accordingly, will base most of the arguments on literary sources.

D. Mackenzie Brown had rightly opined that the most creative period for Indian theory occurs, as in China and Greece, before the beginning of Christian era in the West.[50] He also observed that "Indian political thought cannot be isolated from the main body of Hindu philosophy. In the West, we have accepted a tradition, partly Machiavellian, of a science of government which rests upon its own empirical basis. But the great works of Indian polity, are like the political dicta of Aquinas, one facet of a vast and integrated system of reasoning which poses and interprets the very problem of human existence."[51]

Methodological problems identified by Mahendra Prasad Singh help in a better understanding. The first methodological problem is on the periodisation of Indian culture and history. Divisions such as Hindu, Muslim and British is stereotypical and misleading. Rather the product of cultural-revolutionary transformations and transitions were in:[52]

(a) Aryan-Dravidian acculturation.
(b) Jain and Buddhist protest movements for reforms in the Vedic world view.

(c) Hindu-Muslim encounter and coexistence.
(d) The Western, primarily British, colonial conquest, Indian response and resistance, and the modernisation of Indian tradition.

The second methodological problem relates to the identification and reading of primary texts and classical secondary commentaries of political purport and relevance such as Kauṭilya's *Arthaśāstra.* A third methodological problem (on which we have already thrown some light) is in the observation of the late Indian philosopher Bimal Kumar Matilal who challenged the wrong notion that Indian philosophy is only religious, spiritual, and other-worldly.[53] Mahendra Prasad Singh further identifies the fourth problem (on which like the third, we have already thrown some light) of method on the question of how to study the texts in their appropriate historical and cultural contexts. Traditionally, Indologists have primarily focussed on internal reading of the texts, whereas historians have examined the political, social, and economic context. Students of political thought have primarily been interested in only the political aspects, while historians and Indologists have explored traditions, past, and history systematically.[55] Mahendra Prasad Singh argues, "One sees the faint beginning of political ideas in the Vedas, Upanishads, and epics, and then their crystallisation in the myths of creation of the state in several Brahminical and Buddhist texts. The most full-fledged outlining of the theory of state is found in Kauṭilya's *Arthaśāstra.*"[55]

Some More Challenges in Understanding Indian Historical Traditions and Methods

Two issues would need to be realised for any study of this sort. First is that scholars in the West, and most of them in India and elsewhere are trained in Western theories. This demands that to understand Indian tradition one may have to approach it from a comparative and known perspective which is dominated by the West. As Charles Drekmeier puts it: "An unfortunate feature of a good deal of interpretation of Hindu political thought has been the willingness of Indian scholars, trained in Western history, to force an equation of Hindu and Western theoretical concepts."[56] That is why scholars were comfortable in comparing Kauṭilya to Machiavelli as a short hand. I argue that this caricaturing has done a great harm to Kauṭilya's *Arthaśāstra.* It has also harmed Machiavelli. As Michael Liebig's chapter "Kauṭilya and Machiavelli in a Comparative Perspective" in this volume shows, just *The Prince* is insufficient. To understand Machiavelli and his idea of *raison d'état* (reason of the state) comprehensively, one has to study his *Discourses on Livy's History of Rome*.

The second issue is about the Indian oral traditions and time. It must be appreciated that ancient India relied on oral traditions and the concept of time in its philosophy is not linear but cyclical. This aspect, it seems, was not well understood in the past. Thus, M.A. Stein in his introduction to Kalhana's *Rājatarangiṇi* tells the readers that the Indian mind has never learnt to divide mythology and legendary tradition from true history. Further, on problem of historiography he referred to Alberuni who said "Unfortunately the Hindus do not pay much attention to the historical order of things, they are very careless in relating the chronological succession of their kings."[57] Similarly, writing in 19th century colonial India, when the knowledge of India by Europeans was not comprehensive as it may be now, Gustav Oppert although recognises that the epics and *purāṇas* represent historical branch of Indian literature, expresses his anguish to say, "Our knowledge of the history of ancient Hindus is very limited, and there is not much hope of our becoming better informed, as the most important factor providing such knowledge, i.e. a historical literature or a sufficient number of authentic records, is not existing in India, in fact seems never to have existed".[58] In the past, the Indian historian Hemchandra Raychaudhuri in his first sentence of his introduction to *Political History of Ancient India* (1923) raised this matter to say: "No Thucydides or Tacitus has left for posterity a genuine history of Ancient India."[59] He was right at that point in time. However, such impressions still have a great influence on the common perception of 'Indianness', as getting old and incorrect ideas replaced with new insights or unlearning is not simple. For example, even eminent Chinese Indologist Professor Ji Xianlin maintains that "ancient India had a very weak textual tradition but a very strong oral tradition." Chinese scholars posit that Indians "ignored historical records for oral tradition albeit they have excelled in religion, philosophy and meditation...throughout the history of Indian civilisation, although there are thousands of scriptures passed down from generations to generations, but not a single chronological history or historiography is to be found."[60]

As I show later, this sort of impressions of Alberuni, Gustav Oppert, some of the Chinese scholars, Hemchandra Raychaudhuri and M.A. Stein have since been, to some extent, deconstructed. Indeed, Romila Thapar has argued very convincingly to demolish this myth on absence of historical tradition to say, "While there may not in the early past have been historical writing in the forms currently regarded as belonging properly to the established genres of history, many texts of that period reflect a consciousness of history".[61]

David Shulman in his review of Robert Calasso's book has also corrected this wrong impression that ancient Indian traditions were uninterested in the past, or in facts. He argues:

> After so much eloquent exegesis, it is disconcerting to read a version of the common fallacy that the Vedic Indians (and may be all subsequent Indians) "ignored history"; they were happier, it seems, with their eternal rites and myths. It's high time we went beyond such simple minded notions, which have a veritable antiquity, from al-Biruni in the eleventh century right upto the present.[62]

It is important to revisit what Benoy Kumar Sarkar argued nearly a century ago.[63] Sarkar showed in his writings that it had been incorrectly supposed that the Hindu civilisation is essentially non-economic and non-political, if not pre-economic and pre-political and that its sole feature is ultra-asceticism and over-religiosity.[64] It is with this as the background that the discovery of Kauṭilya's *Arthaśāstra* in 1904 was an event to be celebrated.

Concept of History in Indian Traditions or an Indian Theory of History (Itihāsa)

History "is not a correct translation of the Sanskrit word *itihāsa*. Etymologically, it means what really happened (*iti-hā-asa*). But, as we know, in Indian tradition *purāṇa* (legend, myth, tale, etc.), *gāthā* (ballad), *ititvṛtta* (description of past occurrence, event, etc.), *ākhyāyikā* (short narrative) and *vaṃśa-carita* (genealogy) have been consciously accorded a very important place."[65] It is in later periods, D.P. Chattopadhyaya argues, that change occurred with passage of time and effective presence of Islamic culture. Islamic historians, because of their "own cultural moorings and the influence of the Semitic and Graeco-Roman cultures on them, were more particular about their facts, figures and dates than their Indian predecessors". The Europeans towards the end of 18th century "brought in with them their own views of historiography in their cultural baggage...The introduction of English education in India and the exposure of the elites of the country to it largely account for the decline of the traditional concept of *itihāsa* and the rise of post-Newtonian scientific historiography."[66] Due to this cross-fertilisation, D.P. Chattopadhyaya has a very important point to make, which is, "This is not to suggest that the impact of European historiography on Indian historians was entirely negative. On the contrary it imparted an analytical and critical temper which motivated many Indian historians of 19th century to try to discover our heritage in a new way."[67] This aspect or problem in understanding Indian traditions and methods that is *Itihāsa* will be further elaborated later.

To make readers understand this complex issues of Indian civilisation, it has been correctly pointed out by Mackenzie Brown (for the Western readers) that it is justifiable to follow E.M. Sait's dictum that thinking does not occur in a vacuum – political theory is invariably related to actual problems and conditions and is indeed inseparable from the latter.[68] In her latest book on this theme of history, Romila Thapar argues: "A sense of history and historical consciousness existed, that there were historical traditions emerging from diverse historiographies and that these occasionally took the form of historical writings."[69] In other words, it is a matter of consciousness and the mind. So crisply put by Michel Danino: "It is in this meaning that when we compare anything with Indian concepts, we are dealing not only with different time scales, but with different *mind* scales".[70]

Kauṭilya on History

Let us see what Kauṭilya's *Arthaśāstra* has to say on history. A.K. Sinha has explained that:

> History and *Itihasa* are not merely two words belonging to two different languages and having some resemblance in meaning. They are rather two concepts belonging to two different cultures with different value-systems...Unlike history, *Itihasa* lacks an inherent primary sense of research, investigation and enquiry and therefore, does not emphasise for a factual truth based on specific framework of time and space...[71]

According to Sinha, the *Arthaśāstra* very clearly speaks that *Purāṇas*, *Itivṛtta*, *ākhyāyikā*, *Udāharaṇa*, *Dharmaśāstra* and *Arthaśāstra*, these all consist the *Itihāsa*.[72]

To pin the above down to the text, elaborating the syllabus for training and education of the king, Kauṭilya's *Arthaśāstra* lists: "The three Vedas – *Sāma*, *Ṛg*, and *Yajur* – constitute the Triple. And the *Atharva-veda* and *Itihāsa-veda* are the Vedas."[73] Patrick Olivelle notes: "*Itihāsa veda*: The category *itihāsa* (narrative that are viewed within the tradition as historic) generally apply to two major Sanskrit epics, the *Mahābhārata* and the *Rāmāyaṇa*."[74] Kauṭilya's *Arthaśāstra* also has a detailed syllabus for the education of the king. In *sūtras* 1.5.13-14, it is stated that he should engage in studying Lore (*itihāsa*). Lore consists of *Purāṇas*, Reports (*itivṛtta*), Narratives (*ākhyāyikā*), Illustrations (*udāharaṇa*), Treatise on Law (*dharmasāstra*), and Treatises on Success (*arthaśāstra*). Further, Patrick Olivelle clarifies in the notes by stating that the "The meaning of Reports (*itivṛttas*) is unclear, although a commentary identifies the epics *Mahābhārata* and *Rāmāyaṇa*...It is also unclear what Narratives (*ākhyāyikā*) and Illustrations (*udāharaṇa*) refer to, although some think they may refer to fables and stories, such as *Pancatantra*, also called *Tantrākhyāyika*."[75] Today it is a cliché to say "we learn from history that we don't learn from history" or "we ignore lessons of history at our peril" and so on. Its inclusion as a compulsory subject by Kauṭilya is obviously to know what is right and wrong and as Romila Thapar puts it, "Kings who failed to be familiar with *itihasa* came to grief, but those that knew it succeeded".[76]

Aware of these unique characteristics of the Indian civilisational traditions and literature, now we progress and turn to the intellectual environment at the time of Kauṭilya.

Intellectual Environment

With the above background we now visit Nilima Chakravarti's argument which sets the stage: "In order to trace the essentials of Kauṭilya's thought, we must understand the period of intellectual history of India in which Kauṭilya made his appearance. The Upanisadic thinkers and the Buddha with his followers dominated the scene then. They pointed to the transitory and ever-changing nature of the empirical world. Worldly pleasures were not worth pursuing, they were to be shunned...These resulted in an exaggerated emphasis on asceticism and renunciation."[77] This in turn evoked a sharp reaction from the Lokāyata thinkers who argued that "matter or *deha* alone is real, that there was no life after death, no *Ātman* or soul surviving death, no God either as creator of the world or as moral dispenser. They rejected all sources of knowledge."[78] According to Nilima's understanding, for this reason, philosophers have rightly placed Kauṭilya close to a Lokāyatika.[79] Kauṭilya gave prime importance to *Ānvīkṣikī* or philosophy and logic in *sūtra* 1.2.10 to include *Sāṃkhya*, *Yoga* and *Lokāyata*.[80] It is in this intellectual ferment that the text matured. As Charles Drekmeier argued in his conclusion titled aptly by him as 'Buddha, Kautalya, and Krishna':

> The critical period of ancient Indian history was the age that spanned the Upaniṣ ads and the fullest development of Maurya administration under Ashoka. In these formative years, roughly from the seventh to the middle of the third century BCE, the dimensions of Indian philosophical and social thought were established.[81]

In comparing the present with the past, the then Indian National Security Adviser Shri Shivshankar Menon in April 2014 argued: "*Arthaśāstra* itself emerged from the collision of India's 6th century BCE Enlightenment (*Upaniṣads*, Buddhism, reason) and the power politics of the *Māgadhan* and North Indian state system in subsequent centuries. Both were worlds in rapid change. We seem to be at an analogous historical moment again."[82]

Part II: Some Key Concepts of Statecraft and Foreign Policy

Some Basic Ideas of Political Thinking in Ancient India

Kauṭilya mentions that he has compiled the knowledge and is the grand editor and author of what was known till his times. Although details of the *Arthaśāstra* have been explained in this and other chapters, it is important to get familiar and understand some basic ideas of political thinking in ancient India like the state of *mātsya-nyāya*, the doctrines of *daṇḍa* and *dharma*, the concepts of *sārvabhauma* and *maṇḍala*, and its variations.

In modern International Relations (IR), conditions of anarchy at international level and absence of world governments compel nations to converge towards a balance of power. Here anarchy can be related to the ancient Indian understanding of *mātsya-nyāya* – big fish swallowing up the smaller ones. Before the rise of state, there prevailed a condition of might is right. The strong oppressed the weak, as big fish swallows up the small ones. As characterised by the contract theory of the origin of the state and kingship, the people elected a king to put an end to the state of anarchy. They agreed to pay to the royal person taxes in return for order.

The psychology of men in the state of nature has all the negative attributes where sense of justice (*dharma*) is lost. "Thus arose the desire (*kama*) for possessing things not yet possessed. And this led to their subjugation by attachment (*raga*), under which they began to ignore the distinction between what should be and what should not be done."[83]

Human nature fundamentally is the same across cultures. In elaborating and comparing the doctrine of *daṇḍa*, one Chinese example explains it very clearly. Sarkar in this context argues that:

> In ancient China, Hsun Tze (305-235 BCE) strongly condemned the doctrine of Mencius (373-289 BCE), who had postulated the 'original goodness' of human nature. For, according to his counter-theory, "man is by nature wicked, his goodness is the result of nurture". Su Hw states, "The ancient rulers understood the native viciousness of man…and therefore created morals, laws, and institutions in order that human instincts and impulses might be disciplined and transformed".[84]

Sarkar then gives a similar example of the western-world by mentioning Seneca, the Stoic philosopher of the first century CE, who looked upon the institutions of society as being result of vice, of corruption of human nature. Sarkar alludes also to the Church Fathers having a similar view. Sarkar concludes the argument by mentioning that the verdict of Hindu political thinkers on the nature of man is identical.[85]

Unlike the *Śānti Parva*, part of the *Mahābhārata*, which has the notion of a divine king, for Kauṭilya in the contract theory, the people chose the king.[86] The king was given absolute authority of coercion and for awarding punishment (*daṇḍa*) to the wicked. But, "Kauṭilya holds that unlimited coercive authority would defeat its very purpose and lead once again to *mātsyanyāya*."[87] *Daṇḍa* is a two-edged sword and cuts both ways. On one hand, it is terror to the people and is corrective of social abuse. It is a moraliser, purifier, and civilising agent. It is by administration of the *daṇḍa* that the state can be saved from reversion to *mātsya-nyāya*. On the other hand, *daṇḍa* is also the most potent instrument of danger to the ruler. Its maladministration leads to fall of the ruler:

> In the two-edged sword of the *danda*, then we encounter, on one side, *Staatsraison* (interest of the State), and on the other, *Sittlichkeit* (i.e. morality, virtue, *dharma*, etc.). The conception of this eternal polarity in societal existence is one of the profoundest contributions of the political philosophy of the Hindus to human thought.[88]

In the theory of expansion and war, kings have a natural desire for expansion, while the people look for security and peace, which Kauṭilya says is possible under one leadership. These factors lead to conflict between different states. The king or *swāmī* sets out to conquer first as a *cakravartī*, and later culminating in the concept of *sārvabhauma*. Professor Nilima Chakravarty describes *cakravartī* as the sovereign who rules over the entire circle (*maṇḍala*) of dependent kingdoms and *sārvabhauma* – lord over *sarvabhūmi* – literally the whole area.[89]

Hindu Theory of International Relations

Benoy Kumar Sarkar, writing in the *American Political Science Review* in 1919, perhaps pioneered what he called at that time as the "Hindu Theory of International Relations" basing on extant Hindu texts including that of the recent re-discovery of the *Arthaśāstra* by R. Shamasastry. He clearly spelt out that doctrine of *maṇḍala* underlines the idea of "balance of power", pervades the entire speculation on the subject of international relations. The doctrine of *maṇḍala* is essentially the doctrine of the *vijigīṣu* or *Siegfried*.[90] The theory of state in Sarkar's understanding is thus reared on two diametrically opposite conceptions and dilemma:

(a) The doctrine of *daṇḍa,* which puts an end to *mātsya-nyāya* among the *prajā* or members of a state.
(b) The doctrine of *maṇḍala*, which maintains an international *mātsya-nyāya* or the civil war of races in the human family.[91]

From one anarchy, then, the state emerges only to plunge headlong into another. The doctrine of *maṇḍala* as centrifugal force was counteracted by the centripetal tendencies of the doctrine of *sārvabhauma* (the rule over the whole earth).[92] With the rise of the *sārvabhauma,* the *maṇḍala* necessarily disappears.[93] In *sārvabhauma*, the king has all the other rulers related to him not as to the *vijigīṣu* of *maṇḍala*, i.e. not as to the ambitious storm-centre of an international sphere, but bound as to a *rāja-rājā* (king of kings) to whom allegiance is due as overlord. The doctrine of unity and concord is the final contribution of the *nītiśāstras* to the philosophy of the state:[94]

> The doctrine of *sārvabhauma*, as the concept of federal nationalism, imperial federation, or the universe-State, is thus the keystone in the arch of Hindu theory of sovereignty. The message of *Pax Sārvabhaumica*, in other words, the doctrine of world-unity and international concord is the final contribution of *Nīti-śāstras* to the understanding of the State, and of Hindu philosophy to political science of mankind.[95]

Though Sarkar's formulation may look simplistic, it does help explain the state of international politics even today. Having become familiar with some basic ideas of political thinking in India, it is now the time to see its application in Kauṭilya's *Arthaśāstra.*

Explaining Concepts from Kauṭilya's Arthaśāstra

In its methodology, "Kautilya does not use the historical method in the generic sense of deriving political conclusions and propositions from historical materials".[96] The only inductive historical method is in the illustrative sense in reference to personalities and deeds of ancient history.[97] In the book on 'Concerning the Topic of Training', examples are given to show the necessity of the need to have control over senses such as lust, anger, greed, pride, arrogance and foolhardiness. Kauṭilya gives examples and refers to incidences in the past to impress the leader so as not to get afflicted with vices: such as king Bhoja and Dandkaya by name, who entertained a sinful desire for a brahmin maiden, perished along with his kinsmen and kingdom; and Ravana, not restoring the wife of another, due to pride, perished.[98] Only while prescribing the syllabus for education of the king, he mentions literature related to theistic and non-theistic (materialist) strands. To demonstrate the universal appeal of the text, George Modelski, in 1964, argued:

> Today's students of international relations, ever sensitive to the criticism that their work lacks "historical illustrations" or "empirical-concreteness" should be delighted with Kautilya's complete lack of historical sense…And there is a lesson here, for it is precisely this absence of historical "baggage" and also this abstractness, which ensured that the *Arthasastra* remained suitable for use in instruction centuries after the death of its author.[99]

If we interpret the text with the state of art IR today, then concepts of political virtue (morality), power and order are its guiding variables and this needs to be appreciated and understood.[100] Kauṭilya insists not on the fulfilment of one limited and partial aim but success in all fields. Kauṭilya, although argues for *artha* being his top concern, he does not ignore the balance with *dharma* (moral) and *kāma* (desire/pleasure). In *sūtra* 9.7.60, he writes: "Material gain, spiritual good and pleasure: this is the triad of gain." Kauṭilya's *Arthaśāstra* had guidance on morals that includes the most fundamental and enduring aspect of morals in human affairs that is non-violence or *ahiṃsā*, and control over senses:

> (Duties) common to all are; abstaining from injury (to living creatures), truthfulness, uprightness, freedom from malice, compassionateness and forbearance.[101]

> Control over the senses, which is motivated by training in the sciences, should be secured by giving up lust, anger, greed, pride, arrogance and fool-hardiness. Absence of improper indulgence in (the pleasure of) sound, touch, colour, taste and smell by the senses of hearing, touch and sight, the tongue and sense of smell, means of control over senses; or, the practice of (this) science (gives such control). For, the whole of this science means control over senses.[102]

For Kauṭilya, maintaining and strengthening the power of the state and ensuring the happiness of people are two sides of the same coin. The normative dimension of Kauṭilya's *Arthaśāstra* is securing and expanding the power of the state, securing and improving the welfare of the people and the political unification of the Indian subcontinent.[103] As discussed, the concept of *sārvabhauma* can be understood as 'political unification' of the subcontinent.

What is of interest is that the text makes abstract ideas clear in a practical way. It has also been noted by Modelski that "the strength and the interest of the *Arthasastra* lie in its abstractness and in the systematic quality of its propositions".[104] To engage with this, we now turn to some selected concepts and terms.

Four Upāyas (Approaches or Ways) – Sāma (Conciliation), Dāna (Gifts), Bheda (Rupture) and Daṇḍa (Force)

The four *upāyas* or approaches or ways of realising aim or objective have existed since the period of the epics and the *dharmaśāstras*. The four *upāyas* (approaches or ways) have a wider application, being useful in securing the submission of anyone. The South Indian Jain scholar Somadeva Suri, in *Nītivākyāmṛta,* written in the 10th century, mentions the four *upāyas.* In Sanskrit literature, the *upāyacatuṣṭya* or the "four expedients"; and the *turīya* (the fourth *upāya*) invariably means *daṇḍa* or force. Interestingly, the longevity of the four approaches or *upāyas* continues. The 20th century pioneer of power politics theory, Hans J. Morgenthau, in the chapter on different methods of balance of power in his book *Politics Among Nations: The Struggle for Power and Peace* (1966) mentions: "The balance of power can be carried on either by diminishing the weight of the heavier scale or by increasing the weight of the lighter one." His chapter has the following four sections:

1. Divide and Rule
2. Compensation
3. Armaments
4. Alliances

The four sections are very close to the Kauṭilyan concepts of the four *upāyas* of *bheda* (divide and rule), *dāna* (compensation), *daṇḍa* (armaments) and *sāma* (alliances).[105] In the search for influence of Kauṭilya on Morgenthau, Dr. Michael Liebig found that:

> Hans J. Morgenthau did study Kautilya and does state so in 'Dilemmas of Politics' (Chicago, 1958) where he mentions Kautilya four times and states that Kautilya developed an International Relations theory: "as rare instances of such attempts Kautilya and Machiavelli come to my mind". Among political scientists of the past, he lists Kautilya along with Jeremiah, Plato, Bodin and Hobbes.[106]

Seven Prakṛtis or Saptānga (Constituent Elements of a State) and Need to Take Care of Them

The greatest contribution of Kauṭilya's *Arthaśāstra* recognised by historians has been to conceptualise the state as a set of functions with a comprehensive definition.[107] No other civilisation can claim to have provided such an explanation of the constituents of a state in such detail.

A state is made up of seven parts or elements. These are the *swāmī* (king or ruler), *amātya* (body of ministers and structure of administration), *janapada/rāṣtra* (territory being agriculturally fertile with mines, forest and pastures, water resources and communication system for trade), *durga/pura* (fort), *kośa* (treasury), *daṇḍa/bala* (army) and *mitra* (ally).

Further, Kauṭilya's *Arthaśāstra* warns that the *vyasanas* (calamities) may infect them. Book VIII – 'Concerning Topic of Calamities of the Constituent Elements'– deals with the calamities that affect the various constituents (*prakṛtis*) of the state. It is necessary to take precautions against those before one can start on an expedition of conquest. For example, an army in an operation needs to be maintained and supplied. One of his *sūtras* also indicates when an army may get overstretched or exhausted. For example, out of the many *vyasanas* listed in relation to administration of the army, the following quotation reveals one such situation: "Come after a long march, exhausted, depleted, caught in an unsuitable terrain" (8.5.1).

In the modern age, an apt example is related to the US invasion of Iraq in 2003. Disbanding and dispersing the Iraqi Army was a big mistake as the former soldiers helped and participated in the prolonged insurgency. To correlate, when Chandaragupta Maurya defeated the Nandas, he did not disband the Nanda

Army, as an army is one of the most important constituents or pillars of any state. Having captured the throne of Magadha in 320 BCE, "He used the subsequent years for the consolidation of his hold on the army."[108] In *Arthaśāstra's* formulation, each organ in the '*saptānga*' is vital. No leg must be diseased. Thus, the US would have done well if, after regime change in Iraq, they would have continued with the existing army with minor changes. It is correctly inferred that "the US had trouble resorting security and stability because it had precipitated the virtual collapse of the Iraqi state by undermining its coercive, administrative, legal and extractive institutions".[109] Clearly, institutions which resemble *prakṛtis* must be left intact. In a century where wars are now fought amongst the people, a relevant up-dation of Kauṭilyan aphorism may be: "After defeat of an enemy as in regime change in Iraq, you cannot have stability if you inflict a permanent disaster (*vyasana*) on the *prakṛtis* of the state that you have defeated, especially *daṇḍa/bala* (army)."

***Ṣāḍguṇya* (Six Measures of Foreign Policy):** The problem of the defence of the state is intimately bound up with the question of its foreign relations. It is from hostile states that the state needs to be defended. Foreign policy is summed up in the formula of *ṣāḍguṇya* or six measures. The formula is associated with, though it does not necessarily presuppose, the theory of *rājamaṇḍala* or circle of kings.[110] The six *guṇas* or measures are as follows:

(1) *saṃdhi* – making a treaty containing conditions or terms, that is the policy of peace.
(2) *vigraha* – the policy of hostility.
(3) *āsana* – the policy of remaining quiet (and not planning to march on an expedition).
(4) *yāna* – marching on an expedition.
(5) *saṃśraya* – seeking shelter with another king or in a fort.
(6) *dvaidhībhāva* – the double policy of *saṃdhi* with one king and *vigraha* with another at the same time.

According to Kangle's study:

> The general rule is that when one is weaker than an enemy, *saṃdhi* is the policy to be followed, if stronger than him, then *vigraha* (hostility). If both are equal in power, *āsana* is the right policy, but if one is very strong, *yāna* should be resorted to. When one is weak, *saṃśraya* is necessary, while *dvaidhībhāva* is the policy recommended when with help from another source, one can fight one's enemy.[111] But the general rule may be set aside if various considerations make it advisable to follow a different course. The purpose of all polices is to grow stronger in the long run than the enemy, though sometimes one may have to tolerate temporarily the greater strength of the enemy.[112]

Rājamaṇḍala or **Circle of Kings:** The text lists *rājamaṇḍala* consisting of twelve kings:

(1) *vijigīṣu* (the would-be conqueror).
(2) *ari* (the enemy).
(3) *mitra* (*vijigīṣu's* ally).
(4) *arimitra* (ally of enemy).
(5) *mitramitra* (friend of ally).
(6) *arimitramitra* (ally of enemy's friend).
(7) *pārṣṇigrāha* (enemy in the rear of the *vijigīṣu*).
(8) *ākrānda* (*vijigīṣu's* ally in the rear).
(9) *pārṣṇigrāhāsāra* (ally of *pārṣṇigrāha*).
(10) *ākrāndasāra* (ally of *ākrānda*).
(11) *madhyama* (middle king bordering both *vijigīṣu* and the *ari*).
(12) *udāsīna* (lying outside, indifferent/neutral, more powerful than *vijigīṣu*, *ari* and *madhyama*).

As noted under four *upāyas* above, Morgenthau was also influenced by the concept of *udāsīna*. According to Jayantanuja Bandyopadhyaya, "Kauṭilya's neutral (*udāsīna*) is capable of playing the role of balancer, and is apparently expected to do so". Indeed, when Morgenthau speaks of "splendid isolation" of the balancer, who "waits in the middle in watchful detachment",[113] he may have been influenced (as regards to the general philosophy of Political Realism) by Kauṭilya; for the meaning of the word *udāsīna*, as explained by Kauṭilya in his *Arthaśāstra*, is very close to "splendid isolation" and "watchful detachment".[114]

Before winding up this part, what also needs to be emphasised is that the number 12 does not imply that so many states are absolutely necessary for a circle (*maṇḍala)*; it refers rather to the number of possible relationships that may arise when a state tries to establish its supremacy over a number of neighbouring states. Kangle refers to W. Rubin who thinks that the doctrine of *maṇḍala* was, in its origin, related to the growth of the power of Magadha.[115] Misrepresentation of a neighbour being a perpetual enemy could be attributable to not reading the original and entire text. This needs correction. R.P. Kangle's study of 1960s has fortunately cleared this fog. Kangle refers to Book VII, Chapter 18 and sutra 29.[116]

> The neighbouring princes, *sāmantas*, may normally be supposed to be hostile. But it is possible that some may have a friendly feeling towards the *vijigīṣu*, while others may even be subservient to him. Neighbouring states thus fall in three categories, *aribhāvin*, *mitrabhāvin* and *bhṛtyabhāvin*.[117]

Types of Power – Three Powers (Books VI and IX)

Kauṭilya's *Arthaśāstra* lists and prioritises various types of powers for success in Book VI which deals with the *maṇḍala* theory under the section on peace and activity: "Power is three-fold: the power of knowledge is the power of counsel, the power of treasury and the army is the power of might, the power of valour is the power of energy."[118] In other words, the three powers or *śaktis* are *utsāhaśakti* (the personal energy and drive of the ruler himself), *prabhāvaśakti* (the power of the army and treasury) and *mantraśakti* (the power of counsel and diplomacy). Later in Book IX, "The Activity of the King About to March", of the three powers of the state, Kauṭilya in 9.1.14-16 uniquely maintains that *prabhāvaśakti* (power of treasury and army) is more important than *utsāhaśakti* (power of personal energy) and that *mantraśakti* (power of counsel and diplomacy) is more important than both. This priority and categorisation of force or power for diplomacy is like music to foreign policy makers and scholars in today's international system where diplomacy is considered the best way to resolve or manage conflicts.

A Comprehensive Maṇḍala Theory[119]

Let me summarise with one example in the application of all these concepts – which we may refer to as the *maṇḍala* theory. The sequence is not rigid. To arrive at a decision the thinking process may be as in succeeding paragraphs.

Each *prakṛti* or element of a state needs to be mapped and measured (including that of the *vijigīṣu* or the would-be-conqueror himself). For this, the tool is obviously through intelligence, of which the *Arthaśāstra* is a foundational text.

The entire process of selecting an option has also to take into account what is the capability of the power so described (*śakti*). Then the theory of *maṇḍala* as a conceptual tool has to establish friends, foes, middle power or *madhyama* and neutral power or *udāsīna*. This has to be worked out in a dynamic fashion linked with the intelligence and survey of the state of *prakṛtis*. Measuring capability of *prakṛtis* is an important part which also must indicate the weaknesses of *prakṛtis* that need to be overcome. This is like "knowing oneself and the enemy". If any *prakṛti* is not in order (and is suffering with *vyasana*), then measures need to be taken to get it in order.

Then finally, the application of the four *upāyas* has to be thought through. Issues of morality and justice have to be catered for as well.

The Final Peace

The best summarised guidance in Kauṭilya's *Arthaśāstra* which combines almost all the methods above is on the issue of peace. *Arthaśāstra* states: "1. If there is equal advantage in peace or war, he should resort to peace. 2. For, in war there are losses, expenses, marches away from home and hindrances".[120] It is with this in mind that one of leading strategic thinkers of free India, K.M. Panikkar, in a lecture on Kauṭilya's *Arthaśāstra* stated:

> When the advantages to be derived from peace and war are equal, one should prefer peace, for disadvantages such as loss of power and wealth are ever attendant upon war. Similarly if the advantage to be derived from neutrality and war are equal, one should prefer neutrality.[121]

The need and realisation today, for peaceful solutions without recourse to a force of arms, shows a similar logic as was in the ancient Indian text. The message is similar to the one in the *Human Security Report 2005* which notes that one of the factors that account for the diminution in the incidence of war since 1980 is decline in economic utility of war.[122]

In Book XIII, Means of Taking a Fort, in Section 175 (Storming a Fort) at 13.4.54-62, Kauṭilya talks about various methods of conquests:

> After thus conquering the enemy's territory, the conqueror should seek to seize the middle king, after succeeding over him, the neutral king. This is the first method of conquering the world. In the absence of the middle and neutral kings, he should overcome the enemy constituents by superiority of policy, then the other constituents. This is the second method. In the absence of the circle he should overcome by squeezing from both sides the ally through the enemy or the enemy through the ally. This is the third method. He should first overcome a weak or single neighbouring prince; becoming doubly powerful through him a second prince; three times powerful, a third. This is the fourth method of conquering the world. And after conquering the world he should enjoy it divided into *varṇas* and *āśramas* in accordance with his own duty.

It is clear that the final victorious *vijigīṣu*, the one who consolidates the Indian subcontinent is counselled in *sūtra* 13.4.62 "And after conquering the world he should enjoy it divided into *varṇas* and *āśramas* in accordance with his own duty." I accept R.P. Kangle's explanation on the interpretation of the duty or *svadharma* of the king: "*svadharmeṇa* refers to the king's own duties rather than to those of the *varṇas* and *āśramas*."[123] Some scholars such as Andre Wink take this as the justification of *varṇa* system or religion coming back again into politics.[124] I do not agree with this reading. I agree with Kangle's interpretation and also with that of Buddha Prakash, V.K. Gupta and Satish Chandra given below. Buddha Prakash concludes to say this about Kauṭilya:

> His ideas about centralised administration, salaried civil service, tours of officials, espionage system and money economy embody the spirit of parallel Achaemenian institutions, and his views about the primacy of *Arthasastra* over *Dharmasastra* mark the culmination of the process of the extrication of the science of political economy and secular jurisprudence from the mass of ecclesiastical and customary lore contained in the *sutra* literature under the impact of new thought.[125]

In other words, there was a clear domain of the *artha* literature on issues of statecraft freed from the hold of the Church and clergy. With this distinction the text became universal and secular. Thus, it has been rightly said that:

> *Dharma-sutra* teaches morality and lays down duties of the individual and regards deviation from them as sin. Kautilya is a realist and deals with duties, violation of which are regarded as crimes and punished by the State. Prior to Kautilya, law and religion were intermixed. Kautilya separated the two. It is important to remember that *Dharma* in the tradition of statecraft and in the literature of *Arthasastra* usually refers to *Rajadharma* that is *dharma* of the king and not to *dharma* as a whole. *Rajadharma* is essentially confined to the political domain in which prescriptions of righteousness applicable to individual do not apply in the same manner.[126]

The historian Satish Chandra also removes the doubt on the linkage of religion and politics to argue:

> His public duty or *rajadharma* was to be based on the *Arthashastra,* that is, on principles of politics. This really meant that politics and religion were, in essence, kept apart, religion being essentially a personal duty of the king.[127]

For relationships with other states outside Indian subcontinent, the text does not give any advice on colonial expansion to the *cakravartī*. This is one main positive reason that in Indian strategic culture, colonial conquests have never been attempted as possibly they were not required. In theories of statecraft as we know today, it is this ahistorical theoretical framework that is now to be applied critically and creatively for contemporary international politics. It does not mean that Indian traditions are to be used to spread hegemony and empire – but rather help explain regional and world politics.

Part III: Migration of Tradition in Different forms Outside and within India[128]

Migration and Spread of Indic Traditions and Knowledge to the West

Key ideas and concepts on issues of diplomacy and strategy from Kauṭilya's *Arthaśāstra* were also made into simple instructions for potential kings and for good moral conduct into a book called *The Pancatantra*, whose author Vishnu Sharma acknowledges the debt owed to Kauṭilya's *Arthaśāstra*. "*The Panchatantra* or, which is a book on politics put into fables for early education of princes and would-be statesmen, adopts the term *Nyaya-Sastra* to denote the literature."[129] Books like *Pancatantra* and the *Hitopadeśa* were compiled for the instruction of princess in the way they should go.[130] For example, in Book III of *The Pancatantra*, there is a foreign policy deliberation on issue of war and peace between the warring crows and owls. Here the six measures of foreign policy or options of *ṣāḍguṇya* are demonstrated.[131]

Concepts as stories were exported chiefly in the form of books such as *Pancatantra/Beast Fables*. Sassanid ruler Khosru Nushirwan's ambassador unable to get possession conceived the plan of learning it by rote "and so transmitted to Persia what was regarded as the very quintessence of political wisdom."[132] There are also a tradition which says that the Indian scholar Varahamihira, the author of *Bṛhatsaṃhitā* visited Persia where he was called Buzurmehr. In Persia, he rendered the fables of *Pancatantra* into Pahlavi at the instance of Khosru Nushirwan, king of Persia who ruled from 531-576 CE.[133] The Persian collection in Pahlavi, known as *Kalila wa Dimna*, passed to Arabia and thence, along the highway of a conquering Islam, to North Africa, Spain and Provence.[134] In Spain, it was translated into Hebrew and then into Spanish in 13th century. The Hebrew version was also translated into Latin at the end of that century and published in Germany in 1480, as the source for the 1483 *Buch der Weisheit* (*Book of Wisdom*). It was then translated into Italian in 1552 CE and English in 1570 CE.[135] The intellectual currents from India are best captured by the medieval Arab poet from Baghdad called al-Sabhadi, who said that there were "three things on which Indian nation prided itself: its method of reckoning, the game of chess, and the book tilted *Kalila wa Dimna*."[136] According to Patrick Olivelle:

> The western migration of the Pancatantra is as fascinating story as the Pancatantra itself. The first western translation was into Pahlavi by a Persian doctor named Burzoe, whose dates are 531-79 CE. All subsequent pre-modem western translations are derived directly or indirectly from this Pahlavi version, which is now lost. The Pahlavi version was retranslated into Old Syriac by Bud around 570 CE, of which version only a single defective manuscript exists, and into Arabic by 'Abdallah ibn al-Moquaffa' around 750 CE under the title *Kalilah and Dimnah*, from the names of the two jackal ministers in Book I. All later western translations go back to this Arabic version. The Arabic was translated into Syriac in the tenth or eleventh century and into Greek in the eleventh century. From the Greek we have Latin, German, and Slavonic translations. The Arabic was also translated into Persian, into Spanish around 1251, and in the twelfth century into Hebrew by Rabbi Joel. This Hebrew version was translated into Latin by John of Capua sometime between 1263 and 1278. This Latin rendering was the first Pancatantra version to be printed, around 1480, and became well known throughout medieval Europe. It was translated into Italian by Doni and printed in 1552, and it was Doni's version that was translated into English by Sir Thomas North in 1570 under the title *The Morall Philosophie of Doni*. The repeated retranslations took these versions far from the original Pancatantra, and indeed most Europeans had forgotten that the work originally came from India. Beyond the translations themselves, the Pancatantra influenced Arabic and European narrative literature of the Middle

> Ages, most notably *The Arabian Nights* and La Fontaine, who in the second edition of his *Fables* (1678) states expressly that much of his new material was derived from the Indian sage Pilpay, perhaps a corruption of the Sanskrit Vidyapati (Lord of Learning) or of the common Brahmin title Vajapeyi.[137]

The Cultural Heritage of India records that about two hundred versions in some sixty languages have been traced so far and the *Pancatantra* is second only to the *Bible* from this point of view. It further mentions:

> The resemblance between the fables of *Pancatantra* and those of *Aesop* on the one hand and those of La Fontaine on the other is striking, and the originality and uniqueness of the Indian version have been admitted by almost all scholars.[138]

The essence of Kauṭilya's *Arthaśāstra* endured in later periods as for example in West Asia or Middle East in the Muslim period. According to the historian Rizvi:

> A very comprehensive Arabic *Mirror for Princes* and its later Arabic version entitled *Siraju'l-muluk* was compiled in 1122 by Abu Bakr Muhammad bin al-Walid al Turtushi (1059-c.-1127), who was born in Spain and visited Iran and Iraq. Here he met the seljuq vizier Nizamu'l-Mulk Tusi (1018-92) and was greatly impressed by Tusi's scholarship and political acumen. Even the earlier *Mirror for Princes* had drawn upon the stories of *Kalila wa Dimna*, as translated from the Pahlavi (Old Persian) by Ibnu'l- Muqaff' (d.756). Turtushi's work also shows a definite debt to *Kalila wa Dimna*. He refers also to *Muntakhabu'l- jawahir* (*Selected Gems*), composed by the Indian, Shanaq (Chanakya), as a guide for the monarch. This text, the *Kitab Shanaq fi al-tadbir*, was in fact the celebrated *Chanakya-Niti*, a collection of political aphorisms in Sanskrit,[139] not to be confused with the *Arthasastra* ascribed to Kautilya or Chanakya.[140]

Al-Turtushi's *Siraju'l-muluk* drew upon Chanakya and encouraged rulers to act like the sun, moon, earth, rain, wind, fire, water, and death. From some Hindu sources he presented the widespread analogy of the big fish eating smaller fish (*mātsya-nyāya*) and claimed that this unstable situation was averted only by a monarchy. "Turtushi confidently asserted that the relation of monarch to his people was identical with that of the body to the soul; if the king were virtuous his people would prosper, but if he were not, evil would prevail in his territory."[141] This is somewhat similar to Kauṭilya's core introductory message in rules for the king. "In the happiness of the subjects lies the happiness of the king and in what is beneficial to the subjects his own benefit. What is dear to himself is not beneficial to the king, but what is dear to the subjects is beneficial (to him)."[142]

In Macropedia from Encyclopedia Britannica, 'The Islamic World', at page 119 under 'Migration and renewal (1041-1405)', it is mentioned that The Seljuk were advised by Iranian advisers on "centralised absolutism as it had existed in pre-Islamic times and in the time of Marwanid-Abbasid strength. The best known proponent was Nizam al-Mulk, chief minister to the second and third Seljuk sultan, Alp-Arslan and Malik Shah. Nizam al-Mulk explained his plans in his *Seyasat Nameh,* one of the best known manuals of Islamic political theory and administration." Abu Ali Hasan ibn Tusi (1018-1092 CE) is also his name and his honorific title is Nizam al-Mulk (order of the Realm). More research needs to be done to revisit how this work got influenced by Indian text, more so Kauṭilya's *Arthaśāstra.*[143]

Migration and Spread to Tibet

By far the most thorough work on Indian text is that of the Tibetans. After the introduction of Buddhism in Tibet from India in the 7th century CE a large number of Indian texts were studied and translated into Tibetan. Tibetans, as they visited India for Buddhist education, took the opportunity of translating, with the help of Indian scholars, and preserving various texts of Indian literature. According to Professor Suniti Kumar Pathak, a *Nītiśāstra* is an abridged work out of the voluminous *Dharmaśāstra* and *Arthaśāstra*. *Nītiśāstra* is a study of man and human behaviour or a book of manners.[144] Professor Suniti Kumar Pathak naturally wonders about the considerations the Buddhist Tibetans might have had for translating *Nīti* texts of non-Buddhist authors like Chanakya. He reasons that the impact of Buddhism upon Tibet widened cultural outlook, and this made Tibetan scholars interested in non-Buddhist works.[145] In Tibet, the Indian *Nītiśāstras* are part of the *Tanjur* (*bstan'gyur* – doctrinal teachings given by the subsequent teachers to the Buddha) collection. In the Kar-cha (*dkar chag*) index volume of the Narthan (*snar thaṇ*) edition of the Tanjur, these Tibetan texts are enlisted under the head of *thun mon ba lugs kyi bstan chos* (*sāmānya-nītiśāstra*).[146] Later, during 9th to 11th century CE, the Tibetans composed indigenous *nīti* texts. Non-Buddhist texts such as those related to Chanakya were also translated. Examples being the teaching of Chanakya (*Tsa na ka* in Tibetan) such as *Tsa Na Ka Rgyal Po'I Lugs Kyi Bstan Bcos* (*Cāṇakya Rājanīti-Śāstra*).[147] "The resemblance of thought in the verses shows, the direct influence of Indian *Nītiśāstras* on the Tibetan *Lugs kyi bstan bcos*."[148]

Migration to Southeast Asia[149]

"An inscription states that the 11th century Javanese king named Erlangga subverted his enemy's power 'by the application of the means taught by' the author of the *Arthashastra*, the most famous of all Indian treaties on the policies of a successful *maṇḍala* manager. The *Arthashastra* also contains many precepts useful for a would-be-conqueror."[150] And in the preface to the first edition

(1861) of *The Nitisara or the Elements of Polity* by Kamandaki, edited by Rajendralala Mitra, it is mentioned that:

> From a report submitted by Dr. Frederich to the Batavian Society of Arts and Sciences on the Sanskrit literature of Bali, it appears that the most popular work in the Island on Polity is Kamandakiya Nitisara, and all the Sanskrit books there extant are acknowledged to be the counterparts of purely Indian origin.[151]

Concepts such as *maṇḍala* and other related ideas had traveled to Southeast Asia. Between 200 BCE and 500 CE in Southeast Asia, people "first settled in large nucleated communities, organised themselves into small warring polities".[152] *Maṇḍala* to be sure means alliance based spheres of influence.

Guiding principles and concepts from Kauṭilya's *Arthaśāstra* also radiated to the east to Thailand (the concept of *cakravartī* or 'conqueror of the world'). In Thailand, "The concept of *Cakravartin* indicates that *cakra* or wheel (symbol of sovereignty) of the state chariot rolls everywhere without obstruction. It is believed that Mauryas developed the concept of *Cakravartin*, which was incorporated into Buddhist tradition."[153]

"Early Indonesian societies which adopted either Buddhism or Hinduism shared fundamental assumptions about ideal political structure. Inscriptions refer to kingdom as *maṇḍalas*, a Sanskrit word with a wide range of meaning. Its simplest connotation is a circle."[154] "One founding inscription engraved at Palembang by the ruler of Srivijay in the 680s refers to the outlying polities called *mandala* that he claimed to have brought under his control."[155] In Alan Chong's explanation, "Prior to European colonisation of Southeast Asia, political authority was founded upon concert in a-like patterns of religiously derived centres of virtues and majesty. Hindu and Buddhist beliefs partly explained maritime empires such as Srivijay and Mataram based on large swaths of present-day Malaysia and Indonesia".[156]

Sheldon Pollock has coined the term "Sanskrit cosmopolis" referring to the enormous geographic sweep of Indic culture for centuries spreading not as movement of conquerors, but what I say as 'soft power'. Sheldon Pollock shows how ancient ideas in Sanskrit from India influenced regions beyond the subcontinental boundaries, but not by conquest.[157]

The Indian roots of concept of *maṇḍala* as related to Southeast Asia needs more research. This knowledge of interaction between India and Southeast Asia is not well understood or realised. Iver B. Neumann, in his article[158] quotes Alastair Iain Johnston's understanding of *maṇḍala*.[159] Johnston states that one example was the *maṇḍala* system of premodern Southeast Asia whereby "kingdoms were defined by clusters of declared allegiances rather than territories. Within this system big men were distinguished in a hierarchy of kings, allies and vassals that was fluid." Later in the essay, Iver B. Neumann writes: "That the systematic study of Chinese tribute system and South-East Asian *mandala* system would enrich our understanding of hegemony."[160] It is surprising that these Western authors have not attempted to track the concept of *maṇḍala* to its Indic origins and tradition. It clearly shows that there is a need for scholarship from among the Southeast Asian scholars and also those from India to contribute to enrich International Relations and International Studies with the rich experience both from India and from Southeast Asia.

Taking it to a deeper philosophic-religious level, the idea of a *cakravartī* resonates in Buddhism. Romila Thapar points out that according to Buddhist tradition:

> recurring violence was inimical to the interests of societies in a state system. The harshness of the state was ameliorated in the concept of *cakkavatti/cakravartin*, the universal ruler whose reign is synonymous with law, order and justice. Significantly it is the wheel of law which rolls across his domain and not the *daṇḍa* of chastisement...the concept of *cakravartin* does suggest control over a vast territory. But the concept is not so much that of ruling a geographically vast territory as of centring control, as it were, firmly and securely in a hub of power. The symbolism of the wheel does suggest a differentiation between power at the centre of the circle and at the rim. The domain need not be restricted to the political for in the Buddhist concept the spiritual domain is also open to the *cakkavatti*.[161]

Diffusion within India

Kolff, basing it on R.P. Kangle's translation (6.2.33), argues to show "striking continuity in Indian history. The structural features discussed here clearly inform Kautilya's *Arthasastra* which teaches that the 'power of might' consisting of 'the power of the treasury and army'". Kolff then explains it by relating it to the reign of seventh century king Harshavardhana:

> His preeminence depended on the 'peace and alliance' he was able to realise, in other words, on maintaining himself as the centre of a circle of states (*rajamandala*) as described by Kautilya, the foremost political scientists of pre-modern India whose *Arthasastra* beautifully analyses the constraints put on politics by the configuration of ancient and medieval Indian society.[162]

During the initial phase of the Muslim rule, Ala-ud-din Khalji, who ascended the throne of Delhi in 1296, based his administration on the guidance provided by Kauṭilya's *Arthaśāstra*. The author Barani in his *Tarikh-i-Firoz Shahi* has used ideas from Kauṭilya's *Arthaśāstra* to establish a centralised administration. It was the only known systematic attempt by a medieval Indian ruler to establish a centralised administration and interfere directly with market forces. Similar prescriptions are contained in *Arthaśāstra,* and it is argued by

Kulke and Rothermund that Ala-ud-din knew about the *Arthaśāstra*. Kulke and Rothermund point out that these measures were in keeping with earlier Indian traditions (including those in the *Rājataranginī* chronicle of Kashmir by Kalhaṇa) and do not need to be attributed to West Asian influences.[163] Roy and Alam argue that the *nasihat* (advice) of Zia Barani in his *Fatwa-i-Jahandari* "is a classical work on statecraft which can be compared with Kauṭilya's *Arthaśāstra* and Machiavelli's *Prince*".[164]

Further within India, *Arthaśāstra's* influence continued on Akbar in the Mughal period. In 1937, Benoy Kumar Sarkar was possibly the first scholar to have written about it. He devoted a full section of 21 pages to Abul Fazl's *Ain-i-Akbari* as a Semi-Moslem and Semi-Hindu *Nītiśāstra*.[165] Sarkar showed similarity of the contents of *Ain-i-Akbari* to that of Hindu *Nītiśāstra* including an understanding of the state of *mātsya-nyāya* (logic of fish) as well as *daṇḍa* (punishment), and to get rid of vices (*vyasanas*) and *rājadoṣas* (faults or disqualification of a king).

Rizvi argues that Abu'l-Fazl'Allami (1551-1602) was inspired by a need to rationalise the broad-based policies of peace and concord with all religious communities initiated by his patron, Akbar the Great. Abu'l-Fazl'Allami had access to the Persian translations of the great Hindu epics, the *Mahābhārata* and the *Rāmāyaṇa*, Arabic translation of the *Cāṇakayanīti* and to the Sanskrit works of ancient Indian *rājanīti* (polity).[166] The *kotwals* (principal police officers) during Akbar's reign had various functions: including census of town and villages, gathering daily intelligence, movement of visitors, deterring imposters, controlling bazaar activities, supervising state minting, road safety, recovering stolen property, etc. Interestingly, their duties included eradicating unemployment, investigating the source of income of those who spent money extravagantly and preventing unwilling widows from being incinerated on their dead husband's funeral pyre. "Many of these provisions seem to echo the practices of the ancient Hindu kingdoms, as reflected in the text as the *Arthaśāstra* attributed to Kauṭilya. Akbar was influenced by Hindu advisers."[167] In *Ain-i-Akbari* written by Abul Fazal, Kamla compares, the division of state in Kauṭilya's *Arthaśāstra* at many levels with that of the empire into "*Subas, Sarkars* and *Mahalls*".[168]

Using inscriptions for analysis, S.C. Mishra has demonstrated how *Arthaśāstra* evolved over the centuries by various Indian kingdoms, in particular the time bracket of tenth to twelfth centuries, in a process which led to invention of nicknames of Kauṭilya and the birth of *Cāṇakyanīti* as 'floating wisdom'.[169]

Panikkar alluded that the Hindu kings, to the last, followed the organisation of the Mauryan Empire in its three essential aspects – the revenue system, the bureaucracy and the police. This organisation was taken over by Muslim rulers;

and, in the British period, those doctrines were still in force.[170] The enthusiasm of India's first Prime Minister for Kauṭilya was phenomenal. He devoted six pages to Chanakya in his *Discovery of India*, first published one year before independence in 1946,[171] and, as a symbol, he had the diplomatic enclave in New Delhi named after him as Chanakyapuri.[172] Interestingly, the ideas of Kauṭilya continue to be mentioned for their relevance. A speech by the President of India, Shri Pranab Mukherjee, to the members of the 54th National Defence College (NDC) course and staff mentioned:

> Kauṭilya, in his famous treatise on statecraft, *Arthaśāstra* has given importance to multi-disciplinary approach. Pandit Jawaharlal Nehru, while inaugurating the National Defence College in 1960 had articulated his thoughts and I quote: "Defence is not an isolated subject. It is intimately connected with the economic, industrial and many other aspects in the country and is all encompassing".[173]

The Institute for Defence Studies and Analyses, New Delhi, organised a series of seminars and workshops on Kauṭilya's *Arthaśāstra* since 2012. The proceedings have been published in three volumes that supplement this work.[174]

Part IV: Case Study on Kauṭilya and War

In Kauṭilya's *Arthaśāstra*, as has been discussed, war is the last resort. However, as a comprehensive manual of security, Kauṭilya's *Arthaśāstra* includes details about war. "Kauṭilya's maxims on tactics and strategy are at once wise and sound...He insists throughout on the necessity for constant precaution, on the avoidance of risks, on protection by means of energetic entrenchment and vigilant sentries." Moreover, it emphasises the need for "accurate topographical information and recommends the utilisation of natural features in battles and attention to climatic and metrological changes. He recognises the absolute necessity of a reserve in battle".[175] His details on troop composition and employment in battle provide good guidelines to military commanders even today.[176] The *Arthaśāstra* has key methodological and theoretical ideas and concepts for intelligence analysis, assessment, estimates and strategic planning. The text is a rich repository of the discipline of Intelligence Studies for contemporary relevance.[177]

In the language of international law and norms in war, almost all ideas and concepts are of Western origin like the Latin *jus ad bellum* (the Justice of Resort to War) and its conduct *jus in bello* (the justice of the conduct of war). Academic rigour of International Law will get enriched by utilising some concepts from Kauṭilya's *Arthaśāstra* which seem almost modern.[178]

Conquest and War in the Arthaśāstra

War, to Kauṭilya, was an inevitable and necessary evil. It is here that Kauṭilya introduces in his great work, an innovation of his time – *dharmavijay*. A *dharmavijayī* is 'a just conqueror who is satisfied with mere obeisance'. In actual practice, wars took many ugly forms and Kauṭilya's *Arthaśāstra* does not brush them off under the carpet so to speak. *Dharmavijay* is followed by *lobhavijay* and *asuravijay*. Distinguished from *dharmavijayī* (just conqueror) is *lobhavijayī* that is the one who fights out of covetousness, jealousy and greed for land or money. The worst of the three types is *asuravijayī,* the demon like conqueror who uses forbidden, heinous and unscrupulous methods. Thus, Kauṭilya's *Arthaśāstra* explicates three types of conquests which any conqueror could undertake – *dharmavijay* (a just conquest), *lobhavijay* (conquest of greed) and *asuravijay* (conquest like a demon). Before the discovery of the *Arthaśāstra*, the term *dharmavijaya* occurring in the inscription of Ashoka was a puzzle to the Ashokan scholars.[179] According to Kauṭilya, *dharmavijay* meant that a conquering king was satisfied with the acknowledgment of his overlordship by the inferior or defeated powers as also by others. *Dharmavijay* means a righteous method of warfare where diplomacy and conciliation were pressed into service to avoid actual fighting as far as possible.[180] In an interpretation by the historian R.K. Mookerjee after the conquest of Kalinga, Ashoka (grandson of Chandragupta Maurya) banned all such conquests achieved by violence. Thenceforth, he stood for *dharmavijaya* or cultural conquest as against *asuravijaya* and *lobhavijaya*.[181]

The next and lower level is of how combat is to be prosecuted; it has detailed elaboration of *Yuddha* or War. Three broad categories are mentioned: *prakāśa-yuddha* or 'open fight' in the place and time indicated, *kūṭa-yuddha* or 'concealed fighting' involving use of tactics in battlefield and *tūṣṇiṃ-yuddha* or 'silent fighting' implying the use of secret agents for enticing enemy officers or killing them.[182] Kangle highlights that it is clear that *kūṭa-yuddha* refers to the commonly recognised tactics of battlefield and contains nothing to which objection can be taken from military point of view.[183] In *prakāśa-yuddha* standard military tactics based on a sound military appreciation are to be employed. In book X, Concerning War, it is stated: "When he is superior in troops, when secret instigations are made (in the enemy camp), when precaution are taken about the season, (and) when he is on land suitable to himself, he should engage in open fight."[184] Even though 10.3.26 of Kauṭilya's *Arthaśāstra* mentions "Open warfare (*prakāśa-yuddha*) in which the place and time (for the fighting) are indicated, is the most righteous", human experience indicates otherwise, and does not seem to follow the normative idea as in the text. After the experience of two World Wars and a number of limited wars of 20th and early 21st centuries, it is well known that open fight or *prakāśa-yuddha* no longer exists, not even in space and cyber wars. The reality is that covert action which now must include the cyber domain, targeted killing, political assassinations and unrestricted warfare seem to be the favoured methods (*kūṭa* and *tūṣṇīṃyuddhas*), notwithstanding the theoretical international norms and laws of war.

Kauṭilya's *Arthaśāstra* is a universal manual both for friend and foe, the weak and strong. In Book XII are guidelines for the weaker king. Here, Kauṭilya's *Arthaśāstra* introduces the strategies to be applied by a weak king/ his envoy under attack from the three categories: *dharmavijayī*, *lobhavijayī*, and *asuravijayī*. *Sūtra* 12.1.17 says, "When one of these is making ready to start, he should make a counter-move through peace or diplomatic war or concealed warfare." Here, diplomatic war is called *mantrayuddha*, and *kūṭayuddha* does not seem to refer to the tactics on the field as described in 10.3.[185] Later, in a section in Book XII, Concerning Weaker King and Secret Methods, Kauṭilya's *Arthaśāstra* introduces *gūḍhayuddha* at 12.4.24 "or, agents as hunters, shall in the tumult of an attack, strike him on occasions fit for secret fight". The great translator R.P. Kangle had noted that *gūḍhayuddha* is not the same as *kūṭayuddha* of 10.3. "It is murder pure and simple".[186] Kauṭilya's *Arthaśāstra* only consolidated and summarised the methods and types of warfare and it will be incorrect to say that he propagated *gūḍhayuddha*.[187]

Interestingly, Kauṭilya's *Arthaśāstra* only mentions the victorious kings and concepts such as *dharmavijayī*, *lobhavijayī* and *asuravijayī*[188] and the *yuddhas* as *prakāś*, *kūṭa*, *tūṣṇīṃ* and there is no mention of *dharma-yuddha* in Kauṭilya's *Arthaśāstra*. It could be further argued that if we accept and agree that the text of Kauṭilya's *Arthaśāstra* was fixed by 3rd century CE (after the reign of Ashoka), then Ashoka's empire building, first by violence against Kalinga and then through *dharma* (*dhamma* in Pāli language), may well have been the motivation to include *dharmavijayī* as a just conqueror in Kauṭilya's *Arthaśāstra*. Another important understanding is based on the logic of the text being pre-Ashokan. For example, philosophers such as Nilima Chakravarti have made this puzzle redundant to argue that Kauṭilya "introduced the concept of *dharmavijaya* which was later developed and practiced by King Aśoka".[189]

Winning Peace Through Wars

The two essential conditions for the use of military force to be decisive are: a) The defeated people must accept the fact of defeat and b) the defeated people need to reconcile to their defeat by being treated as partners in international order.[190] In a similar fashion, Book XIII, Chapter 5 of *Arthaśāstra* is devoted to pacification of the conquered territory which is similar to what Michael Howard argues for. There is also fair play in battle or *jus in bello*. It is laid down in the *Arthaśāstra*[191] that when attacking the enemy in open battlefield, or when storming a fort, care should be taken to see that the following categories of persons are not attacked by the troops: (1) *patita*, those who have fallen down,

(2) *paranmukha*, those who have turned their back on the fight, (3) *abhipanna*, those who surrender, (4) *muktakeśa*, those whose hairs are loose (as a mark of submission), (5) *muktaśastra*, those who have abandoned their weapons, (6) *bhayavirūpa*, those whose appearance is changed through fear and (7) *ayudhyamāna*, those who are taking no part in the fight. These dictums about the fair treatment of captured troops and people predate the European origins of International Humanitarian Law and the Law of Armed Conflict.

For the consolidation of an empire, Kauṭilya's *Arthaśāstra* gives a good set of rules as to how the conquered people are to be assimilated and treated. In no way it compares with the extreme view: 'Vae victis' ('Woe to the vanquished!'), the exclamation by the Gaulish Chieftain Brennus, dictating his terms after defeating ancient Rome.[192]

In Kauṭilya's *Arthaśāstra*, it is clearly mentioned that in capturing a fort, the conqueror (*vijigīṣu*) should grant safety to the people. Those who have to be removed from the place where fighting may take place should be settled elsewhere and helped in every way. Destruction of the people is a ruinous policy. According to Kauṭilya, a country without people makes no sense, and there can be no kingdom without a country.[193] In Book XIII, 'Means of Taking a Fort', under Chapter 5 Section 176 are the rules on pacification of the conquered territory. *Sūtra* 13.5.3, for example, states: "After gaining new territory, he should cover enemy's fault with his own virtues, his virtues with double virtues." Further, *sūtra* 4 continues: "He should carry out what is agreeable and beneficial to the subjects by doing his own duty as laid down, granting favours, giving exemptions, making gifts and showing honour." Moreover, in *sūtras* 13.5.7-8, the king is given the following advice for the just and sensible treatment of the vanquished: "He should adopt a similar character, dress, language and behaviour (as the subjects). And he should show the same devotion in festivals in honour of deities of the country, festive gathering and sportive amusements."[194]

War With or Without spilling blood? – Clausewitz and Kauṭilya[195]

In 2014, we began commemorating the Great War Centenary. It is certainly hoped that the scale of bloodshed and violence of the past century will not happen again.

The way the Great War unfolded and got stalemated with unnecessary casualties has led to a number of debates over manoeuvre, attrition and annihilation. The most quoted author about the nature of that war has been Clausewitz, who in his famous book *On War*, penned his thoughts in the 19th century basing it on Napoleonic wars. A powerful imagery exists in the scholarly imagination on Clausewitz in a negative manner. Appalled by the bloodshed and futile loss of lives during the First World War, Basel Liddell Hart called Clausewitz the 'Mahdi of Mass and Violence'. Clausewitzian conception and its resultant bloodshed has also been criticised by Major General J.F.C. Fuller, the high priest of 'manoeuvre war', 'principles of war' and 'philosopher-soldier'. He refers to volumes and pages of the English edition of *On War* revised by Colonel F.N. Maude, and published in 1908 to show how the understanding of Clausewitz has problems.[196] Fuller points out that Clausewitz:

> scoffs at the old idea of 'war without spilling blood', calls it 'a real business for Brahmins.[197]

And Fuller elaborates further to show how Clausewitz thinks about war:

> To introduce into philosophies of war, a principle of moderation would be an absurdity and therefore let us not hear Generals who conquer without bloodshed.[198]

Fuller's penetrating insights show that many of Clausewitz's followers "were completely flummoxed and fell victims to his apotheosis of violence".[199]

Kauṭilya and Bloodless War

What does Kauṭilya offer on war with or without blood? His aphorism is brief. The last *sūtra* 51 in chapter 6 of Book X, 'Concerning Wars', is probably the most popular idea which clearly reveals in a simpler way of a bloodless war as translated by R.P. Kangle thus: "An arrow, discharged by an archer, may kill one person or may not kill (even one); but intellect operated by a wise man would kill even children in the womb." Patrick Olivelle translates 10.6.51 as "An arrow unleashed by an archer may kill a single man or not kill anyone; but a strategy unleashed by a wise man kills even those still in the womb". Surely, J.F.C Fuller and Liddell Hart would have approved of this concept from Kauṭilya's *Arthaśāstra*.

Conclusion

In this chapter, I have related the historical context of Kauṭilya's *Arthaśāstra* with the varied intellectual currents and the identity of the author of this powerful ancient text. The core concepts that seem to be relevant in statecraft and International Relations today have been highlighted. These concepts help explain extant state behaviour. Due to their enduring and universal nature, it seems that core ideas from the text have withstood the test of time. I also relate concepts to modern war including its conduct and the peace that must follow it. The overriding importance of just and bloodless war and the humane treatment of the vanquished is an important take away from the text. Kauṭilya's *Arthaśāstra* only supplements and reinforces the literature on humanitarian laws and norms of war.

Kauṭilya's *Arthaśāstra* is finally getting recognised as a relevant and significant text unearthing a treasure trove of ideas, particularly on strategic thinking, by eminent international academics, especially the community of scholars devoted to International Studies. As has been mentioned, this paper with the help of scholars here may set the stage for the 'Kauṭilyan moment'.

END NOTES

1. I mainly use the majestic and authoritative work by R.P. Kangle. Another translation is by Olivelle (2013). Besides, readers may refer to Sastri (2006).
2. Gautam (2013: 7-8).
3. *Ibid.* cf. Sarkar (2010).
4. Sarkar (1985: 235).
5. Kangle (2010a/b/c).
6. Kangle (2010c: 116).
7. *Ibid.*: 1-3.
8. *Ibid.*: 266.
9. Rao (1958:1).
10. Bhandarkar (1984).
11. Weber (1978).
12. Weiner (1984). Not all what Weiner says seems accurate to me, i.e. "Hindu political thought effectively came to an end with the rise of Islam" (*Ibid.*:112). cf. arguments by me below, and also chapter by Seyed Hossein Zarhani in this volume.
13. Gray (1999).
14. Alder (2014: 3), Gautam (2013).
15. Sihag (2014).
16. Mehta and Pantham (2006: xv-xxiii).
17. Pillalamarri (2015).
18. Singh (2011).
19. Some authors assume that "Kauṭilya" implies being only a realist or Machiavellian and "Aśoka" implies being an idealist. Such work unfortunately does not engage with the rich text and picks up secondary sources. cf. Solomon (2012).
20. Shahi (2014).
21. Bisht (2016).
22. Liebig (2014c).
23. Shoham and Liebig (2016).
24. The word *sutra* means thread, string or clue.
25. Kangle (2010a/b/c), Drekmeier (1962).
26. Kangle (2010c: 1).
27. *Ibid.*: 2.
28. Kangle (2010b: 407), [9.1.17-18]; Kangle (2010c: 2).
29. Kangle (2010c: 2).
30. *Ibid.*: 272.
31. Book Seven, Six measures of Foreign Policy, Chapter One, Section 99, Determination of (Measure in) Decline, Stable Condition and Advancement, sutra 38: "Situated in the

circle of constituent elements, he should, in this manner, with these six measures of policy, seek to progress from decline to stable condition and from stable condition to advancement in his own undertakings". Kangle (2010b: 324), [7.1.38].

32. Kangle (2010b: 387). According to Torkel Brekke's understanding which is based on the work of Andre Wink, "The peoples living in the country regions between two kingdoms belong to both the king and his enemy...the *janapada* is shared with the enemy". This is not the case with R.P. Kangle who in a note to the sutra 27 says "this is because when they are over-run by the enemy they easily transfer their allegiance to him". cf. Brekke (2006: 120), Wink (2001).
33. Thapar (2000c).
34. McClish (2012).
35. Kulke and Rothermund (1998a: 44-45).
36. Prasad and Majumdar (1960: 314).
37. The various schools and predecessors of Kauṭilya whose works are not available or traceable are: Mānavas (school), Bārhaspatyas (school), Auśanasas (school), Bhāradvāja, Viśālākṣa, Pārāśara (school), Piśuna, Kauṇapadanta, Vātavyādhi, Bāhudantīputra, Āmbhīyah (school). cf. Sastri (2006: xxxviif) and Kangle (2010b: 42-56).
38. "Power and Piety: The Mauryan Empire c.324-187 BCE". cf. Singh (2008: 323-324).
39. Jha (2004: 96-97).
40. "Kautilya or Chanakya". cf. Bandyopadhyaya (2005: 1-15).
41. Also spelled as Vishnugupta.
42. Also spelled as Chanakya.
43. cf. "Preface", Aiyar (2013: xvi).
44. Kangle (2010c: 59).
45. Kulke and Rothermund (1998a: 58-59).
46. Like the identities of Homer or Confucius, there is an unending debate on author and date which is not being covered here in detail. It is interesting to know that an Indian sinologist basing it on the logic of Kauṭilya's *Arthaśāstra* to be of 4th century BCE have argued on the absence of mention of any maritime route to China: "Till Kautilya's time in the 4th century BCE land routes were primarily used. That is why we find detailed enumeration of the uttarapatha (the northern, i.e., the North India and Himalayan route including the route across it) and Daksinapatha (the South Indian route) but the routes to East and West, obviously the routes of maritime trade, are not elaborated, probably they were not yet developed in the Mauryan age." Ray (2012: 25).

    On the debate on author and date cf. Trautmann (1971). For rejoinder, cf. Mittal (2000). There is yet another puzzle. There are some scholars who argue that "Kauṭilya the author of the Arthaśāstra was a different individual from Chanakya, the politician of the Mauryan age" (Gajrani and Ram: 2011: 27) and "Chanakya, the Chancellor of Chandragupta Maurya, and Kautilya, the author of Arthashastra were originally two different persons and they were separated from each other by more than five hundred years. As regards Vishnugupta, it also occurs as the name of the author of the Arthashastra, therefore it may be regarded as another name, probably the original name of Kautilya" [cf. Gajrani and Ram (2011: 28)]. Even Kangle had doubts about it. The book ends with: "Seeing the manifold errors of the writers of commentaries on scientific treatise, Vishnugupta himself composed the *sutra* as well as *bhasya*" [Kangle (2010b: 516)]. For this insertion Kangle argues: "The stanza that follows the colophon of the final book is clearly a later edition" [*ibid.*]. We do not engage in this debate here as the Sanskritists and ancient historians are divided over it. For our purpose, the text by itself is very powerful – it is surely like an old matured wine of Indian heritage.

Of special interest is S.C. Mishra (1997). In the foreword, R.S. Sharma explains that S.C. Mishra's work does not base the study either on the Mauryan date of the text or its attribution to the first three centuries of the Christian era. The author has identified four strata in the compilation of the text on the basis of the correspondence between fiscal, military, judicial and administrative terms found in inscriptions on the one hand and their counterpart noticed in the *Arthaśāstra* on the other. Author's conclusions: "text was finally compiled in 12th century CE when the fourth stratum covering the period from 10th to 12th century was added to it. The first stratum belongs to the Mauryan times, the second to the second century CE, and the third to the 5th and the 6th century CE."

47. Kangle (2010c: 60).
48. Singh (2010).
49. Basham (2004: 51-52), Kulke and Rothermund (1998a: 58).
50. Brown (1964: 12).
51. *Ibid.*: 6.
52. Singh (2011: xi-xii).
53. "Introduction" in Singh (2011). cf. Matilal (1990).
54. Singh (2011: xiii).
55. *Ibid.*: xv.
56. Drekmeier (1962: 4).
57. Stein (2009: 29, 32).
58. Oppert (1967: 1-3).
59. Raychaudhuri (1996: 1).
60. As quoted by Yin Zhao (Ti Heng) (2012). In August 2015, I found out from Professor Partrick Olivelle, that Kauṭilya's *Arthaśāstra* has not been translated into the Chinese language.
61. Thapar (2013: 3). The term used by her explains it well as "embedded history" in chapter "Society and Historical Consciousness: The Itihas – purana Tradition". cf. Thapar (2000b: 137-138).
62. Shulman (2015).
63. Sarkar (2013).
64. Sarkar (1985: 17). Alsocf. Singh (1993) and Roy (1981).
65. Pal (2006: xxi).
66. *Ibid.*: xxii- xxiv.
67. *Ibid.*
68. Brown (1964: 11).
69. Gurukkal (2013).1
70. Danino (2011: 9).
71. Sinha (2006: 83)
72. *Ibid.*
73. Olivelle (2013: 67), [1.3.1-2].
74. *Ibid.*: 468.
75. *Ibid.*: 471.
76. "Searching for Early Indian Historical Writings" in Thapar (2013: 57).

77. "Kautilya" in Chakravarty (1992: 167). Similar reasons are given by Nararyan Chandra Bandyopadhyaya (2005: 22-28).
78. Chakravarty (1992:167).
79. *Ibid.*: 167-168.
80. "*Samkhya* and *Yoga* are the two schools from the famous six schools of Indian philosophy. These systems are the pre-Buddhist set of literature called *Sutras*, or aphorism - *Nyaya Sutra* of Gautama (school of logic or analysis), *Vaisesika Sutra* of Kanada (atomic realism/ theism); *Samkhya Sutra* of Kapila (enumeration), *Yoga Sutra* of Patanjali (yoke, application); *Mimamsa Sutra* of Jaimini (enquiry), and *Vedanta* (absolute soul)". cf. Gautam (2015c: 44) note 6. For a discussion of methodology in detail cf. Chousalkar (2004).
81. Drekmeier (1962: 282).
82. Shivshankar Menon, India's former National Security Advisor, Speaking Notes at the International Conference on Kauṭilya, April 9, 2014. cf. Menon (2016).
83. Sarkar (2013: 511).
84. *Ibid.*
85. *Ibid.*: 512-513.
86. "Kautilya" in Chakravarty (1992: 184).
87. *Ibid.*
88. Sarkar (2013). Thucydides has a powerful influence in the western discourse on statecraft. Thucydides' famous Melian dialogue from Chapter XVII is, "The strong do what they can while the weak suffer what they must". Rajamohan (2014) in his column while referring to the project on the renewal of Kauṭilya at IDSA in the *Indian Express* argues that like the Melian dialogue "Kautilya's strategic realism is indeed as hard-nosed as any from the West". By this it seems that he thinks it proper to reduce or convert everything from India to the base of the West, without any argument of concepts embedded in Indian political philosophy of political virtue (*dharma*) which needs to be regulated by *daṇḍa*, or *yogakṣema*. He continues with an example of Melian dialogue: "India's classics have similarly talked about '*matsyanyaya*' – that big fish eat the small. It is not, therefore, a question of East versus West. India must internalise the dominant Western discourse as well as claim strategic thought from ancient, medieval and pre-Independence period of history." The basic difference is that *daṇḍa* must be applied with legitimacy or with *dharma* in mind to avoid *mātysa-nyāya*. This concept is absent in the Greek story of the Melian dialogue. In his short piece, it seems he is suggesting that Melian dialogue is nothing but a policy of *mātysa-nyāya* that Indian must follow rather than overcome. This turns the understanding of the text on its head.
89. Note 198, Chakravarty (1992: 197).
90. Sarkar (1919).
91. *Ibid.*: 408.
92. *Ibid.*
93. *Ibid.*
94. Chakravarty (1992: 199).
95. Sarkar (2013: 527).
96. Varma (1959: 92).
97. *Ibid.*: 92-93.
98. Kangle (2010b: 12), [1.6.1]. Concerning the Topic for Training, Chapter Six, Section 3, Control over the Senses, and Casting out Group of Six Enemies.

99. Modelski (1964).
100. Medha Bisht (2016).
101. This is very close to the Buddhist concept of four sublime states of *Brahmavihar- metta* (loving kindness), *karuna* (compassion), *mudita* (sympathetic joy), and *upekha* (equanimity). Buddhism probably borrowed the concept from earlier Indian traditions.cf. note 2 of Saddhatissa (1970: 65); Kangle (2010b: 8), [1.3.13].
102. The operationalisation of these may be found in Yoga philosophy as Yam (Don'ts) and Niyam (Do's). cf. Kangle (2010b: 12), [1.6.1-3].
103. Liebig (2014b). These ideas, among others, are being explored by the author.
104. Modelski (1964).
105. "Understanding Kautilya's Four Upayas", Gautam (2013b).
106. cf. Michael Liebig's chapter in this volume comparing Kauṭilya and Machiavelli.
107. Thapar (2000a:121-122).
108. Drekmeier (1962: 59).
109. Flibbert (2013).
110. Kangle (2010c: 243).
111. Kangle (2010b: 321-322), [7.1.13-18].
112. Kangle (2010b: 322), [7.1.20ff]; Kangle (2010c: 251).
113. Morgenthau (1978: 194).
114. Bandyophadhyaya (1993: 146). For more on this see the work of Dr. Michael Liebig.
115. Kangle (2010c: 249-250), Rubin (1955: 159).
116. Kangle (2010b: 382).
117. Kangle (2010c: 250). *Aribhāvin* (of hostile disposition), *mitrabhāvin* (of friendly disposition) and *bhṛtyabhāvin* (of a dependent disposition).
118. Kangle (2010b: 319), [6.2.33].
119. This is an improvement of the chapter 4 of my monograph. cf. Gautam (2015c).
120. Kangle (2010b: 325), [7.2.1-2].
121. Panikkar (1952: 25).
122. "Introduction"in Lowe et al. (2008: 45-48).
123. Kangle (2010b: 491). Notes in support of [13.4.62].
124. Wink (2001).
125. Prakash (1966: 17).
126. Gupta (1987: 1).
127. Chandra (2014: 25).
128. Portions of tracing the spread has also been covered by me in chapter 4 "Comparing Kautilya's *Arthashastra*" of my monograph. cf. Gautam (2015c).
129. Jayaswal (1967: 6).
130. Gowen (1992).
131. *Panchatantra*, translated from Sanskrit by Arthur W. Ryder. cf. Ryder (2011: 234).
132. Gowen (1992).
133. Shastri (1969). According to the author, this story is not plausible and if, at all, Varahamihira went abroad, it was Yavana (Greece). Seyed Hossein Zarhani of SAI is known to be working on this and his chapter 'Kautilya's *Arthashastra,* Indian Politico-Strategic Culture and India's Institutional Evolution' with the possible influence of Kauṭilyan ideas on the evolution of political institutions in Islamic Empire, Persia and

Medieval and Mongol India with focus on state bureaucracy may pin down this puzzle with some original archival material. In a meeting at Heidelberg in August 2014, Hussein in his presentation mentioned that he had found out sources to say that a number of Indian pundits (scholars) may have visited Persia.

134. Tharoor (2012: 161).
135. Thussu (2013: 49).
136. As quoted in Amartya Sen (1997).
137. *Pancatantra* translated from original Sanskrit by Patrick Olivelle. cf. Olivelle (1997: xliii-xliv).
138. Bishnupada Bhattacharya (2013).
139. This is also called 'floating wisdom'. cf. Mishra (1993: 198-200).
140. Rizvi (2005: 156-157).
141. *Ibid.*: 157.
142. Kangle (2010b: 47), [1.19.34].
143. cf. Seyed Hossein Zarhani's chapter in this volume.
144. Pathak (1974: 56).
145. *Ibid.*: xiv.
146. *Ibid.*: xiii.
147. *Ibid.*: 33.
148. *Ibid.*: 81.
149. This is based upon a commentary of mine. cf. Gautam (2015b).
150. As quoted by Balbir Singh Sihag in his paper presented at IDSA tilted "Kautilya and National Security", October 20, 2014. Sihag draws attention to its translation being cited by Wolter. For translation of inscription cf. Chatterji (1967: 183), verse 29. The Inscription of Erlangga from Penang- Gungen (Surbaya) of Saka Year 963 inscribed in Sanskrit reads as follows: "There in Saka Year 957 on the eight day of dark half of Kartik on Thursday, the king Vijaya was seized by his own troops through the application of the means (of statecraft) as taught by Vishnugupta (Chanakya) and died soon afterwards."
151. Mitra (1982: i).
152. Stark (2004: 96). The author refers to the concept of *maṇḍala* as described by O.W. Walters. cf. Walters (1999).
153. Indrawooth (2004: 137).
154. Miksic (2004: 239).
155. Manguin (004: 304).
156. Chong (2011: 140).
157. Pollock (2006: 16).
158. Neumann (2014).
159. Johnston (2012).
160. Neumann (2014).
161. Thapar (2000d: 151, 161).
162. "Epilogue" in Kolff (1990: 193-199).
163. Kulke and Rothermund (1998a: 163).
164. Roy and Alam (2011).
165. Sarkar (1985: 529-545).
166. Rizvi (2005: 160-161).

167. *Ibid.*: 190-191.
168. Kamla (2011).
169. Mishra (1997: 197-200). Agarwal (2013: 138) mentions that Chanakya/Kauṭilya was the author of two works –*Arthashastra* and *Neeti Shastra*. However there is no clue to where the manuscripts are of the Chanakya's *Niti Shastra* also called *Chanakyasutra* – which is also termed as 'floating wisdom' by S.C. Mishra (*ibid.*). Due to absence of authentic source documents on *Neeti Shastra* by Kauṭilya, it is difficult to accept the two book theory which I have touched upon in "One Year of *Arthasastra*: Response, Pedagogy and Research". cf. Gautam (2016a: 106-125).
170. Panikkar (1960: 29).
171. I am thankful to Dr. Michael Liebig for drawing attention to Nehru's work. cf. Nehru (1990: 122-25, 141, 163).
172. Allen (2012: 309).
173. In a speech by President of India Shri Pranab Mukherjee on November 13, 2014. cf. Mukherjee (2014).
174. Gautam et al. (2015, 2016a/b).
175. Chakravarti (1987: vii).
176. "Composition of the Army – Then and Now" in Gautam (2016b: 63-82).
177. Liebig in Gautam (2016b: 33-62). cf. Shoham and Liebig (2016). Unlike in Europe or North America, in Indian universities, to the best of my knowledge, Intelligence Studies as a sub-discipline of IR in not a subject. However, if content analysis is done of two international refereed journals then many of the articles may well have been published in any other journal of IR due to an inherent overlap. See *International Journal of Intelligence and Counter Intelligence* from the USA and *Intelligence and National Security* from the UK - both published by Francis & Taylor/Routledge.
178. Jha (2016).
179. Dikshitar (1987: 81).
180. *Ibid.*: 83.
181. Mookerji (1987: 3).
182. Kangle (2010b: 342), [7.6.40-41].
183. Kangle (2010c: 258).
184. Kangle (2010b: 438), [10.3.1].
185. Note to *Arthaśāstra's sūtra* [12.1.17]. cf. Kangle (2010b: 461).
186. Note to *Arthaśāstra's sūtra* [12.4.24]. cf. Kangle (2010b: 469).
187. I notice a problem in L.N. Rangarajan's re-arrangementand translation at page 637. He gives four kinds of *yuddhas*: *Mantrayuddha* (war by counsel), *Prakāśayuddha* (open warfare), *Kūṭayuddha* (concealed warfare) and *Gūḍhayuddha* (clandestine war). He does not mention *Tūṣṇīṃyuddha.* Further, as his work is not in conformity with the progression of books and chapters of the text, he fails to give his views and opinions as a note to a particular *sūtra* or a set of *sūtras* for the reader to make his judgement. This is a must when dealing with the complex text and has been done comprehensively by both Kangle and Patrick Olivelle. It is because of these reasons that work of L.N. Rangarjan may not be the ideal source for research. In orderly placing of *sūtras* (without mixing up and re-arranging as by L.N. Rangarajan), both R.P. Kangle and Patrick Olivelle to me seem to be more suitable for establishing the context according to the books and chapters of the text.
188. It needs to be noted that *Asura* was originally a title of the great Gods Indra, Agni and

Varuna, but later, by a different etymology, it came to mean not-divine, and so a Titanic enemy of God. cf. "Glossary" in Prem (2008: 267).

189. Chakravarty (1992: 203).
190. Howard (1999).
191. Kangle (2010b: 490), [13.4.52].
192. As quoted by Vincent Bernard in the editorial of the special issue on 'Occupation'. cf. Bernard (2012: 5).
193. Kangle (2010c: 260). cf. Kangle (2010b), [13.4.2-5].
194. Kangle (2010b: 491).
195. Based on "*Dharmavijay* (Just War), Winning the Peace and War Without Spilling Blood". cf. Gautam et al. (2015).
196. Fuller (2003: 61-62).
197. *Ibid.*: 61. Reference to the use of term 'Brahmin' in the English edition of *On War*, revised by Colonel F.N. Maude, and published in 1908 are given by Fuller in Book I, page 287. This is the first time I discovered Clausewitz using the word 'Brahmin'. This may have been due to the influence of European Indologists. It was common to refer to the idea of learned Indians or 'professors' as 'Brahmins'. So, it is not unusual or surprising to find that Kauṭilya is often mentioned as Kauṭilya the Brahmin or the Brahmin prime minister or adviser. It is clear that Brahmin refers to an intellectual.
198. *Ibid.*: 61.
199. *Ibid.*

APPENDIX

A Brief Note on the Contents of the *Arthaśāstra*

The best and comprehensive account is to be found in R.P. Kangle's *The Kauṭilīya Arthaśāstra* (*Part II*): Translation with Critical and Explanatory Notes, Second Edition, Motilal Banarasidass Publishers Private Limited, Delhi, Bombay University, 1972, 7th Reprint, 2010. Professor R.P. Kangle was a Professor of Sanskrit and published the work in three parts (Part I is in Sanskrit and Part III is a study) between 1961 and 1965 from Bombay University. Kangle admits that *The Arthaśātra* is a difficult work of XV Books called *adhikaraṇas*. Each Book has chapters. Chapters have sections which comprise of verse(s) called *sūtra*(*s*). The reference to the work has a universal norm. For example Book II, Chapter One, *sūtra* 6 will be written as 2.1.6. Similarly, 10.6.51 will correspond to Book X, Chapter 6, *sūtra* 51.

Method and Books of Kauṭilya's *Arthaśāstra*

Arthaśāstra's unique feature is that it provides evidence of methodology in its composition and hints at the historical setting. On method, the first sentence (*sūtra*) mentions: "This single (treatise on the) Science of Politics has been prepared mostly bringing together (the teaching of) as many treatises on the Science of Politics as have been composed by ancient teachers for the acquisition and protection of the earth" [1.1.1]. The work is very impartial and has advice even for the weaker king and oligarchies. The breakdown of the *Arthaśāstra* is given below:

1. **Book I – Concerning the Topic of Training**: The first *sūtra* (1.1.1) and 15.1.5 mention that this single (treatise on the) Science of Politics has been prepared mostly bringing together (the teaching of) as many treatises on the Science of Politics as have been composed by ancient teachers for the acquisition and protection of the earth. The book deals mainly with training of the prince for arduous duties of rulership. It also discusses the question of the appointment of ministers and other officers necessary for the administration of a state. This prepares the ground for the establishment of a benevolent monarchy.
2. **Book II – The Activity of the Heads of Departments**: This deals with the activity of various state departments and internal administration of a state.
3. **Book III – Concerning Judges:** This deals with the administration of justice and lays down the duties of judges and law.

4. **Book IV – The Suppression of Criminals:** This deals with maintenance of law and order with criminal offences of various kinds.
5. **Book V – Secret Conduct**: The secret conduct described in this Book is that of the king and servants.
6. **Book VI – The Circle (of Kings) as the Basis:** This deals with the circle of kings (*maṇḍala*) and its seven constituents/*prakṛtis* (the king, the minister, the country, the fortified city, the treasury, the army and the ally) of state. The description of the *maṇḍala* in this Book serves as the introduction to the Book VII which deals with *ṣāḍguṇya*.
7. **Book VII – The Six Measures of Foreign Policy:** This deals with the use of the six measures or *ṣāḍguṇya* that can be adopted by a state in its relations with foreign states (peace/treaty, war/injury, staying quiet/ remaining indifferent, marching/augmenting power, seeking shelter/ submitting to another, and dual policy/resorting to peace (with one) and war (with another). This is the longest book and probably is the most understudied by political scientists, due to its complexity.
8. **Book VIII – Concerning Topic of Calamities of the Constituent Elements**: This book deals with the calamities that affect the various constituents (*prakṛtis*) of the state. "It is necessary to take precautions against these before one can start on an expedition of conquest described in following Books."
9. **Book IX – The Activity of the King About to March:** The book deals with preparation to be made before starting an expedition and the precautions that have to be taken at the time. The *vijigīṣu* in the text is expected to 'conquer the world' which implies the conquest of the whole of Indian subcontinent, designated as *cakravartīkṣetra* (9.1.17-18) – "northwards between the Himāvat and the sea, one thousand *yojanas* in extent across."[1] The book also covers the campaigning season and terrain analysis. It also gives details of the type of troops and composition of an army like *maulabala* (hereditary/ standing army), *bhṛtabala* (recruited for a particular occasion), *śrenībala* (troops of guilds and mercenaries), *mitrabala* (the ally's troops), *amitrabala* (troops from enemy), and *aṭavibala* (troops of forest tribes).
10. **Book X – Concerning War:** Deals with aspects of camps, marching, protection of troops, types/mode of fighting, morale, functions of the four arms (infantry, the cavalry, the chariot and elephants), battle arrays, and related matters. The last *sūtra* 51 is probably the most popular idea which clearly shows mind over matter: "An arrow, discharged by

an archer, may kill one person or may not kill (evenone); but intellect operated by a wise man would kill even children in the womb."

11. **Book XI – Policy Toward Oligarchies**: *Saṃgha* (oligarchy) is a form of rule evolved from clan rule. Fairly big states were formed with council of elders to rule over them. The only chapter of the book clearly shows that a *saṃgha* had more than one chief or *mukhiyā*. In some *saṃghas*, the chiefs styled themselves *rājan* or king. It seems to be assumed that the *vijigīṣu* (would-be-conqueror) has or proposes to have suzerainty over the *saṃghas*. The chapter shows how he should maintain strict control over them.
12. **Book XII – Concerning the Weaker King:** The book expands ideas already found elsewhere, particularly of Book VII, chapters 14 to 17.
13. **Book XIII – Means of Taking a Fort:** The capture of enemy forts is recommended mostly through stratagems. Chapter 5 is devoted to pacification of the conquered territory.
14. **Book XIV – Concerning Secret Practices:** Book describes various secret remedies and occult practices intended for the destruction of the enemy. A great deal of magical and other lore is incorporated here.
15. **Book XV – The Method of Science:** This single chapter explains and illustrates the various stylistic devices to elucidate a scientific subject. It refers to 32 devices of textual interpretation called '*tantra-yukti*' or devices of science.

END NOTE

1. Cunningham the British engineer in his book records a *yojana* as 6 and 3/4 miles; and with compensation for the zig-zag routes of carts as 7 and 1/2 to 8 miles. cf. Cunningam (1871).

4

Kauṭilya and Machiavelli in a Comparative Perspective

Michael Liebig

Introduction

In this chapter, I undertake a comparison of Kauṭilya's *Arthaśāstra*[1] and Machiavelli's *Il Principe* and the *Discorsi sopra la prima deca di Tito Livio*.[2] We believe that a comparison of Kauṭilya and Machiavelli, is not only a desideratum in terms of comparative politics and comparative political theory, but also indispensable for the adequate understanding of each of the two political theorists. And such understanding, in turn, is the logical precondition of understanding the contemporary relevance of Kauṭilya and Machiavelli. That their ideas and concepts have remained efficacious up to the present, is particularly evident in India, where the 'modernity of tradition'[3] and the 're-use of the past' (Mitra) are central features of its political system. I think, without thoroughly knowing Kauṭilyan thought, including from a comparative perspective, the analytical understanding of the thinking and behaviour of political and strategic actors in today's South Asia remains perfunctory.

Kauṭilya (often called Chanakya in India) and Machiavelli have rather often been compared. Although most of these comparisons have been made en passant addressing their 'intellectual gestalt', they do indicate that there seems to exist a 'family resemblance'[4] between the two political thinkers. Kauṭilya and Machiavelli have not only been compared by Indologists,[5] but also in the context of Political Science.[6] We select here rather randomly five examples of co-relating the two authors:

Max Weber: "The classical example of a truly radical 'Machiavellianism', in the popular sense of the word, in Indian literature is found in Kauṭilya's *Arthaśāstra*, which dates back to very early pre-Christian times, and is said to be from the time of 'Candra Gupta'. Compared to this, Machiavelli's 'Il Principe' is innocuous."[7]

Jawaharlal Nehru: "Chanakya has been called the Indian Machiavelli, and to some extent this comparison is justified. But he was a much bigger person in every way, greater in intellect and action."[8]

N.P. Sil: "Plato, Aristotle, Machiavelli and Kautilya appear to have derived their outlook on human society from a fundamentally similar ideological base. All of them have almost similar notions of human nature, the need for stability in the commonwealth, and the desirability of righteousness in collective political behaviour."[9]

Roger Boesche: "It is his unrelenting, unsparing realism of Kautilya that makes so many authors liken him to Machiavelli…These republican dreams in the end made Machiavelli a less effective but more likable realist than Kautilya who had no romantic prism refracting his political insights."[10]

Kanti Bajpai: "Kautilya's work is often cited as a key instance of Indian strategic thinking that ranks with Machiavelli's *The Prince*. Whether it has that status is an open question. Our sense is that it does not do so."[11]

In spite of the divergent conclusions that the cited authors draw from their comparison of Kauṭilya and Machiavelli, the fact that they do compare carries three basic assumptions. The comparison is possible and meaningful, because:

1. Kauṭilya and Machiavelli treat the same subject area: politics and, specifically, statecraft.
2. There are likely some conceptual homologies in their respective treatment of the politics and statecraft.
3. There are, equally likely, some significant conceptual differences in their understanding of the politics and statecraft.

As Adda Bozeman notes: "Every comparison carries the assumptions 1) that the phenomena up for juxtaposition are comparable and 2) that they are probably dissimilar."[12] However, the comparison of Kauṭilya and Machiavelli in terms of conceptual homologies and differences must take into account that Kauṭilya is a pre-modern political theorist embedded in South Asian cultural space, while Machiavelli is a political thinker of early modernity in the European cultural context.[13] Therefore, an additional consideration needs to be vectored in, which Bozeman puts as following:

> Further, all comparisons are initiated by the researcher's explicit or implicit choice of norms for measuring relations among phenomena A, B, C, and so forth. And

> in that phase of the intellectual process it stands to reason that the measure of comparison will be provided by the society or culture that the scholar knows best. In fact, no comparison – whether in the context of philosophy, theology, history, economics, the social science, or the arts – can get off the ground unless this kind of extended self-understanding is firmly in place. Next, it is axiomatic that one cannot proceed to comparisons without having reached an understanding of 'the other' on its own terms – be it a social institution, a mind-set, a nation, a language, a form of government, a way of war, or the totality of a foreign civilisation.[14]

In congruence with Bozeman's approach, our comparison between Kauṭilya's *Arthaśāstra* and Machiavelli's *The Prince* and *Discorsi* is methodologically oriented on Comparative Political Theory (CPT), whose main features are outlined by Fred Dallmayr as follows:[15]

- "The teaching of political theory has been confined almost exclusively to the so called Western 'canon', that is, the tradition of political thought stretching roughly from Socrates to Marx or Nietzsche...However, in our age of rapid globalisation, confinement to this canon is no longer adequate or justifiable."
- "Comparative inquiry places the emphasis on cross-cultural encounters"
- "As a subfield of political theory or political philosophy, it [CPT] concentrates not so much on governmental structures and empirical political processes (the concern of 'comparative politics') but rather on ideas, perspectives, and theoretical frameworks as they have been formulated in the past, and continue to be formulated today, in different parts of the world."
- "CPT necessarily includes in its ambit comparisons between 'Western' and 'Eastern' thinkers, as well as between Indian and East Asian or between Islamic and African theoretical perspectives."
- "In terms of methodology, CPT proceeds mainly through the interpretation of texts, utterances and practices, which in turn are embedded in a distinct life-form or cultural way of life... This means that, in approaching and interrogating other cultures, the interpreter is himself or herself called into question – with the result that the attempt to understand alien cultures usually entails also a new or revised self-understanding."

Thus, comparative analysis has to navigate between the Scylla of 'Western universalism' that epistemically hegemonises non-Western cultures and the Charybdis of post-modern 'cultural relativism' which attributes an 'ontological otherness' to non-Western cultures. We believe that the basics of scientific method can and must be applied in addressing the intellectual resources of both Western and non-Western cultures – precisely because scientific method is not the exclusive offspring of Western culture. Thus, transcultural comparison is both possible and meaningful. We share Bozeman's observation that "certain other non-Western modes of comprehending the incidents of government seem, on examination, to refer to precisely, or nearly, the same values that Western nations are now trying to convey."[16]

If textual comparison in these topical areas yields structural homologies between key ideas and concepts of Kauṭilya and Machiavelli, two basic explanations seem plausible. First, an independent, 'parallel' generation of thought-figures in different cultural and historical contexts. For this explanation, Helmuth Plessner's 'covariance' approach[17] and Eric Voegelin's 'equivalences' approach would be relevant.[18] Both authors think that ideas and concepts which have been independently generated in historically and culturally distant contexts, can be structurally homologous.

The second explanation would be a trans-temporal and trans-cultural 'flow' or 'migration' of Kauṭilyan thought-figures – albeit in hybrid recast.[19] If a trans-temporal and trans-cultural 'migration' and hybdridisation of Kauṭilyan thought from South Asia to Europe has occurred, Persian and Muslim cultural space would be key 'transit points'. For the theoretical orientation on the 'idea-migration' hypothesis, we can, in particular, draw on Adda Bozeman's seminal study *Politics and Culture in International History* (1960).

Making a conclusive determination whether homologies between Kauṭilya and Machiavelli are either a case of 'covariance' or of 'idea migration' or both, is beyond the scope of this paper. But we think that, in the pre-modern era, the conditions of the possibility that Kauṭilyan thought has migrated westward, albeit in hybrid recast, across Iranian and Arab cultural space, did exist.

Charles Drekmeier has alluded to the possibility that Machiavelli might have been influenced by Kauṭilya (without, however, indicating how), writing: "It has even been suggested that the Italian [Machiavelli] was inspired by the *Arthashastra*."[20] And Bharat Karnad raises the question: "Could it be, that the *Arthashastra* travelled to Europe, in the manner the so called 'Arabic' numerals, etc., originating in India had earlier done, and provided Machiavelli with the necessary inspiration?"[21]

Karnad's question is indeed fertile and necessary. Subsequent to the textual comparison, we will provide a preliminary sketch of a possible 'flow' of Kauṭilyan thought figures across time and cultures that will suffice to plausibly show that the conditions have indeed existed that Kauṭilyan thought has had tangible influence on Machiavelli.

(A) Textual comparison of Kauṭilya's *Arthaśāstra* and Machiavelli's *The Prince* and *Discorsi*

Kauṭilya and Machiavelli treat the same subject area, but, in order to become productive, the comparative analysis of Kauṭilya's *Arthaśāstra* and Machiavelli's *Prince* and *Discorsi* needs to be broken down into more delineated topics. For this paper, I have selected for the textual comparison the following topical areas:

1. General Characteristics and Methodology.
2. Political anthropology.
3. The state and state power.
4. Statecraft and the idea of raison d'état.
5. The normative dimension of politics.

(a) The Texts' General Characteristics and Methodology

Kauṭilya's *Arthaśāstra* is one of the earliest examples of a scholarly treatise on politico-strategic affairs. The *Arthaśāstra* has an encyclopaedic character covering the (patrimonial) state, public administration, economics, law, foreign policy/diplomacy, military affairs and intelligence. Machiavelli's *The Prince* and *Discorsi* too are comprehensive works but give much less, if any attention to the specifics of state administration, judicial system and the economy. Also, Kauṭilya's treatment of foreign policy is much more extensive, systematic and in-depth than Machiavelli's. Yet, with respect to the methodological structure of Kauṭilya's pre-modern treatise and Machiavelli's early modern political writings, there are evident homologies.

Kauṭilya states in the *Arthaśāstra* that his book was written, "after *going through all the sciences* in detail and *observing the [political] practice*."[22] (Emphasis added)

And Machiavelli writes in the Introduction of the *Discorsi*: "I have endeavoured to embody in it [the *Discorsi*] all that *long experience* and *assiduous research* have taught me of the affairs of the world."[23] (Emphasis added)

The structural homology of the two citations is evident. Kauṭilya's access to theoretical writings on the state and statecraft was wide, even though most of the antecedent Indian literature he refers to is lost.[24] Kauṭilya's historical references are rare and mostly concern mythological figures and occurrences. In the *Discorsi*, Machiavelli refers six times to the Greek political philosopher and historian Xenophon, a student of Sokrates. He seems to have known Aristotle's Politics, as he names him four times by name and uses several of his thought-figures. He refers to Cicero's *De Republica* (four times) and Dante's *De Monarchia* (twice). However, most of Machiavelli's theorisations on the state and statecraft derives from analysing political events of his time and the study of ancient historians, including Herodot, Thukydides, Polybios, Diodorus Siculus, Tacitus and, of course, Livius.

Both Kauṭilya and Machiavelli could draw on their extensive personal experience in political affairs. Kauṭilya was the key adviser, if not 'chancellor' (*mantrin*) of Chandragupta Maurya. Between 1498 and 1512, Machiavelli was the de facto 'foreign minister' of the Republic of Florence conducting diplomatic missions with the German Emperor, the French King, the Pope, Cesare Borgia and many other political figures of the time. Thus, the theorisations of both authors were grounded in the empirical analysis of politics based on participant observation.

Kauṭilya's exposition of the state and statecraft is no 'idealist' or even utopian construction, but rooted in the analysis of political reality using ideal-type methodology (in the Weberian sense). Machiavelli pursues a homologous approach. In the 15th chapter of *The Prince*, he writes:

> But my intention being to write something of use to those who understand, it appears to me more proper to go to the real truth of the matter than to its imagination; and many have imagined republics and principalities, which have never been seen or known to exist in reality; for how we live is so far removed from how we ought to live, that he who abandons what is done for what ought to be done, will rather learn to bring about his own ruin than his preservation. (*The Prince*)[25]

Since Kauṭilya's political theory is grounded in empirical analysis of political reality, his theorems are not to be derived from 'ideological' presuppositions – in religious, metaphysical, moralist or eschatological terms. As Max Weber notes, the *Arthaśāstra* is "devoid of any 'ideology' in our sense of the word."[26] Kauṭilya sees politics as an autonomous sphere with an inherent rationality in terms of theory and practice. Machiavelli's approach is homologue, he too rejects religious, metaphysical or moralist presuppositions in the analysis of politics. Whether he was a-religious, is difficult to determine, but he was certainly – like Kauṭilya – secular. Both stood for a clear separation of the political and religious spheres and rejected the idea that religious institutions and figures should exercise political power.

The *Arthaśāstra* is a theoretical and instructional work, and the same applies to Machiavelli's *The Prince* and *Discorsi*. While works of both authors are scholarly, Kauṭilya gives much more attention to questions of methodology – to which he devotes a whole section of the text (Book XV). He designates his *Arthaśāstra* as a treatise of "political science that his theory-building proceeds methodologically and according to the principles of causality and logical consistency".

It is often argued that Machiavelli's methodology is 'historical'. Indeed, an estimated 50 per cent of the text of *The Prince* and *Discorsi* consist of often detailed historical accounts, primarily from ancient Rome (mainly via Livius), but also from Greek and Asian, notably Persian history, as well as from contemporary history of Machiavelli's life-time. However, *The Prince* and *Discorsi* are no 'history books', but theoretical works on the state and statecraft with extensive historical references. Almost all chapters of the two books, begin with a theoretical statement, only then follow examples from past and contemporary history as to supplement and illustrate the theoretical argument. In contrast, as noted above, Kauṭilya only rarely references events from history or mythology to supplement his theoretical argumentation. Therefore, in principle, there is no methodological difference between Kauṭilya and Machiavelli. E.H. Carr notes that for Machiavelli "history is a sequence of cause and effect, whose course can be analysed and understood by intellectual effort, not (as utopians believe) directed by 'imagination'. Secondly, theory does not (as utopians believe) create practice, but practice theory."[27]

Carr's assessment of Machiavelli's methodological approach is correct; and congruent with Kauṭilya's. Carr is also correct when he sees these concepts as the foundation of the theory of political realism, although neither Kauṭilya nor Machiavelli use the term 'political realism'. What Carr overlooks is the fact that these 'foundation-stones of the realist philosophy' were laid by Kauṭilya – some 1800 years prior to Machiavelli.[28]

(b) Political Anthropology

At the beginning of Book I of the *Arthaśāstra*, Kauṭilya tells us how he sees man's basic anthropological dispositions: affect-driven impulses, greed and striving for dominance: *lust, anger, greed, pride, arrogance and foolhardiness...the group of six enemies* (KA).[29] A ruler must control these basic anthropological dispositions in order to develop the character traits necessary for political leadership. However, 'naturally', affect-driven impulses, greed and striving for dominance are anthropological dispositions of all human beings, not just political leaders.

Kauṭilya's proposition has two main implications: On the one hand, affect-driven impulses, greed and striving for dominance can and must be channeled, controlled and sublimated through personal self-discipline, education, ethics and ultimately (criminal) law. On the other hand, these anthropological dispositions cannot be denied nor eradicated, but need to be taken into account when dealing with politics. Shortly after affirming the necessity of reining in the 'six enemies', Kauṭilya writes:

> 'Material well-being [artha] alone is supreme', says Kauṭilya. For, spiritual good [dharma] and sensual pleasure [kāma] depend on material well-being. (KA)[30]

Thus, Kauṭilya 'realistically' accepts the pursuit of material gain and power as 'facts of life', while avoiding their Sophist-style ideological adulation.[31] That is stressed by Kauṭilya repeatedly in the *Arthaśāstra:*

> Since material wealth is the root of spiritual good and has pleasure for its fruit, the attainment of that utility means attainment of all gains. (KA)[32]

Based upon his anthropological realism, Kauṭilya develops a second line of argument: Because of their basic disposition of affect-driven impulses, greed and striving for dominance, human beings pursue 'selfish' interests – individually or as a social group. By doing so, they get constantly in conflict with each other. Conflicts of interest between individuals and social groups – family, clan, tribe or state – are an anthropological constant in human existence. For Kauṭilya, the acknowledgement of this anarchic reality is a key premise of 'political science'.

Usually, the resolution of conflicts of interest means that the stronger party enforces its will against the resistance of the weaker party. This basic anthropological situation, is expounded by Kauṭilya already on the first pages of the *Arthaśāstra*: The law of fishes – *mātsya-nyāya.* "For, the stronger swallows the weak in the absence of the wielder of the rod" (KA).[33] Kauṭilya argues that primordial mankind had suffered so badly through *mātsya-nyāya* that it came to the conclusion to select and install a ruler endowed with the instruments of power in order to end *mātsya-nyāya.*[34]

For Kautilya, *mātsya-nyāya* or anarchy is the 'state of nature' of human community life. But it can be transformed to the benefit of society by making the ruler, respectively the state, so strong and powerful that the conflicts of interest within society are no longer resolved by stronger individuals or groups at the expense of the weaker ones. The state 'appropriates' *mātsya-nyāya* by monopolising the use of force, thus denying it to its subjects. If *mātsya-nyāya* can be 'domesticated' within a monarchical state, in inter-state relations, 'the law of the fishes' reigns supreme. For Kauṭilya, unrestrained anarchy characterises inter-state relations.

Kauṭilya's political anthropology essentially corresponds to that of Machiavelli. In *The Prince*, he writes: "The desire to acquire possessions is a very natural and ordinary thing".[35] And: "For it may be said of men in general that they are ungrateful, voluble, dissemblers, anxious to avoid danger, and covetous of gain."[36] And, in the *Discorsi*:

> Whoever desires to found a state and give it laws, must start with assuming that all men are bad and ever ready to display their vicious nature, whenever they may find occasion for it. And if their evil disposition remains concealed for some time, it must be attributed to some unknown reason; and we must assume that it lacked occasion to show itself; but time, which has been said to be the father of all truth, does not fail to bring it to light. (*Discorsi*)[37]

> It was the saying of ancient writers, that men afflict themselves in evil, and become weary of the good, and that both these dispositions produce the same effect. For when men are no longer obliged to fight from necessity, they fight from ambition, which passion is so powerful in the hearts of men that it never leaves them, no matter what height they might rise. The reason is that nature has created men so, that they desire everything, but are unable to attain it; desire thus being always greater than the faculty of acquiring, discontent with what they have and dissatisfaction with themselves result from it. (*Discorsi*)[38]

> Whoever considers the past and the present will readily observe that all cities and all peoples are and ever have been animated by the same desires and the same passions; so that it is easy, by diligent study of the past, to foresee what is likely to happen in the future of any republic, and to apply those remedies that were used by the ancients. (*Discorsi*)[39]

For Machiavelli, man's basic anthropological disposition is the drive for material gain and power at the expense of fellow men. He argues that even if men have achieved great wealth, they can indulge in lust. Having attained high social status and great political power over others, they still won't be content and want more which means that conflicts within a state and between states are inevitable. It is 'nature' that has furnished man with these 'passions' and 'ambitions' – and the consequence is anarchy within and between communities of men.

The only way to contain the basic human disposition of lust, greed and domination of others, is the power of the state to force people to behave otherwise through the fear of punishment: "Men act right only upon compulsion…the dread of punishment will keep men better, and less ambitious" (*Discorsi*).[40] And in *The Prince*, he writes: "Love is held by a chain of obligation which, men being selfish, is broken whenever it serves their purpose; but fear is maintained by a dread of punishment which never fails."[41]

Obviously, what Machiavelli states here, is congruent with Kauṭilya's central proposition of political anthropology: "For, the stronger swallows the weak in the absence of the wielder of the rod" (KA).[42]

E.H. Carr correctly notes that, for Machiavelli, "politics are not (as utopians pretend) a function of ethics, but ethics of politics. Men 'are kept honest by constraint'. Machiavelli recognised the importance of morality, but thought there could be no effective morality where there was no effective authority. Morality is the product of power."[43] And Charles Drekmeier notes: "Kautalya, like Machiavelli (with whom he is frequently compared), combined a pessimistic view of man's nature with a belief that man can shape his own destiny... Fatalism persists in Kautalya's world-view, but it is not resignation...The moral order depends upon the continued existence of the state."[44]

(c) The State and State Power

For Kauṭilya, absolute monarchy is the natural form of government, so natural that he refrains from any thorough argumentation with respect to its superiority vis-a-vis other forms of government. In contrast, Machiavelli states. "All states and dominions which hold or have held sway over mankind are either republics or monarchies" (*The Prince*).[45] His principal preference is the republican state, but, under certain conditions, monarchy is necessary. While Machiavelli, principally favours the republican order, there is no axiomatic opposition between republic and monarchy. After all, in the *Discorsi*, the advantages of the republican order are expounded, whereas *The Prince* is promoting monarchy. Friedrich Meinecke is right, when he writes, that Machiavelli "looked at the republic more from above, from the point of view of those governing, than from below, that is broad democracy... Therefore his republican ideal contains all along a monarchical dimension."[46]

Kauṭilya puts enormous emphasis not only on the broad and thorough intellectual education of the ruler, but his character formation. The ruler must be able to control his instincts and affective impulses. "Kings, giving themselves up to the group of six enemies, perished with their kinsmen and kingdoms, being without control over their senses" (KA).[47] Machiavelli argues similarly, a ruler "will chiefly become hated, as I said, by being rapacious, and usurping the property and women of his subjects...He is rendered despicable by being thought changeable, frivolous, effeminate, timid, and irresolute" (*The Prince*).[48]

A ruler's uncontrolled lust, greed and arbitrariness are also key causes for conspiracies to which Machiavelli devotes a whole chapter of the *Discorsi*– it is the longest chapter with 26 pages. Conspiracies come about when a ruler violates the person, honour or possessions of one or several of his subjects.

> It seems to me proper now to treat of conspiracies, being a matter of so much danger both to princes and subjects; for history teaches us that many more princes have lost their lives and states by conspiracies than by open war. But few can venture to make open war upon their sovereign, whilst everyone may engage in conspiracies against him. (*Discorsi*)[49]

For Machiavelli, conspiracies come about when a ruler violates the person (and family), honour or possessions of one or several of his subjects. He sees a second key cause for conspiracies, which is even more difficult to prevent and to detect – envy and ambition. And in that too, he converges with Kauṭilya:

> A prince, then, who wishes to guard against conspiracies should fear those on whom he has heaped benefits as much, and even more, than those he has wronged; for the latter lack the convenient opportunities which the former have in abundance. The intention of both is the same, for the thirst of domination is as great as that of revenge, and even greater…Moreover, men are apt to deceive themselves as to the degree of attachment and devotion which others have for them, and there are no means of ascertaining this except by actual experience; but experience of such matters is of the utmost danger. (*Discorsi*)[50]

Kauṭilya and Machiavelli converge in the view that a ruler, who is incompetent and evil-minded to an extent that the welfare, security or even existence of the state is endangered, has not only lost all legitimacy, but can and should be overthrown. Under such circumstances, conspiracies become legitimate and necessary. With respect to a ruler who threatens the state's existence, Machiavelli proclaims, "there is no other remedy against him but cold steel" (*Discorsi*).[51]

On the subject of conspiracies, we see a far-reaching congruence between Kauṭilya and Machiavelli. The issue of conspiracies permeates the whole *Arthaśāstra*. Conspiracies are addressed by Kauṭilya in terms of causes, political preemption, prophylactic security measures, ways to detect them through the secret service and punishment.

Machiavelli doubts that the foundation of a new state can occur in the constitutional setting of a republic. In order to establish a state, a strong leader is necessary. Equally, when a republic has become corrupted and is faced with internal strife and external threats, a strong leader is needed for its renewal:

> But we must assume, as a general rule, that it never or rarely happens that a republic or monarchy is well constituted, or its old institutions entirely reformed, unless it is done by only one individual... and a wise mind will never censure any one for having employed any extraordinary means for the purpose of establishing a kingdom or constituting a republic. It is well, when the act accuses him, the result should excuse him. (*Discorsi*)[52]

In Machiavelli's view, Romulus, the (mythological) founder of Rome, established constitutional laws with timeless efficacy that could, while originally monarchical, be smoothly adapted to a republican form of government by substituting the king through the two Consuls (one-year term) and a Dictator (six-month term) in times of crisis, elected by the Senate. In contrast to Kauṭilya, Machiavelli does not expound a theoretical, ideal-type model of the state's governmental structure. His role model are the institutions of the early Roman Republic, which are characterised, as Machiavelli emphasises, by a unique combination of monarchical (Consul), aristocratic (Senate) and democratic (citizen assemblies) elements.

For Kauṭilya, the monarchical ruler 'embodies' the state, yet the state is more than the absolutist ruler. Seven state factors (*prakṛti*) constitute the state, and the ruler is just one of them. These 'state factors' are: 1) *swāmin*: the ruler; 2) *amātya*: the minister [government and administration]; 3) *janapada*: the people [in the countryside]; 4) *durga*: the fortress [capital]; 5) *kośa*: the treasury [economy]; 6) *daṇḍa*: armed might; 7) *mitra*: the ally [in foreign policy] (KA).[53] The aggregate of the seven state factors constitutes the state (and allows for a reliable estimate of the state's power potential): "The king and his rule [state], this is the sum-total of the [seven] constituents [of the state]" (KA).[54]

In Machiavelli's political writings, one cannot find such systematic and comprehensive conceptionalisation of the state. However, in *The Prince*, Machiavelli titles the 10th chapter "*How the strength of all states should be measured*" and writes:

> In examining the character of these principalities it is necessary to consider another point, namely, whether the *prince* has such a position as to be able in case of need to maintain himself alone, or whether he has always *need of the protection of others*...I would say, that I consider those capable of maintaining themselves alone who can, through *abundance of men* or *money*, put together a sufficient *army*, and hold the field against anyone who assails them...[States unable to do this] are obliged to take refuge within their walls and stand on the defensive…A prince, therefore, who possesses a *strong city* and does not make himself hated [by the population], cannot be assaulted; and if he were to be so, the assailant would be obliged to retire shamefully. (Emphasis added)[55]

From this citation, we can derive that Machiavelli defines the power of a state by listing the following elements, which correspond to Kauṭilya's state factors:

- A ruler whose policies do not alienate the people – *swāmin*
- A large population (who does not hate the ruler) – *janapada*
- A sumptuously filled state treasury – *kośa*
- A strong army – *daṇḍa*
- A well-fortified capital city – *durga*
- Allies, if the own resources and capabilities are deficient – *mitra*

In this paragraph of *The Prince*, six equivalents of the seven *prakṛtis* are listed. But Machiavelli does not form a systematic and coherent theory which would parallel Kauṭilya's *saptāṅga* theory. However, in other, dispersed text passages, Machiavelli elaborates on the six elements of state listed above.

What about the equivalent of Kauṭilya's second state factor *amātya* – the ruler's advisers, top government and administrative officials? It is missing in the paragraph cited, however, in other text passages, Machiavelli addresses the issue of ruler's advisers and senior government officials:

> The choice of the prince's ministers is a matter no little importance; they are either good or not according to the prudence of the prince. The first impression one gets of a ruler and of his brains is from seeing the men that he has about him. When they are competent and faithful one can always consider him wise, as he has been able to recognise their ability and keep them faithful. But when they are the reverse, one can always form an unfavourable opinion of him, because the first mistake he makes is in making this choice. (*The Prince*)[56]

What Machiavelli states here is quite similar to Kauṭilya's requirements upon the ruler's advisers and ministers as well as the appropriate attitude of the ruler towards them (KA).[57] Both Kauṭilya and Machiavelli share the view that no ruler – even the best and brightest – can rule alone without competent advisers, ministers and administrators. *Rulership can be successfully carried out only with the help of associates. One wheel alone does not turn. Therefore, he should appoint ministers and listen to their opinion* (KA).[58]

Kauṭilya emphatically argues that all matters of state need to be deliberated by the ruler in conclave with his close advisers. He insists that the ruler should consult with his advisers and should ascertain their different opinions along with their reasons for holding them (1.15.35).[59] In the same vein, Machiavelli writes, that "a prince who knows no other control but his own will is like a madman" (*Discorsi*).[60] Fully converging with Kauṭilya's view on the subject, he elaborates:

> A prudent prince must therefore take a third course, by choosing for his council wise men, and giving these alone full liberty to speak the truth to him, but only of those things that he asks and of nothing else; but he must ask them about everything and hear their opinion, and afterward deliberate by himself in his own way, and in these councils and with each of these men comport himself so that everyone may see that the more freely he speaks, the more he will be acceptable…A prince, therefore, ought always to take counsel, but only when he wishes, not when others wish...but he ought to be a great asker, and a patient hearer of the truth about those things of which he has inquired; indeed, if he finds out that anyone has scruples in telling him the truth he should be angry. (*Discorsi*)[61]

In this context, Machiavelli also refers to the intellectual faculties of the ruler and his advisers, stating: "There are three kinds of brains, the one understands things unassisted, the other understands things when shown by others, the third understands neither alone nor with explanation of others. The first is most excellent, the second is also excellent, but the third useless."[62] These sentences of Machiavelli remind us of what Kauṭilya states about the three types of knowledge in statecraft:

1. Immediate knowledge, based on what the ruler himself sees and hears.
2. Mediated, indirect knowledge, based on what the ruler is being told by ministers, spies, diplomats or other 'experts' about occurrences which are distant in space and time, that is intelligence, respectively the product of intelligence analysis.
3. Knowledge inferred from immediate and mediated knowledge with respect to future developments and the ruler's own intended actions, that is intelligence assessments, respectively estimates: "Forming an idea of what has not [yet] been done from what is [has been] done in respect of undertakings is inferred" (KA).[63]

While Machiavelli's third point is a rather banal conclusion, Kauṭilya's third point has exceptional intellectual value, in addressing the key role of inferences in statecraft, notably with respect to the assessment of the situation and strategic planning.

To sum up, Machiavelli does thematise seven factors that make up the strength of a state and they do correspond the Kauṭilya's *prakṛtis*, which constitute the state and the aggregate of which defines the state's power potential. However, Machiavelli does not provide a coherent theoretical frame for these factors through which he measures the state's strength. Similarly, he does not expound a theoretical, ideal-type model of the state's governmental structure. And, he does not elaborate on the institutional and organisational structures of the state's administrative system, which Kauṭilya does so in great (at times, excruciating) detail. Large parts of the *Arthaśāstra* – Book II, III, IV and V – are devoted to the exposition of governmental departments, the justice system, administrative responsibilities and hierarchies, auditing and control mechanisms, job profiles and salary schemes. While the governmental system of the Kauṭilyan state is based on a large, multi-layered and salaried state bureaucracy and the state maintains a standing army, enlarged by mercenary forces in case of war, Machiavelli favours 'amateur' political leaders as well as military commanders, senior administrators and judges, who hold their positions – as in the early Roman republic – for a time only. His prime example being Lucius Quinticus Cincinnatus (519-430 BCE), who was Consul and Dictator twice, but after having successfully accomplished his military and political tasks, he instantly returned to his small farm to live a frugal life as a plain citizen.

Lastly, we turn to the economic sphere that is the role of the economy for state capacity. For Kauṭilya, the economy is the indispensable foundation of state capacity and domestic political stability. Only a flourishing economy generates a rising tax revenue that sustains and expands state capacity without unduly burdening (i.e. pauperising) the population. The Kauṭilyan state actively promotes economic growth, directs and regulates private economic activities and runs a large state-owned businesses. Charles Drekmeier rightly notes: "Several thousand years before Marx, Kautalya insisted that 'in economics lies politics'."[64] In contrast, Machiavelli seems disinterested in economic matters. His treatment of economic issues is rare and lacks analytical depths. In *The Prince*, he writes:

> A prince must also show himself a lover of merit, give preferment to the able, and honour those who excel in every art. Moreover he must encourage his citizens to follow their callings quietly, whether in commerce, or agriculture, or any other trade that men follow, so that this one shall not refrain from improving his possessions through fear that they may be taken from him, and that one from starting a trade for fear of taxes; but he should offer rewards to whoever does these things, and to whoever seeks in any way to improve his city or state. Besides this, he ought, at convenient seasons of the year, to keep the people occupied with festivals and shows.[65]

Such bland statement on economic matters, is more puzzling when we consider the fact that Renaissance Florence was a very wealthy centre of trade and crafts. Moreover, it seems that Machiavelli saw economic prosperity as a threat to political stability by eroding public morale and fomenting social inequality. Machiavelli's ideal citizen is able to adequately – i.e. frugally – sustain his family, but not fixated on private wealth accumulation.

Related to the economic sphere is the issue of corruption. Machiavelli's understanding of corruption is wide-ranging in the sense of an endemic 'social disease' that corrodes public morale first among the elites, then the people and eventually destroys the state – be it a republic or a monarchy. His case in point, is the decay of Roman Republic after having conquered ever more territories outside Italy: family farming was replaced by large estates employing slaves, craftsmen turned into shopkeepers, merchants and large landowners accumulated enormous wealth, which they used for the sale of public offices and the militia army was substituted for a standing army. The once proud Roman citizens became the 'plebs' ready to politically back whoever offered them material benefits. For Machiavelli, Julius Caesar marks the nadir of the decay of the Roman Republic: "Let no one be deceived by the glory of that Caesar who has been so much celebrated by writers...who were corrupted and fearful...Caesar became the first tyrant of Rome, so that city never afterward recovered her liberty" (*Discorsi*).[66]

As in the case of conspiracies, there are remarkable similarities on the issue of corruption between Kauṭilya and Machiavelli. However, Kauṭilya sees corruption in a narrower sense of primarily embezzlement of state property, bribery and abuse of office within the state bureaucracy. But he too sees corruption as a primary threat to the state, which necessitates not only harsh punishment via criminal law, but the employment of the secret service to trace and expose corrupt officials.

While there are multiple and substantive homologies in the conception of the state between Kauṭilya and Machiavelli, there are also substantive differences. One is Kauṭilya's heavy emphasis on intelligence throughout the *Arthaśāstra*. The secret service plays a central role in domestic politics and in the foreign policy of the Kauṭilyan state. In contrast, Machiavelli remains oddly silent on intelligence matters. Unique is Machiavelli's concept of 'renovatio': the combination of institutional continuity and the inherent capacity of institutional reform. He argues, "As all human beings are kept in a perpetual movement, and can never remain stable, states naturally either rise or decline" (*Discorsi*).[67] Herein, Kauṭilya and Machiavelli take similar positions. But, the latter goes conceptionally much further:

> And those are the best-constituted bodies, and have the longest existence, which possess the intrinsic means of frequently renewing themselves, or such as obtain this renovation in consequence of some extrinsic accidents. And it is a truth clearer than light that, without such renovation, these [political] bodies cannot continue to exist; and the means of renewing them is to bring them back to their original principles. For as all religions, republics and monarchies must have within themselves some goodness, by means of which they obtain their first growth and reputation, and as in the process of time this goodness becomes corrupted, it will of necessity destroy the body unless something intervenes to bring it back to its normal condition. (*Discorsi*)[68]

For Machiavelli, the Roman republic had that inherent capacity of 'renovatio' by adapting its institutional practices to new challenges, yet preserving its republican constitutional structure. However, since the final defeat of Carthage in the middle of the 2nd century BCE, the Roman republic increasingly lost its capacity of 'renovatio' leading to a century of civil wars which culminated in Ceasar's dictatorship and the de facto liquidation of the republican order in Rome. While Rome's power and glory continued under Augustus and his successors, in Machiavelli's view, its monarchical system never acquired the capacity of 'renovatio' and thus was doomed to gradual decline. However, Machiavelli does not dispute that monarchies too can have the capacity of 'renovatio':

> We may conclude, then, that nothing is more necessary for an association of men, either as a religious sect, republic or monarchy, than to restore to it from time to time the power and reputation which it had in the beginning, and to strive to have either good laws or good men to bring about such a result, without the necessity of the intervention of any extrinsic force.[69]

For Kauṭilya, the republican political order, means aristocratic-oligarchical rule, has no attraction at all – neither in terms of political practice nor in normative terms. For him, monarchy is the natural and superior political system. While the idea of 'renovatio' is missing in the *Arthaśāstra*, the Kauṭilyan monarchy exhibits a high degree of political elasticity, which is rooted both in the staying power and the plurality of Indian culture.

(d) Statecraft and the Idea of Raison d'État

Adda Bozeman defines the term 'statecraft' as "the sum total of human dispositions, doctrines, policies, institutions, processes, and operations that are designed to assure the governance, security, and survival of a politically unified human group."[70] Statecraft applies to political situations within a state and between states.

In substantive terms, Kauṭilyan statecraft is vectored on three fundamental state goals:

- Maintaining and expanding the power of state.
- Maintaining and expanding the welfare of the people.[71]
- Facilitating the political unification of the Indian subcontinent.

The realisation of these three state goals constitutes Kauṭilyan idea of raison d'état.[72] Kauṭilya provides a substantive explanation of what maintaining and expanding the power of the state means: improving quantitatively and qualitatively the seven state factors *(prakṛti).* Thus, Kauṭilyan raison d'état can be defined as the imperative for the optimisation of the seven *prakṛtis*: "And when the king is possessed of excellences, he makes the [other six] constituents [state factors] perfect with their respective excellences" (KA).[73]

Whatever optimises the seven state factors serves the maintenance and expansion of the power of state as well as the welfare of the people. As Drekmeier notes, the ruler's "action could not be disinterested if the state were to survive and prosper. Thus does the problem of raison d'état develop – before its appearance in the West...For the author of the *Arthaśāstra* the welfare of the state meant ultimately the welfare of the people, and the well-being of his subjects must be rated higher than that of the king himself."[74] The optimisation imperative for the state factors and the commitment to secure and improve the welfare settles the question of Kauṭilyan raison d'état in terms of domestic politics – in terms of modern Political Science terminology we may say, 'internal balancing' has absolute priority. But what about raison d'état in terms of inter-state relations?

Thanks to his *saptānga* theory, Kauṭilya can establish a benchmark for deciding what course of action is to be adopted by the state. The *saptānga* matrix of the seven state factors allows for making a reliable assessment of the correlation of forces between states. Depending on the assessment of the correlation of forces (in terms of the *saptānga* matrix), the state can correctly determine which foreign policy course is consistent with raison d'état. Kauṭilya distrusts political leaders' power instinct and 'lonely decisions' based on gut feelings. Instead, he wants an objective assessment "ascertaining the relative strength or weakness of powers".[75] Based on such an assessment, a precisely defined spectrum of policy options is available: Kautilya's *ṣāḍguṇya* concept cluster. "These are really six measures, because of differences in the situation, says Kauṭilya" (KA).[76] The state must choose between six – not more nor less – foreign policy options:

1. Peace (*saṃdhi*): the rival state is stronger and will likely remain so in the future.
2. War (*vigraha):* the rival is vastly inferior in power.
3. 'Staying quiet', 'wait and see', neutrality (*āsana*): the correlation of forces is balanced.
4. War preparation or coercive diplomacy (*yāna*): one's own power is rising faster than the rival's.
5. Alliance (*saṃśraya):* the rival state's power is rising faster than one's own.
6. Diplomatic double game (*dvaidhībhāva):* highly fluid constellation among states.

What is of critical importance with respect to the *ṣāḍguṇya* theory is its intrinsic connectivity with the *saptānga* theory. "The circle of constituent elements [the seven *prakṛtis*] is the basis of the six measures of foreign policy [*ṣāḍguṇya*]" (KA).[77] The *saptānga* theory provides the benchmark for correlation of forces between states and thus the choice of one of the six foreign policy options. "The conqueror [*vijigīṣu*] should employ the six measures of policy with due regard for his power" (KA)."[78]

Since Machiavelli has not developed a coherent theory of state power that can measure up to Kauṭilya's *saptānga* theory, he can neither develop a concept cluster of foreign policy options (based on the correlation of forces in terms of *prakṛti*) that would correspond to the *ṣāḍguṇya* theory. Nevertheless, we can identify in the *Discorsi* and *The Prince* text-passages that do exhibit conceptual homologies with each of six foreign policy avenues laid out in the *ṣāḍguṇya* theory – without, however, basing them explicitly on the concept of correlation of forces.

Kauṭilya's *ṣāḍguṇya* theory is the application, in the sphere of inter-state relation, of a set of 'methods' for conducting politics in general: the four *upāyas*. Following Max Weber, one may say that the *upāyas* state how a political actor can enforce his will against resistance.

The means [of politics] are conciliation (sāma), gifts (dāna), dissension (bheda) and use of force (daṇḍa). (KA)[79]

For Kauṭilya, there is a ranking among the *upāyas*; its criterion being the amount of effort and cost necessary to enforce one's will upon the other party. The *upāyas* are not an original Kauṭilyan concept, but go back to the oldest sources of ancient Indian political literature.[80] In the *Arthaśāstra*, the *upāyas* are explicitly introduced in the 10th chapter of Book II, but Kauṭilya refers to them throughout the text.

In the following, we first correlate text-passages from *The Prince* and the *Discorsi* to Kauṭilya's four *upāyas*:

(i) 'Conciliation' or *Sāma*: Praise (honest or not) and propitiation that aim at psychologically disarming the counterpart as well as an appeal to mutual interests and benefits (real or not). "But if their conditions be such that their forces do not suffice for open war against the prince, then they seek by every art to win his friendship, and for this purpose employ all possible means, such as adopting his tastes, and taking delight in all things that give him pleasure. Such intimacy will insure you tranquility without any danger, and enable to share the enjoyment of the prince's good fortune with him, and at the same time afford you any convenience for satisfying your resentment" (*Discorsi*).[81]

> It is advisable then at times to feign folly, as Brutus did; and this is sufficiently done by praising, speaking, seeing and doing things contrary to your way of thinking, and merely to please the prince. (*Discorsi*)[82]

> And doubtless, if the Florentines had attached their neighbours to themselves by treaties of amity, or by rendering them assistance, instead of frightening them off, they would now be the undisputed masters of Tuscany. (*Discorsi*)[83]

Rebellious subjects must either be conciliated by benefits or destroyed. (*Discorsi*)[84]

(ii) 'Gifts' or *Dāna*: Means making concessions in terms of tribute, ceasing territory, subsidies or bribery. *Dāna* may mean dispensing with a possession altogether or a mere promise to give away something not yet possessed (like future spoils of war). *Dāna* may also mean refraining from seizing others' possessions by force.

> It is customary for those who wish to gain the favour of a prince to endeavour to do so by offering him gifts. (*Prince: Introduction*)
>
> When there are several [enemies], it will always be a wise plan for the prince to yield something of his possessions to one of them, either for the purpose of gaining him over if war has already been declared, or to detach him from the enemies that leagued against him. (*Discorsi*)[85]
>
> Benefits should be granted little by little, so that they be better enjoyed. (*The Prince*)[86]
>
> As long as you benefit them [the people], they are entirely yours. (*The Prince*)[87]
>
> The [farsighted] conqueror is satisfied with the submission of the people, and generally leaves them their dwellings and possessions, and even the enjoyment of their own institutions. (*Discorsi*)[88]

(iii) 'Dissension' or *Bheda*: The third basic method of politics means sowing discord or *divide et impera*. Through selective preference or discrimination, actors are isolated from each other as to weaken their capacity to resist or to disrupt their (offensive) intentions.

> It has caused me to reflect that the presumption of success should always be in favour of a single power contending against a combination, however superior in numbers and power. For independent of the infinity of circumstances of which an individual can take advantage better than a combination of many, the former will always have the opportunity, with little address, to create divisions between the latter, and thus to weaken any combination...We may therefore with reasonable certainty presume that when a number of princes combine to make war upon a single one, the latter will triumph over combination, provided he has courage and strength enough to resist the first shock and bide events by temporising. (*Discorsi*)[89]

(iv) 'Use of force' or *Daṇḍa*: If *sāma, dāna* and *bheda* fail to enforce one's will against the resistance of others, then the use of force or *daṇḍa*. This concerns, first of all, the state applying its executive power in judicial or extra-judical contexts against its perceived internal enemies. Secondly, *daṇḍa* means going to war with offensive or defensive intentions.

> The dread of punishment will keep men better, and less ambitious. (*Discorsi*)[90]
>
> You must know, then, that there are two methods of fighting, the one by the law, the other by force: the first method is that of men, the second of beasts; but as the first method is often insufficient, one must have recourse to the second. It is

therefore necessary for a prince to know well to use both the beast and the man. This was covertly taught to rulers by ancient writers. (*The Prince*)[91]

A prince, therefore, must not mind incurring the charge of cruelty for the purpose of keeping his subjects united and faithful; for, with a very few exceptions, he will be more merciful than those who, from excess tenderness, allow disorders to arise, from whence spring bloodshed and rapine; for these as a rule injure the whole community, while the executions carried out by the prince injure only individuals. (*The Prince*)[92]

[The issue is whether] cruelties [are] being exploited well or badly. Well committed may be called those (if it is permissible to use the word well of evil) which are perpetrated once for the need of securing one's self, and which afterward are not persisted in, but are exchanged for measures as useful to the subjects as possible. Cruelties ill committed are those which, although first few, increase rather than diminish with time. (*The Prince*)[93]

When a decision has to be involving the fate of powerful cities that are accustomed to free institutions, they must either be destroyed or conciliated by benefits. Any other course will be useless, and, above all, half measures should be avoided, these being most dangerous. (*Discorsi*)[94]

And whoever reads the Bible attentively will find that Moses, for the purpose of insuring the observance of his laws and institutions, was obliged to put a great many persons to death who opposed his designs under the instigation of no other feelings than those of envy and jealously. (*Discorsi*)[95]

Next, we correlate text passages from *The Prince* and the *Discorsi* to Kauṭilya's 'six methods of foreign policy':

(i) Peace (*Saṃdhi*)

[Princes] should carefully examine the extent and force of the evil [adversary], and if they think themselves sufficiently strong to combat it, then they should attack it regardless of consequences; otherwise they should let it be, and in no way attempt it. For it will always happen as I said above, and as it did happen to the neighbouring tribes of Rome; who found out that it would have been more advantageous, after Rome had grown so much in power, to placate and keep her within her limits by peaceful means, than by warlike measures. (*Discorsi*)[96]

I do not mean to say by this, however, that arms and force are never to be employed, but that they should be reserved as the last resort when other means fail. (*Discorsi*)[97]

Therefore, those of our princes who had held their possessions for any years must not accuse fortune for having lost them, but rather their own remissness; for having never in quiet times considered that things might change (as it is a common fault of men not to reckon on storms in fair weather) when adverse times, they only thought of fleeing. (*The Prince*)[98]

One ought never to allow a disorder to take place in order to avoid war, for war is not thereby avoided, but only deferred to your disadvantage. (*The Prince*)[99]

(ii) War (*Vigraha*)

Every one may begin a war at his pleasure, but cannot so finish it. A prince, therefore, engaging in any enterprise should well measure his strength, and govern himself accordingly; and he must be very careful not to deceive himself in the estimate of his strength, which he will assuredly do if he measures it by his money, or by the situation of his country, or the good disposition of his people, unless he has at the same an armed force of his own." (*Discorsi*)[100]

One should never risk one's whole fortune unless supported by one's entire forces. (*Discorsi*)[101]

The object of those who make war, either from choice of ambition, is to conquer and to maintain their conquests, and to do this in such a manner as to enrich themselves and not to impoverish the conquered country. To do this, the conqueror should take care not to spend too much, and in all things mainly look to the public benefit; and therefore he should imitate the manner and conduct of the Romans, which was first of all to 'make the war short and sharp', as the French say. (*Discorsi*)[102]

Whoever impoverishes himself by war acquires no power, even though he may be victorious, for his conquests cost him more than they are worth. (*Discorsi*)[103]

(iii) 'Staying Quiet', 'Wait and See', Neutrality (*Āsana*)

One sees also two cautious men, one of whom succeeds, and the other not, and in the same way two men succeed equally by different methods, one being cautious, the other impetuous, which arises only from the nature of times, which does or does not conform to their method of procedure. (*The Prince*)[104]

In the city of Athens in Greece, Nicias, one of most wise and prudent men, could not persuade the people that it would not be well for them to make war upon Sicily; and the Athenians resolved upon it, contrary to the advice of their wisest men, and the ruin of Athens was the consequence. (*Discorsi*)[105]

Fabius Maximus "could not persuade the people of Rome that it would be advantageous for that republic to proceed slowly with the war, and bear the assault of Hannibal without engaging in battle with him, because the Roman people considered this course as cowardly, and did not see the advantages that would be gained... This occasioned the battle and defeat of Cannae, and almost caused the ruin of Rome." (*Discorsi*)[106]

Everyone knows how Fabius Maximus conducted the war against Hannibal with extreme caution and circumspection, and with an utter absence of all impetuosity or Roman audacity. It was his good fortune that this mode of proceeding accorded perfectly with the times and circumstances. (*Discorsi*)[107]

Irresolute princes, to avoid present dangers, usually follow the way of neutrality and are mostly ruined by it. (*The Prince*)[108]

(iv) War Preparation or Coercive Diplomacy (*Yāna*)

Republics aim to enervate and weaken other states as to increase own power. (*Discorsi*)[109]

For if I desire to make war upon any prince with whom have concluded treaties which have been faithfully observed for a length of time, I shall attack some friend or ally of his under some colour of justification, well knowing that, thus attacking his friend, he will resent it, and I shall have grounds for declaring war against him, or, if he does not resent it, he will thereby manifest his weakness and lack of fidelity in not defending an ally entitled to his protection. And one or the other of these means will make him lose his reputation, and facilitate the execution of my designs. (*Discorsi*)[110]

(v) Alliance (*Saṃśraya*)

I consider to have need of others [allies] those who cannot take the field against their enemies, but have to take refuge within their walls and stand on the defensive [due to their military weakness]. (*The Prince*)[111]

Having created for herself many associates [allies] throughout Italy, she [Rome] granted to them in many respects an almost entire equality, always however, reserving to herself the seat of empire and the right of command; so that these associates (without being themselves aware of it) devoted their own efforts and blood to their own subjugation. (*Discorsi*)[112]

Alliances are broken from considerations of interest; and in this respect republics are much more careful in the observance of treaties than princes. (*Discorsi*)[113]

There is no disgrace is diṣregarding promises that have been extracted by force. Promises touching public affairs, and which have been given under the pressure of force, will always be discarded when that force no longer exists, and this involves no dishonour. (*Discorsi*)[114]

(vi) Diplomatic Double Game (*Dvaidhībhāva*)

We see therefore that the Romans in the early beginning of their power already employed fraud, which it has ever been necessary for those to practice who from small beginnings wish to rise to the highest degree of power; and then it is the less censurable the more it is concealed, as was that practiced by the Romans. (*Discorsi*)[115]

One should never show one's intentions, but endeavour to obtain one's desires anyhow. For it is enough to ask a man to give up his arms, without telling him that you intend killing him; after you have the arms in hand, then you can do your will with them. (*Discorsi*)[116]

> Xenophon shows in his Life of Cyrus the necessity of deception to success...Without these frauds Cyrus would never have achieved the greatness which he did attain. (*Discorsi*)[117]

It is evident that the listed thought-figures of Machiavelli exhibit similarity, if not congruence with the Kauṭilyan concept clusters of the *upāyas* and the *ṣāḍguṇya.*

Kauṭilya and Machiavelli share a consonant idea of raison d'état: maintaining and expanding the power of state and maintaining and expanding the welfare of the people. Yet, Kauṭilya cannot only claim primacy, but a more advanced substantiation of his idea of raison d'état through his concept clusters *saptānga* and *ṣāḍguṇya.* Machiavelli's conceptualisation of raison d'état remains rather abstract, if not vague when he writes that the issue how "to found a republic, maintain states, to govern a kingdom, organise an army, conduct a war, dispense justice, and extend empires" (*Discorsi*).[118] And in the *The Prince*, he writes: "In the actions of men, and especially of princes, from which there is no appeal, the end justifies the means. Let a prince therefore aim at conquering and maintaining the state, and the means will always be judged honourable and praised by everyone" (*The Prince*).[119] These descriptions of the idea of raison d'état is the closest Machiavelli comes to Kauṭilya's much substantiated idea of it. That, however, does not diminish the fact that the idea of raison d'état permeates the political writings of both the authors.

That leaves us with the third component of Kauṭilyan raison d'état: facilitating the political unification of the Indian subcontinent. This third component is fully consonant with two other components of Kauṭilyan raison d'état, but it is not derived from theorising the conceptual essence of statecraft. Instead, it is Kauṭilya's conclusion from the strategic assessment of the political situation of his time. The inescapable need for establishing a pan-Indian state had been demonstrated by the Achaemenid-Persian occupation of north-western India since the middle of the 6th century BCE and even more so by the attempted conquest of all of India by Alexander the Great. However, the impulse for politically uniting the subcontinent is much older and had gained at the time of Kauṭilya an almost normative quality. Drekmeier rightly notes, that the "concept of a state spanning the length and breadth of the subcontinent under the rule of a chakravartin goes back at least to the 10th century BCE."[120] Fueled and reinforced by strategic and normative considerations, Kauṭilyan raison d'état dictates overcoming the political fragmentation of the Indian subcontinent by the means offered with the *ṣāḍguṇya* cluster and establishing a pan-Indian state.[121]

And here, the parallel to Machiavelli is striking: his political writings must be seen in the light of the strategic goal of Italy's political unification and liberation from foreign domination. In Machiavelli's time, Italy was not only politically fragmented, but suffered from serial foreign interferences and outright military invasions by the risings powers Spain and France and to a lesser extent the German emperor. Drekmeier rightly notes:

> Kautalya was faced with the same need for political union in the face of disorder and external threat that confronted Machiavelli in northern Italy...Northern India was comparable in this respect to the Italy of Machiavelli's time.[122]

In *The Prince*, the last chapter is entitled: 'Exhortation to liberate Italy from the barbarians'. Therein, he states that Italy is "without a head, without order, beaten, despoiled, lacerated and overrun" and "this opportunity must not, therefore, be allowed to pass, so that Italy may at length find her liberator" – an Italian prince who takes the lead and unites the country (*The Prince*).[123]

What needs to be added here is that Kauṭilya was successful: the Maurya Empire was established. Machiavelli's passionate appeal, however, was not successful: Italy remained politically fragmented and a pawn in the hands of foreign powers.

I think, this historical background of Machiavelli's political biography is key for his heavy emphasis on the role of '*fortuna*' in politics – particularly bad luck. Kauṭilya too acknowledges the importance contingency in politics: Calamity is *of a divine or human origin, springs from ill luck or wrong policy... It throws out a person from his good, hence it is called vyasana* (KA).[124] Further, Kauṭilya elaborates on calamities: *Visitations from the gods are: fire, floods, disease, famine and epidemic* (KA).[125] Calamities are a fact of life and the political actor must take them into account, but Kauṭilya seems to take a rather detached attitude towards the intricacies of political life. In contrast, the question of *fortuna* pervades both *The Prince* and the *Discorsi*. Machiavelli invokes the tragic fate of several political actors who were ruined by bad luck, but, I think, he has obviously his own political career in mind which ended tragically.

> It is not unknown by me how many have been and are of opinion that worldly events are so governed by fortune and by God, that men cannot by their prudence change them, and that on the contrary there is no remedy whatever, and for this they may judge it to be useless to toil much about them, but let things ruled by chance...When I think about them, at times I am partly inclined to share this opinion. (*The Prince*)[126]

But, Machiavelli is no fatalist. He sets '*virtu*' against '*fortuna*'. His concept of *virtu* is a political one.

It means resolve, steadfastness and farsightedness in politics. Machiavelli's concept of political *virtu* is largely consonant with Kauṭilya's concept of the energy and vigour that distinguish the good ruler: *In the absence of activity, there is certain destruction of what is obtained and of what is not yet received. By activity reward is obtained, and one also secures abundance of riches* (KA).[127] Similarly, Machiavelli argues:

> Nevertheless, that our free-will may not be altogether extinguished, I think it may be true that fortune is the ruler of half our actions, but she allows the other half or thereabouts to be governed by us. I would compare her to an impetuous river that, when turbulent, floods the plains... still when it is quiet, men can make provisions against it by dykes and banks... So it is with fortune, which shows her power where no measures have been taken to resist her, and directs her fury where she knows that no dykes or barriers have been made to hold her…I certainly think that it is better to be impetuous than cautious, for fortune is a woman. (*The Prince*)[128]

> I repeat, then, as an incontrovertible truth, proved by all history, that men may second Fortune, but cannot oppose her; they may develop her designs, but cannot defeat them. But men should never despair on that account; for, not knowing the aims of Fortune, which she pursues by dark and devious ways, men should always be hopeful, and never yield to despair, whatever troubles or ill fortune may befall them. (*Discorsi*)[129]

(e) The Normative Dimension of Politics

The political action guided by raison d'état raises – inevitably so – normative questions. It has often been asserted that Kauṭilyan statecraft is 'pure' power politics bereft of any morality. We believe that this assertion is unsustainable. Kauṭilyan statecraft does have a normative framing – and his idea of raison d'état attests to this. Kauṭilya does not only analyse and synthesise his idea raison d'état in terms of the *saptānga* and *ṣāḍguṇya* theories, but also ascribes to it an intrinsic normative quality that applies to all three components of Kauṭilyan raison d'état:

- Maintaining and expanding the power of state.
- Maintaining and expanding the welfare of the people.
- Facilitating the political unification of the Indian subcontinent.

For Kauṭilya, there is no dichotomy between enhancing the power of the state and enhancing the welfare of the people. He sees the ruler as the 'first servant of the state' and, equally so, as the 'first servant of people'. As Charles Drekmeier notes: "For the author of the *Arthashastra* the welfare of the state meant ultimately the welfare of the people, and the well-being of his subjects must be rated higher than that of the king himself."[130]

In the sphere of statecraft, Kauṭilya denies a fundamental contradiction between purposive political rationality – the state's inherent power logic or state interest – and political normativity in the sense of assuring the well-being of the people. On the entanglement of state interest and political normativity, Kauṭilya writes:

> For, by discarding the good and favouring the wicked and by causing unrighteous injuries... decline [of the state] as well as greed and disaffection are produced among the subjects. Subjects, when impoverished, become greedy; when greedy they become disaffected, when disaffected they either go over to the enemy or themselves kill the ruler. Therefore, the ruler should not allow these causes of decline [of the state] as well as greed and disaffection among the subjects to arise, or, if arisen, should immediately counteract them. (KA)[131]

> And: "If weak in power, the ruler should endeavour to secure the welfare of the people". (KA)[132]

Moreover, in Kauṭilya's view, each of the two value ideas underpinning his idea of raison d'état – enhancing state power and the people's welfare – has a dimension of purposive political rationality and a dimension of political normativity. Charles Drekmeier notes on this problematique:

> There can never be a thoroughgoing divorce of politics and ethics for Kautalya; he never denies that the ultimate purpose of the state is a moral purpose, the maintenance of dharma...He means that moral principles must be subordinated to the interest of the state inasmuch as the moral order depends upon the continued existence of the state...The state was forced to take measures that frequently ran counter to the accepted moral standards of the community. But Kautalya well knew that such policies were all that could save society from collapse. He was led inevitably to a theory approximating the reason of state arguments of 16th century Europe. But he thought to emphasise the fact that such actions were not irresponsible. Indeed it is the duty of the ruler to his subjects that compels him to take drastic steps to ensure their welfare. Survival and progress are recognised as bestowing authority.[133]

Thus, Kauṭilyan raison d'état possesses a superior 'cardinality' in the hierarchy of ethical norms. We might speak of Kauṭilyan raison d'état as the 'supreme norm' for statecraft. As such, Kauṭilyan raison d'état stands above the generally accepted ethical norms. Kauṭilya does uphold generally accepted ethical norms: *Duties common to all are: abstaining from injury to living creatures, truthfulness, uprightness, freedom from malice, compassionateness and forbearance* (KA).[134]

But in the political sphere, there are, rather often, situations where these norms are violated. But as long as such violations occur in the context of political action that aims at maintaining and expanding the power of state and maintaining and expanding the welfare of the people, such violations are necessary and legitimate. For Kauṭilya, raison d'état is the 'supreme norm'. If state action is guided by raison d'état, it is not immoral. For Kauṭilya, there is no fundamental ethical dilemma between societal morality and the supreme norm of raison d'état.

Kauṭilya's position that raison d'état stands above generally accepted ethical norms, is echoed by Machiavelli. But in his case, we can sense that he, unlike Kauṭilya, sees and feels the ethical dilemmas that are inevitably linked with political conduct dictated by raison d'etát:

> For where the very safety of the country depends upon the resolution to be taken, no consideration of justice or injustice, humanity or cruelty, nor of glory or of shame, should be allowed to prevail. But putting all other considerations aside, the only question should be, What course will save the life and liberty of the country? (*Discorsi*)[135]

Often, Kauṭilya's foreign policy theory is seen as blatantly advocating political immorality. Kauṭilyan foreign policy is not about preserving the status quo, but its revision. Other states are to be 'conquered' by whatever means – deceptions, breach of treaty, destabilisations, covert actions and war. However, 'conquest' does not mean imperialist aggrandisement as an end in itself. In the historical context of the *Arthaśāstra's* origination, 'conquest' means the elimination of political fragmentation on the Indian subcontinent. 'Conquest' must serve the political unification of the Indian subcontinent in order to be legitimate. Kauṭilya sets such 'righteous conquest' against 'greedy' and 'demoniacal' conquest. The 'greedy' conqueror is exclusively interested in the spoils of war – "seizure of land and goods" (KA).[136] The 'demoniacal' conqueror's sole aim is pillage, enslavement and destruction. *There are three types of kings who attack: the righteous conqueror, the greedy conqueror and the demoniacal conqueror* (KA).[137]

To sum up: With respect to all five topical areas examined in this paper, there are multiple and substantive differences between Kauṭilya and Machiavelli. However, there are, equally so, multiple and substantive homologies. The degree of conceptual convergence between them is high enough, as to make the possibility of a 'genetic' influence of Kauṭilyan thought upon Machiavelli's political writing a plausible proposition.

(f) The 'Asian Dimension' of Machiavelli's Political Writings

One would expect that Machiavelli's role-models for political leadership all come from the history of Rome. Indeed, most of his prototype leaders are Romans, notably Romulus, the mythological founder of the city, or Fabius Maximus and Scipio Africanus from the time of Rome's victorious third war against Carthage in the 2nd century BCE. Julius Caesar, however, is not among them, Machiavelli sees him as a tyrant who destroyed the Roman Republic. Rather astonishingly, in both *The Prince* and the *Discorsi*, Machiavelli's other role-model leader comes from Asia: the Persian ruler Cyrus II, founder of Achaemenid Empire in the 6th century BCE. In the *Discorsi*, there are five references to Cyrus – 'the King of Kings' – and all of them with almost enthusiastic praise.

> Xenophon takes great pain to show how many victories, how much honour and fame, Cyrus gained by his humanity and affability, and by his not having exhibited a single instance of pride, cruelty, or luxuriousness, nor any other of the vices that are apt to stain the lives of men. (*Discorsi*)[138]

And in *The Prince*, Machiavelli writes:

> Regarding Cyrus and others who have acquired or founded kingdoms, they will all be found worthy of admiration... And in examining their life and deeds it will be seen that they owed nothing to fortune but the opportunity which gave them matter to be shaped into what form they thought fit; and without that opportunity their powers would have been wasted, and without their powers the opportunity would have come in vain.[139]

The prominent place of Persian statecraft in Machiavelli's political writings, is truly remarkable in that it shows that the Italian had no cultural prejudices with respect to statecraft. Bozeman characterises Persia as Eurasia's 'prestige state' in the period between the 7th century BCE and the 7th century CE, "relying on solid bodies of public secular law, stressing the idea of the state as a superior all-encompassing reality, cultivating statecraft through the medium of refined intelligence and communication, and creating specialised bureaucratic services for overseeing affairs of state at home and abroad."[140] Moreover: "The Persian idea of the 'world state' as represented by the 'King of Kings' as well as techniques of government and statecraft were carried not only westward, where they influenced the Macedonians and Romans, but also eastward, where they influenced state-building in India, and perhaps even China...No single document attests to this Persian legacy more faithfully than the Indian *Arthashastra*."[141] Indeed, if there is any exogenous influence on Kauṭilya's concept of the state and statecraft, it would come inevitably from Achaemenid Persia. The empire of Cyrus II extended to the Indus river and included the territory of present-day Pakistan. During the century preceding Kauṭilya, the North-Western Indian states were direct neighbours of the Achaemenid Empire.

Machiavelli's prime source on Cyrus II, is Xenophon's Cyropaedia. With respect to Asian history more broadly, Machiavelli refers to Diodorus Siculus, a Greek historian of the 1st century BCE and his monumental *Bibliotheca Historica*. This 'universal history' covers Egypt, Mesopotamia, Persia and India.

Important is that Diodorus Siculus used extensively Ctesias' work on Persia (*Persica*), which is based on extensive personal experience in the Achaemenid empire, and India (*Indica*) as well as Megasthenes' work on India (also titled *Indica*), mainly based on his observations as Seleucid ambassador at the court of Chandragupta Maurya in Pataliputra.

Machiavelli also makes a reference to the Persian Sassanid Empire (224-651 CE), relating an episode in 503 CE from the wars between the Persians and the Byzantium when the Sassanid ruler Ghobad I (Gabades) conquered Diabakyr (Amida) in eastern Anatolia:

> A striking example of this occurred in Asia, when Gabades, commander of the Persians, having for a long time besieged Amida [Diabakyr] and becoming weary of the siege, resolved to abandon it; and having already broken up his camp, the inhabitants of the place came upon the walls, and, inflated with the thought of victory, assailed his army with every kind of insult, vilifying them and accusing and reproaching them for their cowardice and poltroonery. Gabades, irritated by this, changed his mind and resumed the siege, and his indignation at these insults so stimulated his efforts, that he took the city in a few days, and give it up to sack and pillage. (*Discorsi*)[142]

As to India, Machiavelli knew Diodorus Siculus' 'universal history' which also covers India. Important is that he used Ctesias' work *Indica*, which is based on reports about India that the latter received while staying in Persia. Diodorus Siculus also draws on Megasthenes' work on India (also titled *Indica*), based on his observations as Seleucid ambassador at the court of Chandragupta Maurya in Pataliputra. As Florence was a significant commercial centre with international connections, we can safely assume that Machiavelli was also knowledgeable about contemporary reports on India from merchants and other sources. In the *Discorsi*, Machiavelli tells an episode from the war between an Indian king named Stabrobates and the mythological Mesopotamian warrior-queen Semiramis.

> It was thus that the Indian king acted against Semiramis. This queen, seeing that the king had great many elephants, tried to frighten him by showing him that she had quite as many. She therefore ordered a number of sham elephants made of hides of buffaloes and cows, which she had placed upon camels and sent to the front. But the stratagem was discovered by the king, and proved, not only useless, but damaging to Semiramis. (*Discorsi*)[143]

We do not know the historical events that are echoed in this mythological account nor do we know who this Indian king Stabrobates might have been. But Machiavelli thought it worthwhile to report about it. For Machiavelli's view of Asia generally and (Achaemenid) Persia in particular, the following statement is most remarkable that he states that the virtues of good governance were transferred from Achaemenid Persia to the Roman Republic:

> I think that, as a whole, the world remains very much in the same condition, and the good in it always balances the evil; but the good and evil change from one country to another; as we learn from history of those ancient kingdoms that differed from each other in manners, [yet] the whole world at large remained the same. The only difference being, that all the virtues that first found a place in Assyria were thence transferred to Media, and afterwards passed to Persia, and from there they came into Italy and to Rome. (*Discorsi*)[144]

Take note, for Machiavelli, good governance comes from Asia: the virtues of good governance were transferred from Achaemenid Persia to the Roman Republic.

Eric Voegelin thinks that Machiavelli's political works were written under the 'shadow of Asia', by which he means the impact that the Mongol wars of conquest of the 13th and the 14th century CE had upon European political thinking.[145] Genghis Khan (ca. 1160-1227 CE) and Timur (1369-1405 CE) possessed enormous military power and exceptional military-strategic skill. Genghis Khan created, albeit for only a short time, the largest Eurasian empire ever and Timur's empire did not lag much behind. Europeans looked at these Asian leaders with both awe and admiration because they came close to establishing a Eurasian 'world empire' compared to which Christian Europe looked petty. Timur was seen as "a glowing symbol of the nihilistic grandeur of power without ulterior meaning", as Voegelin puts it.[146] And he adds that "the image of Timur, shaped by the preceding generation is very noticeable as an influence in the formation of his [Machiavelli's] own image of the Prince."[147]

To sum up, the politics of Asia from the 6th century BCE to the 14th century CE do play a significant role in Machiavelli's writings. In other words, his political thinking was not at all as Eurocentric as is generally believed. Therefore, conceptual homologies in Kauṭilya's *Arthaśāstra* and Machiavelli's *The Prince* and *Discorsi* need to be seen in the context of Eurasian space with its manifold trade, political and cultural interfaces.

B. The Hypothesis of a Westward Migration of Kauṭilyan Thought

(a) Putting Kauṭilya and Machiavelli in a Eurasian Transcultural Frame

Unquestionably, cultures and cultural spaces do exist as distinct empirical phenomena based upon diverse histories, collective memories, traditions and habits. That does not mean, however, that cultures are autarkic, instead they interact and thus influence each other via hybridisation. Naturally, political ideas and experiences are part of such cultural interaction and hybridisation. If there exist conceptual homologies in Kauṭilya's *Arthaśāstra* and Machiavelli's *The Prince* and *Discorsi*, we need to consider the question of transcultural migration of political ideas. Such idea migration can take the form of mutual exchange, however there is a directionality in term of time: while older idea aggregates can influence later idea aggregates, the reverse is not possible. Thus, while Kauṭilyan thought-figures might have influenced Machiavelli's thinking, political ideas generated in 1510 CE can have no impact on a political thinker in 320 BCE.

The time distance between Kauṭilya and Machiavelli is roughly 1800 years. Moreover, the spatial distance between Patna (Pataliputra) in India and Florence is roughly 7000 km with high mountain ranges, deserts and the sea in between. In the geographic space between India and Italy, there are several cultural spaces: Indian, Persian, Arab-Islamic, Persian-Islamic, Central Asian-Turkic and European. If we take the time factor of 1800 years into account, the cultural diversity increases further because we have to factor in the cultures of Egypt, Mesopotamia, Levante, Judaism, Greece, Rome, and Byzantium. How should political thought-figures originating in ancient India have migrated enormous distances in time and geo-cultural space and not gotten lost long before they ever could reach Renaissance Italy?

Andre Gunder Frank and Barry K. Gills expound the view that the 'world system' did not start around 1500 CE with European hegemony in trans-oceanic seafaring, science and capitalist economic development.[148] Instead, they argue, a 'world system' centered on Eurasia (including Egypt) has existed since the Bronze Age (ca. 3200-1200 BCE) up to 1500 CE when the modern 'world system' emerged. Within the older Eurasian 'world system' there were repeated 'hegemonic shifts' in economic, political and cultural terms, but that did not affect the system as such and its staying-power. The argumentation of Frank and Gills is focused on the economic sphere, particularly long-distance trade – both overland and sea-borne. They point to the fact that ancient long-distance trade did not only involve luxury goods like precious metals and gems, spices or silk, but staple goods like grain, wine, metal goods (military and civilian) or domesticated animals. Frank and Gills also point to the transport infrastructure of the Eurasian 'world system' consisting of river and sea routes, caravan routes (Silk Road) and highways like the Achaemenid 'Royal Highways' connecting western Anatolia with the Hindukush. Obviously, long-distance trade is key for the migration of ideas, because ideas do not diffuse by themselves but need to be carried by human beings. Thus, traders would likely be the first to communicate what they had learned in distant lands with cultures very different from their own.

Whether it is useful to speak of a trade-vectored Eurasian 'world system' prior to 1500 AD, is debatable, but Franks and Gill have introduced a thought-provoking concept. William H. McNeill notes that in ancient times "the largest and most active transcivilisational market...was based in Eurasia," but he prefers the term "communications network", instead of a Eurasian 'world system'.[149] "Yet markets and trade constituted only part of the communications network that crossed political, civilisational and linguistic boundaries [in Eurasia]. Soldiers and missionaries, as well as refugees and wanderers also linked alien populations together, and carried information."[150]

Another way to approach, that might be correlated with McNeill's concept of the ancient Eurasian communications network, is Karl Jasper's concept of the Axial Age (ca. 800-200 BCE). Discarding a eurocentric position, Jaspers adopts a trans-cultural perspective in that he sees a geo-cultural coherence in Eurasia based on four principal cultural spaces: China, India, Persia and Greece:

> Confucius and Lao-Tse were living in China, all the schools of Chinese philosophy came into being... India produced the Upanishads and Buddha and, like China, ran the whole gamut of philosophical possibilities down to materialism, skepticism and nihilism; in Iran Zarathustra taught a challenging view of the world as a struggle between good and evil; in Palestine the prophets made their appearance from Elijah, by way of Isaiah and Jeremiah to Deutero-Isaiah; Greece witnessed the appearance of Homer, of the philosophers – Parmenides, Heraclitus and Plato – of the tragedians, of Thucydides and Archimedes. Everything implied by these names developed during these few centuries almost simultaneously in China, India and the West.[151]

I leave aside here the question whether Jaspers' Axial Age concept should be seen in the light of the covariance/equivalence approach or in terms of transcultural idea-migration. Important seems to me that Jasper's concept points more to transcultural coherence in Eurasian space than to a random coincidence of cultural fertility. In this context, N.P. Sil opines that there might be "a common reserve of political ideas developed in the Eurasian world at some unknown period in the remote past."[152] This an intriguing idea, worth further consideration.

Voegelin points to the political and strategic dimension of Jaspers' Axial Age conception, correlating it to the "imperial expansion of the Persians, of Alexander [the Great], of the Romans, of the Maurya dynasty in India as well as of the Ch'in and Han dynasties in China."[153]

The infrastructure of the pre-modern Eurasian communications network followed the trade routes, which were also the military roads in the innumerable wars fought within Eurasia. Thus, political and military intelligence information, knowledge of state structures and statecraft, literary texts and other cultural artefacts, scientific knowledge as well as religious and philosophical teachings travelled across Eurasia. With respect to Alexander the Great, Bozeman notes that "his military campaigns were paralleled by scientific field trips, and his negotiations with enemy commanders were interrupted by discourses with Indian sages."[154]

This fine observation is just one of many in Adda Bozeman's seminal work *Politics and Culture in International History*. This work is a groundbreaking conceptualisation of transcultural idea-flows across Eurasia, even if some of her views on some specific aspects thereof might be debatable. Published in 1960, this book has regrettably been mostly ignored in recent decades. Bozeman notes:

> The Greek 'miracle' was prepared for by millenniums of work in Egypt, Mesopotamia, and possibly other regions. It also becomes clearer, as the records are assembled, that many inventions, discoveries, and ideas for which the West used to credit the Greeks exclusively were also – often simultaneously – developed in India and China. The Indians, as well as the Greeks, drew on Chaldean and Assyrian knowledge of medicine, borrowed heavily from Persia and gradually infused scientific thinking into their approaches to the phenomena around them.[155]

Bozeman recognises the significance of Kauṭilya's *Arthaśāstra* as a milestone in the history of realist political thought and in shaping the understanding of statecraft in India up to the present. In her *Politics and Culture in International History*, she devotes eight pages to Kauṭilya and the *Arthaśāstra*:

> Concerning the civil, social, legal, and fiscal organisation of this [Mauryan] state, we have not only the Greek records of Megasthenes but the far more profound expositions of the learned Chanakya. His masterwork, the *Arthashastra*, has been acclaimed as the greatest piece of literature surviving (in part at least) from the Maurya period, and its chapters on foreign policy are said to show the Indian genius for systematic exposition at its best.[156]

However, Bozeman has not addressed the possibility that the *Arthaśāstra*'s key concepts and thought-figures might have migrated westward via Persia and Arab-Islamic space to Europe. Instead, she sees a congruence between Kauṭilyan statecraft and the Achaemenid Persian tradition of statecraft which she explains via a southward idea-transfer from Persia to India. Certainly, Achaemenid statecraft is older than the *Kauṭilīya Arthaśāstra*. But, to my knowledge, we do not possess any endogenous text of Achaemenid statecraft which would even remotely compare to Kauṭilya's *Arthaśāstra*. Moreover, the *Arthaśāstra* draws on ancient Indian statecraft (and treatises on it) which are as old as or older than Achaemenid statecraft.

In the context of this paper, priority of origination of advanced concepts of statecraft is secondary in relation to the transcultural migration of such concepts. And, it seems quite plausible to me that a hybrid convolute of 'older' Persian and 'younger' Kauṭilyan concepts of statecraft migrated – in space and time – towards western Eurasia, including Renaissance Italy.[157]

Nevertheless, Bozeman is on the mark when she emphasises Achaemenid statecraft's unbroken influence across time on the whole Near and Middle East as well as, and particularly so, in the Ottoman Empire. Bozeman also sees important congruences between the Achaemenid Persian tradition and the concept of statecraft in the Byzantine Empire (395-1453 CE). From Byzantium, she argues, the combination of Persian and Roman-Byzantine statecraft exerted major influence on the Republic of Venice in Italy which was up to the 15th century CE the major hub for Western Europe's connections to Asia.

Even though Bozeman does not address the question of a westward migration of Kauṭilyan thought, she does provide crucially important leads which demonstrate that such idea-migration is not only principally possible, but plausible. Her propositions with respect to transcultural idea-flow from Asia to Europe do provide a conceptual avenue which can help to explain homologies between Kauṭilya's *Arthaśāstra* and Machiavelli's political writings.

We now turn, still staying with Bozeman, to two phenomena which are usually seen as quintessential expression of the culture of the European Middle Ages: chivalry and courtly love (troubadours or *minne*). As she points out, it is much more likely that both phenomena come from Asia – India and Persia, to be precise. Commerce and war, paradoxically the Crusades in this case, facilitated the adoption of Asian social values and cultural attitudes in Europe:

> The times [the Age of the Crusades] that witnessed this remarkable evolution of transcultural correspondences were an aristocratic and a martial age, and the hero figure of this age was everywhere the knight, who placed his arms in the service of his God, his lord, and his beloved. The Western European feudal baron, upon whom was incumbent the duty of defending the peace, had his counterpart in the warrior type that had developed among the Byzantines and the Persians, and the aristocratic standards of chivalry and courtly love that were observed throughout Christendom obtained also in the Middle East and North Africa. Whether these ideals and institutions arose independently in each of these realms, or whether they were diffused after having made their appearance first in one society, cannot be said with any degree of certainty. The epic of Firdausi and other poems indicate that the norms of chivalry developed somewhat earlier in Persia than elsewhere, and 20th century scholars have traced the beginnings of courtly love to Bengal, which was famed for its courts of love already in the 7th and 8th centuries CE – three to four centuries before similar customs were cultivated in France. Tantric

> texts embodying the 'new' concept of mystic love reached Persia first, we learn from another source, and there they were translated into Pahlevi by a medical man at the court of Chosroes I [Sassanid ruler, ca. 550 CE]. Recast in Syrian, Arabic, Latin, and Spanish renditions, the idea is then supposed to spread throughout Europe. The assumption is thus at least possible that courtly love, as understood in Europe in the 12th century, did not originate in Southern France (as European scholarship has long maintained).[158]

As the interfaces between the Orient and Occident were particularly strong during the Age of the Crusades, we turn to the chivalric romance *Parzival*, written by Wolfram von Eschenbach (ca. 1170-1220 CE). One of the high points of medieval literature, the epic poem appears to be genuinely European drawing on primordial Celtic and French legends involving King Arthur's court and the story of the Holy Grail. But, there are plausible indications that at least one of the sources of *Parzival* is from Asia. And, for sure, this epic poem has an astonishing Asian dimension – far beyond its name *Parzival*, which may rather point to Persia than to Britain, France or some other place in Europe.

In Eschenbach's text, Parzival's father is Gahmuret, who decides to pursue his chivalric career not in the petty courts of Europe, but in the service of the most powerful ruler on earth – the Caliph of Baghdad. In the service of the Caliph, he is victorious in many battles and highly honoured by him. Eventually, he meets the dark-skinned queen Belakane and marries her. Before their son Feirefiz is born, Gahmuret is gripped again by knight errantry and returns to Europe. There he marries Herzeloyde, but, once again, before their son Parzival is born, Gahmuret returns to Baghdad where he resumes serving the Caliph and soon thereafter is killed in battle. Note, the Christian knight Gahmuret is not fighting against a Muslim ruler, but fights and dies for him. After many complications and adventures, Gahmuret's son Parzival finally becomes a member of the round table of the knights of the Holy Grail. Among them, is the wise sorceress Kundrie who comes from India and makes auguries about what will happen to Parzival. Later, in the poem, Parzival encounters an unknown knight, who, we learn, is a heathen coming from the Orient. The two engage in chivalric duel, in the course of which Parzival's sword breaks. But the foreign knight does not kill Parzival, instead he identifies himself as his half-brother Feirefiz. The two embrace and Feirefiz joins the round table of the knights of the Holy Grail, where he meets Repanse de Schoye and falls in love with her. The problem is that Feirefiz is already married to the Indian queen Secundille, who reigns over the lands at the Ganga. After the Indian sorceress Kundrie informs Feirefiz that Secundille has died in the meantime, he marries Repanse and returns with her to India.

Eschenbach's *Parzival* begins and ends in the Orient and his references to the Middle East and India are multiple. That means, the height of the European Middles Ages, the Orient and India were very much present in Eschenbach's intellectual world. Equally interesting is the source background of this 12th century literary text. The Austrian scholar Friedrich von Suhtschek has pointed to striking similarities between Wolfram von Eschenbach's *Parzival* and the Persian epic poem *Borzu-nama, which ranks* second only to Ferdowsi's *Shahnameh*. The two epic poems were written between the end of the 10th and the beginning of the 11th century CE in Chorasan (south-eastern Iran and Afghanistan). Suhtschek's thesis was initially met with much skepticism, however, in the meantime, it has gained recognition among academic experts in German language and Iran studies.[159]

The purpose of this seemingly odd excursion to the epic poem *Parzival* is to demonstrate that a medieval Europe text of literary genre contains Oriental and Indian thought-figures and is likely heavily influenced or even based upon a Persian source text. Why should not the same apply to texts outside the literary genre like treatises (or practices) of statecraft, which gets us back to the question of a westward migration of Kauṭilyan thought to Europe.

(b) The Westward Migration of the Pancatantra

The collection of beast fables *Pancatantra*[160] is not a literary text in the strict sense, but an instructional text on statecraft that uses stereotypical animal characters ('lion', 'jackal' [corresponding to the 'fox' in European cultural space], 'snake' etc.) as allegories for patterns of political behaviour. The Sanskrit Ur-*Pancatantra* has been lost. Olivelle thinks that its original title was not 'The Five Topics', which he assumes to be an abbreviation of a longer title – 'The Little Story-Book on the Five Topics of Government'.[161]

In spite of its literary format, the *Pancatantra* "is seen and used as a full-fledged scientific textbook of statecraft."[162] Hillebrandt writes: "The samples of political wisdom, which can be found in the *Panchatantra*, a book of fables designed for the instruction of princes."[163] And Bozeman notes, Kauṭilya's *Arthaśāstra* "restates in the language of a systematic political philosophy the cold wisdom that India has traditionally rendered in its celebrated beast fables."[164]

Thus, the *Pancatantra* is the conceptual 'mother' of the 'Mirrors for Princes' genre that originated in ancient India, flourished in Sassanid Persia and in Arab cultural space and eventually reached Europe in the Middle Ages where it remained in high regard among the political and literary elites till the Renaissance.

The *Pancatantra's* westward migration is rather well researched in the context of Indology as well as Cultural and Literary Studies, but not in the context of the history of political ideas. The Sanskrit *Pancatantra* was translated by Borzuya into Old Persian during the reign of the Sassanid ruler Khosrow I Anosirvan (531-579 CE). Soon thereafter, still in the 6th century, followed a translation from Pahlavi into Old Syriac. In the 8th century CE, the *Pancatantra* was translated by Abdallah ibn al-Moquaffa from the Sanskrit or Old Persian into Arabic under the title *Kalila wa Dimna.* The Arab version of the *Pancatantra* became the 'mother' of the translations into Greek, Hebrew and Latin between the 11th and the 13th century CE, which circulated across medieval Europe.[165]

Thus, the migration of the *Pancatantra* can provide a model how thought-figures of Kauṭilya's *Arthaśāstra* might have migrated from ancient India to medieval and early Renaissance Europe. As we shall see in a moment, in the course of its migration, the *Pancatantra* got hybridised, modified and adapted to its new cultural surroundings. It seems likely that sections of the original *Pancatantra* were detached and fused with other texts from Indian, Persian and European antiquity. The book known in late medieval Europe as *The Fables of Bidpai* seems to be an example of such hybrid re-composition.

(c) *Secretum Secretorum – A Transcultural Hybrid of Political Thought*

In 1938, Allan Gilbert published his study *Machiavelli's Prince and it Forerunners,* in which he argues that Machiavelli's inspiration did not only come from the above mentioned political and historical texts of Roman and Greek antiquity, notably Livius' history of the Roman Republic and Xenophon's *Cyropaedia*, but from Mirror for Princes texts that were written in Europe in the period from the 12th century CE up until Machiavelli's lifetime. Among the more prominent authors of 'Mirror for Princes' texts are John of Salisbury, Edigio Colonna, Thomas Hoccleve, Giovanni Pontanus, Diodeme Carafa and Erasmus of Rotterdam. Their texts circulated widely among Europe's political, ecclesiastical and scholarly elites.

An elevated position among the Mirror for Princes books of the period spanning from the 12th to the 16th century CE takes a rather mysterious book – the *Secretum Secretorum* (The Secret of Secrets). Its actual Latin title was *De Regimine Principum* (The Governance of Princes), but it was mostly known by its subheading *Secretum Secretorum.* The book drew the attention of Frederick II Hohenstaufen, Albertus Magnus and Roger Bacon who edited it along with an extensive commentary. Since ca. 1120, an abridged version, and since 1230, the full text (in Latin), circulated at European courts and universities as well as among the higher echelons of the Catholic Church. During Machiavelli's lifetime, the book had been translated into Middle

English, Old French, Italian, Middle High German, Spanish and Hebrew, which indicates its popularity also among the educated lower nobility, merchants and burghers.

In his study, Gilbert examines each of the 26 chapters of Machiavelli's *The Prince* for conceptual homologies with Mirror for Princes texts – among them *Secretum Secretorum*. In nine chapters of *The Prince*, Gilbert identifies evident homologies of key Machiavellian thought-figures with those in the political sections of the *Secretum Secretorum*. Gilbert's findings are indeed remarkable. The homologies are too substantial and numerous as to be dismissed as merely fortuitous. And, conversely, William Eamon speaks of the "pragmatic, almost Machiavellian political advice" in the *Secretum Secretorum,* divulging the "the secrets of effective government".[166]

What is this mysterious *Secretum Secretorum*? The *Secretum Secretorum* purports to be based on letters that the aging Aristotle wrote to his pupil Alexander the Great while the latter was on his campaign to conquer India. Historical research has not found any proof of the existence of such letters by Aristotle. In his study *The Secret of Secrets: The Scholarly Career of a Pseudo-Aristotelian Text in the Latin Middle Ages*, the American medievalist Steven J. Williams writes: "Is the *Secretum Secretorum* a translation of an Aristotelian work? Obviously not. Nor is it in its entirety even the simple reproduction of a Greek *Vorlage*...Moreover, it needs to be said, there is no known extant Greek exemplar of the *Secretum Secretorum* nor any Greek text remotely close to it."[167]

Supposedly, a Greek copy of the *Secretum Secretorum* came into the hands of Arab scholars in the 8th century CE who translated it into Arabic under the title *Book on the Science of Government, On the Good Ordering of Statecraft*. The first (abridged) translation from Arabic into Latin was made around 1120 CE by the (Jewish) converso John of Seville for the Portuguese queen Theresa. About 1230, Philip of Tripoli (in the crusader-controlled part of Syria) made a translation of the complete text from Arabic into Latin. Within a very short period of time, the text reached the court of Frederic II Hohenstaufen in Palermo and the Papal curia in Rome. *Secretum Secretorum* was rapidly disseminating across Europe in this manner. The book features political and ethical advice as one would expect from a Mirror for Princes text, but it also contains large sections on astrological, medical, dietary, cosmological and occult subjects. Its readers seemed to have been equally interested in its political and non-political contents.[168]

In his study on the *Secretum Secretorum,* Steven Williams presents its table of contents:

Preface
Introduction of Anonymous Compiler
Introduction of Pseudo-Yahya ibn al-Bitriq [the putative translator in Arabic]
Aristotle's Introduction
Table of contents
Book 1 - On the Kinds of Kings
Book 2 - On the Position and Character of a King
Practical Political and Moral Precepts
Apology for Astrology
Section on Health
Introduction
Practical Recommendations on Hygiene, Food/Drink, Exercise/Rest; The Four Seasons
The Four Parts of the Body
Diet (Preserving Natural Heat; Healthy Foods; Meat and Fish)
Water
Wine
The Bath
Panacea
Medical Astrology
Section on Physiognomy
Book 3 - On Justice
Book 4 - On Ministers
Philosophical Material (Cosmogony; Powers of the Soul; Sensation; Significance of the Number Five)
Practical Advice Regarding Ministers
Anecdotes to Illustrate the Importance of the Planets in Determining Character: The Weaver's Son; the King's Son
Man the Microcosm
Anecdote to Illustrate the Importance of Faith: The Magian and the Jew
Book 5 - On Scribes
Book 6 - On Ambassadors
Book 7 - On Governors
Book 8 - On Army Officers
An Army's Hierarchy of Authority
Horn of Themistius
Book 9 - On the Conduct of War
Practical recommendations
Astrological advice
Section on onomancy
Book 10 - On the Occult Sciences
Talismans (theory and fabrication)
Alchemy (theory plus the Emerald Table of Hermes)
Lapidary
Herbal (theory and examples)
Conclusion

In the context of this paper, we are only interested in what the *Secretum Secretorum* has to say about political matters and statecraft. While modern historical and philological research has firmly established that the text is no translation of a work by Aristotle, it does eclectically draw on ancient Greek and Hellenistic sources. Williams notes that some text passages seem to be copied from Aristotle's *Nicomachean Ethics*.[169] But, mining Greek and Hellenistic scripts and inserting some fragments thereof, does not make the *Secretum Secretorum* a 'Greek text'. If the text structure and the central idea-contents dealing with politics and statecraft are not of Greek origin, where do they come from?

Since the oldest extant exemplars of the *Secretum Secretorum* are in Arabic, it must be assumed that the text was compiled by Arabic-speaking scholars. But that does not mean that text was actually written by Arabs, because both the text's structure and its idea-contents do not correspond to the tenets of Arab political thought – Caliphate and Sharia. The sections on politics and statecraft in the *Secretum Secretorum* are secular and address agency situated in an autonomous political sphere. Thus, the Arab compilers must have primarily drawn on traditions of political thought that are neither Greek nor Arab. That leaves two options for the conceptual origins of the *Secretum Secretorum*: Iran and India.

Iran does have a pre-Islamic tradition of Mirror for Princes texts. In the Sassanid Empire (224-651 CE) there were such works, which evidently draw on the legacy of Achaemenid Persian statecraft.[170] As noted above, the Sanskrit *Pancatantra*, the ancient Indian Mirror for Princes text, was translated into Pahlavi during the reign of the Sassanid ruler Khosrow I Anosirvan (531-579 CE). During the Islamic era, the Mirror for Princes literature was revived in Iran. In the 11th century CE, Kaykavus ibn Iskandar wrote the *Qabus-nama* and Nizam al-Mulk wrote the *Siyasat-nama* (Book of Government) – two quintessential Mirror for Princes texts. Thus, the origin of the *Secretum Secretorum* could be Iranian.[171]

What about Indian political thought as the central conceptual source for the *Secretum Secretorum*? Steven Williams has wondered: "No one seems to have taken up the idea put forward by Stig Wikander[172] of an Indian origin for the *Secretum Secretorum*."[173] Well, Wikander's idea has been taken up by Mahmoud Manzalaoui in his seminal essay *The Pseudo-Aristotelian 'Kitāb Sirr al-asrār': Facts and Problems on the Origins*.[174] He writes: "But the whole question of Indian influence has now been given more solid ground by Dr. Stig Wikander of Uppsala, in an unpublished paper of which a summary has appeared. The thesis of Dr. Wikander is that there are parallels, though they are never verbal ones, between the contents of Indian Mirrors for Princes and of the Sirr [abbreviation of *Secretum Secretorum* in Arabic]."[175]

Manzalaoui writes that: a) the Persian Sassanid-era mirror for princes '*Letter of Tansar*' also quotes a correspondence of Aristotle with Alexander the Great; and b) the *Secretum Secretorum* contains a list of the necessary qualities of a rulers which is very similar to a corresponding list in the 11th century Persian mirror for princes *Qabus-nama*. But he then adds that even greater homologies exist with Kauṭilya's *Arthaśāstra*: "This Indian Mirror for Princes does indeed contain some notable resemblances to the Sirr... The relevant passages of the Arthasastra are the list of the qualities of a minister[176] and that of the qualities of a king."[177]

Manzalaoui continues:

> The main interest of Wikander, however, is in the specific teachings of the Fürstenspiegel [Mirror for Princes in German], and although he refers in passing to the Nitisastra,[178] his main source of analogues is the Arthasastra of Kautilya, a work attributed to the early third century BCE... Wikander notes that the three-fold classification of Envoys (Sirr, Book VI: Badawi p. 145) is paralleled closely in Kautilya (Book I, cap. Xvi: p. 30). He also points out that the Arthasastra, and other Sanskrit Mirrors for Princes, resemble the Sirr in having sections on the king's qualities and behaviour, on ministers and army matters, and even upon precious stones. There are in fact more resemblances than the abstract of Dr. Wikander's paper reveals. The Arthasastra is a very long and compendious work, with precise instructions on administrative and technical matters, and moral and practical advice to a prince. Apart from the topics already referred to, it also deals, either in a general or a detailed manner, with matters analogous to the contents of the Sirr. The Proem classifies causes into visible (*zihir*) and invisible (*batin*). In advising a king to have a number of counsellors, the Arthasastra (p. 29) quotes Visalaksha's remark that "the nature of the work which a sovereign has to do is to be inferred from the consideration of both the visible and invisible causes". In Book I of the Sirr, Alexander is told to honour men of religion (Bad. p. 77), to lower taxes (Bad. p. 79), to give gifts to his followers (Bad. p. 80), to have compassion upon the poor, and help them with gifts from his treasury (p. 81), to store grain in order to help his subjects in times of famine (p. 82), and to assist men of learning (p. 84). The king who has conquered new territories is recommended in Book XIII, cap. v of the Arthasastra (p. 473) to bestow rewards, remit taxes, award gifts and honours, and hold religious life and learned men in high esteem, and give help to the miserable. In Book IV, cap. iii (p. 254) the king is told to help his subjects in time of famine and dearth both with seeds and provision, and with his own, or his nobles' wealth... A treatment of medicines and of magic [as in the *Secretum Secretorum*] forms the last book (Book XIV) of the Arthasastra (pp. 475 ff.), under the title 'Secret Means'... Kautilya is usually identified with Canakya, author of the Nitisastra.[179] The portions of Canakya's teachings on poisons certainly exist in an Arabic translation (Zachariae, Weisheitssprüche). Canakya's maxims were in fact known to Turtushi, who uses them in *Siraj al-muluk*, attributing them to 'Shabaq al-Sindi'. The sayings of Canakya came to the Arab world via a Persian transmission of the Rajaniti [Indian texts on statecraft]."[181]

A systematic comparative analysis of the *Secretum Secretorum* and Kauṭilya's *Arthaśāstra* is an obvious desideratum of comparative political science. But Wikander's and Manzalaoui's research is substantial enough to make the Indian origin of the *Secretum Secretorum* a plausible proposition.[181] Moreover, their argumentation that Kauṭilya's *Arthaśāstra* (and/or its *Nītisāra* variant) is the prime conceptual source of the political sections of the *Secretum Secretorum,* is eminently plausible.

There can be little doubt that the *Secretum Secretorum* is the product of a "centuries-long 'process of accretion'",[182] in which Greek, Hellenistic, Byzantine, Iranian and possibly some Arab idea-components merged with its original Indian thought-foundation. As in the case of the Indian *Pancatantra*, Kauṭilyan thought migrated first to Iran. From there, already hybridised, central Kauṭilyan thought-figures further metamorphosed in Arab cultural space. Unquestionably, Arab scholars, who could draw on ancient Greek philosophy, proved to be great compilers. They took the Kauṭilyan thought-figures and added Greek, Hellenistic, Byzantine and Iranian inputs – and the result of their translation and compilation work was the *Secretum Secretorum*.

During the 12th and 13th century CE, the Arabic *Secretum Secretorum* was translated into Latin and reached Europe, where it spread rapidly. Its most astonishing 'career' in Europe's political and intellectual milieus effectively ended when Machiavelli's political writings were published. It seems like a case of Hegelian 'Aufhebung': ideas get superseded, yet preserved. As Gilbert writes: "Even if, notwithstanding the wide circulation of the *Secretum Secretorum* for centuries, he [Machiavelli] had not read it, he can hardly have escaped the indirect influence."[183]

Gilbert has shown that there are substantial and numerous homologies between the *Secretum Secretorum* and Machiavelli's *The Prince* – and a comparison with the *Discorsi* would likely yield a similar result. I have shown that there are evident and multiple conceptual homologies between Kauṭilya's *Arthaśāstra* and Machiavelli's *The Prince* and *Discorsi*. The special significance of the *Secretum Secretorum* for us is that it most probably represents the key 'missing link' in the transcultural migration of Kauṭilyan thought to Renaissance Europe.

(d) Frederick II Hohenstaufen: 'Transculturalist' and His 'Kauṭilyan' State

However, the transcultural hybrid *Secretum Secretorum* is not the exclusive indicator of the transcultural migration of Kauṭilyan thought. Benoy Kumar Sarkar has pointed to conceptual parallels between the ancient Indian theory of the *cakravartin* (politically unifying the subcontinent) and the strategic designs of Frederick II Hohenstaufen (1194-1250 CE).[184] Sarkar's lead is indeed interesting.

Frederick Hohenstaufen was the German Emperor, but he didn't spend much time in Germany. He engaged in a long and bitter fight with Papacy rejecting its claim to be the ultimate arbiter not only of all spiritual, but also political issues within European Christendom. Frederick II did not accept any infringements of his political sovereignty by the Papacy and he build up a secular model state in southern Italy – the Kingdom of Sicily – that transcended medieval feudalism and anticipated Renaissance political thinking and practice.

Southern Italy – Sicily, Apulia and Calabria – had been ruled by the Greeks, Romans, Byzantium and Arabs and was taken over in the 11th century CE by (French) Normans. Frederick was the son of the German Emperor Henry VI and the Norman Princess Constance. Orphaned as a child, he grew up in Sicily speaking Volgare (medieval Italian) and mastering Latin, Arabic and German (possibly Provencial and Greek as well). Frederick Hohenstaufen had access to Europe's largest multilingual and multicultural library that his Norman ancestors had build-up in their Palermo palace. Already in his youth, he mixed with Italian, Arab and Jewish scholars.[185] What matters for our paper is the fact that Frederick Hohenstaufen was the key political actor in the transcultural communications network of Eurasian elites. Johannes Fried writes Frederick II Hohenstaufen:

> stood in the center of wide communicative network that extended far beyond Europe and addressed symbolic, theoretical and practical knowledge…Frederick and his court attracted foreign scholars and their knowledge; Latin, Greek, Jewish knowledge; ancient and modern, worldly and spiritual, practical and theoretical knowledge…The Norman Staufer engaged in intellectual exchange with the rulers and scholars of Castile, Aragon, Provence, North Africa, Egypt... The scientific exchanges between the Arab Orient and the Latin Occident were extensive and well-known…Nothing must get lost, from past knowledge new ideas should be generated.[186]

Adda Bozeman adds a crucially important point: India too belongs to Frederick's trans-cultural network. She writes:

> In other words, this medieval emperor was not [no longer] a medieval scholar. For the rationalism that characterised his numerous original experiments in the natural sciences and the elaborate questionnaires that he addressed to fellow scholars in India, Egypt, Syria, Iraq, Yemen, and Morocco pervaded his entire approach to theology, philosophy, logic, mathematics, law and literature.[187]

That in the High Middle Ages, intellectual and other contacts should have existed between Europe and India, seems rather implausible at first sight. That trade connections existed between Southern Europe and India via Byzantium,

Egypt, the Arab Middle East and Persia, is open to scrutiny. Merchants from Venice, Genoa, Florence or Spain (a third of which was still controlled by Muslim rulers) engaged in such long-range trade and thus received some information about India. But, Frederick knew more. The medieval historian Mathew Paris reports in his *Cronica Maiora* that Frederick once had a discussion with Fakhr al-Din, the envoy of the Sultan of Egypt Al-Kamil, about the (Egyptian-Jewish) philosopher Maimonides and latter's comments on Aristotle and Avicenna. In the course of the discussion, writes Matthew Paris, Frederick put forth an argument which he had learned from studying the *'The Book of the Indian Sages'*.[188]

Folger Reichert has investigated the knowledge about India at the court of Frederick II. The court library had a copy of the *Historia des Preliis Alexandri Magni* containing descriptions of India supposedly written by Alexander the Great himself in a letter to Aristotle. The book was ascribed to the Greek historian Callisthenes who, however, was killed before Alexander reached India. Thus, the work is usually called *Alexander Romance* and was written – probably in the 3rd century CE – by an unknown author (Pseudo-Callisthenes). The text contains both valuable observations as well as evidently fictional accounts of Indian life and thought.[189]

Another text at the Palermo library covering India was the *'Book of the Seven Sages'*, which might be the same as *'The Book of the Indian Sages'*, to which Frederick refers to in Matthew Paris' account. This text, also known as the 'The Seven Sages', is a collection of 'narratives of wisdom' that were attributed to a 'Brahmin philosopher' named 'Sindibad' who supposedly lived in the 1st century CE.[190] Reichert also mentions the *Secretum Secretorum* as addressing, inter alia, India. Frederick was familiar with it, since his principal scientific adviser Michael Scotus referred extensively to the *Secretum Secretorum* in his magnum opus *Liber Introductorius,* which mostly deals with astronomy, astrology and medicine as well as philosophy. Ernst Kantorowicz writes in his seminal biography of Frederick: "There are reports that Frederick II had, through his own agents, direct connections – via Egypt – to India. While this cannot be corroborated... that Fredrick was rather well informed about India, we can see in other contexts."[191]

Adda Bozeman argues, in my view convincingly, that Frederick developed a state conception and realised it in his Sicilian kingdom that is decisively shaped by Oriental influences: Achaemenid Persian statecraft, Alexander's Greek-Persian hybrid empire and ancient Indian political thought. These Oriental influences were at least as significant for Frederick as the role-model of the Roman Empire. Bozeman writes:

> As a workshop for the testing of new administrative principles and policies, Sicily-

> Apulia projected clearly the personality of its royal governor. Since Frederick loved wealth and power, his kingdom was to become a thriving, independent, political community which would take dictation from no authority except its sovereign. In the imperial vision this state was to be an end in itself. Since Frederick aspired to encompass the wisdom of all ages and cultures, Sicily was to become the center of all learning. And just as Frederick's mind had been moulded by influences from classical and Christian, Roman and Byzantine, Islamic and Indian sources, so was the government of his state to be shaped to perfection by methods that had proved their superiority in mankind's collected experiences of the art of government.[192]

In 1230 CE, after having spent two years in the Near East, Frederick issued the Constitutions of Melfi – a kind of basic law for the Sicilian Kingdom. In the introduction to the Constitutions, Frederick develops a theory of sovereign rulership: God created man in his own image and gave him domination over all other creatures. Yet, men not only violated God's commandments (thus losing immortality), but also indulged in hateful conflicts among themselves and dispensed with the natural order of common property. Thus, through the nature of things (and divine providence), rulers were selected with the power to decide over life and death in order to contain the evil deeds of their subjects. The governance of these rulers is supervised by the king of kings, and he, Frederick II, is the king of kings. His task is to protect the church as the keeper of the Christian faith, which means that the church is a strictly religious body with neither jurisdiction nor power in political affairs. The king of kings protects the people against (foreign) aggression and internal strife and thus assures peace and justice.

The political theory underpinning the Constitutions of Melfi exhibits evident homologies with two central features of Kauṭilya's political theory: 1) Man's 'selfish' dispositions and the conflictual (anarchical) nature of relations among individuals and communities (*mātsya-nyāya*). And 2) derived thereof, the inherent necessity of a sovereign ruler (state) to suppress these anarchical conflicts through overwhelming power: "For, the stronger swallows the weak in the absence of the wielder of the rod" (KA).[193]

The introduction of Constitutions of Melfi concludes by stating that the most urgent task of the king of kings – Frederick II Hohenstaufen – is to bring peace and justice to the kingdom of Sicily since his youth and absence (due to conflicts elsewhere) have prevented him so far from doing that. The new basic law for the kingdom of Sicily (valid only there) will bring peace and justice by nullifying all previous legislation that contradicts it. Thus Frederick's basic law breaks with customary law of feudalism and introduces a rationally designed legislation serving the stability and power of the sovereign state embodied in its absolutist ruler. The Constitutions of Melfi meant:

- The buildup of a state-wide structure of (state-salaried) officers of the crown with judicial qualifications. For the training of these judicial officials, Frederick founded the University of Naples in 1224 CE. The court of the king was the highest judicial body and the final court of appeal.
- The marginalisation of the jurisdiction of the feudal nobility and the church, since senior church officials were usually feudal landowners also. The right of bearing arms depended on royal permission. The customary right of feuds among noblemen was banned. And, at the expense of the nobility, the equality of subjects before the law was affirmed.
- In line with Frederick's rationalist approach, judgments had to be based on conceivably proof; and trial by ordeal was banned.

As von der Heydte notes with respect to these provisions: the Constitutions of Melfi 'mark the birth of the sovereign state' in Europe.[194] The state upheld its (domestic) sovereignty not only against the feudal nobility, but also against the church – and thus became secular. But that, Bozeman rightly adds, was only possible by drawing on Persian and Indian legacies of statecraft: the sovereign ruler, the centralised state and the role of the judiciary therein, and the separation of the political and religious spheres.

> The commitment to law as the principal guardian of sovereignty reveals the impact of West European, especially Roman traditions...But the purposes that law was designed to serve and the administrative methods by which it was applied were borrowed from the East...They accomplished the single purpose for which it had been drafted: the establishment of southern Italy as a secular, imperial law-state.[195]

Fredrick's Sicilian kingdom had the following features:

- Absolute ruler, who sees himself as 'king of kings' and accepts no political or religious authority above himself.
- Curia regis of counsellors as his principal advisory body and supreme administrative agency, which included: the head of the royal chancellery coordinating political affairs, notably the extensive official correspondence; commander of military forces; chief administrator, notably for fiscal affairs; justiciar, heading the royal supreme court; and one or two senior officials of the royal household.
- Centralised, secular and well-trained state bureaucracy.
- State-salaried and trained system of justice across the state territory.
- Dirigiste-etatist economic policy with state monopolies, abolition of tariffs on trade within the kingdom, regulations for private economic activities and standardised weight and measures.

- A standing army and navy, which meant armed forces outside the traditional feudal setting.
- I have not found explicit references to a domestic and/or foreign intelligence system in the Sicilian kingdom. However, in view of the serial conspiracies against Frederick, mostly instigated by the Papacy, an intelligence organisation at his court can be safely assumed. The same can be said for foreign intelligence, considering his enormous diplomatic activities as well as the multitude of his military campaigns.

When we look at the structure of Frederick's state and his political conduct, we cannot but see homologies with Kauṭilya's ideal-type state and statecraft. That applies for each of the above listed features of Frederick's state. In view of that, Kantorowicz' statement that Frederick "was rather well informed about India" seems eminently plausible. What Frederick had learned about India from written sources and verbal reports, reached him via Islamic cultural space, within which Persian cultural space is of decisive importance. Frederick was fluent in Arabic and did not depend on translations. As mentioned above, the Age of the Crusades, was the historical period in which intra-Eurasian cultural flow was the most extensive and intense since the collapse of the Roman Empire in Western Europe. The crusade which Frederick Hohenstaufen lead in 1228-29 CE was singular in that it involved no armed conflict, but lead to a diplomatic settlement which meant a shared suzerainty over Jerusalem between Frederick and the Al-Kamil, Sultan of Egypt. Bozeman notes:

> Frederick II Hohenstaufen['s] so called Sixth crusade, upon which he embarked in 1227, was unique in the annals, since it was not only cursed rather than blessed by the pope, but also conducted without a single act of hostility against Islam. The explanation for the astounding success of this paradoxical mission must be sought in the complex personality of the richly gifted Holy Roman Emperor himself. As a life-long student on non-Western, especially Arabic, culture forms, the personal friend of innumerable Muslim savants and potentates, and a successful administrator of the multinational kingdom of Sicily, Frederick was thoroughly familiar with the laws, customs, and languages of his official enemy in Palestine. Relying on the store of knowledge that he had personally acquired, and cultivating direct friendly relations with the Muslim leaders, the banned emperor succeeded where all other agencies – ecclesiastical and secular – had failed.[196]

During the year that Frederick spent in the Near East, much of his time was used for diplomatic negotiations with Sultan Al-Kamil and his envoy Emir Fakhr al-Din – both highly educated. Since Frederick could converse with Fakhr al-Din in Arabic much of the diplomatic negotiations turned into discussions of philosophy, science, mathematics – and, of course, state theory and statecraft.[197]

In all probability, Frederick learned of key thought-figures of Indian political theory and theorised statecraft not directly, but in their Persian (and Arab) hybridised forms. Yet, there is no reason to assume that the modifications, cultural adaptations and transformations of the original Indian concepts have compromised their essential idea-contents. The migration of the *Pancatantra* from India to Persia and further on through Arab cultural space prove the point that ideas 'stay alive' while covering enormous temporal and spatial distances. Similarly, the role of the *Secretum Secretorum* as the transcultural 'transmission belt' of Kauṭilyan thought.

Kantorowicz argues that Frederick II Hohenstaufen was educated and intellectually self-confident enough to recognise that (at his time) science, philosophy and statecraft in the Orient were superior to that in the West, and that, therefore, he was determined to personally absorb that knowledge and implement in his 'model-state' in Southern Italy.[198]

(e) Dante's De Monarchia and 'Kauṭilyan Echos' Therein

In his *Hindu Theory of International Relations*, Benoy Kumar Sarkar writes:

> Hindu theory of sovereignty did not stop, however, at the doctrine of a universal *matsya-nyaya*, that is of a world in which each state is at war with all. It generated also the concept of universal peace through the establishment of a *Weltherrschaft* as in Dante's *De Monarchia*... To this theory of the world state we shall now address ourselves. In Europe the idea or ideal of a universal empire took most definite shape towards the beginning of the fourteenth century exactly when the actual development of the modern nationalities was rendering it practically impossible.[199]

Dante Alighieri (1265-1321 CE) is internationally known for his epic poem *La Divina Commedia*, much less is known that he held political positions in his hometown of Florence (1295-1301 CE) and authored a political treatise, *De Monarchia*.[200] As in Machiavelli's case, Dante's political career ended in political prosecution and he was exiled up to his death.

A thorough comparative analysis of Dante's *De Monarchia* and Kauṭilya's *Arthaśāstra* is beyond the scope of this paper. Instead, I will take up Benoy Kumar Sarkar's lead and sketch a few apparent homologies between Kauṭilya and Dante.

De Monarchia, is a theoretical treatise, which, however, also addresses the political situation of his time. Dante stands in the (Ghibelline) tradition of Frederick II Hohenstaufen which means categorically opposing any jurisdiction of religious bodies, first of all the Papacy, over worldly affairs. Against the Papacy's claim of universal supremacy, Dante propounds the concept of a secular 'world monarchy', and, here, Sarkar sees the parallel to the ancient Indian concept of the *cakravartin*.

Dante's argumentation is systematic and stringent, referring to Aristotle (Politics and Nicomachean Ethics), Cicero (De re publica), St. Augustine and Thomas Aquinas, but also the Muslim philosophers Avicenna/Ibn Sina (980-1037 CE) and Averroes (1126-1198 CE). Dante argues, philosophically, referring to Aristotle, that: 1) Particularity is inferior to unity and that the inherent potential of particularity is to develop into a higher unity. 2) By nature, "things hate to be in disorder, but plurality of authorities is disorder, therefore authority is single" (*Dante*).[201] Thus, "whenever several things are united into one thing, one of them must regulate and rule, the others must be regulated and ruled" (*Dante*).[202] Consequently, monarchy is superior to all other forms of government. Only monarchy, world monarchy to be more precise, assures "a check on perverted forms of government such as democracies, oligarchies and tyrannies, which carry mankind into slavery" (*Dante*).[203] Kauṭilya has the same view.

Dante argues that the project of world monarchy has been pursued throughout recorded history. He lists the ancient Egyptians, the Assyrians, the Persians under Cyrus and Alexander the Great. The latter came quite close to establish 'world rule'. However, it was the Romans under Augustus who came the closest in realising a 'world state', which included Asia, Africa and Europe and lasted over an extended period of time. Thus, the Roman Empire is Dante's role model for bringing about a new world monarchy. Here, we see that the Orient is very much present in Dante's intellectual world.

Then, Dante turns to the dialectic of the state's (or ruler's) power and justice. First, he rejects the Christian concept, classically articulated by St. Augustine, that the worldly state is inherently incompatible with divine justice and worldly power is essentially evil. Instead, argues Dante, the state – like all other social communities, beginning with the family – is the natural and inevitable outgrowth of the nature of man. The nature of man is his singular possession of intellectual faculties – seeking knowledge and truth. This 'higher nature' of man, has, according to Dante, the following consequence: "The proper work of mankind taken as whole is to exercise continually its entire capacity for intellectual growth, first in theoretical matters, and, secondarily, as an extension of theory, in practice" (*Dante*).[204]

Next, with thought-figures that remind us of Kauṭilya, Dante argues that there is no principal contradiction between the world monarchy's political agency and ethics. Dante makes two suppositions: First, in the empirical world of politics, justice is neither an abstract postulation nor a given, but to be brought into being by the ruler's energy and activity. Secondly, the principal spoiler of justice is greed (in the broadest sense). From this follows: If the ruler uses his energy and valour towards creating world monarchy, he will become powerful and righteous, because the more powerful he becomes, the less susceptible will he become to greed. The least susceptible to greed is the world monarch, because for him there are no more objects of greed to strive for. "Therefore, justice is the most powerful in the world when it resides solely in the world-governor" (*Dante*).[205]

Dante does not leave the issue with this logical deduction only, and elaborates further: First, justice means the 'common good' or the 'welfare of the people': "Whoever is mindful of the good of the commonwealth is ipso facto mindful of the purpose of right...For if laws are not useful to those who are governed by them, they are laws only in name, not in fact" (*Dante*).[206] And secondly, "citizens do not live for their representatives nor peoples for their kings, but, on the contrary, representatives exist for citizens and kings for peoples...Hence it is clear that though in matters of policy representatives and kings are rulers of others, in matters of aims, they are the servants of others, and most of all the world ruler, who should be regarded as the servant of all" (*Dante*).[207]

For Kauṭilya, the ruler's commitment to the welfare of the people, is the normative foundation of statecraft, which he sees as equivalent with the purposive political rationality of expanding the power of the state. Both Kauṭilya and Dante deny a dichotomy between justice in the sense of promoting the welfare of the people and political rationality aiming at the expansion of state power. Similarly, if not more evident is the homology between the *Arthaśāstra* and *De Monarchia* with respect to the concept of the ruler being the servant of the people, we may note Kauṭilya saying: "In the happiness of the subjects lies the happiness of the king and in what is beneficial to the subjects is his own benefit. What is dear to himself is not beneficial to the king, but what is dear to the subjects is beneficial to him."[208]

Dante and Kauṭilya share the view that violence and war must be ultima ratio in the conduct of the state. Kauṭilya is in no way a follower of *ahiṃsā*, but for reasons of both normativity and purposive political rationality all other means have to be tried before *daṇḍa* is applied. Starting a war unnecessarily is equally immoral as politically (self-)destructive. The same thought-figure is shared by Dante:

> But we must heed the warning that, as in war-like disputes, all possible means of settling the dispute by discussion must first be tried, and that battle is only a last resort... As in medicine all other remedies are tried before steel and fire, which are a last resort, so in disputes all possible other ways of getting judgment must be exhausted before we finally resort to this remedy, as if we were forced to do it by the need of justice.[209]

Finally, Dante's 'world state' is no uniform, hyper-centralised super-state. He takes a pragmatic approach towards the structure of his 'world monarchy' which features what today would be called subsidiarity and plurality:

> It should be clearly understood that not every little regulation for every city come directly from the world-government... Thus, nations, states, and cities have their own internal concerns which require special laws... World-government, on the other hand, must be understood in the sense that it governs mankind on the basis of what all have in common and that by a common it leads all toward peace. This common norm should be received by local governments in the same way that practical intelligence in actions receives its major premises from the speculative intellect. To these it adds its own particular minor premises and then draws particular conclusions for the sake of its actions. (*Dante*)[210]

Dante believes that 'world monarchy' based on ethnic, linguistic, cultural and religious plurality as well as subsidiarity is a realistic political project. He thus writes: "Since our present concern is with politics, with the very source and principle of all right politics, and since all political matters are in our control, it is clear that our present concern is not aimed primarily at thought but action" (*Dante*). [211]

Yet, compared to Dante's concept of 'world monarchy', Kauṭilya's *cakravartin* concept is a lot more realistic. For Kauṭilya, the 'world' to be politically united is limited to the Indian subcontinent. [212] For Dante, 'world monarchy' meant rule over the whole world as known in the early 14th century CE – Eurasia and Africa – "sua namque iurisdictio terminatur oceano".[213] On the Indian subcontinent, a culture prevailed for which ethnic, linguistic, cultural and religious plurality was a given. Europe lacked such a pluralist cultural foundation. Already in the High Middle Ages, the underlying impulse of homogeneity in ethnic, linguistic, cultural and religious terms was far too strong as to be compatible with Dante's design of a 'world-monarchy'. Thus, Sarkar's assessment, cited above, is correct. Dante and Kauṭilya share some important political thought-figures. But there is a decisive difference that Dante was a grandiose political utopian, while Kauṭilya was a political realist.

Concluding Remarks

Sixty-six years ago, Adda Bozeman put forth a conceptual map (in the context of Political Science) that has served as a guide for this paper. She put into question the Eurocentric narrative of the history of state theory and theorised statecraft. Bozeman introduced Achaemenid statecraft, the political thought of the Chinese Legalists, Kauṭilya's *Arthaśāstra* and Nizam al-Mulk into the 'canon' of political theory in general and Political Realism in particular. She recognised that the theory of Political Realism is not the unique and 'pure' offspring of the Occidental tradition represented by the Greek Sophists, Thukydides, Aristotle or Tacitus.

Not only had Bozeman the intellectual courage to state that the modern European political thought was built upon the intellectual foundations laid in pre-modern India and Iran, but also she pioneered the idea of transcultural idea-migration in Eurasia by pointing to the profound intellectual interfaces between the Orient and the Occident in the 12th and 13th centuries CE and the role of Frederick II Hohenstaufen therein. Bozeman's truly innovative approach allows us to see the 'latent presence' of Kauṭilyan thought-figures in the political theory and practice of the 13th century proto-Renaissance as well as the Renaissance itself, uniquely exemplified by Niccolo Machiavelli.

Today, Bozeman's approach can be further substantiated in terms of historical and empirical data and it can be refined through the concept of hybridisation in the context of transcultural flows.

Thus, it can be stated with confidence that the conditions of transcultural idea-migration across Eurasia have existed in the context of which an Indian text on statecraft from the 4th century BCE could have tangibly influenced political theory in late-medieval and Renaissance Italy – missing footnotes notwithstanding. Thus, the evident conceptual homologies between Kauṭilya and Machiavelli might not only indicate 'covariance' or 'equivalence' with respect to these political thinkers, but also point to a transcultural migration of Kauṭilyan thought via Iranian and Arab cultural space to Europe. Yet, that finding does not force us to make a conclusive determination whether the homologies between Kauṭilya and Machiavelli are either a case of 'covariance' or of 'idea migration'. Machiavelli had original and innovative ideas, but these ideas would hardly have been generated if he had not been able to draw on Kauṭilyan thought-figures, albeit in hybrid recast.

The ultimate purpose of this book and the project in which it is situated, has been to contribute to a better understanding of Kauṭilya's *Arthaśāstra* itself by approaching it in a comparative transcultural perspective. And by doing that, we enable ourselves to better understand the latent and manifest efficacy of Kauṭilyan thought in the politico-strategic practices of contemporary India. The 'modernity of tradition' and the 're-use of the past' characterise India's political and strategic practice, but these two concepts have a broader meaning as the comparison of Kauṭilya and Machiavelli has, hopefully, shown.

Kauṭilya's *Arthaśāstra* is certainly a foundational text in the evolution of Political Science, notably IR theory. Kauṭilya's *Arthaśāstra* proves that the conceptual roots of the discipline are to be found in pre-modern Asia. Moreover, the *Arthaśāstra's* vast reservoir of (mostly untapped) ideas can and should be used as conceptual 'catalyst' and 'thought-provoker' with respect to the contemporary puzzles of Political Science.

END NOTES

1. Kangle, R.P. (2010b/1972): *The Kauṭilīya Arthaśāstra* (*Part II*) – English Translation. Delhi: Motilal Banarsidass Publishers. I also use the German translations (from Sanskrit)

of the *Arthaśāstra*. Johann Jakob Meyer (ed.) (1977/1926): *Das altindische Buch vom Welt- und Staatsleben – Das Arthacastra des Kautilya*. Graz: Akademische Druck- und Verlagsanstalt.

2. Lerner (1950).
3. Rudolph and Rudolph (1967).
4. cf. Wittgenstein (1977/1953).
5. cf., I.A. Hillebrandt (1923) and Zimmer (1973).
6. cf. Sarkar (1919), Hillebrandt (1923), Zimmer (1973/1945), Drekmeier (1962), Roy (1981), Sil (1987), Karnad (2002), Boesche (2002a/b), Dixit (2003), Watson (2009), Gautam (2013a), Bajpai et al. (2014)
7. Weber (2008: 203, 1988: 555).
8. Nehru (1981: 123).
9. Sil (1989: 9).
10. Boesche (2002b: 258, 269).
11. Bajpai et al. (2014: 10).
12. Bozeman (1992: 180).
13. For the historical context on Kauṭilya cf. Kangle (2010c), Jayaswal (1943), Kulke (1998); On Machiavelli cf. Voegelin (1951), Meinecke (1962), Hale (1972), Münkler (1987).
14. Bozeman (1992: 180).
15. Dallmayr (2010: ix, x, xi and 3).
16. Bozeman (1960: 7).
17. cf. Plessner (2003). In 1931, Plessner rejected the assumption of mono-linear scientific progress within an exclusively Eurocentric context.
18. cf. Voegelin (1990/1971: 115-133).
19. cf. Mitra (2011).
20. Drekmeier (1962: 204).
21. Karnad (2002: 11).
22. Kangle (2010b: 96), [2.10.63].
23. Lerner (1950: 153).
24. Drekmeir notes: "Since the ruling groups had an interest in limiting the circulation and preventing popularisation of the *Arthashastra* treatises, it is not surprising that few of these works have survived." Drekmeier (1962: 190f).
25. Lerner (1950: 56).
26. Weber (2000: 146 / 2008: 687).
27. Carr (1981: 63f).
28. E.H. Carr is together with Hans J. Morgenthau the founder of the modern theory of political realism in the 20th century. Both political theorists were thoroughly familiar with Machiavelli, but, in contrast to Morgenthau, there is no indication that Carr knew of Kauṭilya's *Arthaśāstra*.
29. Kangle (2010b: 12-13), [1.6.1, 11]. 'KA' means '*The Kauṭilīya Arthaśāstra*'.
30. Kangle (2010b: 14), [1.7.6-7].
31. cf. The 'might is right' argumentation of the Sophists Callicles and Thrasymachos in Plato's *Politea*.
32. Kangle (2010b: 432), [9.7.81].
33. Kangle (2010b: 10), [1.4.13-14].
34. Drekmeier notes on *mātsya-nyāya* or 'law of the fishes': "When asked how fishes live in the sea, a character in Shakespeare's Pericles (Act II, Scene I) answers that they live as men do on land – 'the great ones eat up the little ones'. Breughel's drawing of the big

fish with the many little fish inside is well known, and Swift has a poem on the same theme. This image has been employed by European political writers, and was particularly popular in the 17th century. The simile was used by Boccalini in his *Ragguagli die Parnasso* (1612-13) and by Spinoza in the *Tractatus Theologico-Politicus*" [Drekmeier (1962: 249)]. Of course, *mātsya-nyāya* corresponds to Hobbes' *homo homini lupus* [man is wolf to man].

35. Lerner (1950: 13).
36. *Ibid.*: 61.
37. *Ibid.*: 117.
38. *Ibid.*: 208.
39. *Ibid.*: 216.
40. *Ibid.*: 118, 190.
41. *Ibid.*: 61.
42. Kangle (2010b: 10), [1.4.13-14].
43. Carr (1981, 63f).
44. Drekmeier (1962: 158, 194).
45. Lerner (1950: 4).
46. Meinecke (1960, 37f).
47. Kangle (2010b: 3), [1.1.6].
48. Lerner (1950: 66, 67).
49. *Ibid.*: 410.
50. *Ibid.*: 415, 416.
51. *Ibid.*: 265.
52. *Ibid.*: 137f.
53. cf. Kangle (2010b: 314), [6.1.1].
54. *Ibid.*: 325, [7.2.1].
55. Lerner (1950: 39, 40).
56. *Ibid.*: 85.
57. cf. Kangle (2010b: 15), [1.8-10].
58. *Ibid.*: 14, [1.7.9].
59. *Ibid.*:35, [1.15.44].
60. Lerner (1950: 265).
61. *Ibid.*: 88.
62. *Ibid.*: 86.
63. Kangle (2010b: 17), [1.9.4-8].
64. Drekmeier (1962: 263).
65. Lerner (1950: 142, 211).
66. *Ibid.*: 142, 211.
67. *Ibid.*: 129.
68. *Ibid.*: 397.
69. *Ibid.*:402.
70. Bozeman (1992: 1).
71. It needs to be emphasised that Kauṭilya's commitment to the welfare of the people is no declaratory proposition: "In the happiness of the subjects lies the happiness of the king and in what is beneficial to the subjects is his own benefit. What is dear to himself is not beneficial to the king, but what is dear to the subjects is beneficial to him." Kangle (2010b: 47), [1.19.34].

72. Neither the Kauṭilya nor Machiavelli use the term raison d'état. Yet, the idea 'behind' this category pervades their works. Roughly seven decades after the Machiavelli's death, Giovanni Botero introduces the term 'ragion di stato' in his book *Della Ragione di Stato* and defines raison d'état as: "The knowledge of the means and measures that are necessary to establish, maintain and expand a state" [quoted in Münkler (1987: 169)]. Friedrich Meinecke rightly notes that raison d'état is not the exclusive offspring of European modernity: "An account of this process [the evolution of the idea of raison d'état] from the standpoint of universal history would have to embrace and compare all cultures; it would have to begin by examining the idea of raison d'état in the ancient world, and analysing its relationship with the spirit of that epoch. For both the free city-states and the monarchies of antiquity are teeming with the problems of raison d'état and with attempts to formulate it." [Meinecke (1962: 25)].
73. Kangle (2010b: 386), [8.1.16].
74. Drekmeier (1962: 203f).
75. Kangle (2010b: 406), [9.1.1].
76. *Ibid.*: 321, [7.1.1].
77. *Ibid.*
78. *Ibid.*: 327, [7.3.1].
79. *Ibid.*: 95, [2.10.47].
80. cf. Hillebrandt (1923: 150).
81. Lerner (1950: 403f).
82. *Ibid.*: 404.
83. *Ibid.*: 354.
84. *Ibid.*: 360.
85. *Ibid.*: 322.
86. *Ibid.*: 35.
87. *Ibid.*: 61.
88. *Ibid.*: 302.
89. *Ibid.*: 448f.
90. *Ibid.*: 190.
91. *Ibid.*: 64.
92. *Ibid.*: 60.
93. *Ibid.*: 34.
94. *Ibid.*: 362.
95. *Ibid.*: 498.
96. *Ibid.*: 200f.
97. *Ibid.*: 354.
98. *Ibid.*: 90.
99. *Ibid.*: 14.
100. *Ibid.*: 308.
101. *Ibid.*: 176.
102. *Ibid.*: 298.
103. *Ibid.*: 347.
104. *Ibid.*: 92.
105. *Ibid.*: 249.
106. *Ibid.*: 248f.
107. *Ibid.*: 441.
108. *Ibid.*: 83.

109. *Ibid.*: 287.
110. *Ibid.*: 307.
111. *Ibid.*: 39.
112. *Ibid.*: 292.
113. *Ibid.*: 268.
114. *Ibid.*: 528.
115. *Ibid.*: 310.
116. *Ibid.*: 228.
117. *Ibid.*: 319.
118. *Ibid.*: 104.
119. *Ibid.*: 66.
120. Drekmeier: (1962: 203).
121. While Kauṭilyan foreign policy is 'revisionist' with respect to the multiple states on subcontinent, beyond India's geo-cultural boundaries, the status quo is not called into question. Instead, Kauṭilya, stands for balance of power approach vis-a-vis the Graeco-Persian Diadochi states, China, or the states in Central Asia and the Indian Ocean rim.
122. Drekmeier (1962: 206, 268).
123. Lerner (1950: 95, 98).
124. Kangle (2010b: 321), [7.1.2-3].
125. *Ibid.*: 397, [8.4.1].
126. Lerner (1950: 91).
127. Kangle (2010b: 48), [1.19.36].
128. Lerner (1950: 91, 94).
129. *Ibid.*: 383.
130. Drekmeier (1962: 203).
131. Kangle (2010b: 335), [7.5.19-28].
132. *Ibid.*: 368, [7.14.18].
133. Drekmeier (1962: 201, 260).
134. Kangle (2010b: 8), [1.3.13].
135. Lerner (1950: 528).
136. Kangle (2010b: 407), [9.1.14].
137. *Ibid.*: 460, [12.1.10].
138. Lerner (1950: 72).
139. *Ibid.*: 4f.
140. Bozeman (1992: 99).
141. *Ibid.*: 56, 94.
142. Lerner (1950: 373).
143. *Ibid.*: 459.
144. *Ibid.*: 272.
145. cf. Voegelin (1951).
146. *Ibid.*: 163.
147. *Ibid.*: 155.
148. cf. Frank and Gills (1993).
149. In this paper, I, like Frank and Gills, factor out the question of Africa in the Eurasian communications network. Egypt, geographically located in Africa, is treated as an integral part of Eurasia as a geo-cultural unit.
150. Frank and Gills (1993: xi, xii).
151. Jaspers (2011: 2).

152. Sil (1989: 12).
153. Voegelin (1994: 125).
154. Bozeman (1960: 93).
155. *Ibid.*: 61.
156. *Ibid.*: 119f.
157. The westward migration of hybrid idea-aggregates seems well researched and documented in the case of Indian, Persian and Arab arithmetic.
158. Bozeman (1960: 399f).
159. cf. Suhtscheck (1932: 50-71); Slaye (1989: 93-103).
160. cf. Ryder (1925); Olivelle (1997).
161. Olivelle (1997: xli).
162. Heimann (1930: 196).
163. Hillebrandt (1923: 2).
164. Bozeman (1960: 129).
165. cf. Olivelle (1997): Introduction.
166. Eamon (1994: 49f).
167. Williams (2003: 17).
168. Modern research of the impact history of the *Secretum Secretorum* , however, is mainly focused on its non-political Contents.
169. In contrast to Western Europe, Arab scholars – since the 8th century CE – did have access to Aristotle's works and other Greek and Hellenistic texts and translated them into Arabic.
170. To the pre-Islamic Iranian Mirror for Princes genre belong works like *'Eternal Wisdom'*, *'Letter of Tansar'* or *'Ardashir's Testament'*. cf. Hossein Zarhani, Paper submitted to the IDSA Kauṭilya Workshop, Delhi, May 25-29, 2015; and published in this volume.
171. The *Siyasat-nama* draws on the legacy of Achaemenid statecraft and exhibits homologies with some of the key thought-figures of Kauṭilya's *Arthaśāstra*. Nizam, like Kauṭilya, was both a political theorist and an experienced practitioner of statecraft (in the medieval Persian-Seljuk empire). Bozeman writes on Nizam al-Mulk: "[T]he most striking external evidence of this evolution is to be found in the court life that came to prevail at Baghdad and in the rules of statecraft and diplomacy to which the caliphs of that capital subscribed. That these rules were modeled closely upon the ancient Persian and Byzantine traditions and owed little if anything to Arab and Islamic sources, becomes quite apparent as one reads the *'Book of Government'*, written in the 11th century by the renowned political scientist and vizier Nizam ul-Mulk and used by all the later generations of Persian and Turkish rulers as their leading text in the Muslim art of government." [Bozeman (960: 370f)].
172. Stig Wikander (1908-1983) was a Swedish Indologist and Iranologist. cf. Stig Wikander, "De l'Inde a l'Espagne: L'origine de la Poridat de las poridades," Actas IV Congresso de estudos arabes e islamicos (Leiden: 1971). Wikander's paper for that congress is based on an unpublished essay archived at Uppsala University, Sweden.
173. Williams (2003: 17).
174. cf. Manzalaoui (1974).
175. *Ibid.*: 210.
176. *Ibid.*: 200, 15; Book I, cap. X.
177. *Ibid.*: 200, 308-309; Book VI, cap. i.
178. The *Nītisārā* by Kamandaki is an Indian treatise on statecraft from the late Gupta period (5th or 6th century CE). It is a condensed and simplified variant of Kauṭilya's *Arthaśāstra*.
179. Kauṭilya is also called Chanakya in India, but the author of the *Nītisāra* is Kamandaki.

180. Manzalaoui (1974: 211f).
181. The sections in the *Secretum Secretorum* not dealing with statecraft might have drawn on the encyclopaedic work on Indian philosophy, science and customs by the Persian polymath Al-Biruni (973-1048 CE). His book *Indica* (*Tarikh Al-Hind*) can be seen as the foundational text of Indology.
182. Williams (2003: 17).
183. Gilbert (1938: 88).
184. Sarkar writes that the *cakravartin* concept "fired the imaginations of the Alexanders, Charlemagnes and Fredericks of India throughout the ages" and is comparable to "the Ghibelline imperialism of the Hohenstaufens". [Sarkar (1919: 409, 411)].
185. cf. Kantorowicz (2003), Fried (2003).
186. Fried (2003: 182, 183, 187).
187. Bozeman (1960: 425).
188. cf. Kantorowicz (2003: 171).
189. cf. Gunderson (1980).
190. cf. Grebner (2008).
191. Kantorowicz (2003).
192. Bozeman (1960: 449).
193. Kangle (2010b: 10), [1.4.13-14].
194. Heydte (1952: 55).
195. Bozeman (1960: 449).
196. *Ibid.*: 276.
197. cf. Kantorowicz (2003: 144-154).
198. Frederick II Hohenstaufen encountered the last bloom of pre-modern science and culture in Persian and Arab space. In 1221 CE, the Mongols destroyed the University of Nishapur in Eastern Iran with the second-largest library in the world. In 1236 CE, the Muslim yet multicultural university of Cordoba in Spain was shut down after the city was conquered by Christian Spaniards. In 1258 CE, the House of Wisdom in Baghdad with the world's largest library was burnt down by the Mongols. Thereafter, Bologna, Naples, Paris and Oxford became Eurasia's main centers of learning.
199. Sarkar (1919: 408).
200. Dante Alighieri's *De Monarchia*. cf. Sauter (1974/1913, German translation), Schneider (1984, English translation). The page numbers in citations refer to Schneider's English edition of *De Monarchia*.
201. Schneider (1984: 12).
202. *Ibid.*: 8.
203. *Ibid.*: 17.
204. *Ibid.*: 3.
205. *Ibid.*: 14.
206. *Ibid.*: 32.
207. *Ibid.*: 17.
208. Kangle (2010b: 47), [1.19.34].
209. Schneider (1984: 44).
210. *Ibid.*: 20.
211. *Ibid.*: 2f.
212. Kangle (2010b: 407), [9.1.17-20].
213. For [only] through the ocean is his rule confined.

5

Arthaśāstra: Reflections on Thought and Theory

Medha Bisht

Introduction

Theorising Kauṭilya's *Arthaśāstra* could be a daunting task to begin with. The text is well embedded in the contextual intersection of conceptual nuances inherent in the meanings which are endowed to the realm of state and statecraft. One could define it as the magnum opus of sorts, laying out the rich balance between the feasible and desirable (is and ought), thereby directing a normative understanding of certain choices made by the king (leader).

There are two nodal points that this chapter rests on. First, it explores the possibilities of theorising the *Arthaśāstra* as a text. In order to examine this question I focus on the theoretical relevance of the *Arthaśāstra*. Second, I will problemitise restricting the *Arthaśāstra* to the paradigm driven framework available in International Relations, and instead suggest that going beyond paradigms – towards an inter-paradigmatic space – can be helpful in understanding the meanings of certain concepts and ideas which are articulated in the text itself. In this context, the significance of inter-paradigmatic treatment to understand concepts and ideas, which emerge from cross-cultural encounters, has been emphasised upon. The significance of inter-paradigmatic treatment of the *Arthaśāstra* stems from the belief that the text bears close resemblance to both classical realism and English School of International Relations. This, as has been assumed, could be a useful approach for situating the identity of a text like the *Arthaśāstra* – thus having both ontological and epistemological consequences to make sense of the vocabulary which has been employed in the *Arthaśāstra*. The methodological treatment of inter-paradigmatic space has been inspired from Xianlong Zhang's work who argues that genuine comparisons cannot be made at the level of propositions and concepts, but can only be achieved through inter-paradigmatic conditions, where one has sharp awareness of paradigms' boundaries from which one can attempt to achieve situational communication with other paradigms. This situational comparison can only be pursued at the level of conceptual expression, epistemological thinking (subject-knowing object), and deletion of one/none paradigm.

Thus, basing my arguments on these distinct strands as the framework for offering my reflections on thought and theory, I will be highlighting the normative claims of the *Arthaśāstra* broadly engaging with some of the central concepts that appear in the text. It has been argued that order and morality are central to the understanding of the *Arthaśāstra* not only from the perspective of praxis – the idea of state at the internal and statecraft at the external level – but also from the ontological, epistemological and hence the normative insights that make the text relevant to the broader field of International Relations.

In this context, by undertaking textual analyses, this chapter will adopt a three pronged approach to interpret and analyse the relevance of the text. First, it briefly examines the possibilities of theorising the *Arthaśāstra* as a text. Second, it engages with the conceptual expositions and operational parameters elicited in Kauṭilya's *Arthaśāstra*. The concept of order and its broader relationship with morality has been discussed in this context. Third, it highlights the necessity for going beyond paradigms and moving towards inter-paradigmatic frameworks for situating non-western intellectual resources and their relevance thereby to the field of International Relations. This three pronged approach would not only help in addressing the primary question, which this chapter has identified at the outset, but will also draw attention to the normative relevance of the *Arthaśāstra* which emerges from such analyses.

From Thought to Theory

"How does one understand a theoretical enterprise – one broad enough to encompass the diverse forms of theorising that populate the field?"[1] This is the puzzle that Reus-Smit and Snidal set for themselves to explore the meaning and relevance of theory in International Relations. The broad argument that the authors offer at the introductory chapter of this significant work is that "all theories of International Relations and global politics have important empirical and normative dimensions and their deep interconnections is unavoidable."[2] Given that different perspectives in International Relations emphasise different issues which demand different actions, and which arrive at different conclusions particularly regarding the types of action that is required, they argue that theorising the field therefore has never been able to reside comfortably in a pure normative or a pure empirical inquiry. For them, the dialectics between empirical and normative questions is an inevitable process of theorising itself and this, as they argue, is destined to continue.[3] Not really categorical in stating that the empirical and the normative are two realms of theorising, James Rosenau puts forth the argument that "to think theoretically one has to be clear as to whether one aspires to empirical theory or value theory."[4] For Rosenau, the is-ought distinction is necessary, because both entail a different mode of reasoning, a different rhetoric and different types of evidence. The point of convergence between empirical and normative theory for Rosenau is almost naturally dialectical and would happen in the most organic of all ways, as he argues that "moral values and policy goals can be well served, by putting them aside and proceeding detachedly long enough to enlarge empirical understanding of the obstacles that hinder realisation of the values and progress toward the goals."[5]

Another important discussion while theorising international relations is on the nature and art of theorising per se. Rosenau, for instance, commenting on the art of theorising, creatively argues that thought can only be qualified or elevated to the status of theory when it can provide an explanation for every event. The central distinction, then, between thought and theory is that the latter is based on some central presumptions (or the laws of probability) and some fundamental assumptions regarding the underlying order that political and social phenomenon is based upon. For Rosenau, it is very important to identify an underlying order out of which International Relations springs and understand the laws of probability (exploring the relationship between cause and effect) that govern the explanation for theorising an event. To underline the importance of causal relationship between various variables, Kenneth Waltz differentiates between laws and theories. He argues, "rather than being mere collection of laws, theories are statements that explain them."[6] For Waltz, the key factor that differentiates law from theories is the process of explanation, as explanations reveal why associations exist. The fact that Waltz emphasises that theories are not invented but discovered, underlines the need for identifying an underlying order, which makes sense of the causal hypothesis one intends to examine further. Assertions can both be true or false, the key question in theorisation for Waltz is the potential explanatory value – and this explanatory value as Waltz writes is "gained by moving away from reality – not by staying close to it."[7] While Alexander Wendt in *Social Theory of International Politics* does not disagree with Waltz in this respect, he does emphasise the constitutive nature of theorising, where ideas go deeper in giving meaning to material structures.

A final point which becomes relevant to the art of theorising per se, is the creative force that goes behind in the making of theory. Both Waltz and Rosenau emphasise on the importance of creativity in theory building. It is a discovery of a pattern which can be brought in to an explanatory system.[8] Reus-Smit and Snidal argue that the emphatic thrust of theorising should not be on the nature of theorising but the art of theorising itself. The three critical elements which are a pre-requisite for the art of theorising are – (a) the existence of a referent question about the world we live in or could live in (b) identifying what matters in the 'international' relations political universe and (c) identifying a logical argument (which can be causal or constitutive), where through our argument we mobilise our assumptions. The argument offered is generally in relation to our questions to infer or arrive at new conclusions. These three yardsticks as the authors argue are generally used to theorise the field.

If the *Arthaśāstra* was to be read within the broad parameters associated with the art of theorising, certain factors stand out and attempts could be made to reflect on whether *Arthaśāstra* holds any theoretical value. More appropriately: Does *Arthaśāstra* succeed in theorising the concept of state and statecraft? Juxtaposing the broad arguments which have been laid out, if one was to engage with the primary assertion that the *Arthaśāstra* makes regarding big questions, the answer can be found in the exclusive focus given to the underlying raison d'etre associated with the definition and the purpose of the state. It is most interesting to note in this context that the first half of the text (the first five books) exclusively focuses on the notion of state as a purposive construct.

Similarly, the second question related to relevance of matters in 'international' relations political universe, can be addressed through the pertinent focus that Kauṭilya gives to order. Order was considered central in the *Arthaśāstra*, primarily because of the importance given to the concept of state (through the *saptānga* theory) and statecraft (through the *maṇḍala* theory). As one of the scholars has put it, the state was constituted to get the human race out of human nature. Aseem Prakash writes, "state enabled the citizens to follow their respective *dharma* and to enjoy private property rights."[9] The role, place and meaning of *dharma* therefore is a matter of much deliberation, and in this context its meaning in terms of morality and order becomes significant.

Similarly, the third important element of theorising, entails a logical argument, where one mobilises his/her assumptions. In this context, the details *Arthaśāstra* elicits through *saptānga* theory and *ṣāḍguṇya* theory become significant entry points. The importance of *dharma* and its interpretive angularity for logically understanding the importance of order in the *Arthaśāstra* is insightful from the perspective how critical decisions regarding policy were made. In this context, the following section makes sense of some of these core concepts as they appear in the text which helps in examining the larger attributes that make the text appropriate for theorisation.

The Conceptual Categories: Understanding Morality

The means-end debate has been a recurring dilemma in international politics. This is because when it comes to politics certain unworthy means need to be employed to achieve some worthy ends. The worthy ends in this perspective might be derived from a purely categorical principle of what ought to be done in contrast to a rather consequentialist understanding of the morality embedded in the consequences of an act itself.[10] Unlike the categorical moral reasoning, which locates morality within certain duties and rights, the consequentialist moral reasoning explores logic within the intrinsic quality of the act itself. Indeed both logics employ moral reasoning, though the latter focuses on process and the former on substance. The substance in the *Arthaśāstra* exposes itself in terms of the idea of the state and the purpose and rationale it exists for. Consequences, thus, follow a causal logic, where the end goal stipulated in the *śāstras* (ancient texts/scriptures) is inclined towards maintaining order – and hence maintaining it justifies all means. In this context, it is argued that the ends identified are justified because they are the most appropriate for social and political order. It also needs to be noted that both these views, which emphasise ends over means or vice versa, relate to questions and justification of the moral. This dilemma, as Michael Sandel points, is also one of the great questions of political philosophy.[11]

Given that the relationship dilemma between the ends/means explicitly manifests itself in the debates on political theory and strategic practice, it would be appropriate to explore its logic or justification. In this context, specific philosophies and cultures with which these justifications are embedded or derive their meaning from become significant objects of phenomenological analyses. While much ink has been spilled on this issue particularly in the field of comparative political theory, when it comes to issues of politics and morality, there are three identified frameworks, which address this dyadic connection between the ends and means. These are, (a) anti-morality view, (b) morality as seamless view, and (c) political morality view.[12]

Thus, the end-means debate becomes relevant to questions and logic of state and statecraft because of two reasons. First, it tries to reconcile the logic of morality in politics; and second, it explores the rationale (philosophical and cultural) which goes behind the understanding of a given political action. As argued in this chapter, the logic for action can potentially be interpreted by shedding light on the philosophical debates prevalent at that time. It is this second logic, which makes it necessary to examine the text within the philosophical tradition or the evolution of the history of ideas per se.

Morality and the *Arthaśāstra*

Kauṭilya's *Arthaśāstra* becomes important from the means-ends perspective primarily because it introduces an important element of *dharma* which can also be translated as political virtue.[13] Kauṭilya's notion of *dharma* is significant because it not only has categorical leanings but it also balances desirable elements of polity with the feasible elements of policy. One can also say that this balance can be found at the intersection of morality (*dharma*) and policy (*nīti*) in the *Arthaśāstra*, which was articulated through and embodied in the notion of the state. The state, thus, was a normative construct – an embodiment of *dharma* itself. Prakash defines the state in the *Arthaśāstra* as "a human artefact, which was constituted to get the human race out of human nature."[14] As put by Prakash himself, "the state enabled the citizens to follow their respective *dharma* and to enjoy private property rights. King (was) viewed as a protector of *dharma* but not the sole interpreter of it."[15]

To understand *dharma* at more nuanced level, B.K. Sarkar's explanation is most appropriate. Sarkar subjects the notion of *dharma* within three distinct strands. He writes that in Indian political thought *dharma* can be interpreted as law, duty and justice.[16] The first proposition means that the state differs from the non-state as a law giving institution; second, as a justice dispensing institution; and thirdly, as a duty enforcing institution. This distinction between state and non-state refers to a state of order (*dharma*) and anarchy (*mātsya-nyāya*). It could be appropriate to argue then that the state emerged as an instrument for ordering social relations to minimise the impact of prevalent elements, which could trigger anarchical conditions. In *mātsya-nyāya*, as Sarkar writes, "there is no law, no justice, no duty, the state is infact the originator of law, justice and duty."[17] The preponderance of the state symbolic of order rather than anarchy is therefore very much explicitly visible.

Romila Thapar is of the view that by about 600 BCE the broad patterns of Indian history started becoming much clearer. By this time, permanent settlements in particular areas had given geographical identities to tribes, which were gaining concrete shape due to possession of geographical/territorial areas. To maintain these possessions, therefore, it was necessary that political organisations either in the form of monarchy or a republican government were being contemplated of. Thapar argues that the monarchies were concentrated in the Gangetic plains, the republics were concentrated in the peripheries of these kingdoms. Thus, while tribal loyalties persisted to some extent in the republics, they gave way to caste hierarchies in the monarchies. The republics, according to her, were also less opposed to individualistic and independent opinion than that of the monarchies, which were more inclined to tolerate unorthodox views. Thapar's broad argument is that it was, therefore, the republics that produced leaders such as Buddha – who belonged to the *Śākya* tribe and Mahavira, who belonged to the *Jñatrika* tribe.[18] Thapar notes that one of the most striking characteristics of these non-brahman theories was the Buddhist account of the origin of the state. She cites a Buddhist verse, which captures this view, viz.:

> there was a time in the early days of the universe, when there was complete harmony among all created beings and men and women had no desires, everything being provided for. Gradually a process of decay began, when needs, wants and desires became manifest. The concept of a family led to private property, which inturn led to disputes and struggles, which necessitated law and a controlling authority. Thus it was decided that one person be elected to rule and maintain justice. He was to be the great elect (*Mahāsammata*) and was given a fixed share in the produce of the land as salary. Such a theory suited the political systems of the republics.[19]

In contrast, the monarchical form of government, which is more of our subject of discussion in the *Arthaśāstra*, was centred on and around the Gangetic plains with some of the prominent kingdoms being Kashi, Kosala and Magadha, and it was much later in *Kauṭilīya Arthaśāstra* around 320 BCE that the idea of state was articulated. On the ideational influences of the *Arthaśāstra*, Ashok Chousalkar writes that the *arthaśāstra* teachers were influenced by the course of social revolution and wanted to develop the sources of *artha* to create material prosperity.[20] Different *arthaśāstra* teachers, therefore, represented different schools of thought as they propagated different ideas. According to Kauṭilya himself, there were as many as ten predecessors before him.[21] R.S. Sharma writes that, "according to one calculation the *artha* contents accounts for one-fifteenth of the *Apastamba Dharmasutra*, one twelfth of *Baudhayana Dharmasutra*, one sixth of the *Gautama Dharmasutra* and one-fifth of *Vasistha Dharmasutra*. This points to the growing importance of the subject of *artha*, ultimately leading to the creation of an independent work of the *Arthashastra* of Kautilya."[22] Chousalkar argues that the tradition of *arthaśāstra* was a consequence of the alternative thought that was emerging since the sixth century BCE. The century, according to him, was the beginning of the feudal revolution, when the kings used amoral methods to get things done. Amongst the various schools of thoughts that emerged in ancient India, viz., the supporters of the traditional Brahman religion based on Vedic dogma and sacrifices, the anti-Vedic religious teachers (like Buddha, Mahavira and Gosala), and Lokāyata and *arthaśāstra* teachers, the *arthaśāstra* school tried to understand the cause of new change and advocated that the forces of change could be strengthened with the help of the institution of the state.[23] The institution of the state was thus a unique development in early India. It was regulatory in character, in terms of monitoring the roles of various organs and administrative structures. Thapar writes that theories regarding the origin of state during the Mauryan times experienced a shift of focus from the *rājanya*, who protects the *jana*, to the *kṣatriya* who both protects as well as maintains law and order, and whose control grows out of the notion of sovereignty. Ultimately, when the *kṣatriya* was not sufficient, the state was visualised as the intermeshing of seven limbs (*prakṛtis* or *angas*), among which the king was one of the elements.[24]

An important tool for ordering the society was thus the tool of *daṇḍa* – the rod. Kauṭilya writes:

> the king severe with the rod, becomes a source of terror to beings. The King mild with the rod is despised. The King just with the rod is honoured. For the rod used after full considerations, endows the subjects with spiritual good, material well-being and pleasures of the senses. Used unjustly, whether in passion or anger, or in contempt, it enrages. If not used at all, it gives rise to the law of fishes (*mātsya-nyāya*) – for the stronger swallows the weak in the absence of the wielder of the rod. The people of the four *varṇas* and in the four stages of life, protected by the king with the rod (and) deeply attached to occupations prescribed as their special duties, keep to their respective paths.[25]

As can be perceived from the analyses, *dharma* and order were thus deeply correlated and *daṇḍa* emerged as the means of regulating this order. On the preponderance of *dharma*, the *Arthaśāstra* points out that "in a situation when *dharma* and *niti* contradict each other – *dharma* should provide the direction". Evidence of this can be found in the sources of the law chapter, which states that any matter in dispute shall be judged according to the four bases of justice. These in order of increasing importance are: (a) law, which is based on truth; (b) transaction, which is based on witnesses; (c) custom, i.e. the tradition accepted by the people, the commonly held view of men; and (d) royal edicts, i.e. command of the king.[26] Kauṭilya notes that the latter one supersedes the earlier in the sequence, and therefore the command of the king is supreme. It is further qualified that a just king takes all factors into account. However, a caveat is added which perhaps needs to be noted. Chapter One of Book Three, paragraph 44, reads, "[The King] shall decide, with the help of law a matter in which a settled custom or a matter based transaction contradicts the science of law". Also, "whenever there is disagreement between the custom and *dharma* or between the evidence and the law, the matter shall be decided in accordance with *dharma*."[27]

So, what does *dharma* mean and what significance does it have to the meaning of morality in particular? In other words, how does the *Arthaśāstra* balance the notion of desirability of *dharma* with the feasibility of policy?

Dharma and the *Arthaśāstra*

The meaning of *dharma* can be traced to the *dharmaśāstra* tradition. *Śāstras* have broadly been understood as the systematic study of political life. *Śāstras* also meant authoritative texts/principles/rules laid down in a treatise with given injunctions. *Dharmaśāstras* are referred to as systematic/ authoritative treatises on the general principles and detailed content of righteous conduct. Thus, the principles and rules of *dharmaśāstras* were not just analytical and elucidatory but also authoritative and binding in nature. The *dharmaśāstra* writers thus concentrated on exploring the *dharma* of individuals and social groups, including the government. They discussed the sources of *dharma*, as well as what was to be done, when these conflicted. They also provide a detailed prospectus of duties. Thus, the *dharmaśāstras* were didactic and prescriptive.[28]

Given this distinction, it would be interesting to understand the role and place of *arthaśāstras*, within the *dharmaśāstras*. Bhikhu Parekh further provides a distinction between the *Dharmaśāstras* and *Arthaśāstra*, which is very insightful. He writes:

> In contrast to *Dharmashastras*, the authors of *Arthashastras* were interested in the organisation and mechanisation of *danda*. They concentrated on the nature and organisation of government, the nature and mechanics of power. The way power is weakened, acquired and lost, the source of threat to government and the best way to deal with them. It would however be a mistake to draw too neat a contrast between the two. While it is true that the authors of *dharmashastras* are rather moralistic, and those of *arthashastras* realistic…the former were not particularly naïve and freely acknowledged the political need to disregard moral principles and values under certain circumstances, even as the *arthashastra* writers acknowledged and insisted on the observance of the *dharma*. Thus while the *arthashastra* writers occasionally tended to treat political power as an end in itself, they did not generally lose sight of the moral ends of the government.[29]

The two approaches were thus homologous to each other. They just differed on their subject matter, though the source remained the same – one chose to explore political life from the stand point of *dharma*, the other from that of *daṇḍa* – the difference was thus only in emphasis and orientation. While *dharmaśātras* laid down the *dharma* and was more legalistic and religious in orientation, the *arthaśāstra* while analysing the structure and functions of government, concentrated on institutions and policies and were secular in orientation. Neither approach was complete in itself and had to be read in reference to the other. Thus, it can be said that *Arthaśāstra* bridged the glaring gap between politics and morality. In other words, it bridged then the divide between the *dharmaśāstras* and the *nītiśāstras*. As *nīti* in Sanskrit parlance meant policies, *nītiśāstra* consequently meant an authoritative injunction on policies. Likewise the term *daṇḍanīti* primarily meant authoritative policies on establishing coercive powers of the government.

Dharma in the Indian Political Thought

It would be appropriate here to look at some of the existing debates on the treatment of *dharma* and *nīti* in the evolution of Indian political thought. The political thought in India is generally associated with three main schools. The first was represented by ancient writers like Brahma and Manu – where the primary focus was on the *dharmaśāstras*, which were the legal text books, emphasising what righteous conduct was. The second was represented by Bhṛgu, whose primary focus was on *Śukranītiśāstra*. It focused on issues of policy related to the secular domain and its successor was Śukra. The Bhṛgu school was also named as Bhārgava or Auśaṇas. The third school, meanwhile, was represented by Angīras, and the primary focus was on *arthaśāstras*. Its successor was Bṛhaspati. This third school was named Bārhaspatya and Kauṭilya's *Arthaśāstra* came to be identified with this school.

Arthaśāstra was the mediating link between the secular issues related to *nīti* (policy) and the issues related to *dharma* (morality). It is significant to note as S.V. Puntambekar writes, "Kautilya who mentions other writers on political science makes a solution to both Sukra and Brihaspati, as pioneers in the beginning of his treatise. For him while Brihaspati recognised only economics and politics as sole branch of study, the Ausanas school recognised only politics, as the sole branch."[30] Given Puntambekar's intervention, it also perhaps needs to be noted that the notion of *dharma* as the ethical aspect has not been emphasised by scholars as being a significant part of the *Arthaśāstra*. Instead, it is traced by Puntambekar to Śukra's political thought. However, Anthony Parel's insights in this regard are instructive. He writes that the ideas introduced in the 4th century BCE received their formal recognition in Kauṭilya's *Arthaśāstra*. These ideas were picked up later by authors such as Kamandaki in the fifth century CE, Somadeva in the tenth century CE and the author of *Śukranīti* in the 14th century CE. Parel further argues that one of the most important ideas, that took roots in the *Arthaśāstra* was the relevance of Political Science, as an important discipline. This, as he argues, was to create *cultural conditions necessary* (emphasis added) for the pursuit of four great ends of life – the *puruṣārthas* – which were ethical goodness (*dharma*), wealth and power (*artha*), pleasure (*kāma*) and spiritual transcendence (*mokṣa*).[31] Parel's intervention becomes relevant with regard to the "enumeration of sciences" as mentioned in the *Arthaśāstra*. Kauṭilya writes in Book One, Chapter Two, "Four indeed is the number of sciences", which constituted of philosophy, the three Vedas, economics and the science of politics. He further adds, "since with their help one can learn what is spiritual good and material well-being, therefore the sciences are so called."[32] This holistic approach in the *Arthaśāstra*, which emphasised economics along with politics, material along with spiritual well-being, necessitates that one goes beyond parochialism interms of interpreting both the text and its writer.

While the philosophical interpretation of the *Arthaśāstra* underlines the importance that the text placed on *dharma*, it would be useful to explore the interaction of *dharma* with some key arguments, as articulated in the text and their relevance to some key assumptions that inform International Relations (IR) theory.

Anarchy and Order in IR Theory

If one was to give a primary disciplinary primer in International Relations – anarchy as a concept would stand out in all its prominence. Kenneth Waltz a neo-realist considered anarchy the central structural feature of the international system. The anarchical nature of the international system, with no superior authority, thus made states fend for their own security and survival. The primary contribution of Kenneth Waltz was theorising the international system, and Waltz successfully did so, by laying out three 'ordering principles' of the international system – anarchy, undifferentiated nature of states and distribution of power between states. The international system for Waltz was an independent variable, characterised by anarchy and self-help. It gave rise to competition between states, often seeking to augment their power and enhance their security. The second and third variables elicited by Waltz also hold explanatory potential, as they emphasise on the undifferentiated nature of states and the distribution of power between them.[33] Kauṭilya's *Arthaśāstra* considered the *saptānga* theory a key explanatory variable in influencing the choices of states.

However, it needs to be noted that anarchy, as a concept finds an important place in the *Arthaśāstra*. Known as *mātsya-nyāya*, the concept indeed is central to the understanding of the idea behind the evolution of the state. However, the difference between the Waltzian and the Kauṭilyan notion of anarchy stems from an understanding of anarchy itself.

While the neo-realistic understanding of anarchy forms a deterministic structure within which states operate and their political interests and identities (self-help) are primarily shaped up, the deterministic thrust in the *Arthaśāstra* is not on anarchy but order. This is central problematic, where the *Arthaśāstra* differs from the neo-realist understanding. An appropriate example for arriving at this understanding is the spoke and hub analogy which Kauṭilya uses in Chapter Six. He writes, "Making the king separated by one intervening territory, the felly and those immediately proximate the spokes, the leader should stretch himself out as the hub in the circle of constituents. For the enemy situated between the two, the leader and ally, becomes easy to exterminate or to harass, even if strong."[34] One can sense the necessity of maintaining this order through the circle of states (*maṇḍala*) in Kauṭilya's *Arthaśāstra*. The superiority and inferiority of state within the *maṇḍala* was determined by not only alliances but also the other six constituent elements defining the state – where maintaining and preserving the constituent elements was the *dharma* of the state per se.

The aforementioned argument can be qualified by the rationale, which Hindu political thought posits for the existence of the state, which as stated before primarily can be traced to the beginning of the Mauryan period. In this respect, the distinction, which scholars have used between the state and non-state become significant. As Sarkar writes, "this method was logical as well as historical. That is in the first place, they (ancient thinkers) tried to investigate in what particulars the state analytically differs from the non-state; and in the second place, they tried to picture to themselves, as to how the pre-statal condition could be developed into the statal condition, i.e. how the state grew out of the non-state."[35] This understanding as he points out was reflected in the concept of the *mātsya-nyāya* (the rule of the fishes – the natural order where the big fish eats the small fish). The concept of *dharma*, thus was precisely introduced as an antidote to avoid anarchy.[36] In this respect, one can argue that *dharma*, rendered in the terminology of order, thus becomes a natural corollary to understand how the concept of anarchy or *mātsya-nyāya* in the *Arthaśāstra* was addressed. Order, and therefore not anarchy, is more instructive of understanding the *Arthaśāstra*.

In International Relations, order is the most conceptually animated term in analysing the nature of state interaction. Broadly understood as a "purposive arrangement" of actors, it is often interpreted within an ordered framework, within which states interact with each other. There are four categories which can illuminate a conceptual understanding of order in international relations. The first is descriptive-normative, the second is analytical-descriptive, the third is strategic-structural and the fourth is cognitive-cultural. These brachyological terms broadly convey the meanings associated with the concept of order in varied discourses. While the first category termed as descriptive-normative describes order as a purposive arrangement, the second category analytically elaborates on the nature of order thus laying out and specifying its constitutive elements. The third category broadly conveys the strategic dimension of means and ends debate which is broadly associated with the structural factors focused on ordering relations through alliances or employing balancing strategies. The fourth relates to the cultural, ideational and cognitive frames which are culturally informed and endow meaning to the concept of order not as a universal term but with more cultural specific connotations.[37]

Given the aforementioned understanding, *dharma* as order in the *Arthaśāstra* can broadly be understood within the fourth category. It also needs to be perhaps highlighted that it cannot be divorced from elements which are of strategic, normative and descriptive disposition. While the strategic dimensions become relevant while discussing how order and *dharma* were related in external engagements and domestic governance frameworks, the normative dimensions are illuminated by understanding the link between *dharma*, order, and morality at the domestic level, where the use of just rod was emphasised. Meanwhile, the analytical linkage is laid out in the details of how order is to be maintained at the domestic and external level (through the constituent elements) and the cultural dimension is related to the cognitive-philosophical aspects associated with the Hindu political thought.

Order in the *Arthaśāstra*

To understand the linkage between *dharma* and order, the etymology of *dharma* becomes significant. Dharma stems from the Sanskrit word *Dhṛ*, meaning to hold.[38] Broadly understood as the concept which holds the society together, *dharma* had a special place in ancient state systems as the society was held together by each individual and group doing his or her specific duty. *Daṇḍa* or the power of rod was needed in order to regulate *dharma*.

Bhikhu Parekh writes that "for the Hindu political thinkers, the universe is an ordered whole governed by fixed laws. It is characterised by *Ṛta*, the inviolable order of things. While society becomes an ordered whole when held together by *dharma*, what ordered the societal *dharma* - was the *karma* of the individual."[39] In this context, the *dharma* of king directed the broad contours of political virtue – the qualities broadly identified with that of a just king. An individual's *karma* not only determined his caste but also his *dharma*. The idea of morality as duty (a righteous conduct) is present in the *Arthaśāstra* in different degrees, and is primarily operationalised through the concept of *dharma*. Broadly understood thus, the concept *dharma* can be translated as holding together. One can also say that *dharma* had a special place in ancient state systems as the society was held together by each individual and group doing his or her specific duty. *Daṇḍa* or the power of rod was needed or legitimised to regulate this *dharma*. *Dharma*, thus, was indeed a cognitive prism endowing meaning to order.

One can say that the concept of *dharma* captured the idea of a moral order in the *Arthaśāstra* and this concept of morality balanced pragmatism with virtue. One can also say that the moral order was about thinking strategies or crafting policies, which minimised harm to one's own citizens (duty) and Kauṭilya was very categorical in stating that the interest of the state or the population or subjects in general should be prioritised. The idea of advancing just administration is central to the Kauṭilyan analysis of order at the domestic level.

When transposed to the international level, order does find an important place in Kauṭilya's *maṇḍala* theory – the circle of states. *Maṇḍala* theory represented a unique order of states, wherein one could identify one's foes and allies not only in terms of geographical proximity, but also in terms of their strength and intentions. These operative principles of order can be understood through the articulation of *'the maṇḍala'*. If one moves on to the *maṇḍala* theory one finds that the capacity of the state is important as it constituted the cornerstone of order, which was deliberated upon, as one engaged with actors at the external level. The state qualified with the excellences of the key components of the *saptānga* theory had the potential to become the leader (*vijigīṣu*). The *maṇḍala* theory was so much informed by the respective strength of the state actors that one can frame it as a distinct geo-political order on its own terms. To read *maṇḍala* theory without the state (in terms of its capacity and strength, i.e. material factors) is therefore misconstrued, given the Kauṭilyan emphasis on the *saptānga* theory. *Maṇḍala* theory consisted of the circle of states, consisting of allies, enemies and neutrals. While there were twelve[40] actors which have been identified, for clarity and broad relevance five independent actors existed. The five independent actors, which therefore need to be reckoned with are: the conqueror (dominant state at the centre),[41] the enemy,[42] the ally,[43] the middle king[44] and the neutral king.[45] The rest of the categories were classified as per the sequence established for identifying enemies and allies. These actors were important as they acted as facilitators to measure the success of diplomacy. An understanding on the intent of these actors determined the method which needed to be employed for diplomatic engagement. An important pointer in identifying the intent was the motivation of the actor and its internal cohesiveness – which is embodied in the seven constituent elements. The more qualified a particular state was in terms of seven key elements of the *saptānga* theory, the more susceptible and aware was one to become of its motivation. The *maṇḍala* thus constituted of a total of seventy two elements which was numerically arrived by taking into account the individual attributes of the state, its allies, its enemies, the neutral king and middle king.

A parallel can be drawn to the concept of 'geo-political orders' (international grouping), which Benno Teschke advances. According to Teschke, the constitution, operation and transformation of geo-political orders is predicated on the changing identities of the constitutive units. In Kauṭilyan terms, the constituent units were predicated upon the internal strength, which gave the state a distinct identity of the most dominant state at the international level. If the state declined in terms of its capacity and influence, it no longer was feasibly proximate to achieving the dominant status of the *vijigīṣu* but, at the same time, had policy references in the *maṇḍala*, given the *Arthaśāstra's* emphasis on the policies which need to be adopted by the weak king. Thus, it could, through adaptive posturing (the six methods of foreign policy – *ṣāḍguṇya*), desire to become the leader (*vijigīṣu*). The circle of states was thus a fluid entity, which was prone to transformational elements dependent on state capacity and influence. The inside-outside or the internal-external dichotomy thus seems superficial in the *Arthaśāstra*.

As evident through the discussion above, the details provided by Kauṭilya on sustaining order are significant. Order, thus, was not an arrangement which was fragile. To borrow the words of Stanley Hoffman and transpose it to the understanding here, "order was not temporary to the quantity of power that supported it, nor was dependent on a momentary convergence of interests." The norms of order in the *Arthaśāstra* were reflective more as an instrument of grand strategy seeking to reconcile the desirable elements with the most feasible ones. The broad strategic objective was to augment and strengthen the power of the state in the long term – and *maṇḍala* was a natural corollary to facilitate his end-goal in mind. The reflection of *dharma*, which becomes preponderant to the maintenance of order within the circle of states seems to be particularly relevant in these terms.

Theorising Beyond Paradigms

If one was to frame Kauṭilya as a strategist and his work the *Arthaśāstra* as a work of grand strategy, the ends-means relationship seems to be the most appropriate framework. The departure point for using this frame of analysis is the Kauṭilyan idea of state, which was monitored and regulated, aiming at the optimum use of all possible sources for the benefit of state and its citizens.[46] Ritu Kohli's analysis seems to be most appropriate, and can be considered as a pointer to understanding the Kauṭilyan grand strategy. She writes that, "Kautilya's conception of state was so comprehensive in scope that it regulated even the minutest details like fixing the rates of washer men and even prostitutes." According to her, "Kautilyan state not only subordinated moral principles to the necessities of its own existence and welfare but the same attitude was adopted towards religion which was often used as a means for accomplishing political ends."[47] The understanding of morality which Kohli writes about, was conveyed through the notion of *dharma* being personified by the state. This is well reflected in other writings too. For instance M. Sankhdher writes that, "for Kautilya upholding the *dharma*, good governance was the main aim of the state."[48] This preeminent role and place of state in ancient Indian political thought is instructive in terms of the strategic end which it aimed to serve. The end here being primarily related to the maintenance of social and political stability. An important concept which has been used extensively by Kauṭilya to facilitate this end-goal was the concept of *yogakṣema* – which, as an umbrella concept, ensured the stability of the state. In the Kauṭilyan strategy, *yogakṣema*, thus, can be considered as the primary end goal.

As stated earlier, the *maṇḍala* thus constituted of a total of seventy two elements which was numerically arrived by taking into account the individual attributes of the state, its allies, its enemies, the neutral king and the middle king. The means of arriving at these was by enumerating value on the constituent elements of the set of allies, enemies, middle king and the neutral king – where the conqueror and the enemy were common elements in interacting with the middle king and neutral king. Thus, the conqueror, the ally and the ally's ally comprised one circle, and constituted of eighteen elements – where each of the three actors had their specific six constituent elements in place, i.e. king, councillors, territory and population, forts, treasury and army. Similarly, the enemy, enemy's ally and the enemy's ally's ally comprised of another eighteen constituent elements. The *madhayma* and the *udāsīna* had their respective eighteen constituent elements each in place. All together these included seventy-two constituent elements. Kauṭilya writes, "There are twelve constituents who are kings, sixty material constituents, a total of seventy-two in all. Each of these has its own peculiar excellences."[49] The Kauṭilyan diplomacy was therefore about managing, regulating and balancing these seventy-two constituent elements (the excellences), and therefore can be considered sub-circles of regulating order towards a purposive goal, where order could best be utilised for advancing, guiding and directing the position of a state in the *maṇḍala*, through the use of the six methods of foreign policy (*ṣāḍguṇya*) or the four methods (*upāyas*). In other words these were indicators for aligning and adapting to the exogenous and endogenous structures, and the *maṇḍala* itself was the framework which gave meaning to the inherent inter-relationship between these factors. One can also say, the concept of *maṇḍala* aimed to illuminate the inter-dependence between parts, it was an interconnected arrangement between various parts where the internal and external were inevitably related in the *Arthaśāstra*. The strategies and tactics associated with *ṣāḍguṇya* and *upāyas* are illustration of this inter-connectedness, which needed to be followed and matched up with agile, flexible and adaptive diplomatic practice. From a theoretical perspective, Kauṭilya's *Arthaśāstra* seems most proximate to systems theorisation.

Thus, the definition of morality which emerges from *Arthaśāstra* is relational and is shaped by upholding a certain form of order, which is duty-bound. This order differentiated between the right and wrong and posited a specific argument on what ought to be. The ought in this context is intertwined with the social norms of behaviour and material compulsions, which in the political domain needed to be preserved for the regulation of order and also sustainability of the political system. The primary objective of both statecraft and governance was to advance the preservation of state, the former was done by the *maṇḍala* theory, and the latter was done by seven constituent elements of state.

Thus, when analysed from the frames of anarchy and order, Kauṭilya's *Arthaśāstra* tilts towards the latter than the former. The primary reason for this is the importance of morality (*dharma*) in the *Arthaśāstra*– the personification of which is illuminated through the concept of state per se. *Dharma* in this context needs to be therefore understood in terms of ordering the political system.

Situating *Arthaśāstra* – Within or Beyond Paradigms?

Where does one situate the *Arthaśāstra*, within the broader theoretical discussion in International Relations? If one was to go back to the inter-paradigmatic discourse raised earlier, it would not be an exaggeration to state that English School's idea of international society offered a kind of middle ground or a via media between the extremes of liberal (or revolutionist) and realist view of international relations.[50] Meanwhile, there is also an explicit reference to classical realism – not neo-realism, which has emphasised on the balance of power politics – and hence the need for balancing the international system through statecraft. However, the difference between the *Arthaśāstra* and political realism lies in deterministic influence which the notion of anarchy and order have in the nuances, where the *Arthaśāstra* illuminates extensive details on regulating human nature and thereby the state (order) through a relativist understanding of *dharma* (morality). The explicit emphasis on the *saptānga* theory (state) and the *ṣāḍguṇya* theory (*maṇḍala*) underline the underlying assumption that the regulation of the state and the prescriptions stipulated in the *maṇḍala* – for a state to survive – was to maintain the element of order in the perceived circle of states (or units), which were in continuous interaction with each other.

While power as a concept does not seem anomalous to a discussion on the *Arthaśāstra*, the terms morality and order could appear unusual, unfamiliar and inconsistent. However, given the discussion on the methodology and sources that seemed to have influenced the *Arthaśāstra*, a discussion on morality and order seems pertinent. It is assumed that these concepts as discussed in the field of International Relations might seem to have a useful analytical value – not only in terms of identifying the ontological significance (directed towards understanding the reality) of the nuances that the *Arthaśāstra* brings in, but also identifying epistemological frames (directed towards understanding the relationship with knowledge – epistemology in this context is shaped by ones ontological frame) that are necessary to understand certain non-western perspectives.[51] Epistemological frames are important for guiding the methodology or the process of inquiry that one adopts in the course for understanding how knowledge has evolved over a period of time. Thus, the hermeneutical exercise or the methodology in the context of understanding a text like the *Arthaśāstra* becomes significant because it underlines the symbiotic relationship between ontology and epistemology, where both the frames of inquiry mutually interact with each other, paving way for a reflectivist tradition for understanding and explaining International Relations.[52] Advancing such an argument, Steve Smith argues, both ontology and epistemology are not prior to each other but instead are mutually and inextricably interrelated.[53] It, therefore, can be argued that interpreting and situating the *Arthaśāstra* within the field of International Relations can have a twofold relevance. First, its ontological significance, which means that "the traditional concerns of epistemology are inappropriate for understanding and making sense of our beliefs, since they posit the interpretive or observing subject as in some way prior to question about the nature of being."[54] Second, its epistemological relevance, which "underlines the importance of the embeddedness of all analyses in language and history."[55] In the context of the *Arthaśāstra*, the philosophical-cultural leanings of the text, which organically evolved from the ancient Hindu political thought, becomes relevant. Attempting to counter the arguments where often ontological frames guide epistemological inquiries, Smith highlights the views of Gadamer who comments on the fuzziness which exists between ontology and epistemology. Gadamer, as cited in Smith writes that, "this embeddedness means that notions of truth and reason are themselves historically constituted, so that the kinds of claims about objective knowledge that have dominated epistemological discussions between rationalism and empiricism are fundamentally mistaken."[56] Given this interdependence, juxtaposing the philosophical relevance of the *Arthaśāstra* and its distinct interpretive-reflectivist focus in understanding central concepts – which governed the ideas dictating strategy – become important. It is primarily for this reason that

Kauṭilya's *Arthaśāstra* cannot be situated within or either of the paradigm driven framework (Realism or Constructivism) of International Relations. An alternative-revisionist understanding of the text is emphasised in this context.

Another reason why it could be inappropriate to associate the understanding and meanings of concepts, which stem from the *Arthaśāstra*, to frameworks available in International Relations Theory, is the context of embeddedness of the text in the tradition per se. Most of the concepts employed in International Relations are contextually embedded in the Western philosophical tradition which has often limited contributions from the epistemological and ontological point of view.[57] This argument of embeddedness has been raised by some other scholars such as Terence Ball and Leigh Jenco, who have exposed the limitations of these approaches as they tend to "exclude certain ancient/premodern and preliberal knowledge of political things", thus highlighting possibilities of excluding epistemic contribution of the significant other or marginalised body of knowledge. Leigh Jenco writes, exploration such as this, "seems especially necessary now that political theory and philosophy increasingly recognises the value of historically marginalised thought traditions, but nevertheless continue to engage those traditions using methodologies noted in their own concerns, such as to rectify inequalities of power or to address (mis-)representations of historically marginalised groups."[58] So, it is recognised that while each concept is context specific, nevertheless, it must also be emphasised that undertaking textual analyses of non-western intellectual resources and the relevance it holds for understanding concepts widely used in the discipline and vocabulary of international relations is integral to the task of a student who wants to examine the 'international' in international relations.[59] Studying of contextualised concepts and then juxtaposing them with the generic understanding of concepts per se thus can prove helpful in effectively bridging the incommensurability that exists between the Western and the non-Western ways of understanding international relations. As Farah Godrej points out, "the task of the political theorist must be followed by the project to disturb, provoke and dislocate familiar modes of knowledge through speech and discourse."[61] Given that this debate has animated International Relations to a great extent too, a key question that must be asked is that how does one proceed with such cross-cultural conceptual comparisons, especially when some of the concepts in International Relations owe their genealogy to Western philosophical tradition. This is particularly so, because the danger of conceptual translation is often accompanied by absorbing concepts into a familiar vocabulary, which often dilutes the meaning of certain concepts emerging from other cultures, often making them appear unintelligible.[61] Xianlong Zhang offers a useful way out as a methodological reflection to cross-cultural comparison. Zhang argues that "general comparisons cannot be made on the level of concepts and propositions but can only be achieved through inter-paradigmatic conditions, where we have a sharp awareness of a paradigm's boundary from which we can attempt to achieve a situational communication with another paradigm."[62]

In this context, it is argued that situating Kauṭilya as a realist or constructivist is neither important nor relevant. In fact it can be problematic from the perspective of the genealogies of ideas and traditions, where political realism could appear as a normative theory on its own account.[63] However, where ideas and concepts can help, is in identifying the situational awareness of the text in-between paradigms, and the conceptual nuances that therefore inform such a process, can help in understanding the ontological and the epistemological contribution that non-Western intellectual resources make to concepts used in International Relations.[64]

From a theoretical vantage point, while the *Arthaśāstra* might appear to echo shades of realism, neorealism, constructivism, etc., its explanatory richness stems from the interconnectedness which lay at the foundation the political systems of the time. It thus needs, perhaps, to be reinstated that while much has been written on the realist undercurrents of Kauṭilyan thought (which is both ontologically and epistemologically problematic), few studies have been undertaken to understand Kauṭilya's *Arthaśāstra* from a systems perspective. Upendra Baxi notes that texts like the *Arthaśāstra* "provide analytical value to the work of system theorist like Morton Kaplan."[65] Seeking to establish the contemporary relevance of Kauṭilya, Baxi agrees with ontological and epistemological argument that Drekmeier makes, stating that it "is our responsibility to apply the refinements of methodology and the social sciences in searching out the intended or latent sense of the ideas that confront us. The discovery of meanings that might otherwise remain hidden to us is a nobler employment for our newer knowledge than its restriction to the essentially negative tasks of controverting and deriding."[66] Ontologically, then, Kauṭilya's identity as a system theorist becomes significant and the concepts of power, order and morality find significance within this broader framework. It is for this reason that this chapter intentionally avoids the possibility of studying the concept of balance and order from a realist/neorealist/constructivist perspective. The primary reason for doing so is to trace the identity of Kauṭilya as a grand strategist. Given the relativist understanding of the concepts like morality, order and power, which can be defined/redefined/revisited as per the limits set by each of these theoretical strands, an attempt to understand the *Arthaśāstra* as a text of philosophy and strategy can get compromised in due process. Then, it would be appropriate to treat the *Arthaśāstra* as a work proximate to systems theory – a work which focuses on the notion of order and balance in a political system, and the implication this does hold for understanding the interconnectedness that exists – between the parts and the whole or within the internal and external.

END NOTES

1. Reus-Smit and Snidal (2008: 4).
2. *Ibid.*: 6.
3. *Ibid.*: 8.
4. Rosenau (1980: 31).
5. *Ibid.*
6. Waltz (1979: 5).
7. *Ibid.*: 7.
8. *Ibid.*: 10. Also cf. Rosenau (1980: 19-31).
9. Prakash (1993).
10. Sandel (2009).
11. *Ibid.*: 8.
12. Witze (2012: 137).
13. A detailed exposition of this concept was discussed by the author at the Institute for Defence Studies and Analyses, New Delhi conference.
14. Prakash (1993).
15. *Ibid.*
16. Sarkar (1939: 211).
17. *Ibid.*
18. Thapar (2002: 52-53).
19. *Ibid.*: 53.
20. Chousalkar (1986: 68).
21. Sharma (1990: 158).
22. *Ibid.*
23. Chousalkar (1981:54-55).
24. Thapar (2003: 392).
25. Kangle (2010b: 10), [1.4.8-16].
26. *Ibid.*: 190-196, [3.1].
27. Kohli (1995: 14, 19). *Dharma* has been understood as a matter of law or eternal truth – that is supposed to be the basis of *dharma*; and king, the deliverer of the law. Kangle (2010b: 195-196), note 39 of Kangle (2010b: 195) as well.
28. Parekh (2010: 108).
29. *Ibid.*
30. Puntambekar (1948: 2).
31. Parel, Anthony J. (2008: 41).
32. Kangle (2010b: 6), [1.2.9].
33. Alexander Wendt, in contrast, treats international system as a dependent variable and ideas, according to him, need to be foregrounded in making sense of the material reality of the international system. For him ideas need not be seen in causal terms but in constitutive terms.

34. *Ibid.*: 320, [6.2.39-40].
35. Sarkar (1939: 105).
36. For a detailed analysis cf. Slakter (2011).
37. A detailed analyses of these concepts have been undertaken in Medha Bisht, "The Concept of Order in Arthashastra", *South Asian Survey,* 21(1/2), 2014. (Yet to be released).
38. Parekh (2010: 109).
39. *Ibid.*: 108.
40. *Ari* – antagonist; *Śatru* – enemy; *Mitra* – friend/ally; *Ari-Mitra* – enemy's ally; *Mitra-Mitra* – friend of an ally; *Arimitra-Mitra* – enemy's ally's friend; *Pārṣṇigrāha* – enemy in the rear; *Ākrānda* – ally in the rear; *Pārṣṇigrāhāsāra* – rear enemy's ally; *Ākrāndasāra* – rear ally's friend; *Antarṣi* – weak intervening king; *Udāsīna* – neutral king; *Madhyama* – middle king.
41. Conqueror is a king ready for enlargement. The prerequisite for being a conqueror is a king, who has excellent personal qualities, resources and constituents of his state and follows good policies.
42. Enemy or an antagonist is defined as a king, whose kingdom shares a common border. However, there, not all the kingdoms are enemies worth the attention, as a king *deemed* to be an antagonist is the one, who has powerful excellent personal qualities, resources and constituents. There are vulnerable enemies – the one inflicted by a calamity. One who is weak and without support is a destroyable antagonist and one that has support is an antagonist that can be weakened. Of the most dangerous of all is an antagonist by intent. The characteristics of a destroyable antagonist are: greedy, vicious, trusting in fate, unjust behaviour, does harm to others, mean *mantripariṣad*, with unhappy subjects, powerless or helpless. Note the element of unjust behaviour as one characteristic which weakens the enemy. The inimical neighbours are soulless enemy with an intent on harming the neighbour. Enemy in the rear allied with enemy in the front is a potential source of threat. Enemy is also one who has suffered a calamity and is vulnerable to the attack of the conqueror; and one attacking the conqueror, taking advantage of the latter's calamity.
43. Ally is a king whose territory has a common border with an antagonist. A natural ally is one who is noble by birth or related to the conqueror. An ally by intent is one who needs the conqueror for wealth or personal safety. Interestingly, Kauṭilya adds, kinship can be a source of enmity or friendship. Common interest may bring them together and opposing interest may make them allies. An ally is thus defined as one with the same objective. Vassal neighbours who can be controlled are also allies.
44. Middle King is the one whose territory is contiguous to that of the conqueror and the conqueror's enemy, who is powerful enough to help them, whether they are united or not, or to destroy them individually when they are disunited. Middle King is important because it can influence the balance of power between two groups – the conqueror and his friends on one hand, and the enemy and his friends on the other.
45. A neutral king is one whose territory is not contiguous with those of the conqueror, and the conqueror's enemy, or the middle king (totally outside the area of hostilities) who is stronger than the three and powerful enough to help the three, whether they are united or not, or to destroy them individually when they are not.
46. Kohli (1995: 14).
47. *Ibid.*
48. Cited in *Ibid.*: 19.
49. Kangle (2010b: 319), [6.2.28-29].
50. Buzan (2004).

51. Deepshikha Shahi and Gennaro Ascone have argued for going beyond the Western scienticism, aiming at breaking the epistemological dominance of Western perspectives and reorienting International Relations to post Western understanding. The authors propose the concept of Advaitic monism, wherein the perpetually connected globe has no separate existence apart from Brahman, as the epistemological ground for theorising post-Western IR. cf. Shahi and Ascone (2015).
52. Weaver (1996).
53. Smith (1996: 18).
54. *Ibid.*: 26.
55. *Ibid.*
56. *Ibid.*: 27.
57. Vivekanandan draws attention to this point and situates her analyses from the post-modernist lens of the contextual embeddedness of texts, cautioning against the neutrality of concepts discussed in IR. Vivekanandan (2015).
58. Jenco (2012: 93).
59. Farah Godrej has emphasised the need for a cosmopolitan political thought, where rather than seeking universal values, one should examine the new insights from that of assorted traditions. She argues both Confucius' Analects and *Bhagwadgīta* could not only be seen as objects of contextualised inquiry, but also potential sources of politically relevant knowledge across time and space. Godrej (2011: 162).
60. Godrej (2011: 162).
61. Jenco (2012).
62. Zhang (2010).
63. The literature associated with evaluative realism is significant in this regard. cf. Rengger (2000), Murray (1997), Spegele (1996).
64. David Kang's analyses on Asian International Relations, Kang (2007). Also cf. Mott and Kim (2006) [particularly Chapter One] and Lai (2004).
65. Baxi (1967: 13).
66. *Ibid.*

6

Rājadharma, Legitimacy and Sovereignty in the *Arthaśāstra*

Saurabh Mishra

Introduction

The *Arthaśāstra*, compiled by Kautilya, is an important text that gives a view of a serious tradition of gubernatorial, political, economic and strategic thinking in ancient India. The text has consistently influenced the political and strategic ideas in the vast varieties of Indian literature since ancient times. This, also known as the *Kauṭilīya Arthaśāstra*, is an important text related to the science of governance and politics, precisely "the science of acquisition and protection of the earth" (*yogakṣema*).[1] Kauṭilya asserts that it is a compilation of the knowledge preceding him since ancient times;[2] a repository of traditional concepts and understanding regarding a ruler's conduct (personal and public) in the intrastate and interstate spheres. Kauṭilya's personal positions on certain issues are also present in the form of his comments as he explicitly agrees or disagrees with some of the opinions of earlier scholars.

However, the *Arthaśāstra* has been generally charged by scholars for being extremely amoral/immoral. Scholars like Benoy Kumar Sarkar, D.D. Kosambi, Max Weber, George Modelski and Roger Boesche consider the author of the text as a staunch immoral/amoral realist. This perception about the text is evident in the fact that Roger Boesche criticises him[3] for being an "unrelenting political realist".[4] Boesche remarks:

> Is there any other book that talks so openly about when using violence is justified? When assassinating an enemy is useful? When killing domestic opponents is wise? How one uses secret agents? When one needs to sacrifice one's own secret agent?

> How the king can use women and children as spies and even assassins? When a nation should violate a treaty and invade its neighbour? Kauṭilya and to my knowledge only Kauṭilya – addresses all these questions. In what cases a king spy on his own people? How should a king test his ministers, even his own family members, to see if they are worthy of trust? When must a king kill a prince, his own son, who is heir to the throne? How does one protect a king from poison? What precautions must a king take against assassination by one's own wife? When is it appropriate to arrest a troublemaker on suspicion alone? When is torture justified?...Is there not one question that Kauṭilya found immoral, too terrible to ask in a book?[5]

Arthaśāstra prescribes many things that are not generally accepted as ethical, although it mentions certain texts and traditions which have a lot of ethical deliberations as their core subject. These texts have been suggested as an essential part of the training of the king in governance. Another point is the fact that *rājadharma* is the popular indigenous Indian term for 'political ethics' or the duties and responsibilities of the king/ruler. The legitimacy, authority and sovereignty of the king are connected with the common thread of 'political ethics' or *rājadharma* in a given society that is, for this chapter, the social context of the *Arthaśāstra. Dharma* has been the axis of the Hindu thought on ethics which has a direct relationship with *rājadharma. Rājadharma* is considered as the soul of the indigenous/Hindu theory of state; and the origin/existence and sustenance of the state are related to it. The term is the traditional, primarily ethical, yardstick for evaluation of the performance of the state and the government. This seems to be in contradiction with the general perception created by scholars about the *Arthaśāstra*, the text that is the only ancient Indian systematic text focusing on the "art of governance". However, this is difficult to believe that a society with a strong ethical tradition of *rājadharma* has completely ignored it in its only systematic text available on the behaviour of the king and the state in intra and interstate environment. In the light of these facts, this chapter attempts to understand how the 'unethical' precepts and suggestions within the text of *Arthaśāstra* are explained or defended. In other words, the chapter looks for the ethical thread of the *Arthaśāstra.* It attempts to decipher and describe the ethical philosophical systems within the text and its relevance to the purpose of the *Arthaśāstra* by engaging with a few relevant modern fundamental concepts of political science like legitimacy, authority and sovereignty of the king/state. Therefore, the chapter first explores the relationship of *dharma* and *rājadharma*, the meaning of *rājadharma* within the *Arthaśāstra* and then the issue of legitimacy of king and his actions, his authority and sovereignty; all related to each other with the common thread of *rājadharma*.

The Intellectual Context of the *Arthaśāstra*

The *Arthaśāstra* is indispensably important for the study of ancient Indian strategic, political and gubernatorial thinking as it is the only systematic ancient Indian text written for the purpose of serving as a guide for the king in the ancient Hindu world.[6] The text does not focus on religion or any social or familial aspects in detail. Whatever references have been made to the religious or social aspects in the text, they have been made from the perspective of governance or maintenance of order, legitimacy, authority or hegemony of the king in the state or inter-state socio-political milieu. No hymns or verses have been written in the text to please the gods or any other authority, divine or temporal. This is a deviation from the larger bulk of ancient Indian texts which has been written primarily in the context of the maintenance of the social order based on religion embedded in the *dharmaśastras*. In fact, the text is said to be "essentially a treatise on the art of government".[7]

The *Arthaśāstra* is a departure from the general style of presenting the conceptual and theoretical treasure and the understanding of the ancient Indian socio-political world that has been primarily spiritual in nature. The text, in comparison with the religious style, has been written with a pure academic perspective. It does talk about the relevant social and religious contexts of the time in the very beginning, and later, occasionally, but only briefly, i.e. only what is necessary to understand the contemporary intellectual (ontological, epistemological, legal) and social context of the text that influences its functional and implementation aspects. Thereafter, it becomes a manual with the chapters and clauses focusing on the functional aspects of the gubernatorial and political life of the king (*rāja/vijigīṣu*)[8] of a state.

To look for a possibility of an ethical approach in the text of the *Arthaśāstra*, we need to understand the intellectual and social context of the text. Kauṭilya gives ample insight into the intellectual context of the *Arthaśāstra* in the first five chapters of his Book I, titled "Concerning the Topic of Training". This training is meant for the king to be a good and efficient ruler. He mentions that *Ānvīkṣikī* (the science of enquiry), *Trayī* (the three Vedas – *Ṛgveda, Yajurveda* and *Sāmaveda*), *Vārttā* (economics) and *Daṇḍanīti* (science of politics) are the actual means of knowledge (*Vidyā*).[9] He considers *Ānvīkṣikī* (the science of enquiry) as the "lamp of all sciences", "means of all actions" and as "the support of all *dharma* (laws and duties)".[10] Although there are popularly six orthodox schools of ancient Indian philosophy and several other unorthodox schools, for Kauṭilya, *Sāṃkhya, Yoga* and *Lokāyata* are the ones that constitute *Ānvīkṣikī* (the science of enquiry). The first two of these schools belong to the orthodox spiritual category while the third is an unorthodox materialist, empirical, positivist and atheist school. The orthodox schools are considered to be tracing their roots to the *Vedas* and commonly believing in certain principles and notions like *saṃsāra*,[11] *karma*,[12] *punarjanma* (rebirth),[13] etc. while the others repudiate the authority of the *Vedas*. Elaborating on the importance of the training in *Ānvīkṣikī*, Kauṭilya says:

> Investigating, by means of reasoning, (what is) spiritual good and evil in the Vedic lore, material gain and loss in economics, good policy and bad policy in the science of politics, as well as the relative strength and weakness of these (three sciences), (*Ānvīkṣikī*/philosophy/science of enquiry) confers benefit on the people, keeps mind steady in adversity and in prosperity and brings about proficiency in thought, speech and action.[14]

Kauṭilya, by this, sets the intellectual tone of the text that is based on "reasoning". He advises the use of reason to distinguish the good (*dharma*) and bad (*adharma*) even within the *Vedic* lore, the gain and loss in the context of *Vārttā* (economics) and the relative strengths of the three constituents of *Ānvīkṣikī* in different aspects. So, he, in the beginning of the training of the king calls the aspirer to read the *śāstras* and to attain the knowledge as revealed and suggested by the systems constituting *Ānvīkṣikī* that focused on *gyānapakṣa* (aspect of knowledge) rather than faith or ritualistic religion of any kind.

The text begins with a tribute and salutation to Śukra (named Uśanas sometimes)[15] and Bṛhaspati who are also known as the founders of the *Arthaśāstra* tradition. Although, the main original texts of the two ancient scholars are not available, they have been related to an atheist empirical and positivist branch of philosophy called the *Lokāyata*. The main work on the system, the *Bṛhaspati Sūtra* (approx. 600 BCE) is not available.[16] While Bṛhaspati considers *Vārttā* (economics) and *Daṇḍanīti* (politics) as the only sciences,[17] Uśanas considers only *Daṇḍanīti* as the worthwhile 'science' as it is linked with all other 'sciences'.[18]

Kauṭilya also mentions the "followers of Manu" (the *mānavāh*)[19] while elucidating the sciences relevant to the *Arthaśāstra*. Prof. Kangle warns of confusing this with Manu who is assumed to be the author of the text *Manusmṛti*. He considers that "this (*mānavāh*) refers to a school of *Arthaśāstra* and not to the *Manusmṛti*"[20] which is quite true as the text of the currently available *Manusmṛti* is a much later work. However, the tradition of the thoughts compiled in the *Manusmṛti* is much older than the text of the *Arthaśāstra*. Kangle explains that the *mānavāh* cannot be related to *Manusmṛti* as they accept there are only three sciences,[21] while the *Manusmṛti* names four.[22] Kauṭilya also considers four disciplines as the sciences that are same as in the *Manusmṛti*.[23] This gives a fresh reason to think about the proximity of Kauṭilya to the school of Manu who accepts four sciences including *Ānvīkṣikī* that the *mānavāh* do not consider. Perhaps both *mānavāh* and the author(s) of *Manusmṛti* belong to the same tradition but as different schools which differ on the acceptance of *Ānvīkṣikī* as a science. However, despite the difference on the dates of the compilation of both the *Arthaśāstra* and *Manusmṛti*, they seem to have traces of a common tradition that includes the ideas of both the *mānavāh* and the 'original' tradition that evolved and culminated into *Manusmṛti*. Portions of these texts have similarities and common ideas like the preservation of the *varṇāshramadharma*.[24] John Mckenzie in his *Hindu Ethics: A Historical and Critical Essay* writes that "Hindu scholars regarded this work (*Mānav Dharma Śāstra*) as containing the teaching of Manu, 'the son of the Self-existent', who received it direct from the Creator, Brahmā. Modern scholars are now agreed that *Mānava Dharma Śāstra* is a recast of an old *Mānav Dharma Śūtra*, a lost law-book of the school of the *Mānavans* (*mānavāh*), one of the families which gave themselves to the study of Vedic science."[25] He further says that "its (*Mānava Dharma Śāstra's*) authority was still more strongly established as an outcome of the fiction by which it came to be connected not with the *Mānavans* but with Manu, the father of human race."[26] Mckenzie's proposition points about the commonality of the tradition of the *Mānava Dharma Śāstra* (*Manusmṛti*) and the *mānavāh* as this could not have been rightly or wrongly attributed to Manu without any similarities.[27] This is relevant to understand the intellectual and social context of the text of the *Arthaśāstra*.

Kauṭilya alludes towards the epics of *Rāmāyaṇa* and *Mahābhārata*, although not directly, as he mentions the characters of both the epics like Rāvaṇa and Duryodhana respectively while discussing about the importance of control by the king over his senses and getting rid of 'six vices'[28] in the sixth chapter of Book I.[29] He explained how these two characters perished and lost their kingdom as they had no control over their vices. The precedence of these two epics also helps us in reconstructing and understanding the intellectual and social context of the text of the *Arthaśāstra* as they are windows to the social-political life, values and ideas of their times that have perennially influenced the Hindu mind. Kauṭilya also prescribes that the king should be acquainted and trained with *Itihāsa*, i.e. the *Purāṇas*, *Itivṛtta*, *Ākhyāyikā*, *Udāharaṇa*, *Dharmaśastra* and finally the *Arthaśāstra* that we are dealing with in this chapter.[30] The *Upaniṣads* and *Brāhmaṇa* literature also reflect the ideas of the intellectual ecosystem as elucidated in the *Arthaśāstra*. On the importance of the training of the king within this ecosystem, Kauṭilya says that "from (continuous) study ensues a (trained) intellect, from intellect (comes) practical application, (and) from practical application (results) self-possession; such is the efficacy of sciences."[31] The purpose of the training of the king in the 'sciences' is to make him disciplined so that he is enabled to "enjoy the earth (alone) without sharing it with any other (ruler), being devoted to the welfare of all beings."[32]

Ample literature in the ecosystem deals with ethical issues, both personal and political, i.e. *dharma* and the *rājadharma*. The *Vedas*, *Dharmaśāstra*, *Rāmāyaṇa*, *Mahābhārata*, *Ānvīkṣikī*, etc. contemplate over important ethical questions about the nature and purpose of life like why and how to live. The personal and the social of the king/ruler cannot be isolated from the context and these relevant ethical questions that give meaning to life. This suggests a strong possibility of ethical system(s) within the context and the text of the *Arthaśāstra*.

The Ethical System(s) within the *Arthaśāstra*

The understanding of life or existence of an individual cannot be isolated from his/her socio-political functional aspects. These aspects can be understood by the study of the ontological, epistemological and philosophical systems influencing the consciousness, worldview and thereby the actions of an actor, i.e. the king in the context of this chapter. Not only Indian, but in all societies, the actions of individual actors, whether personal or social, depend on their self-consciousness, worldview, their understanding of the affairs and the environment they are dealing with. This is influenced by their ontological and epistemological convictions. They are at least supposed to act in these lines due to the contemporary social norms and understanding, even if not have faith in them, till they are in their social 'station'. *Ānvīkṣikī* in the *Arthaśastra* is the key to understand the ontological, epistemological and philosophical disposition of the king and the society on political issues. This also reveals the ethical/moral system(s) that is/are relevant to the personal and political levels that are *dharma* and *rājadharma* respectively. The *Sāṃkhya*, *Yoga* and *Lokāyata* schools of Indian philosophy constituting *Ānvīkṣikī* are the windows to the 'political ethics' (*rājadharma*) within the *Arthaśastra*. Before going to the actual constituents of *Ānvīkṣikī*, there is a need to know about the fundamentals of the orthodox Indian philosophy, that is the *Ṛta*, *Saṃsāra*, *Karma* and *Punarjanma*. These concepts are behind each of the orthodox and several unorthodox schools of the ancient Indian philosophy, although the unorthodox approach these terms, especially *punarjanma*, in radically different ways. The first two constituent systems in *Ānvīkṣikī* – *Sāṃkhya* and *Yoga* – have been acknowledged as two different but extremely connected philosophical schools; so much so that they are pronounced and studied together as the *Saṃkhya-Yoga*. The third, *Lokāyata*, is quite different from the two and the central functional philosophy of the *Arthaśastra* as its earliest known propounders, Bṛhaspati and Śukra, have been related to this school.

Sāṃkhya: This is a dualistic system that assumes the simultaneous existence of two fundamental entities in the cosmos – the *prakṛti* and *puruṣa*.[33] The whole perceptional and empirical world, the *saṃsāra*, emerges from the interaction of these two entities. The *prakṛti* is responsible for the material part of creation while the *puruṣa* is the consciousness in the *saṃsāra*. The *puruṣa* gets involved in *karma* (action) as it is inevitable while living in the *saṃsāra* that is full of pain (*duḥkha*) due to the involvement in *karma* and the causality associated with it. The *puruṣa* or the consciousness lives attached and involved in the *saṃsāra* as it assumes its image, generated while its interaction with the *prakṛti*, in *buddhi/mahat* (intellect) as its reality. The intellect gives *puruṣa* the sense of the 'I' and the doer attributing its actions to itself. However, this attribution and involvement in the *saṃsāra* keeps away the *puruṣa* from realising its true nature that is the uninvolved, detached, unagitated self which is stable forever. The agitations within the *puruṣa* is a result of its interaction with the *prakṛti* which carries three *guṇas* (qualities)[34] that are found in all the beings in the *saṃsāra* and are the causes of various feelings and sentiments like joy, grief, anger, etc. The *puruṣa* involved and attached in *karma* is reborn again in any of the different *yonis* (living creatures) depending on the kind of the *karma* and *guṇas* acquired in the previous life. Those who have a balance of good *karma* (full of *sattva*) after death, enjoy in *swarga* (heaven); and the beings acquiring a balance of bad karma (full of *tamas*) suffer in *narka* (hell). After spending their stipulated time, the souls are reborn according to the previous *karma*; and the cycle goes on. The aim of the *Sāṃkhya* is to get rid of this cycle of rebirth and become a free consciousness without any agitation. The reason for the attachment and involvement of the being in *saṃsāra* is *avidyā* (ignorance about the true nature of the *puruṣa*, i.e. both the *prakṛti* and *puruṣa*). The knowledge of the true nature of the two releases the *puruṣa* from all attachment and involvement; and it does not matter what his *karma* (good or bad) has been. The aim is to achieve the state of equilibrium in the *prakṛti* and an unagitated state of the *puruṣa* that is calm and serene forever as they have ever been, without a beginning and end. The state of the attainment of this knowledge is known as *mokṣa*. This can be achieved with the attainment of the knowledge of the two that is possible with the removal of the *Ahaṃkāra* (the sense of 'I' or the 'ego') generated by *buddhi* (intellect). *Sāṃkhya* does not accept the existence of any supreme being (*Īśvara*) that is all powerful and possesses good attributes. For this, there are only two entities - *prakṛti* (just one in number) and *puruṣa* (many in number). Therefore, this is considered as one of the atheist philosophies. But, due to the recognition to the *Vedas*, this is accepted in the orthodox school.[35]

Yoga: This system is only slightly different from the *Sāṃkhya*. There are 25 elements/principles in the *Sāṃkhya* system, while *Yoga* accepts *Īśvara* as the 26th element, adding one more to the system. The rest is similar to the *Sāṃkhya* with an emphasis on the process of the attainment of knowledge (*vidyā*) and getting rid of *avidyā*, i.e. knowing the true nature of the *prakṛti* and *puruṣa*. *Īśvara* is the supreme *puruṣa* who is *nityamukta* (free from bondage and attachment with the *saṃsāra* forever). *Īśvara* is beyond time and directions. He contains all knowledge and majesty. He is just a special *puruṣa* that exists simultaneously with numerous other *puruṣas* and one and the only *prakṛti*, but is not the driver, determinant, preserver or destroyer of the *saṃsāra*.[36]

This school focuses on the various practical processes that help in the attainment of the knowledge of the 'self' and the reality. The system elucidates that the *sattvaguṇa* (the element of the *prakṛti* that signifies whatever is pure, fine, calm and able to distinguish between good and bad) helps attain *mokṣa* (liberation from the cycle of birth and attainment of the true knowledge of *puruṣa*). One can attain *mokṣa* by following *aṣtāṃgikayoga* (eight limbs of *yoga*) – *yama* (self-restraint), *niyama* (observance),[37] *āsana* (right posture that keeps the body and the mind calm and stable), *prāṇāyāma* (regulation of breath), *pratyāhār* (withdrawal of the senses), *dhāraṇā* (steadying the mind), *dhyān* (contemplation), *samādhi* (meditative trance).[38]

Lokāyata: The origins of this system, also known as the *Chārvāka* system, can be traced as far as the *Ṛgveda* but it does not attempt to justify its principles by recognising the authority of the *Vedas*. They hold that the authors of the *Vedas* "were buffoons, knaves, and demons".[39] "All the well-known formulas of pandits…And all the obscene rites for the queen commanded in the *Aśvamedha*, ...were invented by buffoons, and so all the various kinds of presents to the priests."[40] The rituals and the related texts, according to them, "were made by nature as the livelihood of those destitute of knowledge and manliness."[41] Although the main work on this philosophy, the *Bṛhaspati Sūtra* is lost, we can find several comments, statements of position and criticism of the same in other works. This is an atheist school that does not believe in any supreme all powerful being attributed with good qualities, sometimes called as the *Īśvara* by different schools, although in different senses. This is a materialist positivist philosophy. It holds that:

> only this world exists and there is no beyond. There is no future life. Perception is the only source of knowledge; what is not perceived does not exist…As perception is the only form of valid knowledge, matter, which alone is cognised by the senses, is the only reality…The ultimate principles are the four elements: earth, water, fire and air. Consciousness is a material and transitory modification of these elements and will disappear when these elements, from which it is produced, are dissolved.[42]

Further, intelligence is produced in the same way as the consciousness above; the soul is only the body qualified by intelligence and has no existence apart from the body. The most important ideas of this philosophy directly relevant to the purpose of this chapter is that:

> The postulates of religion, God, freedom, and immortality, are illusions. Nature is indifferent to good and evil, and history does not bear witness to Divine Providence. Pleasure and pain are the central facts of life. Virtue and vice are not absolute values but mere social conventions.[43]

As the *Lokāyata* denies any supreme spiritual other worldly authority, it recognises the king (earthly monarch) as the only supreme authority.[44] On the issue of *mokṣa*, it holds that the dissolution of the body as the only liberation. For *cārvākas*, "sustenance and love are the objects of human existence".[45] The way of life suggested by the *Lokāyata/Cārvākas* is summarised as such in the *Sarvadarśanasaṃgraha*:

> While life is yours, live joyously;
> None can escape Death's searching eye:
> When once this frame of ours they burn,
> How shall it e'er again return?[46]

In the presence of the discussed three schools of philosophy within *Ānvīkṣikī* (the science of enquiry), the *Arthaśāstra* takes an eclectic approach towards the purpose of life, i.e. a comprehensive approach including both the spiritual and materialistic together. *Sāṃkhya* and *Yoga* primarily inform the king about the required attitude towards the conduct of life (*saṃsāra*/material) and the inevitability of *karma* (action), while the *Lokāyata* sets the functional and practical activity-oriented fundamentals in the material world. *Lokāyata* provides the principles of materialistic interactions that become the guiding principles of the "science of acquisition and protection of earth."

Ethic of the *Arthaśāstra*: The enquiry through *Ānvīkṣikī* (*Sāṃkhya*, *Yoga* and *Lokāyata*) reveals that the essence and true nature of life is neither good nor bad. According to *Sāṃkhya-Yoga*, the ultimate is *mokṣa* (deliverance) that is knowledge of the true being. The goodness or badness of *karma* in the *saṃsāra* carry no meaning and value after this knowledge; they are meaningful and worthwhile only in the state of *avidyā* (ignorance). The causality of the good and bad *karma* responsible for *punarjanma* dissolves into knowledge. Once attained, all actions, whether good or bad, lose its effect on the individual consciousness and it does not get bound to the cycle of birth again. Action with detachment is the supreme ethic for the *Sāṃkhya-Yoga*. The *Lokāyata* also gets rid of the causality of *karma* as it does not even think beyond the material perceptional world as the good and bad are just conventions. The *Lokāyata* does not look for a transcendental absolute truth and derives its principles just based on the empirical world of sensory experience. Attainment of pleasure and avoidance of pain is the supreme ethic of this school:

> A person is happy or miserable through [the laws of] nature; there is no other cause... The enjoyment of heaven lies in eating delicious food, keeping company of young women, using fine clothes, perfumes, garlands, sandal paste, etc. The pain of hell lies in the trouble that arise from enemies, weapons, diseases.[47]

This is to note that the *Sāṃkya-Yoga* and *Lokāyata* do not conflict with each other in the material world. In fact, all that is propounded by *Lokāyata* in the sensory world is accepted by the *Saṃkhya-Yoga* system within the *saṃsāra*. The difference between them is about the sources of knowledge (as *Lokāyatas* reject inference) and the nature of the 'reality'. There is not any major difference about the functional aspects in the material world but on the limits of pleasure and pain. The point here is that both agree on action (*karma*) and its meaninglessness for the ultimate goal of life (*mokṣa*). Kauṭilya adopts a balanced/equilibrium approach as he elucidates:

> He (the king) should enjoy sensual pleasures without contravening his spiritual good and material well-being; he should not deprive himself of pleasures…(he should devote himself) equally to the three goals of life which are bound up with one another. For, any one of (the three, viz.,) spiritual good (*dharma*), material well-being (*artha*) and sensual pleasures (*kāma*), (if) excessively indulged in, does harm to itself as well as to the other two.[48]

This was his view on the required attitude of a human being towards *sāṃsārik* (worldly) life, specifically for the king who is to be trained in the art of controlling the senses.[49] Together with this, he prioritised "material well-being" at his focus because spiritual good and sensual pleasures depend on it.[50] Therefore, the eclectic/holistic ethic of the *Arthaśāstra*, "the art of governance", combines the both and seems to be convinced with the attainment of pleasure and avoidance of pain with an attitude of detachment from the *saṃsāra* as its central ethical principle.

Dharma and *Rājadharma* in *Arthaśāstra*

Dharma is variously understood in the Indian society. The popular contemporary English translation for the term is 'religion' which is far from close to its meaning. The literal meaning of dharma is derived from the Sanskrit root word *Dhṛ* that means to bear, to support, to uphold.[51] *Dharma* is defined as '*dhārayate iti dharmaḥ*',[52] meaning that attribute which an entity (object or a person) bears is *dharma* of that object or person. This is understood not only with regard to human beings but with all living and non-living entities. *Dharma*, in this sense, is the attribute(s) or quality that is/are retained by any entity. This is also about its behaviour that it bears in an observable framework. The differences in the frameworks give *dharma* its different meanings like law, duty and justice.[53]

The determination of the *dharma* of an entity is a complex issue. The popular Indian schools of philosophies believe in the original cosmic order or law, the *Ṛta*.[54] This expresses itself as the enduring and firm laws of the perceivable universe/creation;[55] and it is approached and explained in different ways by the various systems within *Ānvīkṣikī*. Therefore, the meaning of *dharma* and then the *rājadharma* in the context of the *Arthaśāstra* has to be found in the three schools of philosophy as well as the intellectual-social context of the text. Presumably, the *Ṛta* cannot be defied by any entity existing in the cosmos as it is inherent in the being of everything. The cosmic *dharma* (*Ṛta*)[56] expresses itself in the ethical and the moral order of the universe as understood by the various schools of philosophies both orthodox and unorthodox - "*ekam sat viprāḥ bahudhā vadanti*" (that which exists is one, sages call it by various names).[57] The *Sāṃkhya-Yoga* system in the context of the human being identifies the behavioural pattern and attitude that is to be borne by the individuals for the knowledge (*vidyā*) of the true nature of the 'reality' (*puruṣa* and *prakṛti*); this we can call as *dharma*. The behavioural pattern as provided by this generates *sattvaguṇa* (the quality of purity) that helps the individual differentiate the good and the bad through reason/intellect;[58] and becoming aware of the true nature of the *saṃsāra* as well. *Dharma* in the *saṃsāra* for this system relates with the behavioural pattern and attitudinal set required to be inculcated and borne by the individual to achieve the state of *vidyā*, the true purpose of life (*mokṣa*). However, despite this meaning of *dharma* in the scientific sense, this school accepts the authority of the *Vedas* and other Brahmanical texts that mention *varṇāśrama-dharma*,[59] etc. These texts – *Trayi*, the *Sūtras* by the *Mānavah*, etc. – constituted the Brahmanical social order of the day and the laws governing the society (*dharma* as law). They were substantially governed by the tenets of the orthodox schools of philosophies, including the *Sāṃkhya-Yoga*, claiming them to be based on the cosmic order/*Ṛta*/the reality. The *Mānava Dharmasūtra* is probably the base text for the current text of *Manusmṛti*, as they belong to the same tradition, explaining the traditional Brahmanical/Āryan social order. Although, *Manusmṛti*, cannot be taken as the text to understand the *dharma* in the social context of the *Arthaśāstra* as it was written much later, some of the fundamentals like the *varṇāśrama-dharma* and the Brahmanical cosmology work as a framework of understanding.

The individual *dharma*, according to the *Lokāyatas*, is to do and bear all that gives pleasure and avoid all that is harmful. Given their philosophy, good and bad (virtue and vice) are just conventions according to the laws of the nature. *Dharma*, for them, are not the law books revealed by some other worldly powers and written by *Brāhmaṇs*. This must be societal convention based on empirical truth. The *dharma* in the sense of the *Sāṃkhya-Yoga* that recognises the *varṇāśrama-dharma* in the *saṃsāra*,[60] hence, is repudiated by the *Lokāyata*.

The reason is the origin of the *varṇāśrama-dharma* in the realm of metaphysics or imagination than empirical. This is peculiar to note that the text of the *Arthaśāstra* subscribing the *Lokāyata*[61] as its central philosophy simultaneously subscribes the Brahmanical *varṇāśrama-dharma* based on metaphysics as the ideal (ought to be) social order of the day. This gives a glimpse of Kauṭilya's holistic approach towards the social reality of his times in which an academic text had to acknowledge the powerful and the dominant social order of the day. Therefore, Kauṭilya's view of *dharma* and the *rājadharma*, although the use the term *rājadharma* in the *Arthaśāstra* is disputed, is a peculiar mix of both the orthodox and the unorthodox orders. Only a couple of manuscript copies, out of many available, use the term *rājadharma* as exception at one place.[62] However, *dharma*, in the sense of law, rather than the term *rājadharma* is the normal use in the text. The socio-cultural and interpersonal laws were supposed to be influenced more by the Brahmanical texts, but there were other systems as well, working simultaneously as evident in the text itself, primarily among the forest people (tribes).

Rājadharma: Varuṇa, the Vedic god upholding the cosmic *dharma*/order firmly and enduringly, gives the king in the temporal world the authority to uphold *dharma*. Patrick Olivelle points out a hymn in the *Śatapatha Brāhman* about one of the essential *yajña* (sacrifice), *rājasūya*, for the king:

> Then to Varuṇa the lord of *dharma* he offers a cake made with barley. Thereby Varuṇa himself, the lord of *dharma,* makes him [the king] the lord of *dharma*. That, surely, is the highest state when one becomes the lord of *dharma*. For when someone attains the highest state, (people) come to him (in matters relating) to *dharma*. Therefore, to Varuṇa, the lord of *dharma*.[63]

This implies that the king ought to bear the responsibility of upholding *dharma* (law) in the society thereby the *dharma* of the king (*rājadharma*) being upholding *dharma* (the law) in the society. Although the verse has not used the term *rājadharma,* the meaning is the same as the duty of the king is not only to observe *dharma* in person but also ensuring its observation by others. In this sense the *dharma* of the king is higher in the vertical hierarchy of a society. Therefore, the term *rājadharma*, the *dharma* (duties) related to the institution of kingship/governance, is there for this distinction of the kingly (political) ethics. The term is the traditional ethical yardstick for evaluation of the performance of the state and the government.

The theories of the origin of state (king)[64] give insights about *rājadharma*. It is considered as the soul of the indigenous/Hindu theories of state; and the origin/existence and sustenance of the state are related to it. The *raison d'être* of king generates the *dharma* of the king. According to G.P. Singh, "The *Śānti-Parvan* (*Rājadharma* Section) of the *Mahābhārata* is the earliest valuable semi-historical record on *Rājyaśāstra* or the science of polity."[65] It provides elaborate account of the theory of the origin of state in ancient India. This is relevant to the reconstruction of the *raison d'être* of the state/king in the context of the *Arthaśāstra* as the text indicates its precedence.[66] The *Śāntiparva* is the most cited, influential and popular ancient source for the indigenous theory of state in India. This explicitly uses the term *rājadharma* that further became very popular at some point of time in history. The story of the *Śāntiparva* describes that in the *kṛta-yuga* (origin of the current cycle of time) there was neither the monarch nor the monarchy; neither the force (*daṇḍa*) nor its user (*dāṇḍika*). People were ruled by *dharma* (mutually understood) and they were protecting each other. But, the state did not last long due to want of mutual confidence. People went to Brahmā (the creator) who recommended a sovereign, and a king was elected. Another version of the story in the same text elaborates on the election through "assembly" for "control of violence and crime". This assembly also passed resolutions (laws).[67] The *Arthaśāstra* itself points towards a theory of state when it indicates towards the period of *mātsyānyāya* (the law of fish). The job of the king is to use *daṇḍa* (coercive power) in order to end the state of *mātsyānyāya*, 'the big fish eating the small' or 'the might is right'. The absence of the use of the coercive power by someone in the absence of king gives rise to the *mātsyānyāya* (law of fish).[68] There are other illustrations of the theory as well, although with little variations, throughout the ancient literature. From this, it is deduced that the purpose and meaning of the *Arthaśāstra*, in another words than *yogakṣema* as mentioned by Kauṭilya,[69] is *daṇḍanīti*, i.e. the *nīti* (policy/science) regarding the 'legitimate use of coercive power'.[70] *Daṇḍanīti* is considered as the most important *vidyā* (skill/knowledge) that is responsible for the maintenance of order in society. Kauṭilya is quite clear:

> The means of ensuring the pursuit of philosophy (*Ānvīkṣikī*), the three Vedas (*Trayī*) and economics is the Rod (*daṇḍa* wielded by the king); its administration constitutes the science of politics, having for its purpose the acquisition of (things) not possessed, the preservation of (things) possessed, the augmentation of (things) preserved and the bestowal of (things) augmented on a worthy recipient. On it is dependent the orderly maintenance of worldly life.[71]

Arthaśāstra, through this, states the purpose of the origin of state/king and the use of coercive power as the means to achieve the goal. The text alludes towards the influence of the *Mahābhārata*, and expresses its preference for the *mātsyānyāya* theory. The text is situated in the much later historical context than the Epic Period when states used to be much smaller in size. *Arthaśāstra* is situated in a much evolved time when there were possibilities of large and powerful empires (300 BCE). There are evidences of a 'divine theory of state' as well in the versions of the *Mānava Dharmaśāstra* from the Śunga dynasty period, just after the Maurya Emperors in Indian history, when the rulers found it necessary to hold their place with its help. The origin of Kauṭilya's text by most of the scholars is located in the time window of 300 BCE to 200 CE, that is the time when the *Śungas* also ruled. The tone of the period in central India was a strong monarchy. But, the theoretical twist by a couple of *dharmaśāstra* versions could not sustain, as that was not approved by contemporaries as well as the later revisions of the same text.[72] The *Arthaśāstra*, in the same period, is about the temporal world and the functions and authority of the king as it assumes monarchy as the 'socially accepted' form of government.[73] Thus, from the *mātsyānyāya* theory of state and the *raison d'être* of the discipline of the *Arthaśāstra*, that is *yogakṣema* (acquisition and protection of earth), the expectation of the 'electors' and the 'appointers'[74] of the king from him is twofold – the protection (*rakṣana*) of life[75] and the property of the people.[76] Another important aspect of *rājadharma* in the *Arthaśāstra* is the ideal social order of the text, i.e. the *varṇāśrama-dharma*. The king was expected to protect this order of the day as a part of the *rājadharma*.[77] As the *Lokāyata* accepts laws as conventions of the society, the text accepts upholding the conventions of the *dharmaśāstras* as law; and to uphold that, a duty of the king. However, the following is the statement of principles of the *rājadharma* in the *Arthaśāstra*:

> For the king, the vow is activity, sacrifice (is)[78] the administration of affairs; the sacrificial fee, however, is impartiality of behaviour, (and) sacrificial initiation for him is the coronation. In the happiness of the subjects lies the happiness of the king and in what is beneficial to the subjects his own benefit. What is dear to himself is not beneficial to the king, but what is dear to the subjects is beneficial to (him). Therefore, being ever active, the king should carry out the management of material well-being. The root of material well-being is activity, of material disaster its reverse.[79]

This is to note, here, that the central attitude of the *rājadharma* is activity that is the *rajas guṇa* in the *Sāṃkhya* School. The attitude of the well-being and happiness of the people as the *dharma* of the king has been associated with the word *rājan* since ancient times. Although it originates from the Sanskrit root word *rāt?*, literally meaning a ruler, it has been given a philosophical connotation of *rañj* meaning 'to please'. This philosophical interpretation is accepted throughout the Sanskrit literature; and therefore '*prajārañjan*' (keeping the people happy) as a primary duty of the king. *Rañjan* can also be related with the pleasure of the *Lokāyata* that is the guiding philosophy of the realm of the *Arthaśāstra*.

Legitimacy and Authority

The discussion on *rājadharma* elucidates the principles of state behaviour and action. The purpose of the state would be served essentially with the help of the *daṇḍa* (coercive power) that would bring order by getting the law obeyed. Kauṭilya has described in detail about the state power in a comprehensive manner while discussing on the *sapta-prakṛtis/saptānga* (seven organs) of the state.[80] State power is its capacity to get its writ or will obeyed with or without consent of the people. The state can establish order according to law using brute coercive power. But, people are not just submissive recipient subjects. They have their own conscious agency that works for their benefit and purpose of life and existence. So, the exercise of the state power needs to be accepted by the people in their own material and spiritual well-being. The *Arthaśāstra* lays down the *rājadharma* precisely for these reasons only. It implies that the laws supposed to govern the order in society should have ethical and moral basis acceptable to the people being governed.

Authority is the power of 'right to give orders, make decisions and enforce obedience'. States have authority by the virtue of its existence and monopoly of right to exercise coercive power over others; and theories of state give the rationales of authority of the state/king over the people. The state power getting a set of laws followed may have the authority with it; and the people may obey it with or without their consent. In case of people obeying the law without consent, the state is less stable and the order may be challenged and disrupted in certain conditions. So, the state requires consent of the people to its laws and actions, not just the right to get obeyed (its authority), to make it legitimate. Legitimacy is about the acceptance of the state, king in the context of the *Arthaśāstra*, by the people to obey the laws willingly. The state remains legitimate to the degree of the people's ability to relate their purpose and interests of life with the state's conduct. It is also about the approval of the state's laws and action; and about the moral and ethical principles on which they are founded. For Weber, the concept of legitimacy, "the basis of every system of authority, and correspondingly of every kind of willingness to obey, is a belief, a belief by virtue of which persons exercising authority are lent prestige."[81] He talks about three kinds of legitimacy: legal-rational (law), traditional (customary) and charismatic (personal/peculiar traits/irrational).

The legitimate authority of the king in *Arthaśāstra* was supposed to be based primarily on the traditional and customary laws of the day. The legal-rational sources of the king's legitimacy in the context of the *Arthaśāstra* are difficult to find as it is difficult to define what made the constitution those days. The king was the state in brief; and the customs of his dynasty, in resonance with the theories of the state and its functions in the *Dharmaśāstra* and *Arthaśāstra* traditions, were used to define his jurisdiction and scope of the authority within the kingdom. Therefore, the legitimate authority of the king in Weber's legal-rational sense in the *Arthaśāstra* is based on the theories of the state and the elements of the *rājadharma* as described in the text. The king's right to use coercive power, collect taxes, etc. were considered to be legitimate till he conducted himself according to the *rājadharma*. Kauṭilya mentions the king's 'meting out justice with impartiality' and the 'just use of *daṇḍa*' (coercive power) as important sources of his legitimacy that also falls in the rational category.[82]

There are some pure traditional sources of legitimacy of the king in the *Arthaśāstra*. The king obtained legitimacy to his authority only after an elaborate process of coronation under oath. The oath/coronation songs included the reasons and purpose of his being elected as the king and called him to perform his duties. Several *yajñas* (sacrifices) like *rājasūya*, *aṣvamedha* (horse sacrifice) specified in the traditional texts were performed by the king to reinforce his legitimacy and authority within his territory as well as the *rājamaṇḍala* (the circle of states). He, in the quest to remain legitimate, also had the duty to maintain the Āryan *varṇāṣrama-dharma* within his kingdom.

The king was the ruler of all, including the non-Āryans as well, primarily the forest tribes. The traditional sources of legitimacy of the king primarily focused to address the problem of legitimacy with the dominant and powerful Āryan society. But, a large section of the people within the kingdom and the *rājamaṇḍala* (the circle of states) used to follow different customary and tribal laws. Many of them did not subscribe the Āryan philosophy and the view of life. Even within the Āryans, people were following different sects and customs. The imposition of a homogenous set of law for all would have had a delegitimising effect due to the people unwilling to follow it. Thus, the *Arthaśāstra*, suggested giving way to the practice of customary laws of different people as well, so far as it did not disrupt the mainstream Āryan hegemonic social order. The king was not supposed to meddle up with the customs and beliefs of the people. The text suggests the king even to participate in different cultural functions and customs of his people and accept as his own. The *Arthaśāstra* mentions several social and political interactions and arrangements with the people outside the Āryan order.

The king's personal conduct and qualifications were also responsible for his legitimate authority. The *Arthaśāstra*, for this, provides a rigorous training curriculum for the king. He was supposed to bear the attributes of *rājarṣi* (sage-like king).[83] In the social context of the text, *ṛṣis* (sages) enjoyed the highest order of respect for their knowledge of the ultimate goal of life and the ways to its achievement. The influence of the *Sāṃkya-Yoga* and other orthodox schools expected the attitude of detachment and non-indulgence in *karma* (actions) within the *saṃsāra*. The king was expected to be active but detached from the world; and having control on his senses. In fact, this was expected from every individual in the Āryan society. However, achieving the *rājarṣi* (sage-like king) state of mind is the personal ideal for spiritual and material well-being of the king as well as helping him in stable and long rule. The characteristics of *rājarṣi* in a ruler work like a charismatic source of his legitimate authority, although it is completely based on rational philosophical grounds.

Therefore, the sources of legitimate authority of the king are a mix of rational, traditional and charismatic categories. Here, only 'rational' instead of Weber's 'legal-rational' category has been used, as the theories of state and the *rājadharma* cannot be called as legal in the modern sense.

Sovereignty

The discussion on sovereignty, as we understand today, is a recent phenomenon as compared to the times of the *Arthaśāstra*. Sovereignty conceives the presence of a supreme authority within the state who can take the final call over a decision. It comes attached with a sense of territory thereby including the internal and external dimensions of the sovereign power. Examining the *Arthaśāstra* for the nature of sovereignty would help us know about the true functional aspects and the degree of the distribution of the decision-making power of the state, its constraints or arbitrariness.

Sovereignty is about the functional aspect of the government in a state. Legislation, execution and adjudication are the three primary functions of a government as understood in the modern times. The *saptānga* theory of state in the *Arthaśāstra* was an organic theory of state in which the organs of the state had no real separation of these categories. Among all the seven *prakṛtis* (organs) – *swāmī* (king), *āmātya* (minister), *pura* (fort), *rāṣtra* (people and territory), *kośa* (treasury), *daṇḍa/bala* (force/army) and *suhṛt/mitra* (ally) – the king (*swāmī*) was, in principle, the symbol of all. The whole text of the *Arthaśāstra* was written for the king putting him at the centre of all state activity and the executive of all power. Hence, making the king the head of the government and the supreme executive authority in the state. Sovereign authority can be examined in terms of the legislative, executive and judicial functions of the modern government.

According to Ernst Kantorowicz in *The King's Two Bodies* (1957), "sovereignty is a signature feature of modern politics."[84] Modern polity endorses the idea of a collectivity that is single, unified one, confined within territorial borders, possessing a single set of interests, ruled by an authority bundled into a single entity and holds supremacy in advancing the interests of the polity.[85] This was not the case in the times of the *Arthaśāstra*. Although the king was the sole representative of the state, in fact the embodiment of state, the political society was diverse and decentralised unlike the modern state. It was nothing like a unified collective whole as a nation in the modern times. Unity came through the institution of the king and loyalty of the subjects and the political-administrative officials to him. The loyalty was based on the king's ability to conduct himself according to the *rājadharma* that depended fundamentally on the just use of the *daṇḍa* (coercive power). The state and the government worked under the canopy of the *daṇḍa* (coercive power) that was legitimised by various systems that we have already discussed. The strength of the *prakṛtis* (organs) of the state also increased the king's sovereign power. The king appointed officials who received their positions on the basis of their lineage, intellectual and administrative skills. The lineage and loyalty was important in the social context of the *Arthaśāstra* because they worked as the glue to keep united a state with amorphous territorial boundaries and people across them interacting with each other. Therefore, the exercise of the sovereign power over the subjects in the strict administrative and territorial sense as we understand in the modern days was not possible. "The bureaucratic system of early India was rarely centralised, except in the infrequent periods of empire."[86] The executive sovereign power of the king was not strictly constitutional in the modern sense and therefore it fluctuated with the varying degree of the available *daṇḍa* (coercive power), his legitimacy and the loyalty of officials towards him. The *Arthaśāstra* provides elaborate internal and external punishments through 'secret agents' system that helped keeping the executive sovereign power of the king intact. This is to note that the society did not approve disloyalty towards a legitimate and just king who delivered on his *rājadharma*. The king was supposed to be the sovereign in the executive domain.

The king also delivered the judicial function of the state through the appointment of judges and fixing the procedures of judgment. He also used to deliver judgments, occasionally brought before him. The delivery of justice through courts was a part of the executive sovereignty of the king as there was no concept of the strict separation of powers. Kauṭilya describes the hierarchy of the different legal components of a "matter in dispute":

> A matter in dispute has four feet, law (*dharma*), transaction, custom and the royal edict; (among them) the later one supersedes the earlier one. Of them, law (*dharma*) is based on truth, a transaction, however, on witness, customs on the commonly held view of men, while the command of king is the royal edict…He (king) shall decide, with the help of law (*dharma*), a matter in which a settled custom or a matter on a transaction contradicts the science of law (*dharma*). Where the science (of law) may be in conflict with any edict in a matter of law, there the edict shall prevail; for, there the text loses its validity.[87]

The king is sovereign here, as the "royal edict" prevails in practical executive considerations. This means that in a conflict between the *dharma* (law) as written in the texts (*dharmaśāstras*) and practical contingent situations demanding justice, the "royal edict" prevails as the *dharma* of the day. Still, it is difficult for the king to be arbitrary as the edicts must be based on truth found through *Ānvīkṣikī*. The king used to exercise sovereign powers in terms of judicial functions through edicts but in case of the king's edict being contrary to the science of truth (*Ānvīkṣikī*), he risked losing his legitimate authority.

Sovereignty in the legislative aspects is a peculiar issue in the *Arthaśāstra*, as it has not been mentioned and elaborated. The *Arthaśāstra* repeatedly mentions *dharma* in the sense of law. The tradition of the *dharmaśāstras* formed the legal frame of the society conceived in the *Arthaśāstra*; meaning the legal frame of the Āryan order that was the powerful hegemonic social-political ideology of the time. It was a group of learned people who advised the king on legal matters (*dharma*) but the king did not legislate. The law (*dharma*), remained the law. However, the king could issue "royal edicts" for some guidance to the people. The king in the *Arthaśāstra* as well as in the ancient Indian traditions have been instated as the 'servant of law'. The coronation oath of the king mentioned in the *Śāntiparva* (*Mahābhārata*) indicated towards this fact:

> Mount on the *pratijña* (take oath) from your heart (without any mental reservation), in fact and by word of mouth:
>
> (a) I'll see to the growth of the country regarding it as God himself and (this) ever and always;
>
> (b) Whatever law there is here and whatever is dictated by Ethics and whatever is not opposed to politics (*Daṇḍanīti*) I will act according to, unhesitatingly. And I will never be arbitrary.[88]

Krişna, in a discussion in the *Mahābhārata*, says, "It (duty of the king) is the servant's duty (*dāsya*) which I have to perform under the name of rulership (*Aiśvarya-Vādena*)."[89] The oath of the king and the reiteration of the *dāsyabhāva* (attitude of service) through literature and conventions regulated the behaviour of the king. The notion of '*satya-pratijña*' (true in his vow) and '*a-satya-pratijña*' (false in vow) was highly important and the kings aspired to remain '*satya-pratijña*' to the people. We have an illustration of a hinduised ruler Rudradāman who was anxious to declare in his inscription that he never levied unlawful taxes.[90] These illustrations put sovereignty of law over the king. The king could not decide on the legal matters arbitrarily and was required to submit to *dharma* (law) to remain legitimate. The law was the principal sovereign over the king.

It is quite clear that the nature of the sovereignty of the king in the *Arthaśāstra* was not absolute like the sovereignty of Hobbes and Bodin that required to be indivisible and located solely in the king. They expected the king to possess all kinds of sovereignty – legislative, executive, judicial – at once, making him all powerful and absolute. But, this was not the case in the *Arthaśāstra*. This is also to note that the divinity of the king that emerges through the various songs and oath during the coronation and in some of the ancient theories of state was not meant to make the king as absolute as the God. Prof. Romila Thapar says:

> The maximum references to kings as either incarnations or descendents of the gods coincide with the period of the rise of obscure families to kingship and fabricated genealogies, suggesting that the appeal to divinity was a form of social validation and its significance was largely that of a metaphor.[91]

The king used the symbols of gods for his validity and legitimate use of his charismatic authority. However, the king of the *Arthaśāstra* is the symbolic and executive sovereign in all matters except legislative. He is restricted by law even in the administrative affairs. But, as the executive orders were required to concur with *dharma* (law), the law becomes the sovereign in principle. The king is, in principle, the executive representative of the sovereign *dharma* (law). He is also expected to listen to the counsel of his ministers who are, in turn, expected to advise the king according to *dharma* (law).[92] Therefore, the scope of the sovereignty of the king is limited by *dharma* (law) and the decentralised nature of the state administration. Prof. Thapar also refutes the suggestions of the orientalist scholars that the ancient Hindu king was a despotic monarch. The king in the *Arthaśāstra* strived to preserve and strengthen his executive sovereignty in the internal as well as external aspects of the state, with all explicit or secret tools available to him. But, he just submitted to the *dharma* (law), i.e. *rājadharma*, in the legislative aspects. In the *rājamaṇḍala* (the circle of states) as well, the king was expected to act without violating the *rājadharma*.

On Morality and Ethics of the *Arthaśāstra*

Daṇḍa (force) is the primary tool of the state to maintain *dharma* (order). Although force is essential to end the condition of the *mātsyanyāya* (big fish eating the small), its use against the will of anyone, let alone the people, is fundamentally immoral. The *Arthaśāstra* which is also called as the discipline of *Daṇḍaniti* is based on the use of force. But, the use of force in self-defence and order in the state is considered as perfectly moral; this is corroborated by the ancient theories of state as well. The theories of state are based on the philosophical truth that there is a will and need in the human being to live and sustain. Therefore, the theories give the arrangement of a ruler or superior by giving him the collective power of his electors; and this would be used on their behalf for their protection.

The sense of the 'preservation of life and its sustenance' is a 'good' while its destruction is 'bad' for the three sciences of enquiry (*Ānvīkṣikī*) of the truth.

The *Sāṃkhya-Yoga* philosophy considers these as the truth of the *saṃsāra* while the *Lokāyata* validates these as the law of nature. The use of force against a force that threatens one's life and disrupts a life full of pleasure is a 'good' (a corollary from the *Lokāyata* principles). These principles taken together allude towards use of force as a 'good' for 'protection of life'. Therefore, the use of force is moral but conditional. The same is validated by the principle of '*āpaddharma*' (attributes to be borne in emergency, or the *dharma* in emergency). Several of the ancient Hindu texts and the *Mahābhārata* justify deviation from the normal *dharma* in the conditions of emergency like threat to life. In the *Rājadharmānuśāsana Parva*, Bhiṣma propounded "that the duties at the time of prosperity were different from the duties at the time of adversity because in the adversity, *dharma* assumed the form of *adharma* and *adharma* assumed the form of *dharma*"[93] and that "when there was emergency, the duties of the king were enumerated differently and they did not necessarily accord with the universal laws of morality."[94] This idea was quite popular in the pre-Kauṭilyan *Arthaśāstra* traditions. The *Śāntiparva* mentions that *vijñanbala* (rational practical experience from the phenomenal world) should be used in the times of emergencies to determine one's own *dharma* with the help of one's own conscience. It further elucidates, while men of ordinary intelligence followed the Vedas, wise men followed application of their reason.[95] *Mahābhārata*, through its stories establishes that there is no interest greater than the self-interest and there is no *dharma* greater than the *dharma* decided with the help of one's own conscience. This resonates with the scientific and philosophical meaning of the *dharma* as attributes that are borne by an entity (living and non-living). It also propounds that all relationships are based on self-interest and where there is no self-interest, there is no relationship. The *Arthaśāstra* subscribes this philosophy in its long discussions regarding the internal and external calamities (*vyasanas*) that are faced by a state. So, in a state of emergency threatening the existence and well-being of the state, the state can take steps that are not generally seen as moral.

Kauṭilya suggests resort to violence, deception and secretive punishments to the enemies of the state, both internal and external. But, the most important point about Kauṭilya's approach is that he never suggests violence as the immediate resort. *Daṇḍa*, for him, is the last tool (*upāya*), out of the four, for implementing policies; the other three being *sāma* (conciliation), *dāna* (gift) and *bheda* (sowing dissent). The *Arthaśāstra* holds that the means of diplomacy to achieve political goals are superior and more powerful than violent means. The so called immoral methods of achieving goals become 'moral' and justified in case of politics as it is the realm of incessant emergency. The political actors (kings/*vijigīṣus*) always look for promotion of their interest at the other's expense making it essential for any king to remain vigilant and dissuade any potential or actual threat. Kauṭilya believes that there can be many ways to dissuade people from treason and violence, especially with the help of various combinations of the *upāyas*, before resorting to violence. The use of violence also varies with the nature and intent of the threat.

In a couple of illustrations, the *Arthaśāstra* suggests killing by a king of his relatives, his son and even his wife, in case of treason. But, a careful reading of the text would reveal that this happens not before all other conciliatory and diplomatic *upāyas* fail. Kauṭilya is quite sensitive while using violence as a means of state's internal and external policies. He even discourages the ministers to acquire the throne by treason or in case the king dies without a legitimate heir. He disagrees with Bhāradvāj who suggested that the minister should not miss such an opportunity to become a king with or without violence (secret or explicit).[96] Instead, he suggests an ideal, that the minister should make an effort to get an eligible person elected as the king. If the candidate is still young and immature, he should arrange for his proper training as required.[97] He discourages the minister from usurping power on the grounds of both pragmatism and righteousness (*dharma*).[98] Other allegations against the *Arthaśāstra*, of suggesting immorality, are regarding the violation of treaties, marching against an enemy or an ally. But, all these suggestions have been given in specific political conditions in which the treaty no longer is to be trusted for its benefits, an enemy becomes dangerous and an ally no longer remains an ally. The morality of Kauṭilya is purely guided by the changing nature and dynamics of the political agents in which the 'good' is dynamic in the functional sense. The permanent and absolute 'good' of the state is its self-interest (security and growth). This is the nature of the political realm – a consistent strife for promotion of its interests. However, again, diplomacy and non-violent means are preferred throughout, with violence as the last resort. In principle, violence in the *Arthaśāstra* is a response to a dangerous state of affairs, to a situation of either kill or be killed. The text does not see the political realm as the domain of innocents. Every agent in this space is a potential threat. What the text suggests are various responses to the various degrees of threats. And, for this text, in this space, where others are equally deceiving, for survival and prevalence, one needs not be straight forward.

However, the moral side of the person of the king needs to be catered as well. He is a human being and therefore needs justifications for his own personal and social actions. The king, at first, tries not to be the initiator of violence by becoming a threat to another innocent agent. Only, the need of the nature of politics suggests him for the strengthening of the *prakṛtis* (organs/elements) of the state to become powerful to secure it from any potential threat. In this regard, the training and the king's knowledge of *Ānvīkṣikī* keeps his 'psychological self' intact and coherent. The *Sāṃkhya-Yoga* view of detachment and non-involvement in *karma* (action) suggests the king to take the contradictions of the political realm and all the 'immoral' acts as the duty of his station in society (*saṃsāra*), i.e. *rājadharma*. The *Lokāyata* also puts him above the sense of good and bad. The philosophies explain that there is nothing like moral or immoral, they are the differences in perspectives that we are looking from. Morality lies in the philosophical realm of *avidyā* (ignorance) where one does not know about the holistic reality of the world and the laws governing them, i.e. the *Ṛta* (cosmic order) or the real *dharma*.

The *Arthaśāstra* is based on the ethical thread as explained with the help of *Ānvīkṣikī*. This knowledge enables the king to act differently from the rest who follow the conventional *dharma* (law). It allows him to transgress several boundaries in the social realm and remain at a higher place. The philosophical systems of *Ānvīkṣikī* resolve the confusions of the person of the king about his action being moral or immoral. He, then, can focus resolutely to deliver on *rājadharma* (political duty) toward all his people, who are quite diverse in their customs, beliefs and ethnicity.

Coming back to the social political realm, I could find at least one ethical aberration that is difficult to be explained with the ethical line taken in the text. For example, a disciplined but disfavoured prince of a bad king is suggested to rob "the wealth of rich widows after entering into their confidence, and plunder caravans and sailing vessels after cheating (the men) by administering a stupefying drink."[99] This suggestion is ethically condemnable as the text nowhere explains that the widows and the sailors were somehow responsible for the prince's plight and exile. This is against the normal ethical line in the text of the *Arthaśāstra*. Almost all other seemingly unethical acts conform to the formula of *āpaddharma* (emergency law) in defence of the self and the state. This is strange from an author who, to protect the *rājadharma*, provides for fining the king himself 30 times as the normal amount, if it is found that he punished someone who did not deserve so. However, as the conduct of the prince, here, emerges as an exception out of the ethical line, the context of the related chapter explains that the targets of this prince probably were somehow related to a bad king. Whatever be the case, a small ambiguous aberration is not enough to challenge the general ethical thread of the *Arthaśāstra*. Although the corpus of 'immoral' acts in the text has been explained as *āpadddharma*, many of them would be outrightly rejected by several contemporary social-political and ethical theories. The idealists would always see them as immoral. However, the *Ānvīkṣikī* (science of enquiry) within the text of the *Arthaśāstra* would call the idealists suffering from *avidyā* (ignorance) regarding the true nature of the *saṃsāra* (reality of the world).

Conclusion

The discussion here on the different aspects of the *rājadharma* (political ethics), legitimacy and sovereignty concludes that the *Ānvīkṣikī* (science of enquiry) is the philosophical base and key to understand the actions and policies suggested by the *Arthaśāstra*. The ethics of the text are embedded in a holistic understanding of 'the reality' of being as described by *Ānvīkṣikī*. And, the apparent absence of ethics and moral aspects in Kauṭilya's *Arthaśāstra*, is an illusion due to the influence of *avidyā* or a partial/non-holistic understanding of 'the reality'.

END NOTES

1. Kangle (2010b: 1), [1.1.1].
2. Kauṭilya salutes Śukra and Bṛhaspati before he starts the text of the *Arthaśāstra*. He also mentions other scholars like Uśanas, Manu, Bhāradvāja, Viśālākṣa, Parāśara, Piśuna, Kauṇapadanta, Vātavyādhi, Bāhudantīputra who had preceded him with their views on *Arthaśāstra* and *Daṇḍanīti*. cf. Kangle (2010b: 1, 15-16), [1.1.1, 1.8.1-24].
3. Boesche (2002a).
4. Boesche (2002b).
5. *Ibid.*
6. The definition of the Hindu is very difficult and debated even in the contemporary 'modern' India. The *Arthaśāstra* is a guide for a Hindu monarch from a Brahmanical/Āryan view. There were other contemporary notions of the state as the *saṃgha*, *gaṇarājya*, etc. There were also tribes living in the forests who had their own primitive notions of ruler/state, but the Brahmanical concept of state/king and his authority was the most powerful, prominent and undisputedly dominant notion of the time.
7. Kangle (2010c: 266).
8. The king (*rāja*) when seen in the context of the *rājamaṇḍala* (the circle of states) has been termed as the *vijigīṣu* in the *Arthaśāstra*, the one who desires for victory or conquest. The *rājamaṇḍala* can also be understood as the 'international society' or a region with a variety of states. This is to note that there was no sense of nationalism during the period of the *Arthaśāstra* and the 'international society' in the text can only be understood in terms of an inter-state system.
9. Kangle (2010b: 5), [1.2.1]. *Ānvīkṣikī* has been translated as "the science of enquiry" and "philosophy" by Dr. Sarvepalli Radhakrishnan and Prof. R.P. Kangle respectively. For me, Dr. Radhakrishnan's translated is more accurate. This is also to be noted that although Prof. Kangle has pointed that "in this text *Ānvīkṣikī* is not the science of reasoning or logic, but certain philosophical systems based on reasoning" [cf. footnote 10 in Kangle (2010b: 6-7)], to understand the context of the text of the *Arthaśāstra* we need to take the meaning of *Ānvīkṣikī* in the text as 'the science of enquiry as described in the systems of *Sāṃkhya*, *Yoga* and *Lokāyata*'. cf. Radhakrishnan (1948: 18).
10. Kangle (2010b: 7), [1.2.12]. The six popular orthodox schools of ancient Hindu philosophy are – *Nyāya*, *Vaiṣeśika*, *Sāṃkhya*, *Yoga*, *Pūrva-mīmāṃsā* and *Uttar-mīmāṃsā* (*Vedānta*). Some other unorthodox schools are *Jain*, Budhhist, *Cārvāka*, etc.
11. *Saṃsāra* is the temporal, material, mundane and the perceptional world that can be experienced through the senses.

12. *Karma* is the action of the 'soul' or the 'self' or the '*puruṣa*' while living in the *saṃsāra*.
13. *Punarjanma* means rebirth of the 'self' or the soul or the '*puruṣa*' after an individual's death in the *saṃsāra* due to the kind of its involvement in *karma* (action).
14. Kangle (2010b: 7), [1.2.11].
15. *Ibid.*: 7.
16. Radhakrishnan and Moore (1957: 227).
17. Kangle (2010b: 4), [1.2.4].
18. *Ibid.*: 6, [1.2.6-7].
19. *Ibid.*: 6, [1.2.2].
20. *Ibid.*: 6. Footnote 2.
21. *Ibid.*: 6, [1.2.2].
22. *Ibid.*: 6. Footnote 2. cf. Swāminā (1900: 341-342), [7.43]; Bühler (1886), [7.43].
23. Kangle (2010b; 6), [1.2.1]. *Ānvīkṣikī*, *Trayī, Vārttā* and *Daṇḍanīti* are the four sciences.
24. *Ibid.*: 7-9, [1.3.4-17].
25. McKenzie (1922: 27).
26. *Ibid.*: 28.
27. Bühler (1886: xviii-xliv). About the *Manusmṛti* based on the *Dharma-sūtra* of *Mānavas*.
28. Prof. R.P. Kangle translates the six enemies or vices of a king as "lust, anger, greed, pride, arrogance and foolhardiness." cf. Kangle (2010b: 12), [1.6.1]. But, the translation of '*harṣa*' as 'foolhardiness' is quite ambiguous and misleading as it does not explain the exact nature of foolhardiness and it may be interpreted in many ways. R. Shamasastry had got it correct and translated it as 'overjoy' that may be synonymous to 'foolhardiness' in certain circumstances.
29. Kangle (2010b: 12), [1.6.8]. King Janamejaya, another character from the *Mahābhārata*, has also been mentioned [1.6.6].
30. *Ibid.*: 11, [1.5.13-14].
31. *Ibid.*: 11, [1.5.16].
32. *Ibid.*: 11, [1.5.17].
33. There is only one inert and non-conscious *prakṛti* that interacts with the *puruṣas* that are numerous but of the same quality of the unperturbed and steady pure consciousness.
34. These *guṇas* are *sattva*, *rajas* and *tamas*.
35. For details on *Sāṃkhya* philosophy, see Chatterjee and Datta (2007).
36. Sharma (2013: 163).
37. Observance of purity, bearing of pain and happiness, bearing cold and warmth, self-study, concentrating on the *Īśvara* etc.
38. Hiriyanna (1995: 122).
39. Radhakrisnan and Moore (1957: 234).
40. *Ibid.*
41. *Ibid.*: 233. cf. *Sarvadarśanasaṃgraha*.
42. *Ibid.*: 227.
43. *Ibid.*
44. *Ibid.*: 230.
45. *Ibid.*: 247.
46. *Ibid.*: 228.
47. *Ibid.*: 233. cf. *Sarvasiddhāntasaṃgraha*.

48. Kangle (2010b: 14), [1.7.3-5]. *Dharma, artha,* and *kāma* are known as the *trivarga* (the three categories) of *karma* (action) in the *saṃsāra*. They are also known as the three pursuits of active life. The *trivarga* with another pursuit at different level, that is *mokṣa*, is known as *puruṣārthacatuṣṭya* (four pursuits of human life).
49. Kauṭilya provides in detail for the spiritual and intellectual training of the king; the control of senses is a part of this curriculum. cf. Kangle (2010b: 12-13), Book I, Chapter VI, Section 3, [1.6.1-12].
50. Kangle (2010b: 13-14), [1.7.6-7].
51. Olivelle (2009: 70).
52. That which is borne/carried is *dharma*.
53. Sarkar (1939: 211).
54. McKenzie (1922: 7-8).
55. We, throughout the Indian tradition, note that *dharma* (law or the attributes borne by the cosmos) is enduringly and firmly held by Varuṇa, the Vedic god. According to the *Ṛgveda*: It is through *ṛta* that the rivers flow; the dawn is born of *ṛta*; by *ṛta* the moon and stars keep their courses. Again under the yoking of *ṛta* the moon and the stars keep their courses. Again under the yoking of *ṛta* the sacrificial fire is kindled; by *ṛta* the poet completes his hymn; the sacrificial chamber is designated the chamber of *ṛta*. cf. McKenzie (1922: 7-8).
56. *Ṛta* can be called as the cosmic *dharma* protected and upheld by Lord Varuṇa.
57. *Ṛgveda*, 1.164.46.
58. Sharma (2013/1987).
59. The caste system and the four stages of life.
60. See the intellectual context of this chapter. The texts mentioned in this section, including the *Arthaśāstra* subscribe the dominant and powerful social order of the day, the *varṇāśrama-dharma*.
61. Kangle (2010b: 13-14), [1.7.6-7].
62. The term *rājadharma* has been used instead of *dharma*, in a couple of manuscript copies, in the verse 38 of Chapter I, Book III, *Arthaśāstra*. Prof. R.P. Kangle has taken the use of *dharma* in place of *rājadharma* in this verse as correct and normal. cf. Kangle (2010a: 97. Footnote 38), [3.1.38].
63. Olivelle (2009: 73).
64. *Rājā Rājyamiti Prakṛti Saṃkṣepah*: The king is the symbol of the state and its *Prakṛtis* (elements/organs).
65. Singh (1993).
66. The text mentions the characters from the *Mahābhārata*.
67. Jayaswal (2005: 82). There are several versions of this story that describes evolution from the *Arājak* state (statelessness) to the origin of monarch, the king/state. Some of them elaborate on the process of election. See also *Śāntiparva*, *Mahābhārata*.
68. Kangle (2010b: 10), [1.4.13-15].
69. *Ibid.*: 9-10, [1.4.3, 1.5.2, etc.]; *yogakṣema* also means "*lābhepālane ca*" [1.1.1].
70. legitimate use of force: As used while defining political science by Gabriel Almond and G. B. Powell.
71. Kangle (2010b: 9), [1.4.3-4].
72. Jayaswal (2005: 224-228).
73. Kangle says, "It (*Arthaśāstra*) assumes that monarchy is the normal form of government; hence it is primarily addressed to the king, advising him on how the administration of

his kingdom should be carried on and how he should adjust his foreign policy to the best advantage of his state." cf. Kangle (2010c: 266).

74. Although kingship had become hereditary in the Kauṭilyan times, there was a process of the election of the king by the 'kingmakers', in case there was no eligible heir to the king. How the actual politics worked in the process is a different matter altogether. Kangle (2010b: 312), [5.6.33-36].

75. Kangle (2010b: 28-29, 39, 39, 254-259,259-262, 459), [1.13; 1.16.35; 1.17.2-3; 4.1; 4.2;11.1.55].

76. The purpose of the state is not only the end of the *mātsyanyāya* or the *Arājaka* state (statelessness) but also the "acquisition and protection of earth" (*yogakṣema*). The earth used to be the greatest economic asset in the ancient times.

77. cf. Kangle (2010b: 7-9, 194, 312), [1.3.1-17, 3.1.38, 5.6.35]. There are other examples as well, scattered, that uphold the *varṇa* (caste) system in the text.

78. I have added this (is) for a clarity in the meaning that is intended to be conveyed.

79. Kangle (2010b: 47), [1.19.33-35].

80. The *swāmī* (king), *āmātya* (minister), *pura* (fort), *rāṣtra* (people and territory), *kośa* (treasury), *daṇḍa/bala* (force/army) and *suhṛt/mitra* (ally) are the seven organs of the state. They together, when strong and in good condition, make a powerful state, as they constitute the comprehensive power of the state.

81. Weber (1964: 382).

82. Kangle (2010b: 9-10, 195), [1.4.11-15, 3.1.42].

83. [The king should]... "avoid another man's wife or property as well as doing injury to others, also (avoid) sleepiness, capriciousness, falsehood, wearing and extravagant dress, association with harmful persons and any transaction associated with unrighteousness or harm." cf. Kangle (2010b: 14), [1.7.2].

84. "Sovereignty", *Stanford Encyclopedia of Philosophy*, at http://plato.stanford.edu/entries/sovereignty/ (Accessed on February 20, 2016).

85. *Ibid.*

86. Thapar (1982: 403).

87. Kangle (2010b: 195-196), [3.1.39-45].

88. Jayaswal (2005: 216). cf. also *Śāntiparva* in *Mahābhārata.*

89. *Ibid.*: 165. cf. *Mahābhārata.*

90. *Ibid.*: 220.

91. Thapar (1982: 404).

92. Kangle (2010b: 14), [1.7.9]. "Rulership can be successfully carried out (only) with the help of associates. One wheel alone does not turn. Therefore, he should appoint ministers and listen to their opinion."

93. Chousalkar (2005: 117). cf. *Mahābhārata* (12.128-8-11).

94. *Ibid.* cf. *Mahābhārata* (12.128-37-38).

95. *Ibid.* cf. *Mahābhārata* (12.130).

96. Kangle (2010b: 311), [5.6.24-31].

97. *Ibid.*: 312, [5.6.32-48].

98. *Ibid.*: [5.6.32].

99. *Ibid.*: 44, [1.18.9].

7

Kauṭilya and Sun-Zi: Comparative Philosophical Analysis[1]

M.S. Prathibha

Introduction

Arthaśāstra and *Sunzi Bingfa*[2] (子兵法 Art of War), compiled by Kauṭilya and Sun-Zi[3] (子) respectively represent the greater traditions of the East, India and China. In the Western traditions, logic and reason is attributed to the Greek philosophers and mysticism and shamanism to the Eastern philosophers. Both *Arthaśāstra* and *Sunzi Bingfa* challenge these cognitive conveniences because the texts advocate "knowing" the reality of being while their application of concepts are practical in approach. Both texts study the field of statecraft, answering questions on the nature of war and use of force. Kauṭilya and Sun-Zi attribute to the king, *dharma* and *dao* respectively as the principle source of behaviour. *Sunzi Bingfa* like *Arthaśāstra* cautions the state to take war seriously, and use correct judgment in using the army depending on the situation.

To compare these two texts is not an easy undertaking. In fact, scholars of Chinese philosophy might argue that other philosophers such as Guanzi, Xunzi, or Hanfeizi (political philosophers rather than scholars of military methods and strategy) seem more methodologically appropriate to compare to Kauṭilya. But, this research undertaking is to engage the minds of both Chinese and Indian readers. The enduring quality of Sun-Zi to capture the Indian imagination unlike others, and the propensity of the text to travel across national boundaries demand that these two are compared with depth and analysis. The hope is to widen the scope for other scholars to compare and contrast other ancient Chinese philosophers to Kauṭilya. The engagement of ancient tradition of Chinese philosophy with the Indian intellectual space is imperative given the increasingly closer economic and political engagement between the two countries.

Authorship of *Arthaśāstra* and *Sunzi Bingfa*: Realities of Ancient Past

The authorship of any ancient text does not stand scrutiny without confronting the difficulty in decoding ancient history comprising of competing arguments and interpretations. Similarly, there are various contestations to the historicity of both Kauṭilya and Sun-Zi.[4] However, for a comparative analysis, decoding the essence of both the texts to see the philosophy of both authors while answering pertinent questions is imperative. Kauṭilya, as much as Sun-Zi were speaking to an audience, who though were facing challenges of that time, nevertheless, were concerned about matters that are timeless in their nature. What makes it relevant for contemporary times is that the decision-makers are still grappling with the nature of the use of force on societies, the morality of actions of war, the destruction of people and property, and ultimately, the moral attributes of the states that are engaged in wars (just wars). However, to inform the views of Sun-Zi and Kauṭilya, their ancient history and philosophy is a guide. T.Z. Lavine, in her work *From Socrates to Sartre: The Philosophical Quest*, says that to "understand Plato, we must place him in his culture, in his time".[5] Therefore, to understand Sun-Zi or Kauṭilya, we have to understand their time, their history and philosophical culture of their time.

(a) Sun-Zi and the Zhou Period

The *Art of War* is a product of its time, namely the Zhou dynasty (1045-256 BCE) and its philosophical traditions. Chief among them were Confucianism, Daoism, Legalism, Yin-Yang School, School of Names, and Mohism. The surge of philosophical thought, known as the Hundred Schools of Thought,[6] became the foundation through which the Chinese built their intellectual tradition. The *Art of War* like many others was written during the Eastern Zhou period. The period spanning the Zhou dynasty is critically divided into Western (1046-771 BCE) and Eastern Zhou (771-221 BCE).[7] Eastern Zhou began when King Ping was declared the new king of Zhou in 771 BCE.[8] During the Eastern Zhou, the capital was moved from the west (present-day Xian) to the east, present-day Luoyang (Chengzhou) in 722 BCE. The political, economic and intellectual conditions of the Zhou helped shape the emergence of these traditions.

During the Zhou dynasty, central rule first flourished and a functioning bureaucracy became a characteristic of the dynasty.[9] Particularly, during the

Western Zhou, the political rule was stable and Zhou dynasty, which succeeded the Shang dynasty, took aspects of Shang culture and expanded into Zhou system of moral thought and practice such as the divination rituals.[10] This enabled a culture of continuity. Zhou rulers introduced the "Mandate of Heaven", to justify the defeat of Shang rulers. For them, the Mandate of Heaven (tianming, 天命) gave rulers divine right and by consequence their demise, if they lose the mandate. The rulers lost the mandate if they were unjust, and overthrow of the regime was considered to be legitimate as the ruler was seen to have lost what the heaven had mandated them – the legitimacy to rule the people. However, the successful bureaucratic governance and the central rule through the *Mandate of Heaven* failed to succeed through the Eastern Zhou period.[11] During Eastern Zhou, central control of Zhou rulers weakened considerably leaving small independent fiefdoms, thus resulting in the breakdown of the feudal system that was established in the Western Zhou. Chen Jingpan, in his book, *Confucius as a Teacher*, gives few factors that led to this collapse of order in the Zhou society. He states that the collapse of the feudal system,[12] led to the decline of loyalty to the central rulers and the appropriation of feudal lands to many smaller landholders (Zhou rulers gave land to their male relatives, who in turn gave land to their relatives) led to competition and expansion among them.[13] Thus, many viewed the Western Zhou as the "ideal" period with virtuous rulers; and the Eastern Zhou as a period known for suffering the perils of conquest and wars.

This period of turmoil generated the greatest philosophies in the history of China, and the received texts of the Zhou period later became the classics of the Chinese philosophy. Within the Eastern Zhou, the period is further divided into the *Spring and Autumn*[14] (春秋时代) period (722-476 BCE) and *Warring States* (战国) period (475-221 BCE) until the unification of China under the Qin empire. The two periods could be distinguished through the differences in the nature and intensity of warfare. The *Spring and Autumn* period was dominated by nobles who waged wars for prestige and honour for their small independent fiefdoms. These fiefs by the time of Warring States period became seven big states. Unlike the Spring and Autumn, in the Warring States period, wars were fought among larger independent states and professional generals and often brutal in manner. Spring and Autumn period experienced less intense and small scale wars than compared to the Warring States period.[15]

Sun-Zi's *Art of War*, albeit about war and military strategy, is part of this tradition, generally acknowledged to be part of the School of Strategy (Bingjia 兵家).[16] Thus, the text is a product of the time, when the political and social order had already collapsed. He was also writing during the time when incessant warfare led to the demand of scholar-bureaucrats to advise the kings and lend their expertise. Thus, the *Art of War* was a guide to warfare that advised the king to be in harmony with the people, endorsing the morality of the Zhou period, and the philosophies such as Confucianism and Daoism, which endorsed these values. Sun-Zi's attraction seems to be his preoccupation with using defensive methods, such as stratagems to defeat the enemy instead of outright force. The use of force as the last resort is consistent with Chinese historic tradition of according military with not much significance in the social order.

(b) Sun-Zi's Historicity

According to the textual records of the Chinese traditional history, Sun-Zi was known as Sun Wu. Sima Qian, in his *Records of the Historian*, mentions Sun Wu, and from his account, Sun-Zi lived during the latter part of Spring and Autumn period of the Zhou dynasty. However, scholars argue that the text of *Art of War* allude to a time of professional generals, which was absent during the Spring and Autumn period. Therefore, to many, the *Art of War* and Sun-Zi was a product of Warring States period. Many also doubt Sima Qian's version about the existence of Sun-Zi because of the lack of mention in Zuo Zhuan (Commentary of Zuo). Zuo Zhuan is an ancient text that describes the chronicles of Spring and Autumn period and considered an authority on the history of that period. The controversies surrounding the figure Sun-Zi as the author of *Sunzi Bingfa* is contested as other than *Records of the Historian* and *Spring and Autumn Annals of Wu and Yue* (Wuyue Chunqiu 吴越春秋) there are no other history compilations that mention Sun-Zi as the general of King Wu.[17] Some consider the doubts about the existence of Sun-Zi as a historic figure as "baseless" and argue that the treatise is a product of Warring State period and that the present text must have some added elements after Sun-Zi's authorship.[18]

The answer to the question as to whether Sun-Zi was fact or fictitious has become not as relevant as the placement of Sun-Zi in Spring and Autumn period. The archeological evidence has shown that the received text was indeed written by Sun-Zi, and only clears the earlier confusion of many mistaking Sun-Zi, for Sun Bin, who was the descendant of Sun-Zi, who also wrote another military text, known as the Art of War. The evidence in Mawangtui tombs shows two *Art of War* texts. The texts unearthed from Yinqueshan, kept in the Shanghai Provincial Museum, also contain manuscripts of the Art of War. Thus, going by strict archeological evidence and sophistication of warfare, scholars now agree to a large extent that *Art of War* was written by Sun-Zi, during the Warring States period. But, the traditional histories of China also give few examples of Sun-Zi.

The first reference to Sun-Zi is in Sima Qian's *Records of the Historian* (S*hiji* 史记) that consider him as a native of the Qi Kingdom. According to

Sima Qian, the king of Wu, He Lü read the *Art of War* and wanted to determine the skill of Sun-Zi as a commander.[19] So, he was asked to train the King's concubines. He then proceeded to demonstrate his skill and King He Lü made Sun-Zi his general. Sun-Zi was credited with the success of defeating the kingdom of Chu. He served the king of Wu during the period between 512-506 BCE. After 506 BCE, there is no mention of Sun-Zi in Sima Qian's *Records of the Historian.* In that mention, King He Lü attacks Chu and captures the capital Ying. It is written that Sun-Zi was instrumental into the entry into the Chu capital, Ying. This was the battle of Boju in 506 BCE. According to traditional history, King He-Lü later died of his wounds in 496 BCE, when he attacked Yue Kingdom to be defeated by Kou Chien at Tsui-Li. Sun-Zi, therefore, is hypothesised to have died with his King He Lü. Other speculations include that he died in 482 BCE after helping King Ke Lu's son King Fuchai for a while. In fact, the latter records show that King Wu's trusted advisor Wu Zixu (伍子胥) recommends Sun-Zi to king of Wu. Roger Ames in his study of texts excavated from the Yin-Ch'ueh Shan contends that one of the lost chapters recovered titled 'An Interview with the king of Wu' was possibly the background for Sima Qian's history on Sun-Zi.[20] Therefore, whether the *Art of War* existed during the King Wu's time, or it was constructed in a later period, is subject to various interpretations.[21] Sun-Zi is credited with victory over the Chu army. If his time was during the Warring States period, then his penchant towards refraining from warfare to win could be explained. Warring States period, more than Spring and Autumn period, represented an intensification of warfare, where constant battles drained the resources of states and protracted warfare drove more misery on the common people, the alliances and counter alliances represented a period of intense chaos. In this period, the eleven states signed a non-aggression pact in 564 BCE. Four big states, Jin, Qi, Qin and Chu kept the balance of power during this time. After this period, the Qin united China under the Qin dynasty.

(c) Kauṭilya and Mauryan Empire: Historicity

Kauṭilya, who was also known as Chanakya or Vishnugupta wrote *Arthaśāstra*.[22] Kauṭilya unlike Sun-Zi was considered responsible for the birth of the Maurya Empire. Kauṭilya was credited with helping Chandragupta (324-297 BCE) to establish the Mauryan dynasty in 322 BCE after crafting the fall of Nanda dynasty (345-321 BCE). It was said that Kauṭilya used the local power politics to undermine the Nanda dynasty using the network of spies and intelligence collection. The *Arthaśāstra* is supposed to have been composed around the end of the fourth century BCE.[23] The *Panchatantra* of Vishnu Sharma also identifies Kauṭilya with Chanakya. The contradictions about the authorship and date are due to the challenges associated with Indian history as a whole. It is outside of the scope of this work to detail the debate.[24]

While placing Kauṭilya in his times, history shows that he established a strong central system after the founding of Mauryan Empire. Whereas there had been a breakdown of political stability in China, during Kauṭilya's time, Nanda dynasty was considered to be a great, wealthy and formidable political and military power. Unlike Sun-Zi, the traditional history of India credits Kauṭilya to be instrumental in defeating the Nandas and establishing the Mauryan Empire. Chandragupta and Kauṭilya, together, further improved upon the Nandas and established a stronger bureaucracy and economy. The *Arthaśāstra* is similar to *Art of War*, in a way it is a manual, for those who practise statecraft, thus does not detail the history of that time. The *Arthaśāstra* is different in temperament from the *Art of War*, as it is more detailed in the duties of the king and the management of his state, including warfare. Kauṭilya, unlike Sun-Zi, places greater significance to intelligence system to win wars. Though using intelligence networks could be considered to be defensive, the war advocated in his text is regular warfare.

Philosophy of War and Strategy: *Art of War* and *Arthaśāstra*

(a) The Dao and Dharma

How can one understand the text and its tradition? Kauṭilya draws from the previous works of *artha* and *dharma* literature. Reimagining the historicity of Sun-Zi meant illuminating the Zhou philosophy of tradition. Both authors derive some measure of the philosophical traditions and thus are a continuation of it. The *Art of War* is as much a product of classical literary texts such as the *Zhouyi* (Changes of Zhou), as *Shujing* (Book of Documents) and *Shijing* (Book of Poetry). Although *Zhouyi* or the *Yijing* (Book of Changes) was first a divination text, it is a transportation of Shang culture to the Zhou. *Yijing* was used by rulers as a guide to decision-making. The *Arthaśāstra* on the other hand, imbibes the six schools of thought in Hindu philosophy such as the *Sāṃkhya*, *Yoga*, *Nyāya*, *Vaiśeṣika*, *Mīmāṃsa* and *Vedānta*.

The Art of War's concern about following the *dao* is an example of the enduring concepts in Chinese philosophy to represent an idea that is central to the way Chinese think about the world. The term *dao* is not the prerogative of the Daoists, but existed in Chinese philosophical and cultural consciousness. Maoists like Confucianists are advocating their own version of, "the right" way of *dao*. Daoist texts are themselves an attempt to explain the principles enshrined in *Zhouyi*. Like the Vedas, this is a foundational source for subsequent philosophical texts. *Zhouyi* is used for occult and fortune-telling, the key to understand the way of the universe. This was used earlier for divination; and later for philosophical nature of query. The line statements and hexagrams are supposed to be the authorship of King Wen of Zhou (1099-1050 BCE). The first eight hexagrams are attributed to Fu Xi (c.2800 BCE).

It is not surprising that there has been an effort in linking ancient Chinese military thought to Daoist philosophy due to its adherence to means other than war.[25] Is it possible to associate Sun-Zi with Daoism, when before and during his time, was the golden age of Chinese ancient philosophy with Hundred Schools of Thought? One might also think that if Sun-Zi was endorsing the philosophy of "dao", then material associations such as warfare and victory would not have been endorsed.

Though many would conclude the reluctance to use of explicit violence in the *Art of War* makes it a Daoist text, it is about the study of military methods. This is not an endorsement of Daoism but a rejection of legalism (punishment as a tool to rule). Some might even argue that legalism and Daoism are sides of the same coin, and flow from the same understanding.[26] This is particularly significant as Han Feizi used Daoist notions for the unification of Qin. Later, legalism as a state philosophy was denunciated after the collapse of Qin dynasty, which confirms the notion that the Chinese philosophical tradition rejects punishment or use of force as a predominant and visible tool in enforcing the *dao*.

Yijing (易 经 The Book of Changes), consists of Zhouyi and the Ten Wings (commentaries) evolved during the Warring States period. *Yijing* is considered as one of the Confucian classics because it is purported that the second part of the *Yijing*, which is known as *Yuzhuan* (Ten Commentaries), was supposed to have been written by Confucius. *Zhouyi* (周易), which prevailed in beginning of the Zhou Dynasty, personifies the Yin-Yang dynamics. Here, "yi" means "changes", thus meaning 'changes of Zhou'. *Zhouyi* is the core text that contains the 64 hexagrams and is supplied with line statements. The various scripts of *Zhouyi* have been made available by archeological surveys.[27] *Zhouyi* is signified by *Yin* and *Yang*. *Yin* represents the female, the earth and *Yang* the male, the heaven. This *Yin* and *Yang* have to be in harmony, the way (*dao*) of the universe.

Thus, understanding the *dao* of everthing had various philosophers engage and develop their own systems of thought. *Dao* in general has many meanings, including the "the way", 'road', 'path', 'method'. It could mean the order of the cosmos or relation to the events that affect human affairs. It is said that Confucius was the first to use *dao* in metaphysical sense to mean "the way".[28] In philosophical terms, *dao* is the absolute principle that characterises the universe, the cosmos. It is the harmony of the natural order, one with the cosmos.

There are differences in the way Zhouyi and Daosim look at the way of the *dao*, Wen Haiming explains:

> The Book of Changes explores the *dao* of *tian* for the purpose of understanding human affairs, the Daodejing explores the *dao* of *water* for the purpose of understanding personal events... He further adds: The philosophy of book of Changes is the source of Chinese philosophical thought. Zhouyi philosophy not only serves as the basis for different philosophical schools throughout history, but also as the ultimate origin of Chinese philosophical sensibility.[29]

Confucius, on the other hand, interpreted the *dao* is to be through correct ritual practices, music and literature from the Zhou Dynasty,[30] compared to the Daoist notion that *dao* as something that is not encumbered and flows freely, popularised by the concept *wuwei* (无为). Daoists would later become critiques of Confucian philosophy, renouncing societal expectations, allowing the nature of things to unfold by itself.[31] However, when Sun-Zi illustrates about maintaining harmony, he invokes the *Yijing*, the harmony between the cosmos/ nature and human beings, though in material terms. When Sun-Zi speaks of the *dao*, it is reasonable to understand that he was also well-versed in the ancient and the oracles. That is to say, that Sun-Zi believed in the *dao*, to understand and execute war. William Mott and Jae Kim write:

> Sun Tzu limited and controlled the use of force within Tao in harmony with people. By controlling all forces tightly within Tao, Sun Tzu's paradox explained Tao, while urging the rulers to use economic wealth, social power, and politics as alternatives to wars.[32]

For Kauṭilya, the Hindu tradition of *dharma* occupies a seminal role when the king protects his subjects. Similar to the *dao*, *dharma* also is complex and contains more than one meaning. In philosophical terms, *dharma* is to uphold the order of the cosmos, the rules of the cosmos, to examine the way of life that will contribute to the maintenance of *dharma*. Like *dao*, *dharma* also could be represented at different levels, from representing the order of cosmos to human activities in the society. It could be used to guide human actions, to derive his or her role in the society.

Both, Sun-Zi and Kauṭilya, for instance, favour the king to be in accordance with *dao* and *dharma*. They believe that the king personifies and has to be identified by whether he follows the *dao* and *dharma*. The way of the *dao* in Sun-Zi's context is for the king to be in harmony with his subjects:

> The moral law causes the people to be in complete accord with their ruler, so that they will follow him regardless of their lives, undismayed by any danger.[33]

Here, the ruler has to be in harmony with the people; that is the way of the *dao*. For instance, while waging war, Sun-Zi refers to the moral law of the two sovereigns fighting and, for him, it is important to determine who has the moral law and that determines who should win the war.

Similarly, Kauṭilya distinguishes *dharma* with the qualities of the king. He says that any gain attained by the king during war is determined by whether he is righteous or not. For him, the advantage gained by an unrighteous king as a result of war/diplomacy causes anger among his people.[34] In fact, Kauṭilya adequately explains how to determine the spoils of warfare with wisdom and caution as to whether the king acts on behalf of his advisors, and whether it is done in a "praiseworthy manner".

Thus, translating these principles to warfare, Sun-Zi cautions the commander, to understand the nature of war, the nature of his men, the nature of his enemy, nature of his people, nature of seasons and many more to determine one's decision to launch war preparations or attack an enemy. He mentions the *dao* (道) as one of the moral principles when one looks at war.

The art of war is then governed by five constant factors, to be taken into account in one's deliberations, when seeking to determine the conditions obtained in the field, these are: (i) moral law, (ii) heaven, (iii) earth, (iv) commander, and (v) method and discipline.[35]

Sun-Zi was not upholding the Daoist principle, he was upholding the foundational philosophical idea of the Chinese civilisation. It is not surprising that in the Warring States period the philosophers looked into ancient wisdom to seek inspiration for the chaos and dilemmas of the period. From the Fuxi's Bagua, which itself is a symbolic representation of the *dao*, to the *Zhouyi*'s Yin and Yang, the harmony is personified in Chinese philosophy. Kauṭilya was upholding the Indian philosophical idea of *dharma*, where the human being is supposed to uphold the "right way of life" in connection to the universe. Thus, moral righteousness is placed upon the shoulder of the individual, on how he communicates with the world. While in Chinese philosophy, the *Yin* and *Yang*, represent the continuing and opposite forces existing and correlating together, the Indian philosophy represents *dharma* as the force which upholds the order of the universe. Whereas *dharma* might differ according to many individuals, situation and context, the underlying principle is the individuals' role and duties in a world of complex, changing and multiple realities. An important differentiation between the Indian and Chinese thinking is that the latter considers the cosmic order/world to be continuous, ever-changing, and dynamic without any rigid logic or supposition, and the *dao* represents the right way of life. The different philosophies in China accept the grand philosophical idea of the above mentioned concept of the world/cosmic order (represented in Book of Changes and Yin-Yang) while differing in their versions of the right way to *dao*. The Indian thinking on the contrary, while accepting the world to be changing and dynamic, considers the universe itself subjected to the cycle of creation and destruction, therefore infinite in its existence.

While *dharma* and *dao* represent the normative tradition of both Kauṭilya and Sun-Zi, the context in which these traditions are preserved in the text is important. Since the *dao* is about preserving the harmony between the ruler and the ruled, Sun-Zi advocates a king, who has to be in harmony with his subjects. Kauṭilya also upholds *dharma* in several ways. After capturing a territory, for instance, *Arthaśāstra* does not advocate any destruction, but employs several duties for the king. In the new territory, he should grant favour and exemptions as promised before the acquisition of the territory, to keep the promise to the people of the new territory, such that he should adopt "similar character, dress, language and behaviour".[36] In fact, for the new territory, the king is supposed to not "just release the prisoners and help the distressed, helpless and diseased, but he has to establish a righteous code of conduct". These duties for the new territory show that Kauṭilya expects the king to uphold *dharma* or establish *dharma* in the newly acquired territories.[37] In fact, this normative value is visible in other ways as well. Kauṭilya distinguishes between indiscriminate killings and combat killings. After capturing the fort, Kauṭilya discourages the killing of "those who have fallen down, of the surrendered, the ones who have become terrified at the battle and lost the ability to fight, and who have surrendered."[38]

The war as an instrument is fundamental as it is regarding the use of force and both texts do not use it for unmitigated destruction of the enemy forces. Sun-Zi does not favour in the war of attrition rather winning the war with minimal destruction, therefore observing the ethics of warfare. These ethics do not impinge on their approach to war, which is methodical and clinical in their appreciation of war. Kauṭilya, advises the king to agree for peace if the enemy is equal and destroy an inferior enemy. He does, however, disagree to destroy a weaker king, when the weaker king has retreated to his territory or ready to sacrifice his life. He explicitly says that though this opportunity is very tempting, one has to resist from harassing further a retreating army. This value has to be seen through the purview of *dharma*. While it is understandable and favourable to press one's advantage in war or battle, Kauṭilyan ethics differentiate between ethical conduct of war and winning the war. Another example includes where Kauṭilya encourages the setting up of fire to the enemy's fort. However, while he accepts that starting the fire could help in capturing the fort, he cautions against the "unreliability of fire and its ability to destroy indiscriminately, of all creatures".[39]

The *Sunzi Bingfa* says that a consummate leader cultivates moral law, the *dao*, and strictly adheres to method and discipline. This normative value is important to the ruler as the *dao* ensures that the people are always with the ruler, and follow him regardless of the danger to their lives. For Sun-Zi, the *dao* offers harmony, between the ruler and the ruled, and if this harmony does not exist, chaos will prevail. The *dao* is so important that Sun-Zi appropriates victory to the one which one of the sovereigns has the *dao*. This is the one of the military conditions under which Sun-Zi recommends looking at war. If Kauṭilya argues against indiscriminate killing and destruction, Sun-Zi makes a distinction between persistence and victory. He argues that the goal of a military operation is victory not persistence. Again, the virtue of a small, quick war is preferred over long and lengthy war. In planning a siege, he urges against destroying a nation, he wants to keep it intact; similarly he argues the same for a division or a battalion to be kept intact. Therefore, once the army is captured, there is no need to dismantle it, it is better to keep it intact. Therefore, attacking destructively is not considered an accomplishment. For that, he says, preserving the army is the best, destroying it is the second best.[40] In fact, "preservation" seems to run throughout when Sun-Zi talks about planning offensives in the city, where he describes "the fight under Heaven with the paramount aim of preservation".[41] Sun-Zi abhors senseless warfare, long campaigns, and destruction of the enemy forces, indicating that he sees it as upsetting the harmony of the *dao*. Both texts place importance to the moral nature of decisions and decision-makers. They believe that any actions have to be guided not by material but moral concerns. *Dharma* and *Dao* thus, make the moral thought that guides the actions of rulers.

(b) Method of War: Kauṭilya and Sun-Zi

Arthaśāstra is ahistorical and abstract in its execution. It is not abstract in theory, but in its practical application, concerning with the administrative duties of the king. In fact, compared to *Arthaśāstra*, the *Art of War* represents the strategic thought of a commander to lead an army, thus discarding any reference to historic, social and economic nature of the state. *Sunzi Bingfa* does not idealise actual battle, it places the highest appreciation in defeating the mind of the enemy, his plans and his strategy. Therefore, Sun-Zi's philosophy of war is covert, deceptive as psychological games often do. *Sunzi Bingfa* was thus a departure from the established military culture of the Warring States period. *Arthaśāstra*, similarly, also departs not from the established military culture but the orthodoxy of Hindu religious system. Kauṭilya though acknowledging the Vedas, does not construe the strategy of making war through religious beliefs. He places importance on the king and his virtue, his rule, and his *dharma*. The text encompasses variety of administrative and governance duties for the king, including foreign policy and defence strategy. Unlike Sun-Zi, deception is only one of the strategies that Kauṭilya envisions in his ideal state. In fact, his fascination is keenly towards "intelligence", through secret agents and various forms of information collection/dissension through spies that it has become the hallmark under which he attempts to win military campaigns.

Kauṭilya wrote the text for a king, Sun-Zi for the commander. While Kauṭilya is mathematical about the composition of the army, the forces, the plan to attack, Sun-Zi is poetic and cryptic. Both, however, do converge on a very significant thinking. They caution against devastation and using the army arbitrarily to achieve the goals. While both are willing to use deception or force to achieve an objective, they expect the ruler to be governed by the moral order and preserve the social contract between the ruler and the ruled. Thus, war for both authors is an important element of statecraft. Sun-Zi views war to be important as it concerns survival and life, therefore subjected to intense inquiry (in laying plans). The Kauṭilyan philosophy of war and strategy is to use secret agents, intelligence networks, trickery and deception. This way to plan offensives or to siege a fort is used to overcome the enemy forces. In fact, for taking a fort, Kauṭilya has a section on sedition to instigate trouble and using it to take a fort.[42] Even in the employment of stratagems, Kauṭilya relies on secret agents to penetrate enemy places and cause dissension, gather information, and using various strategies to undermine the enemy forces.[43]

Kauṭilyan strategy and tactics are similar to Sun-Zi as well as distinct in their recommendations. Sun-Zi and Kauṭilya both advocate waiting for the opportune time to conduct battles. Kauṭilya, when laying a siege, recommends that the king should see whether his troops are fully supplied with logistics, when the seasons are favourable but the enemy is suffering from deterioration.[44] Sun-Zi admittedly does encourage to win a war without resorting to fighting. For him, winning every battle is not considered the best, but winning without fighting. A superior military strategy would strike while schemes are being laid. Kauṭilya advocates open warfare, where time and place of the battle are indicated and that as the most righteous form of warfare.

Kauṭilya presents war as an instrument to protect the state from aggression. Kauṭilya recommends a number of variety of battle strategy and tactics. For him, it is necessary to wait for the opportune time, terrain, season, to fight war. Before marching on to attack, ascertaining the strength or weakness of powers, place, time, seasons for marching, time for raising armies, revolts in the rear, losses, expenses, gains and troubles for himself and the enemy is imperative. The terrain should be checked to find whether it is suitable for one's operations, if the weather is cold or rainy and the season suitable or not. According to him, power, place and time are mutually helpful compared to others who choose one or the other. Kauṭilya does not recommend a frontal attack. The unfavourability of the frontal attack is considered as the general principle of warfare. He gives the following as the strategy to follow:

- To use jungle troops and then attack with fresh troops later.
- To use ambush to tire the enemy out by making him believe that he has defeated the troops, and then attack the enemy by using fresh troops.
- To attack an enemy when it is the weakest at protecting his troops, such as when his troops are engaged in plundering or transporting or camping.
- To use deception to conceal a strong force by attacking the enemy with the weak force and then attacking him with the strong one.
- To use deception to lure the enemy by enticing him with cattle and wild animals.
- Attacking the enemy in the morning when it is tired from keeping watch all night.
- There are many places such as desert, forest, narrow path, marsh, mountain valley, uneven ground, where an ambush could be conducted at a favourable time.

In Sun-Zi's philosophy of war, 'the way' to victory seems to be the most important, prudent and the highest. For victory, realising the conditions of the battle has to precede before engaging in battle as the vanquished army would first engage in battle without realising the conditions.[45] While the philosophy of war seems to be victorious without fighting, the philosophy of strategy in Sun-Zi's *Bingfa* is sharply focused on strategic configuration of power *shi*. The concept of *shi* as used in *Bingfa* denotes dynamic power and it could be deployed through forces, which is indicated by the concept *xing*. Sun-Zi indicates in "strategic military power" that:

> the one excels in warfare seeks (victory) through the strategic configuration of power (*shi*), not from reliance on men. Thus, he is able to select men and employ strategic power.[46]

Shi and *xing* are the two concepts that indicate the commander of the army being aware of the complexities of warfare and using the uncertainties to his advantage.

Sun-Zi Recommends

- Entering the war only if it is victorious.
- Gaining strategic advantage (*shi*) by using the conditions of warfare.
- Having a commander who is aware and in turn provoke the enemy in revealing his plans and stratagems.

- Conccaling one own's strategic positioning (*xing*) of troops through deceit.
- Strategic advantage and strategic positioning are always dynamic.

For Sun-Zi, the *dao* of knowing victory is through five principles. These are:

> (1) Knowing when and when not to fight; (2) To know how to handle superior and inferior; (3) Army should be animated by same spirit throughout the ranks; (4) Should take the enemy unprepared; (5) Military capacity and little interference from the political state.[47]

Both Kauṭilya and Sun-Zi employ stratagems in their use of military force and war. For Sun-Zi, one can attack the stratagem of enemy in different ways depending on the context: (i) disputing the mastery of the empire; (ii) forces are ten to one: surround the enemy; (iii) five to one: attack the enemy; (iv) twice as big: divide the army into two; (v) equally matched: could offer battle; (vi) slight Inferior: avoid the enemy; (vii) quite unequal: flee from him.[48] Because for Sun-Zi, the ultimate aim is to break the strategy of the enemy, thus attacking strategy has hierarchical positioning indicating their relative value. Sun-Zi values "prevent enemy's plans" as the best, followed by prevent junction of enemy's forces, attack the enemy's army, and besieging walled cities as the worst policy. For planning a siege, you have to be careful and not send soldiers like a swarm, otherwise it would be disastrous attack. Therefore, the need is to conquer the city without siege, destroy other states without taking a long time, however, victory should be complete and be established everywhere. Because, for him, the result will be that attacking walled cities would take time, three months to prepare shelters and shifting instruments of war and another three months to pile mounts against the walls. With the siege, the army would have to drive many men into the attack thereby losing some of the men. This does not ensure that the town could be under the control of the commander. Therefore, laying siege to the city is the worst strategy.

For Kauṭilya, there are many ways to take a fort. First sowing the seeds of sedition, one is encouraged to instigate the enemy town by installing spies and secret agents to sow dissension. By instigating the enemy, one could take a fort. By laying siege to the fort,[49] when one's army is stronger and the enemy's army is weaker. When attacking the fort, the King should favour who (from the enemy territory) had helped him to attack, the fallen, surrendered, and the people who are scared. In addition, the constituent element of the state is the king, the minister, the country, the fortified city, the treasury, the army and the ally.

One of the strategies that Sun-Zi encourages is to flee if you are not able to wage war, therefore conserving your strengths. This is not termed as cowardice but rather a tactic in the short term so that you could continue the battle later. For Sun-Zi, there should be absolute disinvolvement of political interference in military affairs. He sees this as damaging the military and chances of winning. In formation of battle, he stresses invisibility, invisibility of the army, and vulnerability in the opponent. He always talks about battle as a last resort, then all the victories are accomplished before the battle. Warfare is expensive and the cost of raising an army is high as it includes swift and heavy chariots, soldiers and their provisions and rations. Therefore, Sun-Zi emphasises:

> Short and swift warfare as protracted war costs the state resources of raising and maintaining the army. Cleverness is not waging long wars.

The cost of supplying rations for the army will cause dissension among the people as it would drain their resources. He links the cost of protracted warfare with the dissatisfaction of people.

As military operation is a drain, therefore, it is important to know the conditions of the opponents. Foreknowledge is important, therefore one should use spies – local spy, inside spy, reverse spy, dead spy and living spy. Local spies are hired from among the people of locality, inside spies are hired among enemy officials, reverse spies are among enemy spies, dead spies transmit false information to enemy spies, and living spies come back to report. Therefore, spies are very important and richly rewarded.

According to Sun-Zi, one has to leave the enemy's strong points and attack the weak points of the enemy. Thus, the attacks would be unexpected. He warns against, attacking the army head-on. The attack would rely on speed and efficiency and tactical surprises including attack on soft targets such as border posts. This might involve shifting the forces back and forth on the frontier to keep the enemy guessing. One should initiate a skirmish at one place and withdraw when the enemy sends forces to respond, only to attack somewhere else. By the constant shifting of strategy and with every skirmish, one could understand the responses of the enemy and his thinking. This would also involve manoeuvre, deception and surprise instead of direct attack. But, for Kauṭilya, it is always the destruction of the enemy. Any method used for this purpose is justified; because, if the enemy is not destroyed, one would be destroyed by the enemy. Therefore, he emphasises on a zero sum game for the fight with the enemy.

Kauṭilya looks at two kinds of battles. The open battle and the deceptive battle. He on the first account encourages open battle. However, if certain conditions are not met, then, deceptive battles are seen as the last resort. According to Kauṭilya, deceptive battles are to be taken by the king, if his army is not superior, his instigations at the enemy's base camp is not successful, that he has not taken any precautions against danger and lastly, the terrain is not suitable to him.[50] If such conditions exist, then Kauṭilya wants the king to engage in deceptive battle. Comparing the use of deception between Sun-Zi and Kauṭilya, one notices that Sun-Zi puts more emphasis on deception than Kauṭilya. Whereas Kauṭilya emphasises deception in battle tactics, Sun-Zi emphasises deception in battle tactics and overall strategy. For instance, in Kauṭilya's deceptive battle, even if the enemy is on a suitable terrain than the king, the King can lure the enemy into an unsuitable terrain by pretending that his jungle forces have suffered a rout. Then, the king attacks the enemy with his jungle forces and breaks the enemy's battle array.

Kauṭilya talks about causing dissension in alliance. Sun-Zi talks about causing dissension between the political leadership and ministers, therefore making the enemy's state ineffective to respond. According to the *Art of War*, the enemy should be tired by one's flight, which meant that surprise attacks should constitute military tactics. Sun-Zi talks about using anger to throw the enemy in disarray, as by angering the enemy forces one can sow confusion, making them unclear about their strategy. He also talks about anger in another way, stating that anger is what kills the enemy. According to him, if one enrages one's own officers and troops, they would kill the enemy, which implies huge indoctrination within the troops to hate the enemy. Also, by taking enemy's goods, the soldiers will be incentivised to fight. This reward could be used for making the soldiers overcome the enemy. Therefore, reward system can be used to encourage the soldiers to fight and compete. Once the enemy soldiers are captured, they could be treated well, could be even used to work among one's soldiers. To further confuse the enemy, one has to change uniforms as well. This use of psychological warfare is in abundance in Sun-Zi's strategy, precisely because it attempts coercive ways to ensure victory.

Kauṭilya endorses the establishment of spies in every way, to snoop on government officials, ministers and the likes to collect information from the enemy. He also wants to use different types of spies, such as wandering monks, pupils, traders, holy men, servants.[51] In terms of enemy territory, he differentiates between seducible and non-seducible parties. For instance, ones who are impoverished, filled with self-conceit, and distressed.[52] In terms of army organisation, he advocates having a superintendent of the armoury so that he is in charge of machines that are to be in battle. His job is to keep the machines in good condition, expose them to sun and wind and ensure that they are not damaged by heat. There are also superintendent for foot soldiers, commandant of the army, and superintendent for chariots who would also establish industries for manufacturing of chariots.[53]

After the war, Kauṭilya recommends giving favours to the subjects, helping the people, giving gifts, and also satisfying honours and other gifts to the parties in the enemy camp who had helped the king to acquire victory. The king should partake in the festivals of the newly acquired territory and their customs. This shows a propensity for the integration of the new subjects and the king through conciliation and resolution of conflict. In fact, Kauṭilya distinguishes between the types of victory. For him, the conqueror could be distinguished as to how he treats the newly acquired territory. That is the righteous conqueror, who would be satisfied with submission; greedy conqueror, who could be satisfied with seizure of lands and goods. Kauṭilya recommends the weak king to yield money to the greedy conqueror. There is also the demoniacal conqueror, who would not be satisfied with seizure of lands or goods, but sons, wives and life; and therefore, Kauṭilya recommends the weaker king to take steps to remain out of reach from this type.[54]

Conclusion

For Kauṭilya, established armies and well-connected network of spies are integral to any state. For Sun-Zi, exploiting the conditions of uncertainty and attacking the stratagems and planning of enemy through deception are integral to the state. By surveying both texts we find that, they advocate wisdom of the world of warfare; and do not shy away from the harsher aspects of warfare, rather consider them essential to victory. While being victorious is essential, both are concerned about the morality of warfare and the type of victory that one should aspire for in battle. Thus, both authors are subjected to certain moral compulsions in their decisions to wage wars, and for the political means for it. Both consider the welfare of the people as the foremost duty for the king, thus protection of the people and waging war as the nature of statecraft.

The philosophy of war and statecraft present in both the texts are determined by their respective cultural and civilisational consciousness. Unlike their Western counterparts, both accept ambiguity and deception as part of good strategies to defeat an enemy. The overt use of force for plunder and destruction of property is frowned upon by both authors lending to a unique cultural unity. This is particularly important as contemporary military campaigns increasingly address the destruction of property and livelihood.

END NOTES

1. This paper would not have been possible without the assistance of Indian Council of Social Science Research (ICSSR) Grant Award to conduct discussions with scholars in China. My interactions with scholars of Ancient Chinese philosophy has been helpful immensely in shaping my understanding about Chinese pre-Qin philosophy.
2. This paper uses the Pinyin rather than the Wade-Giles system for most of the Chinese phrases. The chapter does not use Pinyin when referring to a title of book or article in references or footnotes. It should be noted that Sun-Zi is also known as Sun Tzu.

3. Sun-Zi means Master Sun, which is generally used as an ancient title of respect for a learned man in China. For example, Confucius is called Kong Zi (Master Kong).
4. The historicity of Kauṭilya has been detailed adequately in other chapters of this volume.
5. Lavine (1984).
6. Different schools of thought that were predominant during the Eastern Zhou period, the Spring and Autumn and Warring States period, are known together as Hundred Schools of Thought.
7. There are competing ideas regarding the dates of Zhou dynasty. It is perturbed to have started from 1122 BCE. Edward Shaughnessy calculates Western Zhou period as 1045-771 BCE. cf. Pankenier (1992): The author criticises Edward Shaughnessy for ignoring the Yi Zhou Shu to the accounting of the chronology of the early Zhou dynasties.
8. According to Sima Qian, King You had deposed his Queen Shen and son, Yiju and replaced his concubine, Baosi as the Queen. Queen Shen's father Marquess of Shen, together with other nobles and the nomadic tribe Quanrong, killed King You and made the prince Yiju as the King Ping of Zhou. Then King Ping moved the capital to the east from Haojing (near present day Xian), given its proximity to the tribe Quanrong.
9. Twitchett and Loewe (1986: 26).
10. The Zhou rulers used "tian – heaven" instead of "Di – God" as used by the Shang. cf. Chang (2000).
11. Shaughnessy (1999).
12. The feudal system during the Zhou period was considered different from the European notion of feudalism. The Chinese system is called the *chengjian* system.
13. Jingpan (1990).
14. The name Spring and Autumn comes from Spring and Autumn Annals, which is considered as one of the Confucius classics.
15. Twitchett and Loewe (1986: 24).
16. Gawlikowski (1985).
17. Sawyer (1993: 151).
18. Gawlikowski (1985: 171).
19. Chien (1979).
20. Sun-Zi, in Ames (1993: 19).
21. Giles (1910).
22. As other chapters in this volume capture more in detail the various arguments regarding Kauṭilya and the *Arthaśāstra*, this chapter will not detail the various debates surrounding the history and controversies regarding the authorship and date.
23. Refer to P.K. Gautam's chapter in this volume.
24. R.P. Kangle gives a detailed debate about the authorship of the *Arthaśāstra*. cf. Kangle (2010c: 59-115).
25. Rand (1979/1980).
26. Discussion with a Chinese scholar.
27. Shaughnessy (2014).
28. Bo Mou states that Confucius was the first to use *dao* in the metaphysical sense for describing it as "unique moral path that should be walked by any true human being, endorsed by Heaven and revealed to the early sage-kings". cf. Mou (2008: 144).
29. Haiming (2012: 2-39).
30. Mou (2008).

31. Matthews (2010: 176-177).
32. Mott and Kim (2006).
33. Sun-Zi, in Giles (1910).
34. Kangle (2010b: 418-419), [9.4.9-25].
35. Giles (1910: 4).
36. Kangle (2010b: 491), [13.5.3-8].
37. Kauṭilya distinguishes the territory conquered to the territories inherited and reconquest. Most of these duties are referred to the ones that are conquered therefore giving more importance to assimilate the people to the king's rule rather than subjugate them.
38. Kangle (2010b: 490), [13.4.46].
39. *Ibid.*: 488, [13.4.21].
40. Sun-Zi in "Planning Offensives". cf. Sawyer (1994). Sun-Zi says: Preserving the enemy's state capital is best, destroying their state capital second best; preserving their army is best, destroying their army is second best; preserving their battalions is best, destroying their battalions is second-best; preserving their companies is best, destroying their companies is second-best; preserving their squads is best, destroying their squads is second best; subjugating the enemy without fighting is the true pinnacle of excellence.
41. Sun-Zi in "Planning Offensives. cf. Sawyer (1994).
42. Kangle (2010b: 475), [13.1.13].
43. *Ibid.*: 478, [13.2.12, 13.2.37].
44. *Ibid.*: 486, [13.4.4.].
45. Sun-Zi in "Military Disposition". cf. Sawyer (1994).
46. Sun-Zi in "Strategic Military Power". cf. Sawyer (1994:166)
47. Sun-Zi in "Planning Offensives". cf. Sawyer (1994).
48. *Ibid.*
49. Kangle (2010b: 485-486), [13.4.3.].
50. *Ibid.*: 438, [10.3.1].
51. *Ibid.*: 21-24, [1.11.7-8, 1.12.1].
52. *Ibid.*: 31-32, [1.14.4-12].
53. *Ibid.*: 179-180, [2.33.1-10].
54. *Ibid.*: 461, [12.1.30].

8

Fatāwā-ye jahāndāri: Hybrid Political Theory in the Delhi Sultanate

(Perso-Islamic and Endogenous Traditions of Statecraft in India)

Seyed Hossein Zarhani

Introduction

The name and works of Ziyā al-Din Barani or Ziyā Barani (ca. 1285–1357 CE) – one of the most influential historians and political thinkers in medieval India – are barely known among mainstream political theory scholars. Scholars of Indian history are mainly familiar with his *Tārikh-e Firuz Shāhi* (History of Firuz Shāh) that deals with life and time of Delhi Sultans from Ghiyāth al-Din Balban (1266–1287 CE) to Firuz Shāh (1354–70 CE).[1] J. Mehta describes Ziyā Barani as the 'greatest of all contemporary historians of early medieval India'.[2]

While *Tarikh* had been published by Sir Syed Ahmad Khan[3] in the 19th century; *Fatāwā-ye jahāndāri* – Barani's outstanding work on politics – remained unknown until the middle of 20th century. Even after the discovery of the manuscript and the first translation into English by Afsar Salim Khan (1972), *Fatāwā* has generally been ignored or marginalised by political scientists in India, Pakistan and Iran. For example, in the recent *Princeton Encyclopedia of Islamic Political Thought*[4] there is no entry for Ziyā Barani or his *Fatāwā-ye jahāndāri*. This book can be classified as an example of 'Mirror for Prince' or 'Fürstenspiegel' genre. *Fatāwā-ye jahāndāri* is only of Indo-Persian work that is exclusively devoted to political theory during the era of the Delhi Sultanate. In contrast to *Tārikh-e Firuz Shāhi,* Ziyā Barani does not address historical figures or events of Delhi Sultanate in the *Fatāwā*. He wrote *Fatāwā* with a clear intention of instructing Muslim rulers (Pādeshāhān-e Islam) in the art of governance and statecraft. Irfan Habib[5] translated the work's title as 'Opinions on Government', N. Sarkar[6] as 'Decrees on ordering the governed world' and the Encyclopedia Britannica (2015) as 'Rulings on Temporal Government'.

Among the few academic works on *Fatāwā*, there is not only no consensus about the main elements of Barani's concept of politics, but also the interpretations of his work are conflicting and contradictory. For Instance, Varma[7] portrays Barani as a fanatical protagonist of Islam who recommended an all-out struggle against Hinduism. He depicts Barani as a fundamentalist promoting a "religiously militant administration based on dogmatic fanatism". Varma also claims that Barani was a supporter of an aristocracy of religious elites. In contrast, M. Habib and Khan (1961) introduce Barani as the first theoretician who justifies the secular law among Mussalmans. Similarly, Black (2011) describes Barani as an exceptional scholar in seeing a direct opposition between religion and politics. According to Black, "Barani's argument rotates around a clear distinction between state policy and personal morality."[8] Likewise, as I.A. Khan[9] specifies that *Fatāwā* enables us to understand the secular character of the Delhi Sultanate. Quoting Muhammad Habib, Khan (1986) states that *Fatāwā* demonstrates that the Delhi Sultanate was "not a theocratic state in any sense of the word. Its basis was not *Sharia* of Islam, but the *Zawābet* or State laws made by the king." However, Muzaffar Alam rejects the role of Barani as first Muslim thinker who justifies the secular law and writes, "This assessment seems to me anachronistic."[10]

In the same way, there is a debate about the fundamental values that had a direct impact on the *Fatawā*. Roy and Alam[11] note that Barani has been perceived as "conservative, a fundamentalist and a bigot" by some scholars since he was a *Sharia*-minded scholar, who had a hostile view toward the Hindus. In contrast, the Encyclopaedia Britannica (2015) asserts that *Fatāwā-ye jahāndāri* is influenced by Sufi mysticism and Barani "expounded a religious philosophy of history that viewed the events in the lives of great men as manifestations of divine providence."

In view of the contradictory interpretations of Barani's political ideas in his *Fatāwā,* the primary aim of this study is to explore the following questions:

(1) What are the essential elements of Barani's political thought?

(2) Which political, cultural and social background factors influenced *Fatāwā-ye jahāndāri* and Barani's political theory?

(3) What is the influence of a) Islamic political ideas, b) pre-Islamic Iranian political ideas, and c) ancient Indian tradition of statecraft, as articulated by Kauṭilya, on Barani's political thought?

Reviewing the Literature

As mentioned above, before the 1940s, Barani was known only for his *Tārikh-e Firuz Shāhi* (History of Firuz Shāh). That changed when a complete manuscript of *Fatāwā-ye jahāndāri* was discovered and identified by A. Habibullah[12] in the Oriental and India Office Collections, London. The manuscript had originally belonged to Tipu Sultan Library in Mysore, from where it was transferred to London. Due to the fact that last three digits of the date of transcription are 115 (based on Islamic Hijri calendar), Salim Khan[13] concludes that the manuscript was copied from an older version during the 18th century. However, so far, no other copies have been identified. In the last sentence of the introduction of the *Fatāwā*, the author introduces himself as a 'well-wisher of the Sultan's Court, Ziyā Barani'.[14]

As Hardy notes,[15] in the aftermath of partition and the establishment of independent India and Pakistan, intense interest in studying traditions of Muslim political thought in South Asia developed. That interest was connected to questions like the relation between secular law and *Sharia*, citizenship, and Hindu-Muslim relations. Under the supervision of Peter Hardy at London School of Oriental and African Studies (SOAS), Afsar Salim Khan wrote a Ph.D. thesis on Ziyā Barani's political ideas and translated some parts of the *Fatāwā* to English. She published an abridged translation of *Fatāwā* in the *Medieval India Quarterly* (1957). Mohammad Habib combined this translation with an introduction and epilogue which was published in the same journal in 1958. In their *The Political Theory of the Delhi Sultanate,* M. Habib and A.S. Khan (1961) translated additional parts of *Fatāwā* to English and wrote a new introduction to Barani's political ideas. This book introduced *Fatāwā* to English-speaking scholars.

However, only in 1972, was the full text of *Fatāwā-ye jahāndāri* translated into English by Afsar Salim Khan, who had become a professor and head of the department of political science at Peshawar University. Due the fact that there are several omissions and inaccuracies in the English translations, our study also draws on the original Persian text that was published along with the English translation and the introduction of Afsar Salim Khan (1972).

Following this 1972 translation, Barani's *Fatāwā* attracted growing attention among scholars. Hardy (1978) compared and analysed Ziyā Barani's thinking on government in the *Fatāwā-ye jahāndāri* with other eminent Muslim scholars like al-Ghazāli and his *Nasihat al-Moluk*, or Nasir al-Din Tusi and his *Akhlāq-e Naseri*. Irfan Habib (1999) tried to illustrate Ziyā Barani's major ideas on the nature, objectives, and functions of the state. Sarkar (2006) concentrated on the Barani's employment of the 'voice' of Sultan Mahmud of Ghazni in the *Fatāwā* as the main adviser to rulers. Sarkar (2011) also focused on the exercise of government in the capital city (dār al-Molk) provided by Barani. Black (2011) concentrated on the relations between morality and politics in *Fatāwā*. Muzaffar Alam[16] discussed the essential difference of Barani with his predecessors in Muslim space like al-Ghazāli or Nezām al-Molk Tusi as well as his contemporaries in India.

In addition, some scholars compared Barani and his *Fatāwā* with non-Muslim political thinkers. For example, Arbind Das (1996) compared Kauṭilya's *Arthashastra with* Barani's *Fatāwā*. He tried to analyse and compare the two Indian 'Mirrors for Princes' texts in their different historical, cultural and social contexts, with reference to categories such as the theory of kingship, sovereignty, administration, justice or financial organisation. Unfortunately, Das remains silent about the conceivable causes of the considerable similarities between two works and does not thematise the possible continuity of the Kauṭilyan tradition of statecraft in India's political history.

Similarly, Syros (2012) compared Barani's *Fatāwā* and Machiavelli's *The Prince* and underlined the significance of Barani's political ideas from a cross-cultural perspective. Barani and Machiavelli are separated by time and space and lived and wrote in two different political, cultural, and social contexts. However, Syros (2012) acknowledges that there are certain similarities between key ideas of these two writers. He states that Barani's ideas like the pessimistic image of human nature, the distinction between personal morality and politics, the ruler's exposure to various threats, the origins, mechanics, and purpose of government and the ruler's authority during emergencies "bring him peculiarly close to Machiavelli".[17]

Ziyā Barani's Life and Socio-Political Background

Ziyā al-Din ibn Mo'ayyed al-Molk Barani was born in 1285 CE, most probably at Baran (modern Bulandshahr in U.P., southeast of Delhi). He grew up in an India where a century had passed since the establishment of Delhi Sultanate by Persianised Turk Sultans adhering to the Sunni Muslim religion. His birth was coinciding with last years of the reign of Sultan Ghiyāth al-Dīn Balban (1266-1287 CE).

Irfan Habib[18] presents Barani's family background as one of scholars and administrative officials. Hardy[19] notes that Barani was related by descent and marriage to "middle-ranking Muslim service families". According to J. Mchta,[20] Barani belonged to a Turk aristocratic family that settled in India in the first phase of Turk immigration to India. His father Mo'ayyed al-Molk was *Nayib* (Deputy) of Arkali Khan, son of Sultan Ghiyāth al-Din Balban. An uncle of Barani was *kutwāl* (police chief) of Delhi.[21]

Barani himself writes: "The father of this weak individual was a noble (*Sharif*) and my grandmother was a *Syed* [title of descendants of Prophet Mohammad] who performed some miracles."[22] Not only was his father (who had the title of Mo'ayyed al-Molk) *Nayib* (Deputy) of Balban's son Arkali Khan, but also his mother's father Sipahsalar Hisam al-Din was *Hajib* (Chamberlain) of Sultan Balban.[23] Moreover, during the reign of *Khilji* dynasty, Ziyā's father was appointed *Khawaja* (governor) of Baran.

However, Ziyā Barani does not talk about his grandfather (father's father), his name and his job. So it is clear that his father was not a Syed. Moreover, Mo'ayyed al-Molk seems a royal title rather than a real name. Although most of the contemporary historical works presented him as a member of the Turk aristocracy, Barani himself writes he is Indian. Thus, Barani's family background remains opaque for us.[24]

Barani's life and his political ideas were influenced by drastic political and social changes that came in the aftermath of the Mongol invasions of Central, Western, and South Asia. He was born six decades after Mongol invasion of *Khārazm* and *Khorasan* from 1219 to 1221 CE and thirty years after Siege of Baghdad (1258) and Collapse of Abbasid Caliphate. These attacks in many ways impacted the Delhi Sultanate.

Delhi, Mongol Invasion and Indo-Persian Culture

The first consequence of the Mongol invasions is the spreading of Persian language and culture into the North of the Indian sub-continent. As Mohammad Habib notes,[25] India acquired a unique position in Islamic world after Mongol invasion of Central and West Asia (during 13th and 14th centuries) as it was "the only country where *Ajam* culture could flourish". As Bosworth (1984) and Gould (2015) explain, in medieval Arabic literature, *Ajam* [derived from the Arabic root referencing muteness] was the name given to the non-Arabs who lived in Islamic space. *Ajam* applied particularly to Persians. In the early centuries of Islam, the ability to speak Arabic was the main criteria for differentiating Arabs and *Ajam*. Thus, *Ajam* connoted the supremacy of Arabs over 'mute' non-Arabs and consequently had a negative connotation. However, with the rise of Persians in the Caliphate and the revival of Persian culture and language, *Ajam* became a basic ethnic and geographical designation that was a synonym to Persian.

We must add here that *Ajam* culture migrated to India not just as a consequence of Mongol Invasion to Central and West Asia, but, from the 11th century CE onward it was introduced by Turk Sultans who invaded India. Muzaffar Alam, Delvoye, and Gaborieau[26] in *The Making of Indo-Persian Culture* noted that although some of the Turkish Sultans and the ruling families used Turkish as the spoken language, Turk culture never found traction in India. On the other hand, the Turk rulers were steeped in Persian culture. The roots of Indo-Persian culture can be traced to Ghaznavid dynasty that was based in Ghazni in today's Afghanistan. Persian was introduced to India by Sultan Mahmud Ghaznavid, who several times invaded the northwest of the subcontinent and occupied Punjab in 1020 CE.[27] According to Muzaffar Alam,[28] during the 11th century, the new Persian literary culture from Ghazni flowed to Lahore and northern India.

However, Muzaffar Alam et al.[29] specifiy that the maturation phase of Indo-Persian culture took place in the framework of Delhi Sultanate under rule of Persianised Turkish or Afghan dynasties in 13th and 14th centuries such as Mamluk dynasty (1206-1290 CE), the Khilji dynasty (1290-1320 CE), the Tughlaq dynasty (1320-1414 CE), the Sayyed dynasty (1414-1451 CE) and the Lodi dynasty (1451-1526 CE). Although most of these dynasties were not ethnically Persian, they were promoters of *Ajam* culture and Persian literature. Therefore, Persian language and culture flourished under the rule of these dynasties and, as Gould indicates,[30] Persian literature was developed mostly by poets who were not native Persian speakers. Gradually, Persian language and culture became an integral part of the South Asian culture, especially in northern India. More importantly, as Muzaffar Alam (2003) elaborates, because of this cultural flow, northern India became part of Perso-Islamic cultural space. For the *Ajam* cultural world, Delhi and Lahore attained a position and importance comparable to Bukhara, Nishapur, Isfahan, Shiraz, or Herat.

Gould[31] describes *Ajam* as a highly cohesive social, political and cultural configuration within the horizons of the medieval eastern Islamic world. Alam also concentrated on the issues of identity and wrote:

> In the thirteenth century, there was a certain degree of cultural integration with a coherent Perso-Islamic identity (in opposition to the Arab culture) that is identified with the term *Ajam*. The Persian-speaking residents of Delhi and Lahore seem to have considered themselves a part of this world of *Ajam*.[32]

However, Chengis Khan's invasion to the Perso-Islamic world and the subsequent waves of Mongol invasions led to a considerable Persian elite emigration to northern India, which enhanced the role and position of Persian language and culture in India. One of the early manifestations of the emergence of *Ajam* identity and its new imagined territory can be traced in *Lobāb al-*

Albāb (The Essence of Wisdom) that was the first major *Tazkereh* (critical anthology) of Persian poetry.[33] The author of this anthology, Mohammad Awfi (1171-1242 CE), originally was from Bukhara (in today's Uzbekistan) and emigrated to India after Chengis Khan's invasion. Awfi not only considered Persian poets from what is today's Iran as *Ajam*, but also included Abul Faraj-e Runi and Mas'ud Sa'ad Salmān from Lahore, and Nezāmi of Ganja and Khāqāni of Shirvan (both from today's Azerbaijan) as *Ajam* poets.[34]

Awfi was not the only *Ajam* scholar who settled in India. According to historical sources, Delhi in the 14th century CE saw a massive influx of Persian-speaking elites: princes, scholars, merchants, Sufi saints, craftsmen, penmen. For example, Mohammad Qasem Hendushāh-e Astarābādi in his *Tārikh-e Fereshteh* highlighted this migration, writing:

> The kings and princes – who had migrated to India during the reign of previous Sultans – arrived in Delhi during the reign of Ghiyās al-Din Balban [1266–1287]. They were fifteen princes from Turkistan and Transoxiana, Khorasan, Iraq-e Arab, Iraq-e Ajam, Azerbaijan, Sham, and Rome that escaped from Chengis Khan's aggression...Elites such as swordsmen, writers, singers, craftsmen, and artists from every part of the globe gathered in his [Ghiyās al-Din Balban's] court. Most of the Ulama, scholars, Sufi Sheikhs and poets, Amir Khosrow [Dehlavi] was their chairperson, gathered at his son's house.[35]

Not only did these migrant elites influenced the language of the court in Delhi, but also they introduced various Persian scholarly works and poetry. Barani in his *Tārikh-e Firuz Shāhi* illustrated how much *Ajam* culture and Persian poetry was dominant in the court:

> Sultan Mohammad [son of Sultan Balban] had an assembly that comprised from the wise people, scholars, and artists. His [Muhammad Sultan's] companions used to read (to him) the Shāh-Namah, the Divan-e-Sanāyi, the Divan-e -Khāqāni, and the Khamseh-ye Nezāmi. Learned men discussed the merits of these poets in his presence. Amir Khosrow [famous Indian poet] and Amir Hasan were servants at his court.[36]

The migrants who came from Khorasan, Iraq-e Ajam, Azerbaijan and other parts of the *Ajam* world brought the legacy of *Ajam* science, arts, culture, and politics. Although, their home cities like Samarqand, Bukhara, Herat, Tus, Neyshabur, and later Baghdad were devastated by Mongols, Delhi, and its Sultans provided a safe environment for the growth of *Ajam* culture. These developments led to the emergence of new elites (Indian, Turk or Persian) that were highly Persianised. The *Ajam* traditions of these elites were most deeply rooted in northern India.

Ghiyāth al-Din Balban lost his son Mohammad during fighting the Mongols and died in 1287 CE. After Balban's death, his successors could not sustain the dynasty, and later *Khilji* Turks became new Sultans of Delhi. Nevertheless, the

Persian-speaking elites kept their bureaucratic and administrative positions. Ziyā Barani and his family belonged to this elite class and its social status provided an opportunity for his proper education. He had extensive training in Arabic and Persian. Also, he was well-trained in Muslim theology and deeply read in history. After learning Quran and the alphabet, he continued the education during the reign of Alauddin, the new *Khilji* king. In his *Tārikh*,[37] Barani describes the intellectual life of Delhi during the reign of Alauddin with its superb teachers and scholars whose intellectual calibre was "not to be found in Bokhara, or Samarqand, Damascus, Tabriz, Isfahan or in any part of the world...they were equals of Ghazāli and Rāzi." As Barani mentioned,[38] he was a pupil of some of these teachers. He read and studied "several books of ancient and later times in every branch of knowledge", and claimed, "after Tafsir (Quranic commentary), Hadith (Prophet Mohammad's tradition), Fiqh (Islamic jurisprudence), and Tariqat of Sheikhs (Sufism), I have found no science so useful as the science of History."[39] However, Barani had no training in philosophy and this ignorance of philosophy is reflected in his works when he criticises Muslims engaging in philosophy.

During his education, he also was profoundly influenced by Islamic mysticism and Sufi tradition. Later, he became a disciple and friend of Nizām al-Din Awliyā, a famous Sufi Sheikh. Ziyā Barani also had a close relation with the two Indian Persian-speaking poets Amir Khosrow Dehlavi and Amir Hasan Dehlavi.[40]

This privileged background in social status and education enabled Barani to find a job in the court of new Sultan of Delhi, Mohammad ibn Tughlaq (ca. 1300-1351 CE). When Barani was in his fifties, he was appointed as the *Nadim* (boon companion) of the Sultan. It was an important position and, as a major courtier, he had access to power, wealth, and information. Since he accompanied the Sultan on several occasions and had access to information via his observations or another courtier, his *Tārikh-e Firuz Shāhi* depicts a clear image of Delhi Sultanate and power relations in the court.

After Mohammad ibn Tughlaq's death, along with other courtiers, Barani participated in a plan to install his minor son, on the throne. However, Firuz Shāh, who was a cousin of Mohammad ibn Tughlaq, finally became new Sultan. Therefore, Ziyā Barani lost his job and became marginalised and impoverished. Barani wrote his major works *Tārikh-e Firuz Shāhi* and *Fatāwā-ye jahāndāri* after his dismissal. For his *Tārikh-e Firuz Shāhi* used the name of the new Sultan, hoping to find a way back to the court of *Firuz Shāh*. But his attempts were not successful, and he did not dedicate *Fatāwā-ye jahāndāri* to any other ruler. Finally, he died in poverty and loneliness around 1357 CE.

Fatāwā-ye Jahāndāri: A Mirror for Muslim Princes Text

Darling[41] defines Mirrors for Princes as "works reflecting the ideal ruler or giving advice on governance for a current or future king or minister, [that] constitute a well known literary tradition in both Europe and the Middle East." As a popular genre from the ancient era to the Renaissance, in different cultural and social contexts, Mirrors for Princes offer advice and guidance to kings, princes, viziers, and other high-ranking officials. While the European mirrors for princes (Machiavelli's *The Prince* in particular) have been widely studied, non-Western Mirrors for Princes are mostly marginalised by the mainstream of Political Science.

Some authors view Kauṭilya's *Arthaśāstra* as one of the oldest examples of Mirrors for Princes. Even though the *Arthaśāstra* is a genuinely scholarly work with high theoretical and methodological standards, it clearly does also have an instructional dimension.[42] For sure, the ancient Indian beast fables *Panchatantra* – probably older than the *Arthaśāstra* – do belong to the Mirror for Princes genre.

In pre-Islamic Persia (mainly during Sassanid dynasty[43]), works like *Javidan Kherad* (Eternal wisdom), *Name-ye Tansar* (Letter of Tansar), or *Ahd-i Ardashīr* (Ardashīr's Testament) are examples of the Mirror for Princes tradition. These mirrors belong to a pre-Islamic literary genre known as *Andarz* that offered advice on proper behaviour, religion and statecraft.[44] These works originally were written in Pahlavi, however, as Haghighat notes,[45] scholars of pre-Islamic mirrors are faced with the fact that these mirrors for princes are available in manuscripts that were copied after the Islamisation of Persia, or can be found in the Arabic books that contain some translated part of original texts. These kinds of mirrors were translated into Arabic in the first centuries after Islam by translators like Ibn al-Muqaffa (died c. 756 CE). One of most remarkable examples of Ibn al-Muqaffa's work is a translation of *Kalileh va Demneh* from Pahlavi to Arabic. According to Persian traditions, the Sanskrit *Panchatantra* was translated into Pahlavi during the reign of Khosrow I Anošīrvān (531-579 CE). Naṣrullah Munshi translated *Kalileh va Demneh* into new Persian in the twelfth century CE. In the Islamic era, especially in *Ajam* cultural space, the mirror genre emerged in new Persian with a designation like *Andarz* (counsel), *Pand* (maxim), *Nasihat* (advice), and *Wasaya* (instruction), *Maw'ezeh* (exhortation) or *Hikmat* (wisdom, proverb).[46]

In the late eleventh century CE, Kaykāvus ibn Iskandar wrote *Qābus-nāmeh* the first known mirror for princes in new Persian. According to its introduction, *Qābus-nāmeh* was written as a book of advice (*ketāb-e pandhā*) for Kaykāvus' son and successor, Gilānshāh. Soon thereafter, *Siyāsat nāmeh* (The Book of Politics) that was written by Nezām al-Molk-e Tusi (1018-1092 CE) who was the grand vizier of two Turk-Seljuk sultans is commonly recognised as the most outstanding example of the medieval Persian Mirrors for Prince genre. *Siyāsat nāmeh* also known as the *Siyar al-moluk* (The conduct of kings) was manual for a new and inexperienced Sultan based on the pre-Islamic Persian tradition of statecraft typified by the conduct of ancient Persian kings of the Achaemenid and Sassanid dynasties.

Scholars like Aquil[47] claim that *Fatāwā-ye jahāndāri* is not really an example of the Mirror for Prince genre because Barani expressed his political ideas with reference to the history of the Delhi Sultanate; nonetheless, Aquil's study tries to shed light on the normative values and theoretical substance of the *Fatāwā*. Muzaffar Alam (2000) differentiated between two distinct types of Indo-Islamic political treatises that had an immense influence on (Muslim) politics in pre-colonial India: The first is *Adab* that addressed right (political) conduct and the second is concerned with *Akhlāq* (moral qualities). The *Fatāwā* can be seen as a variant of the *Adab* genre that stands in the tradition of *Siyāsat nāmeh*. Affirming that, *Fatāwā-ye jahāndāri* – like the *Arthaśāstra* or *Siyāsat-nāmeh* – is no historical-descriptive text, but it is a theoretical work that also offers practical advice in statecraft.

After reviewing the form and structure of *Fatāwā,* it can be concluded that it was influenced by Nezām al-Molk's *Siyāsat nāmeh.* After a short introduction, *Fatāwā* has twenty-four chapters, albeit named *Nasihat* (advice). In each chapter, after the core thesis as advice, narratives of historical events are presented for illustration and further elaboration. Such anecdotes are mainly about ancient Persian kings, the first four pious caliphs, Abbasid caliphs, other Muslim sultans as well as Alexander the Great, Plato, and Aristotle.

Despite the fact that most of the mirror literature were written for a specific king or vizier, Barani wrote *Fatāwā* as an instruction for (Islamic) rulers in general – his dedication to Firuz Shāh in the title notwithstanding.

Barani's Political Theory in *Fatāwā*

(a) The Conception of Kingship

Although *Fatāwā-ye jahāndāri* was written in India, it cannot be adequately analysed without an eye to main trends in Islamic political thoughts in other parts of Islamic geo-culture. Rosenthal[48] distinguished three main trends in the medieval Islamic political ideas. The first trend concentrated on *Sharia* and the idea of the *Khilafat* (Caliphate), and it was mainly developed by Sunni jurists. Māwardi (972-1058 CE) in his *Ahkam al-Sultaniya* assumed that the *Khalifa* (Caliph) is superior over the *Umma* based on the *Sharia*. In the second trend, Muslim political philosophers like Al-Farabi, Avicenna and Averroes in their *Falsifa* (Philosophy), are strongly influenced not only by *Sharia* but also by the teachings of Plato and Aristotle. In the third trend, the Mirrors for Princes genre offers advice to rulers with a more practical orientation on statecraft as opposed to political jurisprudence and political philosophy. It should be noted here that most of the medieval mirrors for princes in Islamic geo-culture were written in Persian while the majority of philosophical-theological and jurisprudential works were in Arabic.

Tabatabai[49] perceived medieval Persian texts like *Siyāsat nāmeh* as a 'continuation' of pre-Islamic Iranian mirrors for princes that articulate the '*Iranshahri*' (or '*Iranopolis*') tradition of statecraft and Persian kingship. Tabatabai sees in *Iranshahri* thought a consistent pattern of thinking in Sassanid Iran about politics and statecraft, centered on the notion of kingship. *Iranshahri* ideas rotate around key concepts such as the ideal king with *Farrah* (divine authority), the relationships between politics and religion, social strata and justice.

On the other hand, Haghighat[50] recognises the influence on new Persian mirrors by the pre-Islamic Sassanid mirrors but also sees specificities in the new Persian mirrors that were determined by their historical contexts in Islamic Persia.

Most remarkably, Persian was the only language in which mirrors for princes were written in the Islamic world, and this literature emerged in Persia or what we may call the '*Ajam* world'. That is why Tabatabai[51] asserts that the political discourse of mirror for princes that emerged in Islamic period of Persia (or *Ajam* geo-culture) "cannot be considered as a component of so-called Islamic political thoughts." Therefore, these mirrors should be seen as evolved forms of Sassanid political ideas that were written in Pahlavi, but within a new Islamic context.

Tabatabai[52] mostly focused on *Siyāsat nāmeh* as the prime example of the continuity of pre-Islamic Persian political ideas. However, he is unfamiliar with next generation of Persian mirrors for princes that had not been written in Persia, but in India. It seems that *Fatāwā-ye jahāndāri* was strongly influenced by political works that were written in *Ajam* geo-culture such as *Siyāsat nāmeh*. However, it goes beyond the mere imitation of earlier works.

Siyāsat nāmeh as well as *Fatāwā-ye jahāndāri* are rooted in pre-Islamic Sassanid advice literature, but reflect the social and political changes in an Islamic context. In spite of some references to Islam, the Quran, the Hadith and the records of the caliphs, this theory of kingship remains fundamentally alien to the caliphate concept.

As Daryayi shows,[53] *Shāhanshāh* (King of Kings) was the head of Sassanid Empire in Persia. Early Sassanid kings were considered as divine. *Shāhanshāh* was not an ordinary creature and should be respected and obeyed as a divine. According to Daryayi,[54] after further development of Zoroastrian theology, the Sassanian *Shāhanshāh* gradually took on more sacred duties. Like *Ohrmazd* (the Zoroastrian God) who fights chaos in the cosmos, the Shāhanshāh should fight chaos and bring back order to the earth. So "through the order, the well-being of the people was secured and this well-being only feasible through the dispensation of justice by the king." In the context of the pre-Islamic Iranian notion of kingship, *Farrah* is a divine light and can be considered as divine authority, which empowers the king to rule over an empire. Anyone who has *Farrah-e izadi* (God's Grace), "would have the right to succeed or accede to the throne, and his rule would, therefore, be regarded as legitimate".[55] Therefore, according to the notion of kingship in *Iranshahri* tradition, it was assumed that *Shāhanshāh* received his right to rule as a gift from God (*Ohrmazd* or *Ahuramazda*). *Farrah* is a singular privilege which enables him to rule. However, *Farrah* is not a reason for claiming divinity as such. If the *Shāhanshāh* proclaimed outright his divinity or were unjust towards the people, particularly by being unable to maintain peace and stability, he would lose the *Farrah-ye izadi*. Not only in most of pre-Islamic Pahlavi sources and the new Persian *Shahnameh,* is this notion of kingship manifest, but also in the Sassanid artifact *Naqsh-e Rostam,* which depicts Ardeshir (the first Sassanid *Shāhanshāh*) receiving the *Farrah* from Ahuramazda. *Farrah* is symbolised in what looks like a roll of a *Farman* (charter). A stone inscription above Ardeshir's horse states in three languages, "Ardeshir is *Shāhanshāh* (King of Kings) of Iran who is blessed by God. (He is) the son of Bābak Shāh".[56]

Interestingly, several centuries later, Nezām al-Molk – a very strict Sunni and founder of *Nezāmiyeh Madrasah* system for teaching Sunni Islam jurisprudence – dropped the Sunni theory of Caliphate. Instead, under the influence of Sassanid theory of kingship, he adopted the concept of the 'King with the God's grace'. This conceptualisation of kingship clearly differs from the model of *Khilafat* (Caliphate) in Sunni Islam orthodoxy. Nezām al-Molk, at the beginning of *Siyāsat nāmeh* states:

> In every age and time, God (be He exalted) chooses one member of human race, and, having endowed him with godly and kingly virtue, entrusts him with the interests of the world and well-being of His servants. He charges that person to close the doors of corruption, confusion, and discord.[57]

Ziyā Barani too was a very a strict Sunni Muslim. Nevertheless, he also adopted the pre-Islamic notion of kingship (Padishah) without any emphasis on the *Sharia*-based concept of Caliphate. Barani in the first phrase of the first advice writes:

> Padishah is the wonderful creature of Allah (be He exalted).[58]

Comparing *Siyāsat nāmeh* and *Fatāwā-ye jahāndāri*, similar phrases can be identified:

> Almighty God selected Padishah among all other creatures and gave him all glories and greatness of the world.[59]

Like earlier works of pre-Islamic advice literature, Ziyā Barani described King as someone who has God's grace, but no personal divinity:

> As Sultan Mahmud said: O my sons and the kings of Islam! You should know it, and remember it! Kingship is one of the greatest affairs of the world. Because, an individual who was equal with other people in terms of creation, mentality, appearance, and needs is designated by God and he becomes superior and all other sons of Adam are his subjects.[60]

It seems that Ziyā Barani's concentration on the kingship as a political institution has an objective historical background. Nezām al-Molk tried to establish a centralised empire in a divided territory that was under the control of several Khans and tribes. Transformation of the Turk-Seljuk Sultanate into an integrated empire with a centralised administration like Sassanid Persia was Nezām al-Molk's strategic goal. Similarly, Ziyā Barani sought to cope with the political difficulties for Sunni Muslim rulers after the collapse of Abbasid Caliphate in Baghdad. In its early stage, the Caliph as the deputy of the Prophet (not God) symbolised the religious and political unity in the Muslim world. At the beginning of Islam, the Caliph actually possessed dual – pontifex maximus-like – powers and was considered as the temporal and spiritual leader. However, after the rise of the Turk sultanate in the Islamic world, the caliph's temporal power decreased and was limited to Baghdad. Differentiating between authority and power, Makdisi elaborated Caliph-Sultan relations in the 11th century:

> It was the force of attraction between authority and power which brought into conflict the interests of the Caliph and Sultan. In the golden age of the Caliphate, the Caliph possessed both authority and power. When power slipped from the Caliph's hands, the struggle began between him and the holder of power. But the Sultan was always at a disadvantage, for he always was in need of being legitimised; hence his struggle to achieve stability through a reintegration of power and authority to his own advantage.[61]

Scholars such as Ghazāli suggested and formulated the new form of power relations in the Islamic world. Whereas Ghazāli recognised the secular authority of Turk Sultans, he suggested they should formally acknowledge the caliph's legitimacy and symbolically offer him their allegiance. So, the secular Turkish sultans held power, although their moral and religious legitimacy could only be provided by the caliph.[62]

With the collapse of Abbasid Caliphate in Baghdad, the question of moral and religious authority for Sunni Turkish kings had to be addressed. Political instability in Delhi and rise and fall of diverse dynasties in a short period of time can be perceived as the consequence of the collapse of the foundation of political legitimacy in the Islamic world. That is why the Sultan of Delhi, Mohammad ibn Tughlaq, who was faced with various political rivals, found a survivor of Abbasid family in Egypt and offered him his allegiance as the Caliph.[63]

In contrast, Ziyā Barani – even though he was a Sunni Muslim – never theorised Sultan-Caliph relations and preferred to shape his advice with an eye to the pre-Islamic Iranian notion of kingship. In this perspective, the king was considered as the 'shadow' of God on the earth endued with *Farrah.*

Anarchy, Order, and Justice

Ziyā Barani in *Fatāwā-ye jahāndāri*, like Nezām al-Molk and Kauṭilya, considered monarchy as the universal form of government. Nevertheless, Barani's theory of kingship was not limited to *Farrah* notion. He elaborated the concept of kingship with reference to justice and anarchy. The concept of 'justice equals order' was widespread in the pre-Islamic mirrors and *Ajam* literature. However, Barani's conceptualisation of justice and anarchy is closely related to the *Arthaśāstra* in ancient India.

While, Kauṭilya, and Barani are separated in time and political and cultural context, there is some remarkable resemblance between their notions of kingship. Kauṭilya at the beginning of the *Arthaśāstra* introduced basic anthropological features underlying politics. The man is driven by instincts and affects: "lust, anger, greed, pride, arrogance, and foolhardiness".[64] Since, human beings constantly get in conflicts of interests with each other, this anthropological features lead to a pristine situation of anarchy among human beings: the condition of *mātsya-nyāya* (big fish devour smaller fish). Men, fearing for their life and property, decide to install a king who can enforce order and end violent anarchy.[65] Similarly, Ziyā Barani[66] submits his view of the fundamental anthropological features of man at the beginning of the first advice of *Fatāwā-ye jahāndāri*:

> Jealousy, greed, anger, hatred, and evil are inhered within the nature of human beings.

While Barani exempts Prophets, *Awliya* (plural form of Wail, literally means custodian, and Sufi saints or masters in the Sufi context), and people guided by eternal providence, he asserted that anger, greed, and Jealousy are central features of majority of human beings' anthropological constitution.[67] In the fifth advice, he described the condition of anarchy (*Harj va marj*) in which the "oppressors, dominants, unrulies, usurpers, looters, deniers of the day of Judgment violate the property and family of the weak, obedient and helpless people and orphans".[68] For enforcing order (*Intizam*), justice (*adl*) is needed. He defined justice (*adl*) as the antonym of anarchy. According to Barani,[69] establishing justice is the fundamental reason for the supremacy, prestige, and power of kings. The power of the king is necessary to end the condition of anarchy.

Citing a Quranic verse [51:56], Barani argues that the purpose of creation of human beings and *Jinns* ('demons') is the worship of God. In Islamic conception, the Arabic term of *Ebadat* (worship) literally means to be servant or slave. Being a servant of God (*bandagi* in Persian) is attributed to characteristics such as weakness and imperfection relative to God, modesty, humbleness, and obeisance, whereas the necessary attributes of a king – pride, dignity, eminence, and grandeur – are the opposites of those required for devotional servitude. However, these necessary characteristics of kings are essential to ending anarchy, enforcing order and establishment of justice.[70] Such explicit differentiation between personal morality and kings' morality cannot be found in previous Persian or Islamic works on politics. Of course, some schools of Islamic thought based on the concept of *Masliah* (beneficence) in the condition of *force majeure* permitted the short-term abandonment of some rules of *Sharia*, nevertheless highlighting and acknowledging dual morality is an innovative and revolutionary feature of Barani's thought – but one that is consistent with Kauṭilyan political thought.

Question of the Link between Religion and Politics

Edward Gibbon (1737-1794 CE), famous English historian, in his *The History of the Decline and Fall of the Roman Empire*, wrote, "Mohammad (d. 632 CE), with the sword in one hand and the Quran in the other, erected his throne on the ruins of Christianity and of Rome".[71] This image cannot be generalised to Muslim polity in all ages and times. However, the age of Mohammad and what Sunni Muslims call it as the age of the rightly-guided caliphs (632-661 CE) played a significant role in the construction of the notion of politics and religion among Sunni Muslims. In the early Sunni political *fiqh* (jurisprudence), Caliph (*Khalifa*) was considered as the successor of the Prophet and supreme leader of the *Umma* (the community of Muslims). As the ruler of *Umma*, the caliph not only was considered as a religious leader (with the functions such as leading the communal prayers or collecting religious taxes) but also he exercised the temporal roles of the Prophet.[72]

By contrast, pre-Islamic Persian tradition of statecraft had a different perspective about the relation between politics and religion. *Name-ye Tansar*

(Letter of Tansar), a pre-Islamic Sassanid *Andarz*, illustrates the relations between religion and state:

> Do not be surprised that I enthusiastically consider the welfare of the mundane world a prerequisite for the sustenance of the religious conjunctions. Religion and state are born twins. They will never be separated.[73]

Similar notion was repeated in another pre-Islamic Sassanid text *Ahd-e Ardeshir* (*Ardeshir's Testament*):

> Religion and kingship are two brothers, and neither can dispense with the other. Religion is the foundation of kingship, and kingship protects religion, for whatever lacks a foundation must perish, and whatever lacks a protector disappears.[74]

In the Sassanid Empire, Zoroastrianism was the most widespread religion and had the greatest number of believers. The first Sassanid king of kings Ardeshir (226-241 CE) had a family with a Zoroastrian priesthood background and his counselor Tansar supported and strengthened the Zoroastrian orthodoxy. Sassanid dynasty considered themselves as the successors of Achaemenid kings. For the unification of empire, Zoroastrianism could play the role of the state religion. However, the King and royal family were not seen as being (high) priests; yet they fully supported Zoroastrianism. *Mobedan* (Zoroastrian priests) had a high status at the court and in the empire. However, Sassanid kings possessed the temporal power and authority, and they tried to keep the balance between their power and *Mobedan* influence. Religion was also a source of conflict between the Christian Byzantine Empire and the Sassanid empire. The King of Kings of *Iranshahr* was responsible for the protection of Zoroastrianism.[75]

So, in pre-Islamic Persian royal tradition, there were two domains of power. In the first domain, *Shāhanshāh* had the temporal power and he was supported by God's grace. In the second domain, *Mobedan* had the spiritual authority, and they controlled the fire temples. However, the *Mobedan* had no right to intervene in temporal issues. *Shāhanshāh* should support the state religion, try to expand its reach, should respect the principles of religion and act as a faithful ruler. This notion of kingship is entirely different from political *fiqh*, which views the caliph as the successor of the prophet and his temporal and divine authority.

This pre-Islamic idea of kingship and religion became the central foundation of new hybrid Persian mirror for princes like *Siyāsat nāmeh*. This happened in the new context of Zoroastrianism being substituted by Sunni Islam, Sassanid *Shāhanshāh* with Turk Sultans and *Mobedan* with *Ulema*.

Ziyā Barani draws on these concepts and metaphors. Similar to the pre-Islamic Letter of Tansar, he repeatedly states: "Religion and state are born twins".[76] However, Barani did not simply borrow the Sassanid idea but tried to develop it, according to the political context that emerged after the collapse of the caliphate. For the conceptualisation of relations between the state and religion, he articulated a hybrid narration, using Keyumarth, the mythological First Man in the Persian mythology and Seth, the biblical character and Adam's son. He introduced Keyumarth and Seth as twin brothers and stated that they were the first king and the first prophet respectively:

> As it was mentioned in the historical texts of previous nations, Seth (Sheys) and Keyumarth both were sons of Adam, and they were twin brothers. Based on God's comprehensive wisdom, he revealed to Adam and told him, "I will give the prophethood to Seth and his sons in order to guiding other Adam's children to the right way and making them deserving for the heaven and saving them from the hell. [In addition], Keyumarth and his sons in the territory of domination, justice, and beneficence should live with other Adam's children. [Keyumarth and his sons] are responsible for worldly affairs and they make the world habitable for Adam's children."[77]

Accordingly, for the first time in Islamic political thought, Barani explicitly differentiates between prophethood and statecraft. *Dindāri* (practicing religion) and *Jahāndāri* (Statecraft or governance) are two keywords that Barani employed for highlighting this contrast. *Dindāri* is related to spiritual and divine realm and *Jahāndāri* deals with worldly affairs and temporal power:

> *Dindāri* is what Mohammad-ibn Abdullah Qureshi [The Prophet] did. Therefore, everyone that follows his way of life, speeches and practices are *Dindār*. *Jahāndāri* and statecraft are whatever Khosrow Parviz [a Sassanid *Shāhanshāh*] and his ancestors did in *Ajam* (Persia). Then, everybody who follows their way of life, speeches and practices can govern, and all the world obey him.[78]

Barani has a ground breaking new perspective on the distinction between state and religion that was not seen in *Siyāsat nāmeh* or other comparable mirrors for princes. He frankly talked about the difference between Mohammad's pious lifestyle and his pragmatist way of statecraft. According to Barani, Mohammad's miracle is that he as the prophet of God possessed both powers:

> Possessing of *Jamshidi*[79] and *Darvishi*[80] at the same time is the miracle of the prophet of Islam.

He interpreted the failure of the age of the rightly-guided caliphs (632-661 CE) as the result of inattention to necessities of *Jahāndāri* and what today we call 'realpolitik':

> After Mohammad, if Caliphs or Muslim kings want to follow the prophet's traditions and his way of style, the governing is impossible and they cannot even survive![81]

The distinction between the religious and political realm and their inevitable contradictions implies to a turning point in the history of political thought in both Islamic and *Ajam* geo-cultures. Considering the failure of Caliphate model, Ziyā Barani, with a realist perspective transcended the pre-Islamic Iranian notion of kingship to a more secular and realistic conceptualisation that can be compared with Kauṭilya and Machiavelli. Barani discussed the contradictions between statecraft – based on power, material factors and practical considerations – and religion with its idealist notions about morality or ethical premises. He concluded that:

> There is a complete conflict and clear contradiction between Mohammad's way of life and his tradition and Khosrow's way of life and kingship.[82]

Therefore, Muslim kings should follow the manner of '*Akasere-ye Ajam*' (Sassanid kings) and the following old rituals of the Sassanid court that can improve glory of kingdom if employed:

- To make golden crowns and thrones.
- To build castles and palaces.
- To gather treasures.
- To expand personal property.
- To wear silk clothing.
- To build new Harams.
- To punish others even if it is against *Sharia*.

That leaves us with puzzling questions: Why Barani recommended *Padishah-e-Islam* to oppress, intolerantly, Hinduism in India? Why had he an extreme enmity toward Brahmins as the *A'eme-ye-Kofr* (Leaders of Infidelity)? The main answer can be found in the pre-Islamic notion of kingship. A Sassanid *Shāhanshāh* should support the state religion of the empire – that was one of his principal duties. As elaborated above, this notion flowed into the Islamic context with appropriations and modifications. Sunni Islam for the Sunni Turkish Sultan had the same place as Zoroastrianism for the Persian *Shāhanshāh*. That is why Barani several times asked *Padishah-e-Islam* to enforce *Sharia* in Indian society, particularly *Qisas*, *Had*, *Tazir*, and appoint the stern *Muhtasibs* (religious police). Not only he took an extreme stand against Hindus, but also he advised kings to take a stand against Shia Muslims, philosophy scholars, and other non-Sunni Muslims.

Zawābet: State Law and Public Welfare

As was mentioned above, *Fatāwā-ye jahāndāri* cannot be considered as a mere replica of *Siyāsat nāmeh*. Due to the particular political and social context, Barani developed conceptual innovations in his political theory. However, as a pragmatist Muslim political theorist, he realised that enforcing *Sharia* in a multifarious society with growing complexities collides with efficient statecraft. Therefore, Barani strongly emphasised the need for *Zawābet* (secular state laws) in addition to *Sharia*. He remained skeptical about the capability of the realm of *Dindāri* for resolving practical political problems and tried to solve the contradiction between religion and practical politics via differentiation of the two realms. He defined *Manfa'at-e halva Kheyr-e Ma'al* (current interest and final beneficence) as the first and foremost goal of *Jahāndāri* (statecraft or governance).[83] Barani defines *Zawābet* as:

> A rule of action which a king imposes as an obligatory duty on himself for realising goals of statecraft (the interest of the state), and he never deviates from them.[84]

Zawābet, principally, is made by the king. However, they should be implemented after consultation with wise and loyal counselors. Barani realised that *Sharia* was static, and Muslims needed rules of statecraft in response to the change of time and circumstance.[85]

Barani's definition of the goal of state cannot be found in the earlier Islamic political jurisprudence texts and can be only compared with the ancient Indian tradition of statecraft. Barani's idea of the purpose of state can be equated with Kauṭilya's notion of state and what Liebig describes as 'Kauṭilyan raison d'état'.[86] Moreover, *Zawābet* can be compared with the concept of *rājadharma* as it was understood by Kauṭilya. The concept implies that the principles of *dharma* are the base of state's authority. Thus, the fulfillment of king's duties and responsibilities – based on *rājadharma* – is the central factor for the stability of society and the happiness of the people.[87]

According to Barani, the king, and his government should follow the religious *Sharia*, but at the same time, they should obey the *Zawābet*, as the state's laws and regulations, in the name of '*istihsan*' (the public good or welfare). If these laws violated the *Sharia*, the principle of the necessity of '*istihsan*' (the public good) should be called upon in their favour.[88]

Zawābet should be based on four pre-conditions:

1. It should not violate the *Sharia* and the religion.
2. It should be congruent with the elites' interest and the aspirations of the masses. It should not be source of people's suffering.
3. Precedents or similarities with these rules should be found in the reign of earlier faithful kings.
4. If it was against *Sharia*, but its non-implementation would cause damage to the people, it can be adopted.

As a result, as Ahmad[89] indicates, Muslim rulers of both Delhi Sultanate and the Mughal Empire (1526-1750 CE), were not mere executors of *Sharia* law in India. As Barani formulated it, Muslim rulers adopted and implemented *Zawābet* that was secular in essence. Iqtidar Alam Khan states:

> That the Delhi Sultanate as well as the Mughal empire were far from being Islamic theocracies and actually carried within their state organisations many overtly secular features that are fully borne out by the observations of Barani and Abu al-Fazl on the problems of sovereignty.[90]

Conclusion

The subject of this study is political theory in the era of the Delhi Sultanate – specifically Ziyā Barani's political theory as articulated in his *Fatāwā-ye jahāndāri*. The core objective of this study is to answer these three questions:

1. What are the essential elements of Barani's political thought?
2. Which political, cultural and social factors influenced *Fatāwā-ye jahāndāri* and Barani's political theory?
3. What is the influence of a) Islamic political ideas, b) pre-Islamic Iranian political ideas, and c) ancient Indian tradition of statecraft, as articulated by Kauṭilya, on Barani's political thought?

Regarding the first question, the political ideas of Barani are based on his distinction between '*Jahāndāri*' (Statecraft, literally means world-keeping) and '*Dindāri*' (practising religion). Barani's argumentation emphasises a clear distinction between state policy and personal, religion-derived morality. Therefore, for Barani, the unity of these two realms was possible only as a miracle with Prophet Mohammad. Thus, Islamic rulers should follow the Sassanid tradition of statecraft as the best way of '*Jahāndāri*'. Furthermore, the idea of *Zawābet* as state laws that are established by the king for the public good is another distinctive feature of Barani's political ideas.

Regarding the second question, the collapse of the Abbasid Caliphate and the rise of questions of political legitimacy, political instability in the Delhi sultanate and the immigration of Persian speaking elites to Delhi are the objective factors that impacted the formation of Barani's political theory.

Finally, this study shows how Barani's political thought was influenced by pre-Islamic Sassanid tradition of statecraft. Moreover, his ideas can be seen as the continuity of Nezām al Molk's political thoughts and his *Siyāsat nāmeh*. Similar to pre-Islamic Iranian political ideas, he introduced king as the 'wonderful creation' who is God's deputy on the earth. Also, similar to the role of Sassanid kings for the protection of Zoroastrianism, the king of Islam should protect the official religion (Sunni Islam). However, his ideas cannot be seen as the mere copy of Persian political thought. *Fatāwā-ye jahāndāri* features innovative ideas like:

- The theoretical foundation of kingship.
- The theory of justice versus anarchy.
- The separation between the realms of state and religion.
- The necessity and importance of secular law.

As of now, there is no tangible evidence that Ziyā Barani had access to ancient Indian works on statecrafts such as Kauṭilya's *Arthaśāstra* or similar Indian works. However, the *Fatāwā-ye jahāndāri* does contain thought-figures that appear homologous with ideas in the *Arthaśāstra*. Thus, it can be stated that the *Fatāwā-ye jahāndāri* is a hybrid text with Islamic, pre-Islamic Persian and ancient Indian thought-components. Research digging deeper into the latter idea-component is a desideratum.

END NOTES

Note: For the transliteration of Persian words, the author has followed the 'Iranian Studies scheme'.

1. cf. Auer (2015), Jauhri (2001), Kolff (2008), Moosvi (2009), Singh (2008).
2. Mehta (2009: 15).
3. Barani (1862).
4. Bulliet et al. (2012).
5. Habib (1999: 24).
6. Sarkar (2006: 327).
7. Varma (1986: 218-220).
8. Black (2011: 166).
9. Khan (1986: 5).
10. Alam (2000: 220).
11. Roy and Alam (2011: 30).
12. Habibullah (1941: 210-211).
13. A.S. Khan in Barani (1972: 3).
14. Barani (1972: 2).
15. Hardy (1978: 127).
16. Alam (2004: 31).
17. Syros (2012: 545).
18. Habib (1999: 20).
19. Hardy (1988).
20. Mehta (2009: 15).
21. Habib (1999: 20), Hardy (1988).
22. Barani (1862: 350).
23. Habib (1981: 307).
24. cf. Barani (1938: 71).
25. Habib (1981: 59).
26. Alam et al. (2000: 23).
27. Chopra (2012: 31).

28. Alam (2003: 133).
29. Alam et al. (2000: 24).
30. Gould (2015: 91).
31. *Ibid.*: 92.
32. Alam (2003: 134).
33. Awfi (1982).
34. cf. Gould (2015).
35. Hendushāh-eAstarābādi (2008: 267-268).
36. Barani (1862: 66-67).
37. *Ibid.*: 352.
38. *Ibid.*: 352-353.
39. *Ibid.*: 9.
40. Habib (1999: 21).
41. Darling (2013: 223).
42. We do not delve here into the never-ending disputes among Indologists about the authorship and dating of *Arthaśāstra:* The first position expounds that Kauṭilya is the author of the *Arthaśāstra* and it was written at the end of fourth century BCE in India. Some other Sanskrit philologists claim that the *Arthaśāstra* is a compilation of multiple text components written by several (unknown) authors between the fourth century BCE and fifth century CE. cf. Liebig (2013: 101).
43. The Sassanid (Sassanian) Empire was the last pre-Islamic Persian empire, ruled by the Sassanian dynasty from 224 to 651 CE.
44. Luce (2010: 1916).
45. Haghighat (2012: 2).
46. Luce (2010: 1916).
47. Aquil (2008: 168).
48. Rosenthal (1958: 1-10).
49. Tabatabai (2006: 77).
50. Haghighat (2012: 3).
51. Tabatabai (2013: 115).
52. Tabatabai (2006, 2013).
53. Daryayi (2010: 41).
54. *Ibid.*: 42.
55. Katouzian (2003: 235).
56. cf. Ghiasabadi (2012).
57. Nizam al-Mulk (2002: 9).
58. Barani (1972: 3).
59. *Ibid.*: 88.
60. *Ibid.*: 147.
61. Makdisi (1970: 262).
62. March (2012: 113).
63. Barani (1862: 491-492).
64. Liebig (2014b: 4).
65. *Ibid.*: 5.
66. Barani (1972: 3).

67. *Ibid.*: 4.
68. *Ibid.*: 66.
69. *Ibid.*: 67.
70. cf. *Ibid.*: 68-69.
71. Gibbon (2003: 893).
72. Bosworth (1960: 948).
73. Quoted in Hunter (1998: 42-43).
74. Quoted in Lambton (2013: 41).
75. cf. Daryayi (2010), Tabatabai (2006).
76. Barani (1972: 333).
77. *Ibid.*: 333-334.
78. *Ibid.*: 140.
79. Jamshid is the mythological First King in the Persian mythology. cf. *ibid.*
80. Darvish is Persian word, meaning 'poor', literally. In the context of Sufism, it has been used in the same manner as the Arabic word "*Faqir*" to refer to Sufi holy men who have given up worldly life for a spiritual and devoted life. cf. *ibid.*
81. Barani (1972).
82. *Ibid.*
83. *Ibid.*: 217-218.
84. *Ibid.*
85. *Ibid.*: 219.
86. Liebig (2014b: 13).
87. Narayan (2004: 21).
88. Barani (1972: 217-223).
89. Ahmad (2009: 148).
90. Khan (1986: 4).

References

Agarwal, Deepa (2013): *Chanakya – The Master of Statecraft*. New Delhi: Penguin India.

Ahmad, I. (2009): "Genealogy of the Islamic State: Reflections on Maududi's Political thought and Islamism". *Journal of the Royal Anthropological Institute*, 15(1), 145-162.

Aiyar, C.P. Ramaswami (2013): *The Cultural Heritage of India, Volume II – Itihasa, Puranas, Dharma and Other Sastras*. Belur Math, Ramakrishna Mission.

Alam, M. (2000): "Shari'a and Governance in the Indo-Islamic Context". In: Gilmartin, D. & Lawerence, B.B. (Eds.), *Beyond Turk and Hindu: Rethinking Religious Identities in Islamicate South Asia*. Gainesville: University Press of Florida, 216-245.

Alam, M. (2003): "The culture and politics of Persian in precolonial Hindustan". In: Pollock. S. (Ed.), *Literary Cultures in History: Reconstructions from South Asia*. Los Angeles: University of California Press, 131-198.

Alam, M. (2004): *Languages of Political Islam in India 1200-1800*. London: C. Hurst & Co Publishers Ltd.

Alam, M. / Delvoye, F. N. / Gaborieau, M. (2000): "Introduction". In: Alam, M. / Delvoye, F.N. / Gaborieau, M. (Eds.), *The making of Indo-Persian Culture : Indian and French Studies*. New Delhi: Manohar.

Alder, Bruce Currie / Kanbur, Ravi / Malone, David M. / Medhora, Rohinton Medhora (2014): "The State of Development Thought". In: Alder, Bruce Currie / Kanbur, Ravi / Malone, David M. / Medhora (Eds.), *International Development: Ideas, Experience, & Prospects*. Oxford: Oxford University Press.

Allen, Charles (2012): *Ashoka*. London: Little Brown.

Ames, Roger T. (Trans.) (1993): *Sun-tzu - The Art of Warfare*. The First Translation Incorporating the Recently Discovered *Yin-ch'üeh-shan texts*. New York: Ballantine Books.

Aquil, R. (2008): "On Islam and Kufr in the Delhi Sultanate: Towards a Re-interpretation of Ziyā 'al-Din Barani's Fatawa-I Jahandari". In: Datta, Rajat (Ed.), *Rethinking a Millennium – Perspectives on Indian History from the Eighth to Eighteenth Centuries*. New Delhi: Aakar Books, 168-197.

Auboyer, Jeannine (1965): *Daily Life in Ancient India from 200 BC to 700 AD*. London: Weidenfeld and Nicolson.

Auer, B. (2015): "Pre-modern Intellectual Debates on the Knowledge of History and Ziyā al-Din Barani's Tarikh-I Firuzshahi". *Indian Economic and Social History Review*, 52(2), 207-223.

Awfi, M. (1982): *Tazkira-e Lubabul Albab* (M. Abbasi Ed.). Tehran: Fakhr-e Razi.

Bajpai, Kanti / Basit, Saira / Krishnappa, V. (Eds.) (2014): *India's Grand Strategy – History, Theory, Cases*. New Delhi: Routledge.

Bandyopadhyaya, Jayantanuja (1993): *A General Theory of International Relations*. New Delhi: Allied Publishers Limited.

Bandyopadhyaya, Narayan Chandra (2005): *Kauṭilya or An Exposition of His Social Ideal and Political Theory*. New Delhi: D.K. Publishers. First Published in 1927.

Barani, S.H. (1938): Ziauddin Barani. *Islamic Culture*, 22(1), 76-97.

Barani, Z. a. D. (1972): *Fatawa-yi Jahandari* (A. S. Khan, Trans. and Ed.). Lahore: Habib Press.

Baranī, Z., a. D. (1862): *Tārikh-e Firuz Shāhi*. Edited by Sayyid Aḥmad Khān. Calcutta: Bibliotheca Indica.

Basham, A.L. (2004): *The Wonder that Was India*. Third revised Edn. London: Picador.

Baxi, Upendra (1967): *Kautilyan Principles and the Law of Nations*. Department of Jurisprudence and International Law, Institute for Advanced Studies in Jurisprudence: University of Sydney.

Behera, Navnita Chadha (2007): "Re-imagining IR in India". *International Relations of the Asia-Pacific*, 7(3), 341-368.

Bernard, Vincent (2010): "Editorial: Occupation". *International Review of the Red Cross – Humanitarian Debate: Law, Policy and Action,* 94 (885), 5-11.

Bhabha, Homi K. (1994): *The Location of Culture*. London and New York: Routledge.

Bhandarkar, D.R. (1984): "Asoka's Place in History". In: Bhatia, H.S. (Ed.) *Political, Legal and Military History of India - Volume II*. New Delhi: Deep & Deep Publications, 239-254.

Bhattacharya, Bishnupada (2013): "Sanskrit Prose". In: Chatterji, Suniti Kumar (Ed.), *The Cultural Heritage of India, Volume V – Language and Literature*. Belur Math: Ramakrishna Mission, 253-272.

Bisht, Medha (2014): "The Concept of Order in Arthashastra". *South Asian Survey*, 21(1/2). (Not yet released).

Bisht, Medha (2016): "Revisiting the *Arthasastra*: Back to Understanding IR". In: Gautam, P.K. /Mishra, S. / Gupta, A. (Eds.), *Indigenous Historical*

Knowledge – Kautilya and His Vocabulary, Volume II. New Delhi: IDSA/ Pentagon Press, 20-33.

Black, A. (2011): *The History of Islamic Political Thought – From the Prophet to the Present*. Edinburgh: Edinburgh University Press.

Boesche, Roger (2002a): *The First Great Political Realist: Kautilya and his Arthashastra*. Lanham, USA: Lexington Books.

Boesche, Roger (2002b): "Moderate Machiavelli? Contrasting the Prince with the *Arthashastra* of Kautilya". *Critical Horizons*, 3(2), 253-276.

Born, Lester Kruger (1928): "The Perfect Prince: A Study in Thirteenth- and Fourteenth-Century Ideals". *Speculum,* 3(4), 470-504.

Bosworth, C.E. (1984/2011): "Ajam". *Encyclopaedia Iranica,* at http:// www.iranicaonline.org/articles/ajam (Accessed on December 2, 2016).

Bosworth, C.E. (Ed.) (1960): "Khalifa". In: *Encyclopaedia of Islam* (2nd Edn.). Lieden: Brill.

Botero, Giovanni (1589): *Dela Ragion di Stato*, quoted in: Münkler, Herfried (1987), *Im Namen des Staates – Die Begründung der Staatsraison in der Frühen Neuzeit*. Frankfurt and Main: Fischer.

Bourdieu, Pierre (1990): *The Logic of Practice*. Stanford: Stanford University Press.

Bozeman, Adda B. (1960): *Politics and Culture in International History*. Princeton, NJ: Princeton University Press.

Bozemann, Adda B. (1992): *Strategic Intelligence & Statecraft*. Washington DC: Brassey's.

Brekke, Torkel (2006): "Between Prudence and Heroism – Ethics of War in the Hindu tradition". In: Brekke, Torkel (Ed.), *The Ethics of War in Asian Civilizations – A Comparative Perspective*. London and New York: Routledge.

Brown, D. Mackenzie (1964): *The White Umbrella – Indian Political Thought from Manu to Gandhi*. Berkeley and Los Angeles: University of California Press.

Bühler, G. (Trans.) (1886): *Manusmriti: The Laws of Manu*. Oxford: The Clarendon Press.

Bulliet, R. / Cook, D. / Euben, R. L. / Fahmy, K. / Griffel, F. / Haykel, B. /Moosa, E. (2012): *The Princeton Encyclopedia of Islamic Political Thought*. Princeton: Princeton University Press.

Buzan, Barry (2004): *An Introduction to the English School of International Relations*. Maiden: Polity Press.

Carr, E.H. (1981): *Twenty Year's Crisis, 1919-1939 – An Introduction to the Study of International Relations*. London: McMillan. First Published in 1946.

Chakravarti, P.C. (1987): *The Art of War in Ancient India*, Delhi: Karan Publications.

Chakravarty, Nilima (1992): *Indian Philosophy: The Pathfinders and the System Builders (700 BC to 100 AD)*. New Delhi: Allied Publishers Limited.

Chandra, Satish (2014): *History of Medieval India*. Reprint. Orient Blackswan. First printed in 2007.

Chang, Ruth (2000): "Understanding Di and Tian: Deity and Heaven from Shang to Tang Dynasties". *Sino-Platonic Papers*, No. 108.

Chatterjee, Satischandra and Datta, Dhirendramohan (2007): *An Introduction to Indian Philosophy*. New Delhi: Rupa.

Chatterji, B.R. (1967): *History of Indonesia – Early and Medieval*. Meerut: Meenakshi Prakashan.

Chien, Szuma (1979): *Selections From Records of The Historian*, Translated by Yang Hsien-yi and Gladys Yang. Beijing: Foreign Language Press.

Chong, Alan (2011): "A Society of the Weak, the Medium and the Great: Southeast Asia's Lessons in Building Soft Community among States". In: Astrov, Alexander (Ed.), *The Great Power (Mis)Management – The Russian-Georgian War and its Implications for Global Political Order*. Surrey: Ashgate, 135-158.

Chopra, R.M. (Ed.) (2012): *The Rise, Growth and Decline of Indo-Persian Literature* (2nd Edn.). New Delhi: Iran Culture House.

Chousalkar, Ashok S. (1981): "Political Philosophy of Arthashastra tradition". *The Indian Journal of Political Science,* 42(1), 54-66.

Chousalkar, Ashok S. (1986): *Social and Political Implications of the Concept of Justice and Dharma*. Delhi: Mittal Publishers.

Chousalkar, Ashok S. (2004): "Methodology of Kautilya's Arthashastra". *The Indian Journal of Political Science*, 65(1), 55-76.

Chousalkar, Ashok S. (2005): "The Concept of Apaddharma and the Moral Dilemma of Politics", *Indian Literature*, 49(1), 115-127.

Collier, David and Levitsky, Steven (1997): "Democracy with Adjectives: Conceptual Innovation in Comparative Research". *World Politics*, 49, 430-451.

Collier, David and Mahon, James E. Jr. (1993): "Conceptual 'Stretching' Revisited: Adapting Categories in Comparative Analysis". *American Political Science Review*, 87(4), 845-855.

Coupland, Reginald (1944): *The Indian Problem: Report on the Constitutional Problem in India*. Oxford: Oxford University Press.

Croissant, Aurel and Merkel, Wolfgang (2004a): "From Transition to Defective Democracy? Mapping Asian Democratization". *Democratization*, 11(5), 156-179.

Croissant, Aurel and Merkel, Wolfgang (2004b): "Introduction: Democratization in the Early Twenty-first Century". *Democratization*, 11(5), 1-9.

Cunningham, Alexander (1871): *The Ancient Geography of India*. London: Trübner& Co.

Dallmayr, Fred (Ed.) (2010): *Comparative Political Theory*. New York: Palgrave Macmillan.

Danino, Michel (2011): *Cultural Specificities in the History of Indian Science*.

IIC Occasional Publication 34. New Delhi: India International Centre. (Lecture delivered on September 12).

Darling, L.T. (2013): "Mirrors for Princes in Europe and the Middle East: A Case of Historiographical Incommensurability". In: Classen, A. (Ed.), *East meets West in the Middle Ages and Early Modern Times – Transcultural Experiences in the Premodern World.* Berlin: Walter de Gruyter.

Daryayi, T. (2010): *Sasanian Persia: The Rise and Fall of an Empire* (Reprint). London [u.a.]: Tauris [u.a.].

Das, Arbind (1996): *Arthashastra of Kautilya and Fatawa-i-Jahandari of Ziauddin Barani: An Analysis.* Delhi: Pratibha Prakashan.

Diamond, Larry (2002a): "Elections without democracy: Thinking about hybrid regimes". *Journal of Democracy*, 13(2), 21-35.

Diamond, Larry (2002b): "Thinking about Hybrid Regimes", *Journal of Democracy*, 13(1), 21-35.

Dikshitar, V.R. Ramachandra (1987): *War in Ancient India.* Delhi: Motilal Banarsidass. First Edn. Published in 1944.

Dixit, J.N. (2003/2004): *India's Foreign Policy 1947-2003.* Delhi: Picus Books.

Douglas, Mary (1966/1996 reprint): *Purity and Danger – An Analysis of the Concepts of Pollution and Taboo.* London: Routledge.

Drekmeier, Charles (1962): *Kingship and Community in Early India.* Stanford, CA: Stanford University Press.

Eamon, Willam (1994): *Science and the Secrets of Nature: Books of Secrets in Medieval and Early Modern Culture.* Princeton: Princeton University.

Edwardes, Michael (1965): *Everyday Life in Early India.* London: BT Batsford.

Encyclopaedia Britannica (2015). "Ziyā 'al-Din Barani", *Encyclopaedia Britannica*, at http://www.britannica.com/EBchecked/topic/52608/Ziyā -al-Din-Barani (Accessed on May 8, 2015)

Flibbert, Andrew (2013): "The Consequences of Forced State Failure in Iraq". *Political Science Quarterly*, 128(1), 67-95.

Fludernik, Monika (1998a): "The Constitution of Hybridity: Postcolonial Interventions". In: Fludernik, *Hybridity and Postcolonialism – Twentieth-Century Indian Literature.* Tuebingen: Stauffenburg-Verlag.

Fludernik, Monika (Ed.) (1998b): *Hybridity and Postcolonialism: Twentieth-Century Indian Literature.* Tuebingen: Stauffenburg-Verlag.

Forster, Regula and Yavari, Neguin (Eds.) (2015): Mirrors of Princes Reconsidered. Harvard: Centre for Hellenic Studies.

Frank, G. and Gills, B.K. (1993): *The World System – 500 years or 5000.* London: Routledge.

Frankel, Benjamin (Ed.) (1997): *Roots of Realism.* London: Routledge.

Fried, J. and Kailer, T. (Eds.) (2003): *Wissenskulturen – Beiträge zu einem forschungsstraegischen Konzept.* Berlin: Akademie Verlag.

Fried, Johannes (2003): "In den Netzen der Wissensgesellschaft – Das Beispiel des mittelalterlichen Königs- und Fürstenhofes". In: Fried, J. / Kailer, T. (Eds.),

Wissenskulturen – Beiträge zu einem forschungsstraegischen Konzept. Berlin: Akademie Verlag, 141–194.

Friedl, Christian (2005): *Studien zur Beamtenschaft Kaiser Friedrich II. im Königreich Sizilien (1220-1250)*. Wien: Verlag der Akademie der Wissenschaften.

Fuller, J.F.C. (2003): *The Conduct of War 1798-1961 – A Study of French, Industrial, and Russian Revolution on War and Its Conduct*. First Indian Edn. Dehradun: Natraj Publishers. First published in 1961.

Fürstenberg, Kai (2015): *Panchayati Raj in India: The Evolution between 1947 and 1992*. Heidelberg: Electronic Resource, Heidelberg University.

Gajrani, Shiv and Ram, S. (Eds.) (2011): *Kautilya*. New Delhi: Commonwealth.

Gallie, W. B. (1955/1956): "Essentially contested concepts". *Proceedings of the Aristotelian Society*, New Series, 56, 167-198.

Gautam, P. K. (2013a): *One Hundred Years of Kautilya's Arthashastra*. Delhi: Institute for Defence Studies and Analyses (IDSA Monograph Series).

Gautam, P.K. (2013b): "Understanding Kauṭilya's Four Upayas", *IDSA Comment*, at http://www.idsa.in/idsacomments/UnderstandingKautilyasFourUpayas_pkgautam_200613 (Accessed on January 10, 2016).

Gautam, P.K. (2015a): "*Dharmavijay* (Just War), Winning the Peace and War without Spilling Blood". In: Gautam, P.K. /Mishra, S. / Gupta, A. (Eds.), *Indigenous Historical Knowledge – Kautilya and His Vocabulary, volume I*. New Delhi: IDSA/Pentagon Press, 87-95.

Gautam, P.K. (2015b): "Shared Heritage of Ancient Statecraft between Southeast Asia and India". *Insight Southeast*, 4(2), 9-13.

Gautam, P.K. (2015c): *Kautilya's Arthashastra – Contemporary Issue and Comparison*. Delhi: IDSA Monograph Series No. 47. New Delhi: IDSA.

Gautam, P.K. / Mishra, S. / Gupta, A. (Eds.) (2015): *Indigenous Historical Knowledge – Kautilya and his Vocabulary, volume I*, Delhi: Institute for Defence Studies and Analyses/Pentagon Press.

Gautam, P.K. / Mishra, S. / Gupta, A. (Eds.) (2016a): *Indigenous Historical Knowledge – Kautilya and his Vocabulary, volume II*, Delhi: Institute for Defence Studies and Analyses/Pentagon Press.

Gautam, P.K. / Mishra, S. / Gupta, A. (Eds.) (2016b): *Indigenous Historical Knowledge – Kautilya and his Vocabulary, volume III*, Delhi: Institute for Defence Studies and Analyses/Pentagon Press.

Gawlikowski, Krzysztof (1985): "The School of Strategy (bingjia) in the Context of Chinese Civilisation". *East and West*, 35(1/3), 167-210.

Ghiasabadi, Reza Muradi (2012): "Evolution of the Names Iran, Arya, and Fars (Persia) in Ancient Texts", *Persian Studies*, June 3, at http://ghiasabadi.com/what-is-iran-en.html (Accessed June 27, 2015).

Ghosh, Partha (2007): *The Politics of Personal Law in South Asia: Identity, Nationalism and the Uniform Civil Code*. Delhi: Routledge.

Gibbon, E. (2003): *The History of the Decline and Fall of the Roman Empire* (H. Friedrich-Muelle, Ed.). New York: Modern Library.

Gilbert, Allan H. (1938): *Machiavelli's Prince and it Forerunners*. Durham: Duke University Press.

Giles, Lionel (1910): *The Art of War*, Translated. Norwalk: The Puppet Press.

Godrej, Farah (2011): *Cosmopolitan Political Thought: Method, Practice and Discipline*. New York: Oxford University Press.

Gould, R. (2015): "The Geographies of Ajam – The Circulation of Persian Poetry from South Asia to the Caucasus". *The Medieval History Journal*, 18(1), 87-119.

Gould, S. (2002): *The Structure of Evolutionary Theory*. Cambridge: Harvard University Press.

Gowen, Herbert H. (1992): "The Indian Machiavelli or Political Theory in India Two Thousand Years Ago". *Political Science Quarterly*, 44(2), 173-192.

Gray, Colin S. (1999): "Clausewitz Rules, OK? The Future is the Past- with GPS". *Review of International Studies*, 25, 161-182.

Gray, Stuart (2014): "Reexamining Kautilya and Machiavelli – Flexibility and the Problem of Legitimacy in Brahmanical and Secular Realism". *Political Theory*, 2014, 42(6), 635-657.

Grebner, G. and Fried, J. (Eds.) (2008): *Kulturtransfer und Hofgesellschaft im Mittelalter – Wissenskultur am sizialianischen and kastilischen Hof im 13. Jahrhundert*. Berlin: Akadmie Verlag.

Gunderson, Lloyd (1980): *Alexander's Letter to Aristotle about India*. Meisenheim am Glan: Verlag Anton Hain.

Gupta, V.K. (1987): *Kautilyan Jurisprudence*, New Delhi: Self-published Printed Edition.

Gurukkal, Rajan (2013): Book review of *The Past Before Us: Historical Traditions and Early North India* by RomilaThapar, Ranikhet: Permanent Black. In: *Seminar* 650, October, 75-79.

Habib, I. (1999): "Ziyā Baranī's Vision of the State". *The Medieval History Journal*, 2(1), 19-36.

Habib, M. (1958): "Life and thought of Ziauddin Barani". *Medieval India Quarterly*, 3, 197-252.

Habib, M. (1981): *Politics and Society during the Early Medieval Period – Collected Works of Professor Mohammad Habib*, volume I, (K.A. Nizami Ed.). New Delhi: People's Publishing House.

Habib, M. and Khan, A.U.S. (1961): *The Political Theory of the Delhi Sultanate* (including a translation of Ziauddin Barani's Fatawa-I Jahandari). Allahabad: Kitab Mahal.

Habibullah, A. (1941): "Re-evaluation of the Literary Sources of pre-Mughal History". *Islamic Culture*, 15(2), 207-216.

Haghighat, S.S. (2012): *Persian Mirrors for Princes: Pre-Islamic and Islamic*

Mirrors Compared. Paper presented at the New Approaches to the History of Political Thought.

Haiming, Wen (2012): *Chinese Philosophy*. Cambridge: Cambridge University Press.

Halbwachs, Maurice (1991): *Das kollektive Gedächtnis*. Frankfurt am Main: Fischer.

Hale, J.R. (1972): *Machiavelli and Renaissance Italy*. Harmondsworth, UK: Penguin.

Hardy, P. (1978): "Unity and Variety in Indo-Islamic and Perso-Islamic Civilization – Some Ethical and Political Ideas of Ḍiyā 'al-Dīn Baranī of Delhi, of al-Ghazālī and of Naṣīr al-Dīn Tūsī Compared". *Iran*, 16, 127-135.

Hardy, P. (1988): "BARANĪ, ZĪĀ-AL-DĪN, Indian-born Muslim historian who wrote in the period of the Delhi sultanate", *Encyclopaedia Iranica*, at http://www.iranicaonline.org/articles/barani-zia-al-din (Accessed on May 2, 2015).

Hegewald, Julia (2005): "Domes, Tombs and Minarets: Islamic Influences on Jaina Architecture". In: Adam Hardy (Ed.), *The Temple in South Asia, Volume 2 of the Proceedings of the 18th Conference of the European Association of South Asian Archaeologists*. London: British Association for South Asian Studies and the British Academy.

Hegewald, Julia (2006): "From Siva to Parshvanatha – The Appropriation of a Hindu Temple for Jaina Worship". In: Catherine Jarrige & Vincent Lefèvre, (Eds.), *South Asian Archaeology 2001,* 2 volumes. Paris: Editions Recherches sur les Civilisations, 517-523.

Hegewald, Julia (2012): "Building Citizenship: The Agency of Public Buildings and Urban Planning in the Making of the Indian Citizen". In: Mitra, Subrata (Ed.), *Citizenship in the Era of Globalization: Culture, Power and the Flow of Ideas*. Heidelberg: Springer.

Hegewald, Julia and Mitra, Subrata K. (Eds.) (2008), *Re-use: The Art and Politics of Integration and Anxiety*. Delhi: Sage.

Heimann, Betty (1930): *Studien zur Eigenart indischen Denkens*. Tübingen: Mohr.

Heinisch, Klaus (Ed.) (1968): *Kaiser Friedrich II. in Briefen und Berichten seiner Zeit*. Darmstadt: Wissenschaftliche Buchgesellschaft.

Hendushāh-e Astarābādi, M.Q. (2008): *Tārikh-e Fereshteh – Az Āghāz ta Bābur* (History of Fereshteh: From Beginning to Babur). Edited by M. Nasiri. Tehran: Anjoman-e Āsārva Mafākher-e Melli Iran.

Heydte, Friedrich August von (1952): *Die Geburtsstunde des souveränen Staates*. Regensburg: Verlag Josef Habbel.

Hillebrandt, Alfred (1923): *Altindische Politik*. Jena: Fischer.

Hiriyanna, M. (1995): *The Essentials of Indian Philosophy*. Delhi: Motilal Banarsidass.

Howard, Michael (1999): "When are Wars Decisive?", *Survival*, 41(1), 126-135.

Hunter, S. (1998): *The future of Islam and the West – Clash of Civilizations or*

Peaceful Coexistence? Westport, Connecticut, London: PRAGER/Greenwood Publishing Group.

Indrawooth, Phasook (2004): "The Archaeology of Early Buddhist Kingdoms of Thailand". In: Glover, Ian and Bellwood, Peter (Eds.), *Southeast Asia – From Prehistory to History*. London and New York: Routledge,120-148.

Jaspers, Karl (2011): *Origin and Goal of History*. London: Routledge.

Jauhri, R. (2001): *Medieval India in Transition–Tarikh-i-Firoz Shahi – A First-Hand Account*. New Delhi: Sundeep Prakashan.

Jayaswal, K.P. (1943): *Hindu Polity: A Constitutional History of India in Hindu Times*. Bangalore: Bangalore Printing and Publishing Company Limited.

Jayaswal, K.P. (1967): *Hindu Polity: Constitutional History of India in Hindu Times, Parts I and II*. Bangalore: The Bangalore Printing and Publishing Company Limited.

Jayaswal, K.P. (2005): *Hindu Polity: A Constitutional History of India in Hindu Times*. Delhi: Chaukhamba Sanskrit Pratisthan.

Jenco, Leigh K. (2012): "How Meaning Moves – Tan Sitong on Borrowing Across Cultures". *Philosophy East and West,* 62(1), 92-113.

Jha, D.N. (2004): *Early India – A Concise History*. New Delhi: Manohar Publishers.

Jha, U.C. (2016): "Methods and Means of Warfare: Kautilya and Contemporary Laws of Armed Conflict". In: Gautam, P.K. / Mishra, S. / Gupta, A. (Eds.), Indigenous *Historical Knowledge – Kautilya and His Vocabulary, volume II*. New Delhi: IDSA/Pentagon Press, 64-83.

Jingpan, Chen (1990): *Confucius as Teacher – Philosophy of Confucius with Special Reference to its Educational Implications*, Beijing: Foreign Language Press.

Johnston, Alastair Iain (2012): "What (If Anything) Does East Asia Tell Us About International Relations Theory?" *Annual Review of Political Science*, 15, 53-78.

Kamla (2011): "Abul Fazl: Governance and Administration". In: Singh, M.P. and Roy, Himanshu (Eds.), *Indian Political Thought – Themes and Thinkers*. Noida: Pearson, 42-53.

Kang, David (2007): "Getting Asia Wrong: The Need for New Analytical Frameworks". *International Security*, 27(4), 57-85.

Kangle, R.P. (2010a) (Ed.): *The Kauṭilīlya Arthaśāstra (Part I)*. Delhi: Motilal Banarsidass.

Kangle, R.P. (2010c/1965): *The Kauṭilīya Arthaśāstra (Part III)* (A Study). Delhi: Motilal Banarsidass Publishers.

Kangle, R.P. (Trans.) (2010b/1972): *The Kauṭilīya Arthaśāstra (Part II)* (English Translation). Delhi: Motilal Banarsidass Publishers.

Kantorowicz, Ernst H. (2003): *Kaiser Friedrich der Zweite*. Stuttgart: Klett-Cotta.

Karnad, Bharat (2002): *Nuclear Weapons and Indian Security*. Delhi: Macmillan India.

Katouzian, H. (2003): "Legitimacy and Succession in Iranian History".

Comparative Studies of South Asia, Africa, and the Middle East. 23(1/2), 234-245.

Khan, A.S. (1957): "Fatawa-I Jahandari". *Medieval India Quarterly*, 3(1/2), 13-87.

Khan, I.A. (1986): "Medieval Indian Notions of Secular Statecraft in Retrospect". *Social Scientist*, 14(1), 3-15.

Kissinger, Henry (2014): *World Order – Reflections of the Character of Nations and the Course of History.* New York: Penguin.

Kohli, Ritu (1995): *Kautilya's Political Theory – Yogakshema, the Concept of Welfare State.* New Delhi: Deep & Deep Publications.

Kolff, Dirk H.A. (1990): *Naukar, Rajput and Sepoy – The Ethnohistory of the Military Labour Market in Hindustan, 1450-1850.* Cambridge: Cambridge University Press.

Kolff, Dirk H.A. (2008): "A Millennium of Stateless Indian History?", In: Datta, Rajat, *Rethinking a Millennium – Perspectives on Indian History from the Eighth to the Eighteenth Century, Essays for Harbans Mukhia.* New Delhi: Aakar, 51-67.

Kühnhardt, Ludger (1988):"Staatsordnung und Macht in indischer Perspektive – Kautilya Chanakya als Klassiker der politischen Ideengeschichte". *Historische Zeitschrift*, 247(2), 333-355.

Kulke, Hermann (2005): *Indische Geschichte bis 1750.* München: Oldenbourg.

Kulke, Hermann and Rothermund, Dietmar (1998a): *A History of India.* 3rd Edn. London and New York: Routledge.

Kulke, Hermann and Rothermund, Dietmar (1998b): *Geschichte Indiens.* München: Beck.

Lai, David (2004): *Learning from the Stones: A Go Approach to Mastering China's Strategic Concept, Shi*, Monograph, Strategic Studies Institute, US Army War College.

Lambton, A.K.S. (2013): *State and Government in Medieval Islam.* London: Routledge.

Lavine, T.Z. (1984): *From Socrates to Sartre: The Philosophical Quest.* New York: Bantam Books.

Lerner, Max (Ed.) (1950): *The Prince and the Discourses.* New York: The Modern Library.

Lewis, O. and Steinmo, S. (2012): "How Institutions Evolve: Evolutionary Theory and Institutional Change". *Polity*, 44, 314-339.

Liebig, Michael (2013): "Kautilya's Relevance for India Today". *India Quarterly*, 69(2), 99-116.

Liebig, Michael (2014a): *Endogene Politisch-Kulturelle Ressourcen: Die Relevanz des Kautilya-Arthashastra für das moderne Indien,* Baden-Baden: Nomos.

Liebig, Michael (2014b): "Kautilya's *Arthashastra*: A Classic Text of Statecraft and Untapped Political Science Resource". In: *Heidelberg Papers in South Asian Comparative Politics*, No. 74.

Liebig, Michael (2014c): "Statecraft and Intelligence Analysis in the Kautilya-*Arthashastra*". *Journal of Defence Studies*, 8(4), 27-54.

Lijphart, Arendt (2009): "The Puzzle of India's Democracy". In: Mitra, Subrata (Ed.), *Politics of Modern South Asia, Critical Issues in Modern Politics*, volume 1. London: Routledge, 36-60.

Lindberg, Steffan (2007): "Institutionalization of Party Systems? Stability and Fluidity among Legislative Parties in Africa's Democracies". *Government and Opposition*, 42(2), 215-241.

Lowe, Vaughan / Roberts, Adam / Welsh, Jennifer / Zaum, Dominik (Eds.) (2008): *The United Nations Security Council and War and Practices Since 1945*. Oxford: Oxford University Press.

Luce, M.D. (2010): "Mirror for Princes (Islamic)". In: Classen, A. (Ed.), *Handbook of Medieval Studies - Terms - Methods - Trends*. Berlin: De Gruyter.

Makdisi, G. (1970): "The Marriage of Tughril Beg". *International Journal of Middle East Studies*. 1(3), 259-275.

Manguin, Pierre-Yves (2004): "The Archaeology of Early Maritime Polities of Southeast Asia". In: Glover, Ian and Bellwood, Peter (Eds.), *Southeast Asia – From Prehistory to History*. London and New York: Routledge, 282-313.

Manzalaoui, Mahmoud (1974): "The Pseudo-Aristotelian "Kitāb Sirr al-asrār". Facts and Problems". *Oriens*, 23/24, 147-257.

March, A.F. (2012): "Constitutionalism". In: Bulliet, R. / Cook, D. / Euben, R. L. / Fahmy, K. / Griffel, F. / Haykel, B. / Hefner, R. W. / Kuran, T. / McAuliffe, J. / Moosa, E. (Eds.), *The Princeton Encyclopedia of Islamic Political Thought*. Princeton: Princeton University Press, 112-115.

Matilal, B.K. (1990): *Language and Reality – Indian Philosophy and Contemporary Issues*. 2nd Edn. Delhi: Motilal Banarsidass.

Matthews, Warren (2010): *World Religions*. Wadsworth: Cengage Learning.

McClish, Mark (2012): "Is the Arthasastra a Mauryan Document?", In: Olivelle, Patrick / Leoshko, Janice / Ray, Himanshu Prabha (Eds.), *Reimaging Asoka – Memory and History*. New Delhi: Oxford University Pres, 280-309.

McKenzie, John (1922): *Hindu Ethics: A Historical and Critical Essay*. London: Oxford University Press.

McNeill, W.H. (1993): "Foreword". In: Frank, G. and Gills, B.K., *The World System – 500 years or 5000*. London: Routledge.

Mehta, J. (2009): *Advanced Study in the History of Medieval India* (Vol. III). New Delhi: Sterling Publishers Pvt. Ltd.

Mehta, V. R. (1992). *Foundations of Indian Political Thought*. Delhi: Manohar.

Mehta, V.R. and Pantham, Thomas (2006): *Political Ideas in Modern India: Thematic Explorations*, Vol. X, Part 7. New Delhi: Centre for Studies in Civilizations/Sage Publications.

Meinecke, Friedrich (1960/1924): *Die Idee der Staatsraison in der neueren Geschichte*. München: Oldenbourg.

Meinecke, Friedrich (1962/1924): *Machiavellism – The Doctrine of Raison D'etát and its Place in Modern History*. St. Louis: Transaction Publishers.

Menon, Shivshankar (2013): *Keynote Address at IDSA Conference on Kauṭilya, October 8, 2013,* at http://www.idsa.in/keyspeeches/Kauṭilyas Arthaśāstra Amb Shivshankar Menon NSA (Accessed on December 5, 2015).

Menon, Shivshankar (2016): In: Gautam, P.K. / Mishra, Saurabh / Gupta, Arvind (Eds.), *Indigenous Historical Knowledge – Kautilya and His Vocabulary– Volume III. New Delhi:* IDSA/Pentagon Press, New Delhi, xvii-xix.

Metcalf, Thomas R. (1998): *Ideologies of the Raj*. Cambridge: Cambridge University Press.

Meyer, Johann Jakob (Ed.) (1977/1926): *Das altindische Buch vom Welt- und Staatsleben – Das Arthacastra des Kautilya*. Graz: Akademische Druck-und Verlagsanstalt.

Miksic, John N. (2004): "The Classical Cultures of Indonesia". In: Glover, Ian and Bellwood, Peter (Eds.), *Southeast Asia – From Prehistory to History*. London and New York: Routledge, 234-256.

Mishra, Atul (2014): "Indigenism in Contemporary IR Discourses in India: A Critique". *Studies in Indian Politics*, 2014, 2(2), 119-135.

Mishra, S.C. (1993): *Evolution of Kautilya's Arthasastra: An Inscriptional Approach*. Delhi: Anamika Prakashan.

Mitra, Rajendralala (Ed.) (1982): *The Nitisara or the Elements of Polity by Kamandaki*. Calcutta: The Asiatic Society. First Published by Baptist Mission Press, Calcutta, in 1861.

Mitra, Subrata K. (1988): "Paradoxes of Power: Political Science as Morality Play". *Journal of Commonwealth and Comparative Politics*, 26, 318-337.

Mitra, Subrata K. (1990a): "Between Transaction and Transcendence: The State and the Institutionalisation of Power in India". In: Mitra, Subrata K. (Ed.), *The Postcolonial State in Asia: Dialectics of Politics and Culture*. London: Harvester.

Mitra, Subrata K. (1994): "Flawed Paradigms: Some 'Western' Models of Indian Politics". In: Samurthy, T.V. (Ed.): *State and Nation in the Context of Social Change*. Delhi: Oxford University Press, 219-245.

Mitra, Subrata K. (1999a): "Effects of Institutional Arrangements on Political Stability in South Asia". *Annual Review of Political Science,* 2, 405-428.

Mitra, Subrata K. (1999b): *Culture and Rationality: The Politics of Social Change in Post-colonial India*. Delhi: Sage.

Mitra, Subrata K. (2000): "The Nation, State and the Federal Process in India". In: Schmidt, Ute Wachendorfer, (Ed.), *Federalism and Political Performance*. London: Routledge.

Mitra, Subrata K. (2011): *Politics in India – Structure, Process and Policy*. London: Routledge.

Mitra, Subrata K. (2012): "From Comparative Politics to Cultural Flow – The Hybrid State and the Resilience of the Political System in India". In:

Stockhammer, P.W. (Ed.), *Conceptualizing Cultural Hybridization: A Transdisciplinary Approach*. Heidelberg: Springer, 107-132.

Mitra, Subrata K. (Ed.) (1990b): *The Post-colonial State in Asia: Dialectics of Politics and Culture*. New York: Harvester Wheatsheaf.

Mitra, Subrata K. and Fischer, Alexander (2002): "Sacred Laws and the Secular State: An Analytical Narrative of the Controversy over Personal Laws in India". *India Review*, 1, 99-130.

Mitra, Subrata K. and Liebig, Michael (2016): *Kautilya's Arthashastra: An Intellectual Portrait – The Classical Roots of Modern Politics in India*. Baden-Baden: Nomos.

Mitra, Subrata K. and Singh, V. B. (2009): *When Rebels become Stakeholders*, Delhi: Sage.

Mitra, Subrata K., (Ed.), (2009): *Politics of Modern South Asia, Critical Issues in the Modern Politics,* 5 volumes. London: Routledge.

Mittal, Surendra Nath (2000): *Kauṭilīya Arthaśāstra Revisited*. Project of History of Indian Science, Philosophy and Culture (PHISPC), Monograph No.11. New Delhi: Centre for Studies in Civilizations/Munshiram Manoharlal Publishers Pvt Ltd.

Modelski, George (1964): "Kautilya – Foreign Policy and International System in the Ancient Hindu World". *The American Political Science Review*, 58(3), 549-560.

Mookerji, R.K. (1987): "The Foundation of the Maurya Empire". In: Nilakanta Sastri, K.A. (Ed.), *A Comprehensive History of India, volume II – The Mauryan and Satavahans, 325 BC-AD 300*. New Delhi: People's Publishing House. First published in 1957.

Moosvi, Shireen (2009): "Medieval Indo-Persian Historiography". *Different Types of History*, 14(Part 4), 59-69.

Morgenthau, Hans J. (1958): *Dilemmas of Politics*. Chicago: University of Chicago Press.

Morgenthau, Hans J. (1978): *Politics Among Nations – The Struggle for Power and Peace*. New York: Alfred A. Knopf.

Morris-Jones, W.H. (1964): *The Government and Politics of India*. London: Hutchinson University Library.

Mott, William and Kim, J. (2006): *The Philosophy of Chinese Military Culture – Shih vs Li*. New York: Palgrave MacMillan.

Mou, Bo (Ed.) (2008): *History of Chinese Philosophy*. London and New York: Routledge.

Mukherjee, Pranab (2014): Speech by the President of India, Shri Pranab Mukherjee call on by members of the 54th NDC course and staff of National Defence College on November 13, at http://www.security-risks.com/security-trends-south-asia/india-defence/president-address-to-ndc-course-3827.html (Accessed on April 30, 2015).

Münkler, Herfried (Ed.) (1990): *Niccolo Machiavelli – Politische Schriften*. Frankfurt/M: Fischer.

Münkler, Herfried (1987): *Im Namen des Staates: Die Begründung der Staatsraison in der Frühen Neuzeit*. Frankfurt am Main: Fischer.

Murray, Alastair (1997): *Realism – Between Power Politics and Cosmopolitan Ethics*. Edinburgh: Keele University Press.

Naipaul, V.S. (1979): *India: A Wounded Civilization*. New York: Penguin.

Nandy, Ashis (1983): *The Intimate Enemy*. New Delhi: Oxford University Press.

Narlikar, Amrita and Narlikar, Aruna (2014): *Bargaining with Rising India: Lessons from the Mahabharata*. Oxford: Oxford University Press.

Nehru, Jawaharlal (1981): *The Discovery of India*. Delhi: Indian Council for Cultural Relations.

Nehru, Jawaharlal (1990): *The Discovery of India*, Delhi: Oxford University Press.

Neumann, Iver B. (2014): "International Relations as a Social Science". *Millennium: Journal of International Studies*, 43(1), 330-350.

Nizam al-Mulk (2002): *The Book of Government, Or, Rules for Kings (The Siyar Al-Muluk, Or, Siyasat-Nama of Nizam Al-Mulk)* (H. Darke, Trans.). London: Routledge.

North, Douglass (1990): *Institutions, Institutional Change and Economic Performance*. Cambridge: Cambridge University Press.

Oevermann, Ulrich (2008): "Charismatisierung von Herrschaft und Geltungsquellen von Gerechtigkeit im Prooemium der Konstitutionen von Melfi des Kaiers Friedrich II". In: Grebner, G. / Fried, J. (Ed.), *Kulturtransfer und Hofgesellschaft im Mittelalter – Wissenskultur am sizilianischen und kastilischen Hof im 13. Jahrhundert*. Berlin: AkadmieVerlag, 43-98.

Olivelle, Patrick (Ed.) (2009): *Dharma – Studies in Its Semantic, Cultural and Religious History*. Delhi: Motilal Banarsidass Publishers.

Olivelle, Patrick (Ed.) (2013): *King, Government and Law in Ancient India*. Oxford: Oxford University Press.

Olivelle, Patrick (Trans.) (Ed.) (1997): *Pancatantra – The Book of India's Folk Wisdom*. Oxford: Oxford University Press.

Oppert, Gustav (1967): *On the Weapons, Army Organisation, and Political Maxims of the Ancient Hindus, with Special Reference to Gunpowder and Firearms*. Ahmadabad: The New Order Book Co. First published in 1880.

Pal, Manoj Kumar (2006): "Old Wisdom and New Horizon". In: Chattopadhyaya, D.P. (Gen. Ed.), *History of Science, Philosophy and Culture in Indian Civilization*, Vol. XV, Part 5, Project of History of Indian Science, Philosophy and Culture (PHISPC). New Delhi: Centre for Studies in Civilizations/Viva Books.

Panikkar, K.M. (1963): *The Foundations of New India*. London: Allan & Urwin.

Panikkar, K.M. (1960): *A Survey of Indian History*. Third Edn. Bombay: Asia Publishing House. First published in 1947.

Panikkar, K.M. (1952): *The Principles and Practice of Diplomacy*, Occasional Paper No. 6. Delhi: Delhi School of Economics.

Pankenier, David W. (1992): "The Bamboo Annals Revisited: Problems of Method in Using the Chronicle as a Source for Chronology of Early Zhou. Part 2: The Congruent Mandate Chronology in Yi Zhou Shu." *Bulletin of the School of Oriental and African Studies*, 55(3), 498-510.

Parekh, Bhikhu (1999): *Colonialism, Tradition and Reform: An Analysis of Gandhi's Political Discourse*. Delhi: Sage.

Parekh, Bhikhu (2010): "Some reflection on Hindu tradition of Political Thought". In Fred Dallmayr, *Comparative Political Theory: An Introduction*. New York: Palgrave Macmillan.

Parel, Anthony J. (2008): "Gandhi and the Emergence of the Modern Indian Political Canon". *The Review of Politics*, 70(1), 40-63.

Parmar, Aradhana (1987): *Techniques of Statecraft – A Study of Kautilya's Arthashastra*. Delhi: Atma Ram & Sons.

Pathak, Suniti Kumar (1974): *The Indian Nitisastras in Tibet*. Delhi: Motilal Banarsidass.

Pillalamarri, Akhilesh (2015): "Chanakya - India's Truly Radical Machiavelli", *National Interest*, January 29, 2015, at http://nationalinterest.org/feature/chanakya-indias-truly-radical-machiavelli-12146 (Accessed on January 18, 2016).

Plessner, Helmuth (2003): *Macht und menschliche Natur*. Frankfurt am Main: Suhrkamp.

Pollock, Sheldon (2006): *The Language of the Gods in the World of Men – Sanskrit, Culture, and Power in Premodern India*. Ranikhet: Permanent Black.

Prakash, Aseem (1993): "State and Statecraft in Kautilya's Arthashastra", A paper presented at the Fall Semester Mini- Conference organised by the Workshop in Political Theory and Policy Analysis, Indiana University, Bloomington, December 11 & 13, 1993.

Prakash, Buddha (1966): *Glimpses of Ancient Panjab*. Patiala: Punjabi University.

Prasad, Beni, and Majumdar, R.C. (1960): "Political Theory and Administrative System". In: *The History and Culture of the Indian People, The Age of Imperial Unity*. 4th Edn. Bombay: Bharatiya Vidya Bhavan, 303-334. First published in 1951.

Prem, Sri Krishna (2008): *The Yoga of the Bhagavad Gita*. New York: Morning Light Press.

Puntambekar, S.V. (1948): "Some Aspects of Sukra's Political Thought". Paper in the Tenth Indian Political Science Conference, January 1948. *IJPS*, 9(2/3), 1-12 & *IJPS* 9(1), 71.

Radhakrishnan, Sarvepalli (1948): *Indian Philosophy* (Volume II). First published in 1923. London: George Allen & Unwin Ltd.

Radhakrishnan, Sarvepalli and Moore, Charles A. (Eds.) (1957): *A Source Book in Indian Philosophy*. Princeton: Princeton University Press.

Rajamohan, C. (2014): In his column on the renewal of Kautilya at IDSA. In: The *Indian Express*, September 3, 2014.

Rand, Christopher C. (1979/1980): "Chinese Military Thought and Philosophical Taoism". *Monumenta Serica*, 34, 171-218.

Rangarajan, L.N. (Ed.) (1992): *Kautilya – The Arthashastra*. Delhi: Penguin Books India.

Rao, M.V. Krishna (1958): *Studies in Kautilya*. Delhi: Munshi Ram Manohar Lal.

Ray, H.P. (2012): "The Southern Silk Route from China to India". In: Shuying, Wang and Deepak, B.R. (Eds.), *India-China Relations: Civilizational Perspectives*. New Delhi: Manak Publications.

Raychaudhuri, Hemchandra (1996): *Political History of Ancient India – From the Accession of Parikshit to the Extinction of the Gupta Dynasty*. With a commentary by B.N. Mukherjee. Delhi: Oxford University Press. First published in 1923.

Reichert, Folger (2008): "Geographisches Wissen in der Umgebung Friedrich II". In: Grebner, G. and Fried, J. (Ed.), *Kulturtransfer und Hofgesellschaft im Mittelalter – Wissenskultur am sizilianischen und kastilischen Hof im 13. Jahrhundert*. Berlin: Akadmie Verlag, 131-147.

Reinhardt, Volker / Saracino, Stefano / Voigt, Rüdiger (Eds.) (2015): *Der Machtstaat – Niccolo Machiavelli als Theoretiker der Macht im Spiegel der Zeit*. Baden-Baden: Nomos.

Rengger, Nicholas J. (2000): *International Relations, Political Theory and the Problem of Order*. London: Routledge.

Reus-Smit, Christian and Snidal, Duncan (2008): *Between Utopia and Reality: The Practical Discourses of International Relations*, Oxford: Oxford University Press.

Ritschl, Eva and Schetlich, Maria (1973): *Studien zum Kautilya Arthasastra*. Berlin: Akademie-Verlag.

Rizvi, S.A.A (2005): *The Wonder that Was India Volume II – A Survey of the Indian History and Culture of the Indian Sub-continent from the Coming of Muslims to the British Conquest 1200-1700*. London: Picador. First published in 1987.

Rosenau, James N. (1980): *The Scientific Study of Foreign Policy*, revised Edn. London: Frances Pinter.

Rosenthal, E.I.J. (1958): *Political Thought in Medieval Islam – An Introductory Outline*. Cambridge: Cambridge University Press.

Roy, Gandhi Jee (1981): *Diplomacy in Ancient India*. New Delhi and Patna: Janaki Prakashan.

Roy, H., and Alam, M. (2011). "Zia Barani – Good Sultan and Ideal Polity". In: Singh, M.P. and Roy, H. (Eds.), *Indian Political Thought: Themes and Thinkers*. Noida: Pearson Education India, 30-41.

Rubin, W. (1955): "Inter-State Relations in Ancient India and Kautilya's

Arthasastra". *Indian Year-Book of International Affairs*, volume IV. Madras: Indian Study Group of International Affairs, University of Madras.

Rudolph, Lloyd and Rudolph, Susanne Hoeber (1967): *The Modernity of Tradition*. Chicago: The University of Chicago Press.

Rudolph, Llyod I. and Rudolph, Susanne Hoeber (1987): *In Pursuit of Lakshmi: The Political Economy of the Indian State*, Chicago: The University of Chicago Press.

Rudolph, Susanne H. (1987): "Presidential Address: State Formation in Asia – Prolegomenon to a Comparative Study". In: *The Journal of Asian Studies*, 46(4), 731-746.

Ryder, Arthur W. (Trans.) (1925): *The Panchatantra of Vishnu Sharma c. 1199*. Chicago: The University of Chicago Press.

Ryder, Arthur W. (Trans.) (2011): *Panchatantra*, 34th Edn. New Delhi: Jaico Publications. First Jaico Edition in 1949.

Sabine, George H. (1973): *A History of Political Theory*. New York: Hold, Rinehart and Winston.

Saddhatissa, H. (1970): *Buddhist Ethics: Essence of Buddhism*. London: Allen & Unwin.

Sandel, Michael (2009): *Justice – What's the Right thing to Do?* London: Penguin Books/Allen Lane.

Sarkar, B.K. (1919): "Hindu Theory of International Relations". *The American Political Science Review*, 13(3), 400-414.

Sarkar, B.K. (1939): *The Political Institutions and Theories of the Hindus: A Study in Comparative Politics*, Delhi: Chuckervertty, Chatterjee & Company, Limited.

Sarkar, B.K. (1985): *The Positive Background of Hindu Sociology: Introduction to Hindu Positivism*. Delhi: Motilal Banarsidass. First published in 1937.

Sarkar, B.K. (2010): "The German Translation of the Kautilyan *Arthasastra* – Meyer's Humanism". In: Mittal, P. and Dua, Geeta, *Kautilya Arthasastra – Collection of Articles from the Indian Historical Quarterly, Indian Antiquary, Indian Culture, and Calcutta Review,* in Two Volumes. Delhi: Originals.

Sarkar, B.K. (2013): "Some Basic Ideas of Political Thinking in Ancient India". In: *The Cultural Heritage of India, Volume II – Itihasa, Puranas, Dharma and Other Sastras*. Belur Math, Ramakrishna Mission, 509-529.

Sarkar, N. (2006): "The Voice of Mahmūd – The Hero in Ziyā Baranī's Fatāwā-I Jahāndārī". *The Medieval History Journal*, 9(2), 327-356.

Sarkar, N. (2011): "An Urban Imaginary, ca. 1350 The Capital City in Ziyā' Barani's Fatawa-I Jahandari". *Indian Economic & Social History Review*, 48(3), 407-424.

Sartori, Giovanni (1970): "Concept Misformation in Comparative Politics". *The American Political Science Review*, 64(4), 1033-1053.

Sastri, Ganpati Mahamahopadhyaya T. (2006): "General Introduction". In: Unni,

N.P. (Trans.), *The Arthasastra of Kautalya* with the commentary "SRIMULA" Part 1 and 2 (Adhikaranas), Delhi: New Bhartiya Book Corporation.

Sauter, Constantin (Ed.) (1974/1913): *Dante Alighieri – De Monarchia*. Aalen: Scientia Verlag.

Sawyer, Ralph D. (1993): The Seven Military Classics of Ancient China. New York: Basic Books.

Sawyer, Ralph D. (1994): *The Art of War*, Translation, Oxford: Westview Press.

Schabinger, Karl Emil (Ed.) (1987): *Nizamulmulk – Das Buch der Staatskunst. Siyasatnama*. Zürich: Manesse.

Schama, Simon (1989): *Citizens: A Chronicle of the French Revolution*. London: Penguin.

Scharfe, Hartmut (1968): *Untersuchungen zur Staatsrechtslehre des Kautalya*, Wiesbaden: Harrassowitz.

Schneider, Herbert W. (Ed.) (1984): *Dante – On World-Government*. Indianapolis: Bobbs-Merrill.

Sen, Amartya: (1997): "Indian Traditions and the Western Imagination". *Daedalus: Journal of the American Academy of Arts & Sciences*, 26(2), 1-26.

Shahi, Deepshikha (2014): "*Arthashastra* beyond Realpolitik – The 'Eclectic' Face of Kautilya". *Economic and Political Weekly*, 69(41), 68-74.

Shahi, Deepshikha and Ascone, Gennaro (2015): "Rethinking the absence of post-Western International Relations theory in India – 'Advaitic monism' as an alternative epistemological resource". *European Journal of International Affairs*, 22(2), 1-22.

Sharma, Chandradhar (2013): *Bhāratīya Darśana: Ālocan aur Anuśīlan*. First Published in 1990. Delhi: Motilal Banarsidass.

Sharma, R.S. (1990): *Sudras in Early India: A social History of the Lower Order Down to Circa AD 600*. Delhi: Motilal Banarsidass Publishers.

Shastri, Ajay Mitra (1969): *India as Seen in the Bṛhatsaṃhitā of Vārāhamihira*. Delhi: Motilal Banarsidass.

Shaughnessy, Edward L. (1999): "The Western Zhou". In: Loewe, Michael and Shaughnessy, Edward, *Cambridge History of Ancient China – From the Origins of Civilization to 221 BC*, Cambridge: Cambridge University Press.

Shaughnessy, Edward L. (2014): *Unearthing the Changes – Recently Discovered Manuscripts of the Yijing and Related Texts*. New York: Columbia University Press.

Shoham, Dany and Liebig, Michael (2016): "The Intelligence Dimension of Kautilyan Statecraft and its Implications for the Present". *Journal of Intelligence History*, 15(2), 119-138.

Shulman, David (2015): "At the Heart of Hinduism", Book Review of Robert Calasso's *Ardor (2014)*, translated from the Italian by Richard Dixon, Farrar, Straus and Giroux, *The New York Review of Books*, Vol. LXII, No.1, January 8, 49-51.

Sihag, Balbir Singh (2014): *Kautilya – The True Founder of Economics*. New Delhi: Vitasta Publishing.

Sil, Narasingha P. (1989): *Kautilya's Arthashastra: A Comparative Study*. New York: Peter Lang.

Singh, G.P. (1993): *Political Thought in Ancient India*. New Delhi: D.K. Printworld.

Singh, Mahendra Prasad and Roy, Himanshu (Eds.) (2011): *Indian Political Thought: Themes and Thinkers*. Noida: Pearson.

Singh, Upinder (2010): "Politics, Violence and War in Kāmandaka's *Nītisāra*". *The Indian Economic and Social History Review*, 47(1), 29-62.

Singh, Upinder. (2008): *A History of Ancient and Early Medieval India: From the Stone Age to the 12th Century*. Noida: Pearson Education India.

Sinha, A.K. (2006): "A Historiographical Approach to Ancient Indian Culture". In: Sinha, A.K. (Ed.), *Facets of Indian History*, New Delhi: Anamika Publishers.

Slakter, David (2011): "On *Mātsyanyāya*: The state of Nature in Indian Thought". *Asian Philosophy: An International Journal of the Philosophical Traditions of the East*, 21(1), 23-34.

Slaye, Walter (1989): "Friedrich von Suhtscheck und das Parsiwalnama". *Zeitschrift der Deutschen Morgenländischen Gesellschaft*, 139, 93-103.

Smith, Steve (1996): "Positivism and Beyond". In: Smith, Steve / Booth, Ken / Zalewski, Marysia (Eds.), *International Theory: Positivism and Beyond*. Cambridge: Cambridge University Press, 11-46.

Solomon, Hussein (2012): "Critical Reflections of Indian Foreign Policy – Between Kautilya and Ashoka". *South African Journal of International Affairs*, 19(1), 65-78.

Spegele, Roger D. (1996): *Political Realism in International Theory*. Cambridge: Cambridge University Press.

Stark, Miriam T. (2004): "Pre-Angkorian and Angkorian Cambodia". In: Glover, Ian and Bellwood, Peter (Eds.), *Southeast Asia: From Prehistory to History*. London and New York: Routledge.

Stein, M.A. (Trans.) (2009): *Kalhana's Rajatarangini – A Chronicle of the Kings of Kasmir*. First Indian Edn. in 1990. Delhi: Motilal Banarsidass.

Stepan, Alfred (2008): "Comparative Theory and Political Practice – Do We Need a 'State-nation' Model as well as a 'Nation-State' Model?" *Government and Opposition*, 43(1), 1-25.

Stockhammer, P.W. (Ed.) (2012): *Conceptualizing Cultural Hybridization – A Transdisciplinary Approach*. Heidelberg: Springer.

Suhtscheck, Friedrich von (1932): "Wolfram von Eschenbachs Reimbearbeitung des Parsivalnamä". *Clio* 25.

Swāminā, Tulasīrām (Ed.) (1900): *Manusmṛti*. Meerut: Adhyakṣaswāmī Press.

Syros, V. (2012): "Indian Emergencies – Baranī's Fatāwā-I Jahāndārī, the Diseases of the Body Politic, and Machiavelli's accidenti". *Philosophy East and West*, 62(4), 545-573.

Tabatabai, J. (2006): *An Introduction to Political Thoughts in Iran (Daramadī bar andīsha-yisiyāsīdar Īrān)*. Tehran: Kavir.

Tabatabai, J. (2013). "An Anomaly in the History of Persian Political Thought". In: Boroujerdi, M. (Ed.), *Mirror for the Muslim Prince: Islam and the Theory of Statecraft*. New York: Syracuse University Press, 107-121.

Thapar, Romila (1982): "Ideology and the Interpretation of Early Indian History". *Review* (Fernand Braudel Center), 5(3), 389-411.

Thapar, Romila (2000a): "From Lineage to State". In: Thapar, Romila, *History and Beyond*. New Delhi: Oxford University Press.

Thapar, Romila (2000b): "Society and Historical Consciousness: The Itihas – purana Tradition". In: Thapar, Romila. In: *History and Beyond*. New Delhi: Oxford University Press.

Thapar, Romila (2000c): "The Mauryas Revisited". In: Thapar, Romila, *Cultural Past: Essays in Early Indian History*. New Delhi: Oxford University Press, 462-515.

Thapar, Romila (2000d): *History and Beyond*. New Delhi: Oxford University Press.

Thapar, Romila (2002): *Early India – From the Origins to AD 1300*, New Delhi: Penguin Books.

Thapar, Romila (2003), *Cultural Pasts – Essays in Indian History*, Oxford: Oxford University Press.

Thapar, Romila (2013): *The Past Before Us: Historical Traditions of Early North India*. Ranikhet: Permanent Black.

Tharoor, Shashi (2012): *Pax Indica – India and the World of the 21st Century*. New Delhi: Allen Lane/Penguin.

Thussu, Daya Kishan (2013): *Communicating India's Soft Power: Buddha to Bollywood*. New York: Palgrave Macmillan.

Tillotson, Giles (2008): *Taj Mahal*. London: Profile Books.

Trautmann, Thomas R. (1971): *Kautilya and the Arthashastra*. Leiden: E.J. Brill.

Twitchett, Denis and Loewe, Michael (1986): *The Cambridge History of China, Volume I, The Chin and Han Empires, 221 B.C-A.D.220*. Cambridge: Cambridge University Press.

Varma, V.P. (1959): *Studies in Hindu Political Thought and Its Metaphysical Foundations*, Delhi: Motilal Banarsidass.

Varma, V.P. (1986): *Ancient and Medieval Indian Political Thought*. Agra: Lakshmi Narain Agarwal Publishers.

Vivekanandan, Jayashree (2015): "The Text as Tradition". In: Gautam, P.K. / Mishra, S. / Gupta, A. (Eds.), *Indigenous Historical Knowledge: Kautilya and His Vocabulary, volume II*, New Delhi: Pentagon Press, 3-19.

Voegelin, Eric (1951): "Machiavelli's Prince – Background and Formation". *Review of Politics*, 13(2), 132-168.

Voegelin, Eric (1990/1971): "Equivalences of Experience and Symbolization in History". In: *The Collected Works of Eric Voegelin, volume 12*. Baton Rouge: Louisiana State University Press, 115-133.

Voegelin, Eric (1994): *Autobiographische Reflexionen*, München: Wilhelm Fink Verlag.

Walters, O.W. (1999): *History, Culture, and Region in Southeast Asian Perspective*. Revised Edn. New York: Southeast Asia Program, Cornell University (in cooperation with the Institute for Southeast Asian Studies, Singapore).

Waltz, Kenneth (1979): *Theory of International Politics,* United States of America: Mc Graw Hill, 1979.

Watson, Adam (2009): *The Evolution of International Society*. London: Routledge.

Weaver, Ole (1996): "The Rise and Fall of the Interparadigm Debate". In: Smith, Steve / Booth, Ken / Zalewski, Marysia (Eds.), *International Theory: Positivism and Beyond*. Cambridge: Cambridge University Press.

Weber, Max (1964): *The Theory of Economic and Social Organisation*. New York: The Free Press.

Weber, Max (1978): "The Religion of Asia". In: Runciman, W.G. (Ed.) and Matthews E. (Trans.), *Max Weber – Selections in Translation*. Cambridge: Cambridge University Press, 192-205.

Weber, Max (1988): *Gesammelte Politische Schriften*. Tübingen: Mohr/UTB.

Weber, Max (1994): *Weber - Political Writings* (Ed. by Peter Lassman). Cambridge: Cambridge University Press.

Weber, Max (2000): *The Religion of India – The Sociology of Hinduism and Buddhism*. Translated by Hans. H. Gerth / Don Martindale. Delhi: Munshiram Manoharlal Publishers.

Weber, Max (2008): *Religion und Gesellschaft. Gesammelte Aufsätze zur Religionssoziologie*. Frankfurt am Main: Zweitausendeins.

Weiner, Myron (1984): "Ancient Indian Political Theory and Contemporary India Politics". In: Eisenstadt, S.N. / Reuven Kahane / David Shulman (Eds.), *Orthodoxy, Heterodoxy and Dissent*. Berlin: Mouton Publishers, 111-129.

Werner, Michael and Zimmermann, Benedict (2006): "Beyond Comparison: Histoire Croisée and the Challenge of Reflexivity". *History and Theory*, (45), 30-50.

Wikander, Stig (1971): "De l'Indeal' Espagne: L'origine de la Poridat de lasporidades". In: Actas IV Congresecretumsecretorumo de estudosarabes e islamicos. Leiden: Brill.

Williams, Steven J. (2003): *The Secret of Secrets – The Scholarly Career of a Pseudo-Aristoleian Text in the Latin Middle Ages*. Ann Arbor: University of Michigan Press.

Wink, Andre (2001): "Sovereignty and Universal Dominion in South Asia". In: Gommans, Jos J.L. and Kolff, Dirk H.A. (Eds.) (2001): *Warfare and Weaponry in South Asia 1000-1800*. New Delhi: Oxford University Press, 99-130.

Wittgenstein, Ludwig (1977/1953): *Philosophische Untersuchungen*. Frankfurt am Main: Suhrkamp

Witze, Stephen de (Ed.) (2012): "Means/Ends". In: Bessusi, Antonella (Ed.), *A*

Companion to Political Philosophy: Methods, Tools and Topics. Burlington: Ashgate Publishing Company, 135-148.

Wolf, Günther (Ed.) (1966): *Stupor Mundi – Zur Geschichte Friedrich II. von Hohenstaufen*. Darmstadt: Wissenschaftliche Buchgesellschaft.

Zaman, Rashed Uz (2006): "Kautilya: The Indian Strategic Thinker and Indian Strategic Culture". *Comparative Strategy*, 25(3), 231–247.

Zhang, Xinaglong (2010): "Comparison Paradox, Comparative Situation and Interparadigmaticy: A Methodological Reflection on Cross-Cultural Philosophical Comparison". *Comparitive Philosophy,* 1(1), 90-105.

Zhao, Yin (Ti Heng) (2012): "Bimbisara, Buddha, and Buddhism: Reconstructing the Linkages through Chinese Buddhist Sutras". In: Shuying, Wang and Deepak, B.R. (Eds.), *India- China Relations: Civilizational Perspectives,* New Delhi: Manak Publications, 45-74.

Zimmer, Heinrich (1969): *Philosophies of India*. London: Routledge.

Zimmer, Heinrich (1973): *Philosophie und Religion Indiens*. Frankfurt/M: Suhrkamp.

Zimmer, Heinrich (2011): *Philosophies of India*. Delhi: Motilal Banarsidass Publishers.

Zorn, Rudolf (Ed.) (1966): *Niccolo Machiavelli – Discorsi*. Stuttgart: Kröner.

Index